GW00385420

THE YOUNGEST SON

By the same author

SPORT
Table Tennis Today
Table Tennis

POLITICS
The Traitor Class
Plot Against Peace
Germany's New Nazis

SCENARIO
(with Walter Meade)
Scott of the Antarctic

CINEMA
Film World

TRAVEL
Land of Blue Sky

AUTOBIOGRAPHY
With Eisenstein in Hollywood

PORTRAIT OF THE AUTHOR AS A VERY YOUNG MAN

THE YOUNGEST SON

Autobiographical Sketches

by

IVOR MONTAGU

1970

LAWRENCE AND WISHART

LONDON

SBN 85315 208 x

For

HELL

Printed in Great Britain by
The Camelot Press Ltd., London and Southampton

CONTENTS

ACKNOWLEDGMENTS

THANKS ARE due to Collins & Harvill and to Penguin Press for permission to use the quotations on page 7; to the Radio Times Hulton Press Picture Library for the double portrait taken by Sasha to the People's Press for the *Daily Worker* picture of the S.C.R. simultaneous chess display, and particularly to Bancroft Clark for his photographs taken in Hungary in 1924 and in the Soviet Union in summer 1925. The origin of the early illustrations is not in all cases clear but among those that have been identified are photographs by Bassano & Vandyk Studios; Elliot & Fry; Grove, Son & Boulton; Speaight; Grosvenor Studios; and Bitterne Park Studios (H. Mines). Most of these are now in the collection of the Hon. Mrs. Oliver Frost. The Easton Glebe snapshot is by the author.

AMBER LIGHT

THESE autobiographical notes extend over the years 1904 to 1927—in terms of the author's age, up to 23.

When I started to write them I came across a warning from D. B. Bromley:[1]

> "What we remember is often a seriously distorted version of what we originally experienced. We not only forget parts of what we knew, we also tend to introduce made-up parts and to distort and rearrange the whole pattern of our experience. We simplify and rationalise, so that recall is easier and our thoughts are more coherent. We tend to remember a few salient facts rather than a mass of details; we tend to assume that something happened because it fits in with our reconstruction of past events; we seem to remember that certain persons and events were connected when they were not, or that events happened in a particular order when they did not."

Cross my heart, I have done my best to get the memories right, but it is only fair I pass on this warning to the reader. As of now—as American efficiency experts say, making three words do the work of one—I have no idea whether they will prove of interest to anyone or whether they will ever be continued. If I persist it is because I am encouraged by the opinion of Giuseppe di Lampedusa:[2]

> "There are no memoirs, even those written by insignificant people, which do not include social and graphic details of first-rate importance."

I. M.

Rousay, Orkney.
1967-68

[1] *The Psychology of Human Ageing* (Penguin, 1966).
[2] *Two Stories and a Memory* (Collins & Harvill, 1962).

I

FAMILY ALBUM

In the nurse's arms—W.S.

§ 1

AT THE top was a skylight. This topmost floor was inhabited by housemaids and we were not encouraged to go there. A wooden gate shut off the stairs leading to it from our landing, not for moral reasons but to give them privacy. It also prevented the successive toddlers from venturing up the staircase by themselves and falling down, though sometimes we were accompanied to the top floor and helped up a steep open sort of fixed steps to where we could raise a trapdoor with our heads and play deliciously among the crowded boxes. A similar safety gate cut off the possibility of venturing downward to bother the grown-ups below.

There were four of us in the end. The eldest brother; then a gap of two years and the next brother; then three years and me; a wait of five and my sister.

The nursery rooms made up a corner of the second floor. In the day nursery a huge and ornate carved cupboard had been sliced in half, so that one half served its original purpose, with the wall as backing, and the other half, with a door opening down to the ground, shut off a window and a pantry. Round the fireplace were beautiful blue and white tiles, some representing sleepy cats, the others combining to make a big picture of the house itself. As we grew up, my brothers moved out of the nursery to bedrooms along the street side of the landing. First, my eldest brother to a big bedroom with art nouveau stork and flower patterns. Then the middle one, with me soon joining him, to share a smaller bedroom next to it. And eventually I had to myself the smallest bedroom, nearest the day and night nursery, in which remained my sister and the nurse. The landing was a huge linoleumed play space. After my first visit to the theatre—all the children so far arrived went together to *Henry V* when I was four—we acted the comedy scenes as we remembered them upon that landing. I remember waiting for my cue on the bottom steps above the gate, and then kneeling down and wooden swords and much business about "Eat the leek". (Ivor is a Welsh name so I certainly had to play Fluellyn.) And we had a huge mattress spread out to learn ju-jitsu. Much later, for my sake, there was a table-tennis table.

The next floor down was somewhat awesome, for there my parents lived. There they slept and my father relaxed and read and my mother worked and entertained. In any case they were not to be disturbed. There we were allowed to descend and be shown off to visitors, if we were clean and well-behaved, and thence my mother, and less frequently my father, would ascend and open the little gate and pay their children visits. My mother would often kiss the children good night. She was, as I now know, very youthful in those days, and in white satin for her formal balls she must have looked a picture. When my grandfather died, and my father became a lord and wore black knee-breeches with a sword, as did my eldest brother, we others thought they looked rather silly, although we dared not say so.

The landing on this floor was fairly dark so that you naturally slowed down and walked on tiptoe. One thing could light up on its own—my father's collection of japonaiserie in two big cabinets along one wall. I remember how the light shone on yellow netsukes and lacquer in black and red and gold, with one tiny jar of pale-blue enamel that I thought must be the colour of heaven. My mother had a dressing-room, and a boudoir for her tea-guests with flimsy furniture in French and English marquetry. The joint big bedroom with its enormous white bed, made splendid by pleated blue silk at its head, had a magic door in the corner that led nowhere; when you opened it and then squeezed yourself in as close as it would shut with you inside, you found yourself between two full length mirrors and peering at endless reflections of yourself in both directions.

My father's dressing-room, into which you were not of course supposed to go, had an enormous bath in a sort of box, so that if you were feeling extremely venturous and absolutely *knew* that no grown-up would come back and catch you, you could get inside and pull down the lid and feel terrified, like the Earl's daughter in *The Mistletoe Bough*. The library was on this floor too. Like the nursery above it, it had a round, light, window-seated recess in the angle of the house, with cushions you could kneel on to look out. In one corner was my mother's desk with a desk-lamp, and green boxes and japanned black files. Here she sat working to arrange her dinner-parties, or at something she called the "May League", which I afterwards understood was some kind of charity connected with Queen Mary which did something on the latter's birthday. Also in the corner was a cupboard in which my mother kept her sweets. This was always locked, but I soon found out that most of the furniture keys fitted most of the furniture locks, something I believe she never knew. There was an art nouveau fireplace, a heavy Turkey carpet in green and red, heavy bookcases around the walls surmounted with art nouveau parchment wallpaper in blue and gold, and heaviest of all were my father's desk and armchair. Here he did much reading, his legs stretched out, heavy spectacles on his nose, soft slippers on his feet. No one else was allowed to sit in this chair.

Wherever there was space, huge family portraits hung, including a gigantic eighteenth-century group by Devis where the next staircase led downward to the hall. This was the large inner hall, a place of Spanish metal candelabra and Spanish chairs in scarlet silk, an oaken table with silver tray for visitors' cards, and a huge fireplace that was never used, with blue William de Morgan ceramics round its chimney-piece. Four ways led out of this hall, the first into the drawing-room with its parquet floor and picture screens and Kashdan rugs and price-less golden French furniture (dreary it seemed to me) and crystal chandeliers which glittered when they were lit. I hated this room. The floor threatened slipperiness, you were never allowed in it except after hours of washing and polishing and then it was full of people who embarrassed you. And there was a great French grand piano, where mother sang, and singing bored me. The second outlet was to a narrow outer hall, where footmen took the hats and cloaks. The third led to the dining-room. This was a relaxed place of easy luxury, warm wooden panelling, table, sideboards—all of oak—chairs in light chestnut-coloured leather studded with big brass nails, glass, serving hatch, Cromwellian ceiling and Jacobean curtains. Admission here was a sign of increasing privilege to which we in turn succeeded as we grew. The last door led to the basement. It was a blessed solid door that shut out noise and, once it closed behind you, you could safely clatter down to the uncarpeted friendliness below stairs, the kitchen warmth, the mysteries of the coal-cellars; and, if you were very good, you might clean the knives in a machine with apertures of different sizes and a handle to be turned.

From bottom to top of this tall building ran a lift, a pokey claustro-phobic thing, hidden behind frosted glass in the extreme corner of each floor, its slow progression scarcely animated by hydraulics, a lever to guide it and an endless pole on which to pull to make it start. A wooden flap to bear the tea-things occupied the best part of its space. Between that and its open front there was safe room hardly for one grown-up, but sometimes a child might squeeze behind its passenger as it groaned slowly, interminably aloft. From bottom to top did I say? Not quite. Not exactly a personnel lift, nor a luggage lift, it was a *servants'* lift, to carry trays or washing baskets or themselves invisibly past the gentlemanly regions when untimely menial presence might offend convention. And so, of course, it stopped above the grown-ups', at the children's floor. Its rightful users had to get out and hump their own personal burdens up the last steep staircase to their nests above.

Two doors gave egress from the house. The "front", for family or visitors, was massive brown and iron-bound with a brass chain. Beside it on the outside in a niche was a smooth wooden seat where, after a walk, having run the last stretch home, you could sit and wait for the nursemaid to arrive and ring the bell. Broad white stone steps led down from here to the street. The "back" door, so called though oriented identically, was directly underneath, whence white steps, awkwardly twisting, climbed to finish at a metal railing set to protect the basement-well from being tumbled into by passers-by. Round the corner, behind more railings, a dingy patch of balding grass and a sorry, peeling plane tree. The whole house comprised one-third of a block, which I, much later, learned had earlier been a single dwelling belonging to the financier of whose ennoblement *Punch* wrote:

"... but honours without honour would be a Baron Grant."

Across the way, porters and mansion flats. Beyond, the bustling High Street and the park. This was 28 Kensington Court, the house where I was born.

It is now the Gambian Embassy.

§ 2

MY FATHER married my mother when he was 29 and she was ten years younger. It is characteristic of the sort of man he was that when his sons grew old enough to be interested in such things and asked him, he told them, as a matter of course, that 29 was the right age for a man to marry and that it was good for a man's wife to be about ten years his junior. This without a smile or any suggestion of awareness of the personal application. He was heavy, like his furniture, not ill-looking in his way, with a high bare forehead and a black walrus moustache that later turned to grey, six feet tall and growing heavier as he grew older. He was a man of great authority and some dignity. He ate well. At one time he was President of the Hampshire County Cricket Club. I remember a Bournemouth Festival at which rugged John Daniel, captain of Somerset at cricket and England at rugby, stared in open-eyed amazement at the vast bulk in the luncheon pavilion forking up the salad that was the only part of the pavilion set-lunch his religious principles allowed him on such occasions. "Do you always eat only lettuce?" was the query the cricketer could not suppress.

My father worked at the Bank. This was somewhere in the city, a far-away place to which, in fawn covert-coat bought at Swears & Wells, I would be taken by complicated routes to see an only-hazily-apprehended Lord Mayor's Show. What he did there I neither knew nor was capable of guessing, though I do remember being taken once and shown what I now know were vaults with gold and silver ingots. At home, in spite of his large desk, he did not work, at least not at paper work, but relaxed in the capacious, padded chair. (In the house, only my mother used a secretary.) He read the *Times* and the *Daily News*—he was a faithful Liberal—and no one might look at these newspapers until he finished them. For his books he used a bookmark. I would see him go out to play golf in knickerbockers and later I was allowed to accompany him, but of course I was in bed before he played bridge, which he did extremely well. He also enjoyed jigsaws. He subscribed to a club which sent him in succession boxes containing innumerable pieces and little booklets in which you either wrote "correct" or enclosed a paper with the outline of the missing bits.

"Mustn't touch puzzle" were words I learned before I could pronounce them. The veto was absolute only for his absence, however. He was a sociable man and welcomed participants at the baize-covered puzzle table, but you had to learn not to let your hand hover, obscuring sight of the pieces, to put back any lifted piece exactly where it came from if it did not fit where you expected, and never to put the last ones in when he was not there to see. Of course my parents did entertain, copiously, to lunches, dinners, and later on week-ends in the country, and in this fashion no doubt he would work in an unobvious way, for thus business was frequently concluded or the atmosphere prepared for it. The library was pointed out to me, for example, as the place where, in 1916, the bribe was fixed that "brought Rumania into the war". Did he not have a Rumanian order—of the Golden Fleece or something—as he had of the Japanese Sacred Treasure (second-class)—to prove it?

My mother was very pretty, gay, charming, vivacious, young—as I have said—constantly ready to laugh and pleased by jokes (although they sometimes had to be explained to her). I have mentioned also that she managed the household, kept the accounts and arranged the hospitality. I constantly saw her at work, giving the orders for the day or coping with the crises. She also took singing lessons. She was perpetually, visibly, busy. Of what would today perhaps still be called, though not respected as, their private life, I know nothing. The word "love" when first I learned it, I heard applied only to the relation supposed to exist between parents and children. At no time did I ever see anything between my parents applicable to the sense I later learned it to possess as a special relationship between grown-ups. My mother showed towards my father only affection, admiration, complete reliance; my father to my mother only devotion and pride in her grace and accomplishments. Occasional squabbles I heard, mostly from my mother's side and tinged with the air of a child playing at independence; never a quarrel. I grew up without knowing that divorce or adultery happened to people except in books and newspapers. My father's fortunate marriage lasted nearly thirty years. I am certain he was happy and I think my mother was. She survived him another forty.

Only after both were gone did I learn from one of their contemporaries something of which I had had no inkling, but which, with hindsight, I find not only credible but illuminating, that is, that my father's family had originally thought it a misalliance.

§ 3

BE THIS as it may, there was no sign of constraint or mistrust perceptible among the various ramifications of their two families at the time I became conscious of my surroundings, no trace of any "two sides" that could penetrate the consciousness of a child. The trouble about the relatives was not at all in their attitude to one another, which was amiability itself—spiced by a little friendly narking—but in their sheer numbers. This both confused and terrified me. It is in the nature of things that children should be born into a family circle. Of course some are "only-children", or children of solitary or isolated parents. But most count a reasonable quota of uncles, aunts, cousins and the like. Mine were legion. If I begin with one lot it is only for the purpose of convenience.

In my father's bookcase, to which I had access with my knowledge of the magic interchangeability of keys, stood a magnificent tall slim volume bound in red leather tooled with gold. It stood next to the massive and equally sumptuous MS volumes of his tour to Japan when a young man. The thin one was the family pedigree. Turn over the first page and you found the Montagu arms. Not just the crest already familiar to me from the notepaper, with the neat stag labelled with a small banner and the motto underneath "Swift yet sure", but something far more impressive and complicated, with two rather tame looking spear-bearing retainers, one on either side, and a rather wavy sort of frilled object I believe is called a "tent of Judah". After this, however, you were in for a disappointment. There was my father recorded, whom I knew. And before him my grandfather, whom I also knew. Nothing else.

Really, the family on my father's side was, and is, much more numerous than this. And curiously enough, despite the pedigree, it was not in truth the "Montagu" family, as would have been shown more clearly had the volume been less reticent. Much later, only a few years ago in fact, there fell into my hands a likewise slim but much smaller and less inspiring production—"The History of the Samuel Family of Liverpool". It is like a telephone directory in that everyone seems to be in it. I can remember my mother saying firmly and scornfully one morning of Harriet Cohen, at the time one of the most highly regarded pianists in England: "She's mad. She thinks she's related to us." But this book tells me she was indeed related, and so with several others I have heard disdained in the same way. They are in the index. No one is missing.

(This work was commissioned from my cousin Ronald, by profession a genealogist, by the late Howard Samuel, whom I never met until a few months before his death. At least it was he himself told me he was its "angel", and he is in there too.)

I knew that I had four names: Ivor Goldsmid Samuel Montagu. Goldsmid for my maternal grandfather. I knew that my brother Stuart had been called Stuart Albert Samuel Montagu, and that my brother Ewen was Ewen Edward Samuel Montagu, and that their second names were Colonel Goldsmid's first and second. My father's brothers, too, had that tell-tale S. as an initial, the significance of which was never plain. What I did not know until I surreptitiously prised open the leaves of this beginning of the family tree, was that, strictly and legally, we were hyphenated and that all our names should have terminated Samuel Samuel-Montagu. The explanation of the mystery (solved much later) was that my grandfather—of Liverpool like the Beatles—just simply changed his name, presumably for business reasons, from Montagu Samuel to Samuel Montagu, and while he did not like to keep or use the hyphen or the Samuel in business, he did not like to let the original surname altogether go. The Montagus, like most other human beings, were adept at wanting to have their cake and eat it.

Anyway, this is how it came about that, in the noble version, the family in so strict a sense appears to start abruptly. I remember, with juvenile quixotry, feeling that there was something somehow derogatory about this change of name, it was sailing under false colours. So evidently did Hilaire Belloc, who composed the rhyme:

> Lord Swaythling, whom the people knew,
> And loved, as Samuel Montagu,
> Is known unto the fiends of hell
> As Mr. Moses Samuel.

It is perhaps not a very clever verse (although I repeated it with zest as soon as I discovered it, feeling myself very independent and naughty the while). There can be little doubt of "the people's" love for my grandfather, whose funeral cortège was followed—so I understand,

I was not present—by thousands in Whitechapel, where for many years he had sat as a Liberal member of parliament. There is nothing in the quatrain beyond the assumption implicit in Hilaire Belloc's stereotype of any Jewish financier to show that hell had any concern with my grandfather, and, though I should now fault him for certain traits of character I had no knowledge of as a child, it is not these that Hilaire Belloc was thinking of (or indeed would have blamed him for). Nevertheless I did for some years dream that "when I was twenty-one" —the far-off target of every child impatient to be grown-up—I should revert to the "authentic" name of Samuel. Come that age, the idea had long been abandoned, not perhaps for the practical reason that my name by then had already been used a good deal in publications, public organisations, etc.—for at that age I was still quixotic—but because the more rational reflection had superseded it that, if honesty be the paramount consideration in a surname, that of ones' own father is at any rate more relevant than that of any remoter fore-runner.

The change of name was never spoken of in our family, but not because of self-consciousness; it just simply did not arise. My father was quite ready to tell jokes about name changes. One good one related to an elderly immigrant, more recently from central Europe, who confided to my grandfather that he was worried at the effect upon customers of his impossible name of Uhrschlüssel. Some time later he came along with letters patent certifying that he had improved it legally and in good order. "I am kvite English now," he beamed to my grandfather. "I call myself Vuchky." And my middle brother was once smart enough to score a legitimate bull's eye against his form-master at Westminster. Mr. Sargent, an extremely able and intelligent man who, incidentally, was an authority on toxic mushrooms, was holding forth grandiloquently in the English lesson on the pronunciation of *o* as *u*, especially before two consonants, (exemplified in London, Monday, etc.) "For instance, you there," he said, misguided enough to point at Ewen, "your ancestors called themselves Muntagu." "Oh no they didn't," came the too easy reply, "they called themselves Samuel."

My mother impressed upon us very early that there was no *e* on the end. The *e* tended to be "common". Maybe, but absence of it could entail consequences. An incident cherished in the family but certainly *not* related to the children at an impressionable age demonstrated this. My grandfather was the second Jewish peer in Britain (Rothschild was the first). Like his predecessor, he was a banker and rude people said he bought the title, first a baronetcy, then a barony. Who knows? Certainly he was widely celebrated for philanthropic exercises, no doubt there were the usual contributions to the party funds. "Political and public services" it is ambiguously called. When his name appeared in the honours list, there was the customary question of the title. Courtesy demands that a new creation should not repeat the hallowed label of a predecessor without the latter's consent. My grandfather wrote to ask leave of his neighbour of a few miles away in the New Forest, the then Lord Montagu of Beaulieu. Pat came the answer: "I have no objection to sharing my name with you, if you will share your money with me." So that was why my grandfather had to fall back upon calling himself Lord Swaythling, taking this style from the village and railway station on the old Southern Railway near his old country house at South Stoneham a few miles from Southampton. With heavy humour he called my father, as my father occasionally did his own eldest son: "St. Denis", this being the station one further down the line.

True Victorians, my grandfather and grandmother had ten children, six girls and four boys. Henrietta (whom we called Netta—my father backed the famous 100 to 1 Derby winner Signorinetta because of her), Louis (my father), Marian, Ethel, Edwin, Florence, Lionel, Lily, Gerald, Elsie. I know their names by now, but I still do not know the correct order, except that I am pretty sure Netta came first (she died only the other day, a few hours before her annual flight to holiday at her estate in Northern Ireland, an indomitable 97 with a wooden leg), and I think my father came next. I am not at all sure which was the youngest and could not tell for certain without looking it up. Anyway a lot of them were married, they had yet other surnames, a quiverful of children each, the total of first cousins at its apogee added up to twenty-two. But there were also second cousins. And first and second once removed. To Samuels and Cohens (my paternal grandmother was a Cohen and they too are no inconsiderable breed) alliance added Franklins and Harts and Myers and Waleys. And farther away seemed to be more complicated names like Montefiore (you will find them all in the monograph). There were even some from Belgium and others—or were they just business connections?—from Petersburg. Any of them were liable to muster at a family gathering. And all the Aunts and most of the Uncles were very stout. In one room the effect was terrifying.

There is an event in the Jewish year which does, just so, unite all the family in one room. This is the Passover, less a religious ceremony than a domestic institution, although it includes many prayers and psalms. No one near-related can have any excuse for being absent from it. (With what envy, years later, did I admire the courage of my middle brother, the first to play truant for a single year—at a motor rally—and the aplomb with which his wife, subjected to the uncharitable inquisition: "Where is Ewen?", replied, firmly and conclusively across the table: "He is not here.") But kin more remote, Jewish staff or visitors staying in the house, even the casual passer-by straying from the street, on this night all are traditionally welcome. A silver goblet for Elijah—he vanished under odd circumstances (he was *seen* on his way to heaven but, after all, who knows when he may be coming back)—symbolises the readiness to accept the unexpected guest, and it must be filled with wine anew every time the cups of the rest are filled. The gathering takes place in the house of the head of the family, who acts as master of ceremonies. He himself, and no priest from outside, reads everything in Hebrew. The tables blaze with white linen and every participant from a well-off Jewish family such as ours has a personal silver wine-mug, presented at birth. When I first joined in, the affair was held in my paternal grandmother's long and solid dining-room, gleaming with mirrors. Afterwards it moved to our drawing-room.

The character of the service has been often described. It celebrates the saving of the Jewish people from bondage in Egypt, the rescue by means of the ten plagues, the exodus, the parting of the waters of the Red Sea and the survival of the ordeal in the wilderness, culminating in their seizure of Palestine and victory over the local inhabitants. (That was the first time; in our day this has been repeated, but with aid of outside powers more mundane than the outstretched arm of God.) It is intended as an experience of deep emotion in the life of every Jewish child, reminded that particularly at this time of year have his people often been threatened, the Paschal ceremony, from the Middle Ages to the nineteenth century, having been a frequent occasion of ritual murder accusation and pogrom. In turn each youngest child present is the centre of the gathering. It is for the youngest to open the main proceedings by his enquiry, "Wherefore is this night different from all other nights?" This is called: reading the *Munishtana*. The name derives from the Hebrew of the question that opens the reading (*Munishtana ha laiyelo ha zay mikol ha lailaus*?). And the rest is answer.

I learned to read my question when I was 6, not an unusually early age for the accomplishment. It may be trying for nervous children but my impression is that it is for most—as it was for me, a vain child—

not altogether unpleasant to be for a moment the centre of attention and afterwards encouraged by polite applause. Whoever is youngest for each year must continue the chore, however, providing the peg on which the rest is hung. Until another sprig turns up from another collateral, he cannot be relieved, and after a while he begins to revolt inwardly against being thus publicly singled out as the most junior and least grown-up. I was lucky, however, a girl cousin taking it on after a year or two.

Of course, in an Orthodox family like ours, with the answers too in Hebrew, the child fails to understand a word of it, though he can do his best, with the help of his mother keeping the place, to follow an English crib. There is little time to be bored, however, for every few paragraphs the reading is interrupted by a ritual injunction: "Eat the unleavened bread", "Drink the third cup", "Eat the bitter herb" (this I liked, especially when it was parsley), "Fill the fourth cup". Half-way through you stop for a smashing cold supper: smoked salmon fried salmon and sole and plaice, puddings and jellies, cheese and *matzos*—our banquet was the work of a superb cook, a warm Catholic Irishwoman. Then you resume with a goodly quantity of choruses to join in, and finish with songs that have been pop for hundreds of years. Looked at like that, it is not too bad for the child. As no doubt intended, it keeps him going, right up to the good-byes said in the hall as the visitors wrap up with overcoats and white silk scarves around their necks against the spring night air. Here we all expressed the traditional wish "*Shono ha bo v Yerushalayim*" ("Next year in Jerusalem") to one another, though what any of us would have said if we could have supposed that there was really danger of us meeting anywhere next year except in our comfortable homes I dare not imagine.

Of all the service, I liked best when we banged on the table at the lines thanking God for his grisly disposal of two particularly anti-Israelitish kings; and of course the curse was a thrill.

Incidentally, about that curse. Provoked, it is said, by the persecutions at Passover time, there is a stage when the doors of the room must be opened and an invocation to the Lord: "Pour out thy wrath upon the heathen" is solemnly read. After my grandfather's death, my father officiated as his natural successor. (Incidentally, after *his* death, my eldest brother, as next, went on reading the service, by my mothers' side, for forty years, for so long as she was alive, though by the end of that time the faith, or at least the observance, of some of the celebrants had worn pretty thin otherwise. Neither my eldest brother nor my father could really understand Hebrew, but they had learned to read it and practice made them pretty fluent.) After a year or two my father announced that he would no longer read this passage, he had rather be cursed than curse (a thought which, evidently, had never occurred to my grandfather) and walked out of the room to withstand its blast outside the door, followed, in this as in so much else, by my eldest brother. An uncle—Reggie it may have been—had to take over and stumble through the paragraph, while my mother and the rest of the company rather uncertainly sat tight. The following year, however, two of my aunts, backed by others, threatened to accompany my father, and it was soon evident that no one liked to take responsibility for uttering the curse. Here followed a most interesting and characteristic scene. It turned out that my father objected to the common stand. He did not wish himself to be a party to cursing, but he did not want the curse to be abandoned, for it was a part of a tradition. However, on this rare occasion, he was overborne and there were no more maledictions in our family.

Diverting though the glitter and sing-song could be to a child, the sheer magnitude of the company to be coped with made the event a burden. Of all present one was in turn the cynosure, by all to be inspected, measured, weighed: "And what have you been doing lately?" (Incidentally, though the point runs somewhat ahead of the chapter, what an ordeal this was for my wife, when eventually, for a year or two after the discovery of our marriage, she accompanied me to this still overwhelming gathering, just for both sides to show—or make show, as the Beatles say—that there was no ill-feeling.) And withal they were all so kind! Never in all my life did I meet from any relative anything but kindness, or at least—so it could never be resented—an action which was not kindly meant. I think it was just the abundance of those present, the difficulty of disentangling them, of deciding who belonged to whom, that was so trying. Apart from the few children one sometimes played with, which cousins were attached to which aunts and uncles? Which husband, even, was the property of which aunt? That gentle and shy one there, the flower painter, he was Ethel's husband surely. And when, in clear tones, the three best voices took over part of the refrain singing, that gentle other one must be his eldest son, but whose were the two great girls, the fair thin one and the sturdy ruddy one? The uncles sibling to my father were easiest. The lean, bald one who quizzed me through his monocle and called me Solomon (he never came to Passover) I knew was Edwin, the politician.

The erect one with a heavy black moustache who said little and stared at his wife who was slimmer than all the other women and wrote plays, that was Gerald. Lionel we knew best, he was a bachelor, he owned race-horses and we early heard he was called "Cardy" at his clubs. We loved him because if he came to stay at Christmas he gave each of us a golden sovereign. I could even distinguish some of the once removed cousins, the still-Samuels; Herbert, with his dignified, clipped speech; Stuart, who was in the bank, had done something —could it have been disgraceful?—that had led to him being thrown out of Parliament (I later learned it was the somewhat technical offence of being simultaneously M.P. and partner in a firm with a Government contract, to do with silver bullion and India); Gilbert, who drew up deeds and things, and tried to be funny for us and so was considered eccentric. I even knew the Belgians, kind Ernest and thin Dora and the father with a white beard like the pictures of King Leopold. It was the aunts, so like in shape and mostly with families in tow, that constituted the main difficulty, except for two: Lily, engaged in good works, and her selfless shadow and chaperon elder sister Marian, for these lived alone and were unmarried.

Unravelling them while they were together was only part of it. You might run into them separately anywhere and thank the wrong one for her presents. Especially might you meet cousins anywhere, above all, north of the Park, where they abounded. (Most of them lived in Bayswater, which we were taught was markedly inferior to Kensington.) Some of them might venture into Kensington Gardens—a sort of no-man's-land. And if you made a mistake, what a fool you would feel! I conjecture that it is as a consequence of this problem that I have grown up with, and have to this day, a horror of mistaking people, or addressing them wrongly in person or on envelopes, although I am told this is a phobia and sensible people one addresses do not really mind.

Such a half-way meeting place was the abode of my paternal grandparents at 12 Kensington Palace Gardens. Of the first Lord Swaythling I have little direct memory. At foreign embassy receptions, Ben Tillett, glass in hand, used to lay the other hand on my shoulder and present me to everyone in listening distance, saying, "This boy's grandfather took the chair at the first meeting of the dockers' union" and I would feel appropriately proud. I must have seen my grandfather often, for he did not die until I was seven years old, but all I remember is a vague picture of a small man in black with a patriarchal grey beard, and how much of this image is veritable memory and how much due to the splendid portrait of him by Orchardson I do not know. Somewhere I read that *his* father was a watchmaker; I can only guess whether that was a polite euphemism of the period for pawnbroker. In my Aunt Lily's privately-printed memoir, you may read of my grandfather's opening opportunities in a financial house in the north, his coming to London as a rising young employee-with-a-future, and his venturing on his own to found the private bank that still, now as a limited company, bears his name.

But obvious between the lines of my aunt's tribute, as well as available from other printed sources, spring out not only the conscience and uprightness, the public well-doing and the benevolence by-his-standards to his family, but also the almost maniac expectation that all his sons would follow him in banking, the cruelty and humiliation inflicted on Edwin because he preferred politics, and the financial bonds tightened around this second son almost to the latter's attainment of cabinet rank, as well as the puritan harshness and separation inflicted upon Lily when she felt a call to follow a more liberal modern form of Judaism than the orthodox practices sanctified for him by habit and tradition. In all this I see, though much mellowed by a more permissive era, the pattern of my father.

His widow Ellen, my Grandmamma, I knew much better. Every Saturday we used to walk—riding was forbidden on the Sabbath and although the journey up the hill was not really far even for my little legs I was always lazy—half-way up Palace Gardens to No. 12, next door to what is now the Soviet Embassy. The rooms were large and softly carpeted. The furniture was so solid it was impossible for my puny strength to budge. Backing on the park was a big garden in which I cannot distinctly remember playing though we must have done so sometimes, and above all there were always the aunts and cousins. My Grandmamma was a kind, placid soul, squat and heavy like all the family women, black-clad with a white cap over her white hair, a full face with velvety lined cheeks and a twinkle behind her pince-nez. She gave me chocolate-meringue finger-biscuits that I especially liked and let me read the old *Punches*. These were on the shelves at one end of the room, volume after volume, right from No. 1. Here, crouched on the floor behind some huge armchairs, safe from interruption, out of sight and apparently out of mind of the others with their prattle and tea cups, I went through the whole lot. I did not like, or understand, very much of the earlier ones, whose highest humour seemed the pun, but of the darker brown ones with the years in Roman figures on the spine I read all the picture captions and studied all the cartoons. Gladstone, Harcourt, Salisbury, Dizzy and the rest became familiar figures. Indeed, in some sort this was perhaps my first school of politics.

§ 4

THE RELATIONS on my mother's side were less confusing. It may have been that they were more picturesque. It probably is because I did not encounter them congregated in the mass. They turned up more as individuals. Although they would be in and out of our house, or various of us would visit them, and no distinctions apparent to a few-years-old's eye affected our relationships with them, they did not go in for family ceremonies. In fact, although I in no way noticed this particularly, they were not Jewish. Or rather, only just at one corner was the Jewish connection enough to have made the marriage possible.

My mother's father was the link. He was a person of some distinction, Colonel Albert Edward Goldsmid, the first Jewish colonel in the British Army and founder of the Jewish Lad's Brigade, a sort of counter and adjunct to the Church Lads' Brigade and forerunner of the Boy Scouts. I never saw him. He died before I was born. Not long before, for my mother was already pregnant and, taking the risk that I might turn out a girl, he left me two keepsakes—the walking stick curiously carved with emblems of the four nations of the British Isles presented as a memento by Edward VII to all officers who had done duty as adjutant to him at Balmoral, and a gold watch that still ticks away assiduously and keeps accurate time if I wind it up.

It is an interesting sidelight on my mother's attitude to me that she kept these relics until I was more than forty years old, and even then only entrusted them to me reluctantly and after much importuning.

The forbears of "Grandbertie", as we called him, had been Christian converts and I was often told the story of how the impulse was early born in him to revert to Judaism. It appears that his Christianised parents had taken their little boy with them one day when they were out visiting and he had learned of his Jewish ancestry from the gossip of the coachman as the two sat together waiting on the box. Then and there, the story ran, he had resolved to return to the original family faith. I have always seen the characters in this story in my mind's eye, side by side and muffled up, with the snow falling and the warm steam rising from the great rumps and swishing tails of the carriage pair in front of them. But I am sure now that this wintry detail can only have been embroidery, based on some childish experience of my own. His marriage was no less romantic. As a young subaltern he had fallen in love with the most beautiful of the granddaughters of his commanding officer, while stationed on the south coast. As a penniless junior officer, with few prospects, and Jewish too, he could expect no recognition, and the two used to meet surreptitiously, himself wearing disguise, on a seat on the sea-front until they resolved to run away. The young hero of this somewhat *Vanity Fair* episode was not broken, but transferred. His wife knew little of the facts of life, so that, after a suitable interval, my mother was born "unexpectedly", as she used to put it, in Belfast.

The only image by which I knew Grandbertie was that in an engraved portrait, which hung on the stairs and was framed with so much diffuse white around the head and shoulders that I could only think of him as a grown-up, balding version of those celestial cherubs or *putti*—there were several coloured representations of such in my mother's room—who flutter head and shoulders around Heaven and of whom the French savant, on being asked whether they ever sit down, replied politely: "*Ils n'ont pas de quoi.*" But an indirect personal representative remained in his mount of the South African campaigns, a tall quiet pony named Waterboa, a sandy bay. I was never old enough to ride it—our riding lessons came later, in London, at a school in Knightsbridge and on leading rein round Rotten Row. There does, however, exist a picture of the chubby curly-haired child seated alarmedly on Waterboa (a hand holding the steed off-screen), and I can remember being driven behind the animal in the trap.

I did not miss my maternal grandfather because my maternal grandmother had almost immediately remarried, and so the symmetry agreeable to a child remained intact: on the one side Grandmamma and Grandpapa; on the other Granny and her new husband, my godfather Captain de Vere Beauclerk, late of the same cavalry regiment as my dead grandfather. I always supposed him a jilted admirer who had stayed lifelong bachelor for love.

This latter gallant officer I knew well, for he often played golf with my father. His face was battered by some boxing exploit in the mess, and it is recorded of me (of course I do not myself remember) that, on my offering one day to do up his boots, buttoned at the sides in the fashion of the period, he replied: "No, thank you, I am old enough and ugly enough to do that for myself", only to be rewarded by a limpid look from the brown eyes of the infant and the question: "Is that because of your nose?" Anyway, he did one thing for me for which I have reason to be grateful: put me down at birth for the M.C.C. (Thirty years passed before my name was reached and then I was so hard up I could barely scrape the dues together.) When, later on at school, I realised from the history lesson that, as a Beauclerk, my stepgrandfather was descended from Charles II and Nell Gwyn, I basked in as much glory as if he had been my own congenital ancestor.

There were two daughters of the runaway marriage. The second, Carmel, had been trained to play the harp, which she did sometimes in flowing white robes in our drawing-room. It seemed to me a somewhat ridiculous instrument, perhaps because inappropriate to earth, and I liked her playing no better than my mother's singing, which all the guests applauded. I shall have much more to tell of my Aunt Carmel later, as circumstances brought us into the same line of battle when I was growing up. Suffice it here that my mother was, even as a child, the managing one, keeping the petty-cash accounts, counting the pins and buttons, running the whole small family in excellent preparation for her later life's blossoming as châtelaine. With two sisters in a family of so sterling a father, the Freudian will not be surprised to hear that, as children, little love was lost between them, and I have today a photograph—from my mother's collection but once owned by my granny—showing the two just turned into double figures and facing the lens with somewhat equivocal expressions, due—as I later learned from Carmel—to my mother keeping a deadly grip on her arm with her finger-nails to ensure that she "behaved" during the pose.

Granny wore black mostly, like Grandmamma, especially after being widowed the second time, but she was much more fashionable. You could see how pretty she had been. She used to take me to Lords for the Eton and Harrow match, and give me strawberries and cream on the lawn behind the pavilion. She often stayed with us and everyone liked her, although she was not awfully good at bridge—which she played a great deal—and sometimes irritated my father by not making up her mind. Towards the end she never could remember how many trumps were out; and this became a family byword, for we did not realise it was the first symptom of her illness. She died, at the end, with little memory or movement. My mother took me, in my late teens, to visit her in a country sanatorium. Sad as this story is, she was really not unhappy, for she sat peacefully and white, all but unconscious of what passed about her.

The house was full of splendid portraits and groupings of Goldsmids of long ago, painted by minor masters. Of Goldsmids of the present I remember clearly only a modest and timid young woman, sweet to me and everyone, who would appear for brief periods and then slide away, leaving the exact degree of cousinship quite uncertain. The Hendrikses, on the other hand—my mother's mother's family—were very lively. All, or at least a number, of that long ago C.O.'s grand-daughters were still going strong. There was even, at first, *their* father, a thin gentleman who seemed endless when unfolded out of his chair before my tiny eyes when I was taken in my best to visit him in Vicarage Gate. They had an Empire-building tradition. One ancestor, Sir John Littler, was depicted on our walls with drawn sword, riding a horse; while sundry writhing or slaughtered bodies of Indians lurked in the dark background amid ruins of some town he had destroyed. (My mother also showed us an exciting and very soft-textured shawl, looted by him from Tippoo Sahib's sultanas at the taking of Hyderabad.) The two sisters we knew best had never married. They had seen the Empire and the Continent together, and now settled down together. One of them was small and plump, and worried about everything. She was known as Aunt Bumby, or Auntie B. The other was tall, serene, greyer and never perturbed about anything. She was Aunt Ethel, or rather Great-Aunt Ethel to distinguish her from the other one, my father's sister. Both seemed awfully old. Auntie Bumby would rattle on, her stories were incredible, impossible, invariably described misfortune and nobody believed her: "Do you know what that sort of snake does? It ties itself in a knot to the rafters, and then lowers itself down. When its head was a few inches from my pillow . . ." Auntie Ethel was generally silent, but from time to time would interrupt with a hoarse cackle and: "Nonsense, Beatrice." Aunt Bumby had a sausage dog to which she was devoted and which followed her everywhere. It was smooth-haired and looked horrible. One day, I remember, it was sick on the library carpet. My father took a long-handled steel shovel from the fireplace and tried to scoop the mess into the fire. But the shovel had an incised pattern so that everything came through and this only made matters worse. Great-Aunt Ethel had an aquarium with small freshwater fish and a special one, a catfish with whiskers, that lay, velvety brown, on the bottom and was supposed to rise up when thunder was in the air, only it never did. She used to let us feed them with ants' eggs. The aunts often asked me round to their ground-floor flat, which was quite near and to which the nursemaid used to take me. Here I was allowed to play the pianola —I am quite unmusical but I got a lot of fun out of watching the patterns of holes move across the paper roll of music and jabbing the pedals vigorously with my feet. The only piece whose name I now remember is the "Barcarolle", perhaps because of the pun.

The two great-aunts who had families we saw less often. One was married to a soldier, Uncle Blobs; we went to see him in Netley Hospital, where he lay wounded during the First World War. The husband of the other was the family doctor, a splendid bluff old veteran, all mustard plasters and bedside manner, who dragged us unfailingly through the whole gamut of childish maladies. We loved Uncle Jack, and he reciprocated. To me he was especially indulgent, dishing out excuse certificates—headaches in summer, chilblains in winter—whenever there was something on at school I wanted specially to miss. The price? Only to stand his merciless, penetrating chaff.

His son, Hugh, was our favourite cousin (although a "once removed"). His slightly cynical air and knowing smile, his constant traveller's tales, made him the hero of his younger kinsmen. What adventures he had had! What places he had been to, and what events he had seen! He had been with bandits in Mexico, reported rebellions in Algeria. He handled, and showed us, pistols; even gave father a book he had written about them. In the First War he was with Intelligence, and presented me with pieces of the first Zeppelins that had been brought down; some twisted wire from Cuffley and a crosspiece of aluminium strut. How we laughed at his cleverness when he told us how his department had launched the account of the German corpse factories and of how the Hun was using the myriads of trench-war casualties for making soap and margarine. He explained that he had originally thought up the idea himself to discredit the enemy among the populations of Oriental countries, hoping to play upon the respect for the dead that goes with ancestor-worship. To the surprise of the authorities it had caught on, and they were now making propaganda out of it everywhere. The tears ran down his cheeks as he told us of the story they had circulated of a consignment of soap from Germany arriving in Holland and being buried with full military honours. But, even for us, the taste of some of his tales began to grow sour after he became a Black and Tan.

We none of us ever saw him after this, at least I did not. But years later I read a story in a newspaper about how he had despatched his daughter and a friend to transport General Franco by subterfuge to Spain in an aeroplane to start the Civil War.

§ 5

I WAS born into the midst of this flock on 23 April 1904, St. George's Day—the anniversary (according to consensus) of Shakespeare's birthday, one day away from Lenin's.

For each of her four children, Mother kept what she called a Life Album. This was a thick, dark-covered book with pages of strong cardboard. From the day each was born, she pasted between them written accounts of all that happened to the particular child, or tucked in photographs, press cuttings, certificates. A few years before her death she distributed them among us. I still have mine, but do not intend to turn to it to help out recollection. In a self-portrait, what is most relevant, surely, is what I can remember—it would lose authenticity through others' brush-strokes.

Two episodes I am quite certain are included in this Album. Each occurred soon after I was four, yet even without opening the book I can remember every detail. You will find there, I am sure, the photo with the Bath Club medal. It is pinned on my bathing suit as there I stand—tiny, frail, sweet as sugar (the camera cannot lie). I was 4 years and a few months when I swam the length of the Bath Club baths—I do not know what distance that was—the youngest to that time and a record that stood for several years. As a matter of fact, I should have done it already on my fourth birthday; but my first try occurred late in the afternoon of that very day and, having earlier celebrated by consuming a surfeit of my favourite Fuller's cake with the vanilla icing, I had, at two-thirds of the distance, to pull into the side to let everything come up again. You will also find a poem I composed about the same time. My mother wrote it down to my dictation:

The wily flea
Climbs up a tree
And hides among the branches.
But when comes down
The man from town,
It bites him on the haunches.

Believe it or not, my parents consulted an "expert"—not in zoology surely—and his opinion is solemnly recorded that it showed a sense of scansion remarkable in one so young and promise of a great future as a poet. This prophecy at least has been belied, for although I have spoiled much paper in sixty years I have only three times dared to touch the skirts of the muse—and then always as a helper, never a creator. Once, when Herbert Marshall was writing his competition-winning English translation of the new Soviet National Anthem, I was proud to "improve" one line. The second time was when, working in the cutting-room on the English version of Dziga-Vertov's *Three Songs of Lenin* for the Film Society, I pontifically "corrected" for him the verse translation of a young volunteer cutter sent us by the G.P.O. Film Unit, by the name of Auden. And the third was in Peking, when I became involved in a three-cornered collaborative effort to render into the language of our hosts some quatrains written by the wonderful and tragic poet Nazim Hikmet. The originals were written in Turkish, he explained them to me in French, I translated them into English and then our Chinese colleague put them into Chinese. As a matter of fact, I did later on also translate Hikmet's moving poem about the Hiroshima child, and this was printed. I thought it could also be made into a film, but the project, like so many film ideas, never came to anything.

Most of my earliest memories are concerned with events around the age of 4. I have often wondered at the talents of memoir writers who can begin with definite recollections of what happened at 2 and 3. With me, anything so early is vague and formless. Crying in the dark, perhaps, and being comforted in someone's arms. Toys—a Noah's ark with wooden animals, a teddy bear called Grumpy (I have him still), coloured alphabet building blocks.

(A scientific footnote is desirable here. I provide an instance of the phenomenon called by psychologists "Coloured thinking". That is: I associate colours with such things as numbers, letters, days of the week. Until, in the twenties I think, I read in *Nature* of this as a not uncommon occurrence but one rare enough to deserve study, I had always taken it for granted that it was normal and universal to do so. If I had half-reflected about it at all, I had supposed it to be due to childhood experience of first-seen lettering, such as my alphabet blocks. But this was a misplaced assumption because, after all, they were only red and blue. For me Sunday is a sort of sandy orange, Monday is blue,

Tuesday pale yellow, Wednesday green, Thursday brown, Friday dark grey, Saturday light grey; A light red, B dark blue, C yellow, D pale orange, E grey-blue; 1 white, 2 metallic blue, 3 orange, 4 dark blue, 5 yellow-green, 6 red, etc.)

At 4 I nearly lost a finger. Granny Beauclerk's flat was on the sixth floor of a corner block on the High Street where Barker's other shop now stands. Impatient, I used sometimes to run up or down the stairs instead of waiting for the lift. Either way, young, chubby legs with little weight to carry can outdistance the guardian grown-up and win space for experiment on-your-own. One day I chose to put my hand through the grille protecting the lift-well to touch the big fascinating wheel that rose and fell with the lift, paying out its suspension. The wheel was sticky, and kept the tip of my little finger. Screams brought repairs, but the fourth and fifth fingers of my left hand are still bent over to remind me of it.

At 4 I had an encounter with the Princess of Wales. Above all I hated to be brushed and combed. One rainy afternoon while this rite was being carried out with extra zeal, I was told that this was because the Princess—my mother's "May"—was going to visit us and for her I must "look my best". I knew, of course, that she would come in a golden coach, bedecked with jewels and drawn by many horses, and I ensconced myself on the window seat of the corner embrasure in the nursery, commanding a view of all three access streets, and there waited, nose glued to the pane, so that the spectacle should not escape. With howling and much ill-grace I was dragged downstairs and set astride a footstool, impatiently jockeying upon it while the ladies in the library drank their tea and talked until—"Can I go now?"—I was released to dash upstairs back to my vantage point. I could not believe afterwards that I had missed my thrill, and felt thoroughly cheated. I think I noticed that one of the ladies was wearing grey. She certainly was not wearing a crown.

Soon afterwards my mother's maid, a tall, craggy woman with rugged features, called Clinging, vanished from ken and later I learned that the Princess had coveted and annexed her. This made me sorry, for once, when I had run in from outside in a tantrum, Clinging had come down the stairs to comfort me and, as she stilled my howls and wiped my tears away, bidden me compose myself. "Don't you know there is an East wind?" she said. "If you make a face, and the East wind blows, you stay like that for ever. That's why I look like I do," she added.

This frightened me and carried absolute conviction though even then I decided she must be a wit.

At 4 also I learned to read, my mother helping me from a book with old-fashioned pictures: *Reading without Tears.* I did not find this difficult, though writing legibly was quite another matter, perhaps because I began to try too early. The first books I was given, that birthday, were *The Biography of a Grizzly* by Ernest Thompson Seton and Scott's *Ivanhoe.* Of the first I read every word, many times; adored, admired and suffered with the bear. I eagerly sought after the author's other works and this may well have started me off on natural history. Scott was stiffer. The beginning and end are still vivid enough with me today, but the middle is a blank. Afterwards I tried *The Talisman,* but did not get very far with that either, though I remember Saladin's outdoor parlour trick with scimitar against sword. Of course I did not disdain picture books, like *The Animal's Rebellion,* and spent halfpennies on my meed of comic papers like *Chums* and *Comic Cuts.* Anyway, from then on I loved reading and when forbidden, for there was an idea around that too much reading accounted for my short sight—I had to have glasses very early—disobeyed. The nursery-landing lavatory or, more dangerous, under the bed with a candle, were my refuges for reading-orgies.

Around 4 came our first governess, *Tantchen.* She was an elderly German, with her hair in a severe bun, a yellow unsmiling face bearing several sprouts of hair, a blouse tight at neck and wrists with white frills. We teased her of course, but she was a good soul and not only talked to us in German but wisely taught us out of *Struwwelpeter* and *Max und Moritz.* French came somewhat later, via a rather nebulous Count. An endeavour was made to teach me the piano, but poor Miss Weissberg, whose task this was, could make no impression on my disdain for music. To win my acquiescence, she brought me presents of lead soldiers. In vain! I scorned our ten-finger exercises and played with the bribe instead. My favourite was a charging knight with visor down and shield and armour in a black and yellow pattern.

Soon after 4, too, came my baby sister, Joyce. (Though this I nearly prevented for, as my mother told me much later, I had been restless and kicked her violently when, in the first months of her pregnancy, she had shared her sleeping compartment with me on the Scottish night express.)

And around 4 came the only nurse and nursemaid whom I really remember, and who from then on were the root and refuge of these childish years. How can it be otherwise in rich families? It is the nursery staff who dress, wash, feed, walk out with and discipline each child. They are the constant companions, encouragers, audiences of the children, sharing the nursery landing with them and reigning there as rulers. Whatever the affection of the parents, they can but be occasional interventions, courts of appeal for crime, bestowers of unpredictable blessings, gods out of a machine dwelling in a sort of reverse Olympus on a lower floor. For years nurse and nursemaid were my closest confidantes, an unfailing source of *love without fear*. And yet how little I know about either of them. I suppose it is in the nature of a child to be an egotist, and the process of growing up tempers this egotism with experience. Today I can recognise how much they devoted to us of their own lives. Of course we loved them, kissed them, clambered on their laps, bought them presents out of our pocket money; but the extent of our universe was *our* thoughts and needs and wishes. We took *theirs* for granted.

They were ever cheerful, patient with our tantrums, kept discipline with humour. I was a wilful child. My memories are keenest of disputes and punishments, yet I think I cannot have been as objectionable as my recollections paint me or those around could not have been so tolerant and kind towards me. Perhaps one's memories are most vivid when one is most frustrated. I had very definite dislikes about food. I did not like boiled milk, either its taste or the skin on it. I would not eat rice. Here I was so obdurate the parental appeal court had to be called in. The rejected dishes were presented again and again, cold. It did no good. To this day I cannot touch milk or rice. By my parent's order I was stood in corners. But I was never beaten. My father did beat his sons, after interviews in his dressing-room, with his belt. It was Ewen who got it worst, guilty or innocent. (Is this why he has now become, by profession, a sort of judge?) Ewen was the middle one, so he could naturally gravitate either upwards or downwards for company in various enterprises. If a common undertaking with Stuart turned out badly and had to be paid for, Stuart seldom suffered; he was the eldest and consequently was believed; Ewen paid. If mischief concerted by Ewen and me went awry, Ewen was older than I and must have influenced me. I always escaped. I was Mother's pet.

But our nursery guardians had their own ways of handling us. I remember a holiday at Margate' the only holiday we ever spent away under their curatorship, without our parents. High-spot was a pierrot show at the bandstand on the promenade. We never forgot a song by a man with a much-married wife: "I'm 'Enery the Eighth, I am, I am", and a riddle that long remained for us the height of wit: "Have you anything in the shape of bananas?" "Yes, sausages." But once I lost my temper and ran away. Nurse and nursemaid must have been frantic as they searched through the crowds. When they thought to come back to our boarding house to look for me, there I was, on the bed, changing my socks—a pretext I had thought up as possible excuse for my sudden return. But Mabel (the nursemaid's name was Mabel Ponder) had her revenge. I had set my heart on taking part in the competition at fishing from the pier, set for later in the week. Mabel came with me to help me with my line, and she persuaded me that banana skin was the ideal bait for attracting such fishes as might lurk below. Behold me, earnestly allowing her to tie the fragments on and vainly persisting with my task for hours. Only about fifty years later did she explain her motive: "Why should I stick all those nasty worms on hooks? With bananas I was sure that anyway I shouldn't have to take off any wriggling, slimy fish." Fortunately for my faith in human nature, at the time I had simply thought her choice of lure was based on peculiar knowledge.

Mabel came to us at the age of 14 about ten years my senior—though of course at that time the gulf of authority made the difference appear much greater. She was a comely girl, all pink and freshness, the sort anyone looking at her would suppose an English country rose. Actually her home was Woolwich. All I knew about her then was that she had parents there and, I think, two sisters. I know little more about her now although she has devoted her whole life to our family, having stayed on with my sister as her maid and living with her still, although into her 70s. In middle life she struck up a deep friendship with Mrs. Hynes, our Irish cook, and went with her to early Mass. In spite of much illness, the Catholicism she then adopted has added serenity to her natural cheerfulness. It was usually Mabel who took me out, into Kensington Gardens, shopping in the High Street, everywhere. In the gardens I bowled an iron hoop, or sailed a boat on the Round Pond. Why is it that the boats painted white and green always seem to go faster than the others? We visited a richly-stocked toyshop called Lorberg's, where we bought Meccano sets and plasticine, and I used to get other people to take me out so I could buy her hairpins or pins with white and black heads as a "surprise" for Christmas. My destination for such gifts, I blush to admit, was not Barker's, where the family had an account, or Derry & Toms, which stood midway of the three large Kensington stores, but Ponting's, for that was cheapest. Every time that I pass through Woolwich now, or go to Highbury to see the Arsenal play, association of ideas makes me think of Mabel.

Perhaps loyalty to place, a simple enough concept to a child and therefore the only personal fact he can seize, is the only way in which he can reciprocate the loyalty he receives. Nanny was a Scotswoman. We knew her name was Agnes. The surname was less important to us; I later knew it was MacMichael. She came from Kirkcudbright, which we learned to pronounce correctly, swallowing six of its ten consonants. I remember the veil with small black spots that she put on when we went out together. I loved her instantly, and immediately became a patriotic Scot. With joy I discovered that my mother had, on the Hendriks side, both Stuart and Campbell "blood", a rare combination in view of the usually murderous dealings of these clans with one another (it was a catchword of my mother to say, when she had a headache, that it was the two clans fighting one another). Of course we went to Burns Nicht and St. Andrews Nicht at the Albert Hall. I wore a kilt, with sporran, dirk and buckle (the tartan I preferred, of course, was Royal Stuart), even imagined that I liked the singing and the pipes. At Hallowe'en we bobbed for apples. Soon, with the help of a glossary, I was reading Burns and "Wee Macgregor" too. I devoured a big history book with pictures called *Scotland's Story*, and later in school rejoiced whenever the English were beaten in the internecine wars. I was furious at Flodden.

(Incidentally, it cannot be so very long ago that Willie Gallacher yielded to my persuasion and got me a tam-o'shanter to wear whenever the Scots came to Wembley for the biennial battle. It turned out to have feathers on it, not at all like Wee Macgregor's, and far gaudier than I should dare to don. I felt a real Sassenach when, on my demurring, he explained that evidently what I had meant to ask for was a Kilmarnock Bunnet.)

Nanny was one of a family of twelve brothers and sisters. I met a sister once, bethinking myself of her and looking her up, in the Glasgow hotel where she worked as a receptionist, to borrow a pound when, in my late teens, I was stranded there after a zoological expedition. Nanny left the family some time, I think, after I did, to get married. For years of my childhood she was the being I most trusted, around whom the world revolved. Afterwards I only met her once, when on one of my rare later visits to my mother; she, by then a widow, was also paying a call. We exchanged how d'ye dos. I kissed her cheek. Is the gulf between generations always so impassable?

§ 6

WHEN I was 6, rising 7, a big change occurred in our lives. My father decided to build a country house.

Up to that time we had taken other people's houses each summer. My memory of these varies very much in intensity and detail. The first of them, I think, was in Denham, and I remember very little about it except that in the garden in front of the house there was a grassy slope and I loved rolling down it. The new-mown grass that sticks to one's clothes has a gorgeous sunshiny smell. About Cornwall I remember very much more, especially Kynance Cove, and water whirling round, and rocks and souvenir lighthouses made of grey granite. There was a walk we made over mud flats that seemed endless to my stumbling legs and, at the end of it, thunder-and-lightning teas, where toast was spread with Cornish cream and then you were allowed to take a spoon with golden syrup and make the lightning flashes zig-zag all across it. Most of the time I spent splashing among the seaweed of rock pools with a book by Edward Step, catching transparent shrimps in a little white net on a bamboo pole or picking anemones off the rocks to take home to the bath. Most of these were beadlets, of course, but one day I was excited to find a dahlia. Sometimes we were allowed to go fishing, and we soon learned how to put the lugworms on the hooks and lower the line till we felt the weight touch the bottom. I learned, too, how to quiet a crab by holding it behind its back and blowing in its face. Once there was a shoal of mackerel in the harbour mouth, and we rushed out in a motor-boat and took the mackerel off the line, five or six at a time, as fast as we could throw it to the water. Perhaps it was before then that we went up to Lossiemouth—the long night journey which my kicking heels made so precarious. My father took his golf clubs from Hanger Hill, but all that I can remember is long, flat-stretching sands, as far as you could see, studded with tiny sea shells of every shade of colour, and a kind lady called Miss Grant. The granite here was pink. And after that I remember a holiday at Swanage, which I was determined to visit because of being entranced by the Reverend Hutchinson's *Extinct Monsters and Creatures of Other Days*, and my mother taking me as far as she dared let me drag her along the point, searching for fossils; but we found none and I had to be content with a few bought after our return at a shop in Cromwell Road: a perfect ammonite, a shark's tooth, a bit of backbone, a sea urchin and a brittle star. I was allowed to go by myself to Uncle Blobs and Auntie Vi, who were at a farm near Winchelsea, and there I was persecuted by a big turkey cock and had to defend myself with a stick, but a young Silver Campine chick made friends and followed me everywhere, so that I insisted on taking it home.

Before my paternal grandfather's death in 1911, and while he and Grandmamma were living at South Stoneham, we often used to visit them there. The house was long, and coloured dark rose-red. At the entrance side, beyond the shrubbery, was the village, where you could get brandy-balls. Inside were stone passages and the same heavy comfort as at his house in London. To one side was croquet, and the rear windows gave on to a vast lawn with mighty cedars on it, stretching right away down and down to reach the salmon pool. This pool was tidal. The bottom end of the grounds was bordered by that famous trout stream, the Itchen. The public road passed over the stream, to run south and east of my grandfather's estate. The Itchen ran in two branches under this road, one to go direct under an old water mill, mentioned in Domesday Book and still functioning (we were sometimes allowed to visit it, if not a nuisance, and sniff the ripe floury smell), and the other, controlled by sluices, to tumble first into the huge salmon pool and then flow out of it under an arch where the top touched the water at high tide, thus passing under the road by an alternative route to rejoin the general flood that broadened to reach Southampton Water and the docks. At high water, first my grandfather, then my father, with favoured guests, would fish for salmon. The proper costume was tweedy. With knee-breeches and stockings turned down at the knee, a tweed cap and a carefully selected batch of multi-coloured flies or silver minnows, my father and later my eldest brother too would cast, standing on a breakwater that ran down into the whirling white water, a keeper beside them to net and gaff. I was not allowed to fish from there, but I was allowed to get in the rowboat when, at low water several times a week, it would tow a great net right around the pool; then I might scramble out on the stones in waders, and help pull in fish of all kinds: huge monster salmon, eels, and lampreys with their pouting mouths. All flapped and wrestled with the mesh till taken out and stunned with short wooden clubs.

Turning northward and edging the Itchen bank, the grounds first passed a water garden, where the green grass was deceptive and you had to stretch as wide as you could and tiptoe from stone to stone to reach the sundial without the wet coming over your shoes, and then entered a dark wood, which wound in islands and peninsulas around a labyrinthine lake. Here all was quiet, and fishing seemed much nicer. Here I could be good for hours, the sunlight stealing in patches through the trees, making the midges dance in its beams and showing, where it struck the water, everything clear through the shallow, cold fresh depths to the dead branches and decaying leaves of many autumns set fast in ooze, the caddis flies creeping on the bottom, the water-boatmen near the surface, or the bright metallic beetles and water-skaters racing over the surface film. You were supposed to watch your float, and of course you had to where the sun was at the wrong angle, but mostly you could choose a place where all the fish themselves were seen—dace, roach and perch. You had to hold your breath as the victim ventured forward with tiny movements of his fins and pursed his lips to probe the maggot, earthworm or crumbling wodge of dough dangling as lure. My favourite was the perch, with his shadowy black bars and red prickles.

Once a year there was a big fête, when tents covered the lawns and you could drink lemonade and get your fortune told. Not till I was older did I go to stay, by myself, at the house at Hythe—the Kent one—where Granny Beauclerk lived in second widowhood. This one was tiny by contrast: it was set on a hill so steep it made you puff, and surrounded by dense beds of yellow Rose of Sharon among whose roots and leaves spiders, earwigs and woodlice revelled to make me happy.

My father and mother cannot have liked the house at South Stoneham, and at any rate my father did not wish to wait on inheritance to provide him with his own country home. But he did like the fishing. (After my Grandmamma's death, when the house was sold as a hostel to what later became Southampton University, he at first kept the salmon pool.) His solution was to buy and put in order the decaying property of Townhill Park, much bigger in extent and with shooting rights over yet vaster fields and woods.

The western margin of our new home-to-be confronted the eastern border of my grandmamma's place some two miles distant and across the river.

First came the tow-path. Imprudently bathing from here—so we were told—a footman, favourite of us youngsters, was drowned soon after we came to live here. Was this the truth, or a story made up to suit our age and conceal a more sinister accident while he was drunk? Anyway, we peered over the edge at the shuddery green weeds which had trapped him, gently stirring in the current not far below. Then came a wide water-meadow, criss-crossed with ditches, flooded and even dangerous at the height of the spring tides. Here waterfowl abounded, sometimes snipe and always peewit—in the right season we gathered plovers' eggs by the basketful for my father's breakfast.

Alongside this expanse ran the drive. At the gates, always left open, lived the keeper with his exhibition of crucified predators—owl and sparrowhawk, stoat and weasel—set there ostensibly as a warning to their surviving kin but no doubt really to impress my father with his prowess, for in those days before animal ecology no doubt each was as ignorant as the other about the disadvantage of such executions. This entrance was about three-quarters of a mile from South Stoneham, about a mile from the tram terminal at Bitterne (the Roman Clausentum), where you could clamber to the empty top-deck in front of Nanny or Mabel and wait for the vehicle to start, and about a mile from Townhill itself.

When it had quitted the flat water-meadows on its left, this drive up to the house divided. To the right, as the back drive, it passed ploughed and grazing farmland and a distant copse of tall, open beeches, carpeted with moist moss. This arm, at the top of the hill, approached the house through a maze of subsidiary buildings, a veritable "town". The other fork, to the left, curved upward in a wide sweep, skirting a dense tangle of bluebell wood (my father was always careful to call it wild hyacinth) and rising to the turning circle at the front door. Another, much shorter, drive left this circle to the north-east joining a lane to another village—with a better sweetshop—Westend, and, much further away, the woods where the pheasants and partridges were reared for slaughter.

I suppose I am, strictly, a Londoner, being Kensington-born and brought up in the Gardens, like Peter Pan. But from that time on so much of my growing up was centred on Townhill, first holidays but then week ends as well, that all my local patriotism is coloured by Hampshire and Southampton. I wear the cricket tie and the Saints' cherry stripes, and have lived to see the one team county champions and the other reach the First Division. All that, however was in the future. When my father bought Townhill, I was too young even to realise where it was. All I remember clearly is tramping along vast tree nurseries in the rain—my father was a great planter of saplings—and being allowed to choose a silver birch for "my own"; barrows and scaffolding and excavations across which planks ran precariously or squelched deliciously in the mud; ha-has and pits shallow enough to climb down into and share with fascinating frogs.

The following year, the house would be rebuilt and we should come to live there, and presently in London I should go to school.

II

GROWTH FACTORS

With his satchel—W.S.

§ 1

THE REFURBISHED house at Townhill was big and white, inside and out, with a red roof.

The western edge of the house consisted of long verandahs with basket-work chairs and cushions. Above them, attached to the first floor, was a sort of red-tiled patio bordered by a low white wall for safety, with access from my mother's bedroom and the nurseries. The southern verandah had a long refectory table where we ate out of doors sometimes, when the weather was fine. A rare cork-tree grew upward from its floor through the patio-roof above; my father had built carefully round it.

The gardens this side of the house began with a level terrace of stone flags and grassy lawns, straw targets for darts, and swinging canvas-canopied settees for lazy visitors. A big mulberry tree with a seat round its trunk stood near, and stone steps and banks of turf led to great shady oaks and elms and vast herbaceous borders and a rose garden with one rose—a miniature climber not unlike a tiny Alexandra but pink and white—named after my mother. Yew hedges separated clock golf from croquet, bowls from lawn tennis, and a big ironwork gate gave on to a sunken rock-garden with a goldfish pool, set in a rectangle of pergola clad in lemon verbena. I used to pinch the thin scented leaves and hold them up for visitors to sniff.

Beyond this again another iron gate led to the cricket field, a ha-ha and the woods.

The house was shaped like a big L, the shorter piece facing north, the longer west. To the inside, the south-east, the hill fell most sharply, so here were windows of a third, lower, floor and, nestling in the L's arm, a cement rectangle where we would roller-skate or play stump-cricket with tennis balls.

Beyond were shrubs and gravel roads, flats for menservants, cottages for gardeners, the cowhouse with its prize Jerseys, a dairy, stables and poultry-houses, pigsties and potting-sheds, barns and toolrooms and a furnace-room for heating, which we children were forbidden to enter. Here, too, were the kitchen-gardens that provided fresh vegetables each day, their walls specially zigzagged to ripen successive crops of stone fruit—my father said the nectarines were best; the hot-houses for cantaloupes and muscats, the orchards that specialised in Ribstons; the acres of fruit enclosed in wire cages or under netting, where you could crawl to catch butterflies or liberate songbirds that had entered through the holes.

Later the biggest of the barns was turned into a garage for our first car, a Lorraine-Dietrich, and the coachman learned to drive. He never looked comfortable, however, in chauffeur's clothes; his gnarled face had been better suited by top hat and cockade than by the flat driver's cap. Our real chauffeurs, one of whom had waxed and pointed moustache-ends, went better with their uniform or dungarees as they washed and polished and repaired in the later specially built new garage.

Inside the big house, the windows and white walls made all the rooms light.

The class structure was clearly reflected in the geography: On ground floor and first floor U to the north, less U to the south; the basement and the extra top floor at the extreme south end were definitely non-U. My room on the first floor was almost central.

On the first floor the north part had its own lavatories and bathrooms the corner of the L itself comprised my mother's and father's bedroom —as in Kensington really my mother's room; I don't think I ever saw my father in bed before the illness from which he died. My mother we often saw there when she was working at her writing table, or in the mornings when she was having her hair done by her maid. She had long, glossy, dark hair and was always being congratulated on its "natural wave". I could not understand this, having seen what I had seen, but my wife assures me you can "do" your hair not only to transform but to maintain its nature.

Next to it, also as in London, was my father's dressing-room, and next to that a much more luxurious blue bathroom, with sunken bath in mosaic of blue and many other hues.

In this U short arm were the bedrooms of my elder brothers and also single and double suites including another grand bathroom for "best" guests. For how many persons? Five or six perhaps.

My own bedroom came just opposite the grand staircase down. I did not mind at all that this "territory" was cramped. Bed, chest of drawers and chair were all crowded together in the poky space. When, later on, I was allowed a room of my own at Kensington Court, I was a good deal older and insisted on its being furnished according to my taste, which was abominable and ran to a chequer-board pattern in startling black and yellow. Here I accepted without demur the general colours of the house, white above, green carpet below. The only object of my own individual choice was a huge Ponting photograph, made on Scott's last ill-fated Antarctic expedition. May Wilson, who ran a girl's club and was frequently with us, was a sister of Scott's nearest companion, Edward Wilson, so the disaster was a big happening to us children. She was white-haired, wore pince-nez, pronounced "girl" as "gel" and "vase" as "vayz", and was always cheerful and never cross. We saw the film and were taken to the photograph exhibition. At the latter a plump child was playing on the floor and we were told he was Peter Scott. I was rather shocked because the bright blue tunic he wore appeared to be his sole, imperfect covering. We were each allowed to buy one picture. Stuart and Ewen each chose a version of the ship "Discovery" amid icebergs. I chose killer whales.

Down two steps were the nurseries where Nanny lived with Joyce. In the south end were less spacious one- and two-room suites and the back staircase. The extra top floor at this end was for the bedrooms of women servants. One was not supposed to go up there but might, when small, to visit Mabel. Besides maids, there lived there the housekeeper, who had keys at her belt, and Mrs. Hynes. I have since often wondered why Mrs. Hynes stayed on with us, for she really was so good at her profession of cooking that visiting tycoons used to tempt her with double or treble salary. I think her Catholicism gave her a sense of duty and also she had a genuine regard for mother who had a great interest in food and its preparation, collecting a whole library of exotic recipes. In general my parents rarely parted with any of their staff—only when they had to, as when Clinging was whisked away. Indeed I was quite oldish before I realised that anyone but a cad could part with a servant, any more than a decent person would drown a pet.

Ground floor level at this end accommodated minor guest overflow and, as regulars, those who were not quite guests *or* family, and yet patently even to a child not ordinary servants, for they ate above the salt. Such for instance were my mother's secretaries, her accompanists and our tutors. I remember only two of each. Our first tutor was a slim diffident young man called Butterwick; the next, a sturdy one called Harvey was much regretted when he left for India—in him the cricket team lost a mighty hitter of sixes. Our favourite of the pianists was Ella Ivimey. Her whole family were musicians right far back and she told a story of one discovering in an obscure church register an entry: 'Ivimey, bass horn' only for it to become too evident, when the proud kinsfolk gathered, that the medieval script should correctly have been deciphered as: 'Ivimey, base born'. The other, a rather weedy youth in my opinion, used to show me unequivocally affectionate letters written to him by Lytton Strachey.

All her life my mother had only two secretaries. The first Miss Turner, an elderly spinster whom we called Beanie, used to hold her little finger straight up above her teacup and was superlatively mild. We all made game of her and adored her. After the First World War, she was succeeded by Miss Becker, who, together with Mrs. Hynes' former deputy, Nancy, stayed on with my mother and helped look after her until my mother's difficult end of life and death at 86. Miss Becker had a hard time, for her duty was to be everyone's confidante and make all run smooth, soothing us when it didn't. Neither secretary, it is interesting to note, typed; in those days all personal letters had to be written in clear longhand, for typing was considered impolite.

The basement is quite easy to explain. Here were staff dining-rooms, kitchen, sculleries, pantries, storerooms, coal cellar.

North of the back staircase, toward the U section of the ground floor, ran a corridor with wide windows on the inside of the L—here they were "first floor", looking down on the playground. On the outside came first a special pantry, where lifts with serving hatches ran down to the kitchen; then the big dining-room.

Next, forming the outside corner of the L and giving on the north-west verandah, came the garden-room, with furniture of soft red plush and bookcases I soon raided for Kipling and Sherlock Holmes (Madame Mishu, the Rumanian ambassador's wife, found *Three Weeks* there and spent a whole week-end reading it on the sofa, an elderly sphinx-like black-clad gnome); the actual corner, a boudoir of chintzes and cretonnes and card-tables for the grown-ups; and round the corner, an outer hall, whose carpet could be taken up for dancing, and a "cloaks", where implements for outdoor games were stacked.

Inside the corner of the L was the inner hall, where the main staircase that began at my room on the first floor, ended. Here the gong would ring for mealtimes, and here before dinner the company would assemble in evening dress to wait until all were present before they went in. My family were very hot on dressing for dinner (as may be guessed I hated it, I could never master my cuff-links or studs) my Uncle Lionel was reputed to have dressed in stiff shirt and dinner-jacket even when hunting big game in the Sudan. We were more often a glittering than a dowdy crew while waiting. I remember in particular that Rosita Forbes, a really first-class explorer in the field who to conquer society had felt obliged to wear enormous hats, used to keep us there for what seemed hours before at last making a dramatic entrance at the staircase top, bare-shouldered and with long train sweeping the stair-rods.

Inside also was a gunroom that served as my father's study. The gun-cupboards were kept tight-locked, so if he were not there I might go into it to consult the *Encyclopaedia Britannica* (the 11th, the best, the last fully British, edition of course). I would fly to it at every argument with my father and spend painful hours there on my knees, turning over the thin paper and searching among the small print. Perhaps this was an important part of my education, for we were both opinionated, both stubborn and I was always overruled. I would turn to it to confute him, but he had an infuriating habit of settling matters, whenever my dredging had turned up something worth quoting, by the bland formula: "The Encyclopaedia is wrong."

Right at the end of the short arm on the ground floor was the schoolroom, where our tutors were supposed to make us work. Here in huge cupboards reaching to the ceiling were toys and magic lanterns, books and collections. Bird's eggs, which we had learned to blow, scrap-books, transfers, cigarette cards, my eldest brother's stamps, my insects, killing-bottles, stones and fossils, later on my microscope and slides. One collection of mine which was *not* there was a small case of sample precious and semi-precious stones which someone—I don't know who—had given me. This my mother kept safe, which gave me an inflated idea of its value. There was a diamond in it the size of a pin's head.

My mother read a lot to us at first. She especially liked comic stories of families but would keep stopping to ask what was really happening when she could not grasp the descriptions, or else to laugh when she did. We all had our own favourites, starting with the Beatrix Potters and going on to the E. Nesbits. I think that each of us brothers would secretly have liked to have the Phoenix or the Psammead on his side. We all had a go at what we could get out of Arthur Mee's eight fat red volumes. My specials, curiously enough, were fairy stories: "Cossack" and "Russian" ones with pastel-coloured covers and particularly a fat red schoolbook-looking thing—I have it still, the cover loose—*Scandinavian Folk-Lore*, with tales of ghosts, trolls, elves, early Norse Christians and the like.

Not long before his death and with the First World War well behind, my father fulfilled a dream and built on a "music-room", and a new boudoir for my mother, to replace the school-room.

In these were mingled all the finest *objets d'art* that he had inherited as heirlooms from my grandfather, together with new acquisitions he had long coveted but for which hitherto he had had no space. Only the Samuel Montagu silver was missing—that had already been loaned to the Victoria and Albert Museum. A parquet dance floor had strewn upon it no fewer than four precious blue and yellow Chinese carpets. Each wall panel of the ballroom consisted of a polished walnut masterpiece so exquisite that the craftsmen who made them wept when they learned that pictures were to cover them. The paintings for this duty, perfectly illuminated, were those my father and grandfather had collected: two Gainsboroughs, a Ruysdael, a Turner, a Van Dyck, a Reynolds, the great Constable of "The Young Waltonians". The Raeburn, the Guardi, the Pieter de Hoogh and the Morland went into the boudoir. A grand piano in a special casing trimmed with gilt occupied one corner. Crystal chandeliers hung from the ceiling. Lacquered side-tables bore a huge bull's-blood vase and blue and white porcelain. My father confessed it had always been his ambition to own a Coromandel screen. Here, in this room, there stood not one such screen but two.

(One day I threw open the doors to Joe Beckett, heavyweight champion of Great Britain and Ireland, and switched on the glittering lights. Joe's appraisal: "What a place for a gymnasium!")

While this final addition was a-building, my eldest brother Stuart took the architect aside and made him show him the plans. Ewen and I were envious of these confidences but Stuart explained: "After all, I shall have to live in this place longer than father will." We were shocked at this attitude, considering it unfeeling. We were wrong of course. The system of primogeniture which obtains no less among the English landowning classes than in the Jewish tradition seeks to safeguard continuity by endowing the eldest son not merely with title and entailed property but with the fortune to maintain it. Stuart was only foresightedly fitting himself to carry out a duty that would morally be imposed.

But things did not work out that way. After my father's death much befell in the world, and consequently therefore in the family, otherwise than everyone expected. My brother parted with the house, which he could not keep up. It was sold, and all its contents; the entail on the heirlooms was broken. The pictures, headed by the glowing Constable, went off to Christie's. I, for whom Townhill had so much been my home that I considered myself a Sotonian, not a Londoner, never went back. I did not attend the sale. I could not tell you even now what became of the house, for I have never asked.

§ 2

THE SUMMERS always seemed more sunny in childhood. The cold of winter was chiller—I can remember skating in Regent's Park and red golf balls on the snow as my father's mittened fingers lit his pipe with fusees on the course at Hanger Hill. Pea-soupers were thicker too—more than once the footman had to get down off his box and feel our way for us from flare to flare in front of the horses as we came back from some November matinée. Yet the weather cannot be so different, it must be only that extremes stick in the memory.

Anyway, the young country mouse has this advantage over the young town mouse: the pattern of the seasons is more marked.

Spring came with flowers. Primrose-picking in the woods would come round always just before my birthday, with violets "and a-nen-o-mes" as prizes too. A little later the nearest of our copses would be one great blue carpet with wild hyacinths. My father came upon a little girl-robber there one year, trespassing. She dropped her armfuls and fled. My father, a just and reasonable man according to his lights, reflected that though she ought not to trespass there the harm was done; much better now she should take her booty than leave it there to rot. He gathered the fallen hyacinths in both arms and ran after her, intending to restore them. This must have been a fearsome spectacle to the child, already intimidated by his bulk and status as Justice of the Peace. The more he puffed and ran, the faster she flew, the bluebells scattering behind them both. It is a good mark for him that he could see the funny side afterwards.

By late May and June I would be parting the rushes on the Itchen's bank, peering at caddis-larvae crawling on the bottom in their armour, while father cast over the surface and the mayfly rose and fell. Or I would be lying amid the growing hay listening to bumble-bees, watching trapped grasshoppers jump out of my opened fists.

Summer was the season for car-trips, still an adventure on which punctures were common and could make you late for meals. When we travelled from London the ladies wore veils over their hats and we stopped half-way to picnic on the Hog's Back. We would go westward to the New Forest or eastward to the garden of a Mrs. Sinkins. Could it have been she of the pink? We went to Winchester Cathedral and the tombstone which says: "Here lies a British Grenadier, who died from drinking cold small beer", but the warning was lost on me for I still do not know the meaning of "small' in this context. We shuddered in Romsey Abbey at the box with the skull of the Saxon girl whose perfect features and flaxen hair were supposed to have vanished away the moment the lid was lifted and the skin was touched.

We went to the docks, to see the big liners, White Star and Cunard, and hear them hooting. Sometimes our party boarded them to "see around", or see off passengers my parents knew. (Curious that though my stomach is fair in an open boat even on a rough sea, it gets queasy on shipboard in harbour just from the smell of paint). Sometimes on our own steam yacht hired for the summer we would run up Southampton Water past Netley Hospital until we could see the Needles. On the way back we would be allowed to fish a little, usually off Lee-on-Solent, but by that time mother was always in a hurry to be home.

Once Uncle Lionel took us to Frank Hartigan's racing stables at Andover where his racehorses were trained. It rained hard as we walked round on duckboards and gave a lump of sugar or an apple over the half-door to one or other that looked out. In honour of this visit, much later I used to put sixpences with a street bookie on horses from the stable. Uncle Lionel's "best ever" was White Heat, a sixth in the Derby, that afterwards was unbeaten over hurdles for a time. Our farthest journey was to Salisbury Plain to see a day of flying. I vaguely remember a Bleriot and that in that era monoplanes were spoken of as faster than biplanes. A queer V-shaped tailless aeroplane was mentioned, invented by somebody called Dunne. I distinctly remember a high wind and Colonel Cody's moustache.

But above all, summer was cricket. I loved the game, not because I was bidden, but because of the feel of short turf under my feet. I was cricket mad, whether as player or as watcher, or even as imaginer shut up in my room, for I captained both sides, made up out of Wisden, in vast competitions of paper cricket by myself. At the County Ground I had found a niche, but neither in the Pavilion, where grown-ups bothered you, nor among the public, where you were expected to keep still. I had flannelled my way into the score-box, where the child was allowed to sit in the cool dark depths and help move the big poly-faceted wheels that hung above to register each run. A kiosk in the corner of the ground sold refreshments; penny sticks of Fry's chocolate cream, red, orange, yellow or white in semi-circular section, sucky sweets and fizzy lemonade. The best of these bottles were the ones with a glass blobble stuck in the neck, which you pushed down with your thumb, but there were also the more modern ones that we have nowadays, with metal caps. Trying to lever one of these latter off one day in the recesses of the score-box, I burst the neck of its bottle and cut an artery at the bottom of one of the fingers I had wrenched previously in my granny's lift. The blood bubbling out scared me, but unwittingly I took the best course, closing my small fist tight around my balled-up handkerchief, and running howling for dear life round the ground back to the pavilion, where an SOS call soon brought a doctor to make more stitches.

After that I always watched from the balcony of the professionals' dressing-room. The amateurs I knew by sight: E. M. Sprot, the captain, a huge slogger with a bristling black moustache who, I thought at first, must be a pirate; gangling A. Jaques, the bowler, who had such a good season just before the war and then got killed. But the Pros tolerated me and became friends and heroes.

My passport to the dressing-room was Jimmy Stone, the wicket-keeper. He came to Townhill and coached us, teaching me to keep my bat straight and the handle well forward. I knew every one, as each came in sweating from the field to don fresh shirts or strap on his accoutrements. Red-coloured Alec Bowell, who always opened the batting and threw in so sharp from cover, with ears that stood out like side-lamps; Hampshire's twin post-war bowling pillars, Alec Kennedy, with a chest of black fur, and Jack Newman, who always bowled with his sleeves down and was miserable about the catches that others missed; earlier, E. R. Remnant, small and dapper, whose run was only two or three steps before he produced a twister from behind his back.

But my special gods were, of course, Philip Mead and the rugged giant George Brown, man of mighty frame, left-hand smiter with the bat, fast right-hand bowler with the ball, most daring of silly mid-offs in the field and England's scratch wicket-keeper in its hour of need. My heart was in my mouth each time Mead (C. P.) left us on the balcony to go out and take guard—always middle-and-leg which of course we children imitated—tugged at the peak of his cap and looked round the field, before laying the foundation for one of those big scores with a single tapped to leg. I rejoiced when Brown (G.) sent me to fetch his shoes. "No, not those fairy boots, those over there—the ferry-boats." He reproved me for drinking my favourite tipple, sodawater, saying it would fizz inside me and stop me running. I felt honoured by the advice, but did nothing to change my ways.

I drank in gossip, hoarded till now. Mead had done disappointingly badly on a tour to Australia. Apparently there had been bad blood between him and J. W. H. T. Douglas, who had taken over the captaincy. On board ship, Phil had woken in the night and tried to climb out of the porthole, moaning that Johnny was after him. Another day I was in the dressing-room when Mead came in chuckling from a century against Yorkshire. "If only Wilfred could bowl to me all day from both ends." (This was Rhodes, at that moment accounted one of the best bowlers in England, who was being so disrespectfully referred to.)

My worst moment as hero-worshipper came during the war when, already 12, I ran across the grounds at Lords and caught a man in white with my autograph book during the special match played to celebrate its centenary. As he signed the book he asked me: "Do you know who I am?" and I, who had forgotten, was stumped until I saw the signature C. B. FRY. What I have not forgotten since was his expression. If only it had been someone else!

Fry, it may not be generally known, was the agent in introducing into the 1921 Test match team the three Hampshire cricketers who rescued England when Australian fast bowlers Gregory and McDonald were cutting down the flower of England's batsmen. The selectors, at wits' end, tried to dig out Fry, who after holding Ranji's hand at Versailles throughout the Peace Conference, was now safely installed as schoolmaster-commandant aboard his Hamble training ship. They remembered that the great athlete had always been sound against the fastest bowling.

Fry, who had no Test ambitions by then, agreed to think it over. He made a few handsome county scores but then came the crux. I can see him now as he brought off a spectacular running catch fielding fairly deep. Brown was fielding near him and said, as they changed over, "Wonderful catch, sir, for a man at your time of life." "Ah," responded the great man, "but I always was a wonderful cricketer, George, you know." After his second knock he reached the pavilion and came painfully up the aisle between the cheering members. As he passed us he exclaimed, quite audibly and with evident satisfaction: "The finest innings of my life!"

What we did not know was that the innings we had just seen was also to be his last. He had suffered agonies from lumbago all the time that he had been batting. Fry told the selectors he could not play in the Test, they must pick Tennyson. Lionel Tennyson was captain of Hampshire then, but his batting average for the county was in the 20s, his bowling in the 50s. To put him in the Tests appeared absurd. But Fry knew he was a devil-may-care fellow who feared nothing. The selectors gave in to Charles Fry.

I saw the result in the following Test at Lords. Again the Australians ran twice through the English team. Only Woolley, batting perfectly around the wicket, withstood them. In the first innings Tennyson, going in low in the order, scraped and floundered for a score of 5. His second innings was a repetition of the first. At about the same score, Carter, usually a prince of wicket-keepers, standing back, dropped an easy catch that Tennyson had put straight into his gloves. Had the wicket-keeper held the catch, which he must have done nine times out of ten, this would simply have been the end of a curious experiment. As it was, it became a turning point. Tennyson went on to make seventy instead of seven and was appointed captain for the last two matches in the series.

In the fourth at Leeds he made another high score with a split hand. When he went into the fifth, he had Mead and George Brown at his side. George stood behind the wickets to strengthen the weakness in England's batting and Mead made the highest score by an Englishman at home against Australia up to that date, 182 not out.

We were all older then, but not too grown-up for this excitement. We knew Tennyson well and, as everybody else did, liked him. He used to stay at Townhill for all the county matches at the Southampton ground. He was always ready for a wager. During an important game at Lords, he broke two ribs and put himself out of play for weeks, boxing Lord Dalmeny in the dressing-room. His wife was a pretty, China-doll sort of woman, and after dinner at Townhill, when she had left with the other ladies he would, for a bet, call her Pekingese to him and, amid the port and the cigars, flick nuts at it, hitting the poor brute on the nose every time.

I ran into him at the Albert Hall during Beckett's second fight with Frank Moran. Joe had lost the first—Frank Moran had held his neck on the blind side of the referee and pulled him on to a punch on his adam's apple; now, in the return, Moran put Joe down in the first round. I bet Lionel Tennyson £5 that nevertheless Joe would this time get up and win, which he did in the fifth, but I never saw Tennyson again and he never paid me. Perhaps this was fair, because I had not got the money to pay him if Joe had not got up; but I would have found it somehow.

Ewen and I saw every ball bowled in that fifth test at the Oval from the professionals' dressing-room directly behind the bowler's arm. We took George Brown back up to London on the Monday morning, Ewen driving and I having chickens all the way lest he should run into something and upset George's eye. I learned the expression "Chinese drive" when an England batsman (nameless) played forward to a ball on the off so that it went off the edge for four behind the wicket on the leg. I watched a brilliant piece of gamesmanship when Charlie Parkin, bowling the first ball of the Monday morning, as though let it slip out of his hand so that it shot up into the skies like a donkey drop and came straight down, with the Australian batsman stepped back and watching it as if frozen, to miss the wicket by a hairsbreadth. Charlie must have been practising that one all the week-end.

The last time I met the Hampshire Pros was one year later, when I was 18 and for some reason in the Midlands. All England was ringing with the story of how Warwickshire had got Hampshire out for 15 and of how Hampshire, following on, had made 521 in the second innings and won by more than 100 runs. I found myself on the train and in their compartment. They had just accomplished one of the most extraordinary feats in cricket history but what fascinated me was that, instead of basking in a shared glow of pride or engaging in mutual congratulations (Brown had made over 170 and there were other centuries), these men, normally on such good terms, spent the whole journey in recrimination and blaming each other—"if only you had not done this or that"—for what had happened in the first innings. I think I understood then, for the first time, the strain of top-class sport on its practitioners.

Our own efforts, certainly, were at a lower level, though they sometimes roused passion. The match of the year was always the meeting between the two country houses, ours at Townhill and Grandmamma's at South Stoneham, played home and away in alternate years. One season, on Grandmamma's ground, there was an awful moment when our head gardener, batting, blocked the ball and, finding it near his crease, picked it up and rolled it back to the other end, where Grandmamma's head gardener was bowling. The bowler, Fred Rose, to everybody's consternation at once called "How's that?", and the umpire had no alternative but to give our man out. Nobody at Townhill spoke to Fred for two years.

As for me, my actual playing career was undistinguished. My two brothers and I each went eventually to the same preparatory school. The eldest—Stuart—kept wicket for the school team when he was there. As each left prep school, the other came, slipping into the vacant place, and soon the Townhill team had three would-be wicketkeepers. Of course there could be no question which of us would occupy the post, and I did not enjoy playing longstop to retrieve the occasional 4 byes that slipped past my eldest brother. I could not bowl. I could scarcely bat. I could catch reasonably well and was not frightened to stop the ball. But where to put me in the field to hide me? All my life I have suffered from a sad disability in athletic terms. Sh . . . I cannot throw. It is absurd to race along the outfield, stopping a certain boundary, and then, as the applause dies down, stand like a stuffed dummy, waiting for another fielder to run towards you, or throwing the ball so that it only reaches halfway to the wicket. And close-wicket fielding is not safe for small children.

So my only destiny at Townhill was as a hopeful stone-waller near the bottom of the card. Curiously enough, though my loyalties were all Hampshire, it was Hendren of Middlesex (I suppose because I imagined, quite falsely, that I resembled him in figure) whom I took as pattern. Whenever I went to the crease I stood up, looked around, raised my bat vertically and like him twiddled it in my hands. With me, however, alas this magic was less potent. My best season was the last. I batted all through it and was proud of an average of five point something with a highest score of three.

Let it be recorded here that since these days I have only played cricket three times more. Once for Schoolboys versus Members at Queens Club. Once for Film and Stage versus Lord Ebbisham's team of Lords and Commons at Welwyn. (Anthony Asquith took on the safer job of scorer.) And once for the *Daily Worker* against Transport House. This was just after the Second World War. Political Black Lists were at their height of venom, but for the English cricket is religion and even the Right-wing, which could isolate us Communists from the rest of the Labour movement in all else, did not dare interfere with the sacred cow of sport. We nearly won the match, too, and would have done, if it had not been for a sticky bureaucrat half-way down their batting order whom nothing could winkle out.

Bats were in short supply, then, and difficult to get. I had a privileged source, as MCC member, and got a new one at Lords' to pass on to the team. I thought perhaps I would steal a march on our opponents and, very daring, for the first and only time ever, fixed up an hour's hard batting practice at the nets.

The ground at the Lord's nets was extremely sodden and the two hard-bitten old pros who faced me saved their wind by devoting themselves exclusively to slow spin. I tried to watch their fingers, and the ball on to the bat, with grim determination. No matter how carefully I thrust the bat forward it was invariably inside or outside the break by about three inches. As this happened for about the fiftieth time the senior of my tormentors spoke, his tone as impassive as his leathery face. "Very difficult wicket, sir," he said.

§ 3

IN AUTUMN came the shooting parties. Lists of guests to stay would be made out, day-visitors arrived ready in cloth caps and tweed knee-breeches. Each of my elder brothers grew up to be allowed a gun, first a four-ten, later a twelve-bore. As will be later related, I followed differently. At this time shoots for me meant going out at lunchtime with the ladies, traversing muddy ruts and helping the house-servants to cover trestle tables with linen, spread our waterproof sheets and unpack the hampers. We would find some trampled corner of a field or bare ride in the woods with straggling branches leafless against the sky. My special friends—keepers and underkeepers—would be lording it amid rows of corpses spread out to count by braces: pheasant or partridge, rabbit and hare, pigeon and woodcock. The beaters, their ale hastily consumed behind the hedges, would be trudging off across country in readiness to drive the game towards the first after-lunch stand.

Sometimes, if good, I was allowed to take station immediately behind the elbow of my father, or of some favourite guest, and watch the marksman blaze away with two double-barrelled shot-guns loaded and handed to him alternately. Even then I counted it no very worth-while change for the rocketing bird to become a falling bundle of feathers in mid-air, and be retrieved by the dogs to send to some poor relation. I coveted the blue jay's feathers that boastful guns sometimes wore in their hatbands or conferred on ladies, but I never asked for one.

I do not think any human casualties occurred at our battues—elsewhere they may have been common. I remember Sir Alfred Mond (afterwards first Lord Melchett), a New Forest neighbour and frequent participant in father's shoots, being twitted for having put several beaters in hospital at one of his own not long before. He pooh-poohed the affair as trivial: "Rubbish, it was only small-shot. A few days comfortably laid up in hospital and they'll be right as rain. They get well paid for it. They like it." He may have been right, but I did not believe him.

Winter was Christmas, and New Year the Servants' Ball.

The Jewish calendar includes a festival called Chanukah, recalling a magic endurance of holy lamp oil in short supply during a Temple siege by the Romans. At this, too, candles are lit and presents exchanged and it takes place around this season. My mother was always careful to maintain the ceremony and explain its meaning to us children, but it was a strictly small-scale inner-family affair. It was Christmas that was the annual excitement celebrated by the entire household and a packed house-party of guests, mostly regulars. Better said, perhaps, Yuletide, in the full pagan form of the English tradition. The Christian side of the affair slid by unnoticed, Catholic members of the staff, or guests, being off to early mass and back again before the rest were about.

We looked forward to the same visitors every year. I have already spoken of our cupboard love for Uncle Lionel's gold. "Presentwise", as the fashionable verbal form would have it nowadays, we children did extremely well at Christmastime. Everyone brought us tribute. It is much easier, and cheaper, when visiting rich hosts to show appreciation by giving something to the children than to think out something that the parents lack. Ungrateful beneficiaries of this system, we smoothly took it as our due. The question in our greedy minds as each favourite guest arrived was never "whether" but "what". Bottom for welcome was anything *useful*, such as a box of handkerchiefs or a pair of socks. Surely anyone sensible must realise that to be acceptable a gift must be a total luxury? The useful was provided automatically by our parents at non-present times.

Another form of ingratitude, at least in my spoilt bringing-up, was resentment at the obligation to write thanks—called by my mother a "bread-and-butter letter" and imposed by her meticulously if the donor of any gift were not personally staying in the house. A gift was not a gift, I argued, if attached to it were the strings of having to write back. I would sit sullen and wordless before the white, presently blot-bespattered, page. Maybe this early training accounts for the clichés and empty phrases that to this day creep so abundantly unbidden to my pen.

The nursery was the sorting office. Here, wrapped to disguise their shape, our presents for each other would be handed over. Here also we would make up the stockings for parents, guests and nearest staff. By custom there must be a sprig of holly in each top and a tangerine in each toe. Our own were made up in I know not what secret place, and I blush to admit that often a stocking proved inadequate, a pillow-case had to supplement it. Looking at anything before 7 a.m. was not encouraged. As soon after that as was decent we might lug our prizes in to mother and unveil them in order, youngest first, by her bedside before helping to open hers.

The evening before we had always been allowed up late, for ghost stories. We would sit in the dark round the stone fireplace in the outer hall, lit only by the glowing fire. Everyone had to try to tell one; Hugh Pollard's were the best. Then, still in the dark, fiery snapdragon would be brought in. Nobody might be cowardly enough to funk snatching the raisins and nuts sprinkled with brandy out of the darting flames—even if, as I, not liking them, he did so only to pass them on.

Nevertheless, the breakfast gong would go at half-past-nine next morning as on any ordinary day.

Christmas morning breakfast was no different from any other breakfast. Breakfast at Townhill with guests staying there was always an enormous meal. The only difference at Christmas was that we children might eat less, having already spoiled our appetites by tasting the sweets in our stockings.

Choice at breakfast was unlimited. There was porridge for those that liked it, with brown or white sugar or golden syrup, and grape-nuts or post-toasties with cream from the Jersey cows. On a sideboard covered with a thick circle of plateglass stood lidded silver dishes, each heated by a methylated spirit flame below. Inside these might be kippers or bloaters; smoked haddocks in milk; eggs fried, poached or scrambled, or baked in little ramekins; fish cakes or egg cakes; kedgeree—which I never touched, not liking rice; smoked beef—we never served ham or bacon; kidneys on toast. Sardines would be in a dish with a porcelain fish on top.

We served ourselves *ad lib* from this sideboard. Servants did not attend in the dining-room at breakfast. They answered a bell, to receive the timing in minutes if a boiled egg were wanted, or replenish the tea or coffee or the racks of toast.

Ad lib on the dining-room table itself were butter pats, marmalade, jams—always including my favourite strawberry (Tiptree Little Scarlet) but sometimes home-made and sometimes exotic (my father went in for guava) and honeycombs in season (made fun by an occasional dead bee). Lastly, fresh fruit. And, as I did not take tea or coffee, my individual soda-water syphon. No one burst.

Rereading this, I notice I do not list caviare among the foods available. As a matter of fact we never served caviare at Townhill. My mother did not like it, and though my father sometimes had some in

Kensington it was alleged to be an acquired taste, not for children. Not unnaturally, like the fox without the grapes in Aesop's fable, I decided that it must be a taste not worth acquiring and when I first visited Russia after my majority never touched it. This was a pity because in that year (1925), possibly for some reason of transport, it was more abundant in the Soviet cities than butter. I never really tasted caviare until I got back to England, when everyone who gave me a "come-back" celebration, starting with H. G. Wells at the White Tower, put on caviare especially as an appropriate honour and I had not the moral courage to refuse. This *made* me like it, which was a pity, for I have never since been able to afford it and of course only the best, the big grey-grained kind, will do. Incidentally, to protect my father from a misconception, I should record that this apparent selfishness of his about caviare was no doubt based on a sincere belief that others would not appreciate the stuff as much as he. He was not ordinarily mean and we were brought up to look on as the height of infamy a perhaps legendary Lord Portsmouth who was said to have kept two grades of cigars, one for himself, the other for his guests.

After this beginning we would go out for crisp, no doubt necessary, walks before lunch, along the drive or else in the woods.

Lunch had usually three or four courses, as well as cheese and fruit. Dinner followed the same pattern except that—as I resented—a savoury took the place of cheese. We always served salad *with* hot meat and vegetables, not only with cold meats as an English table d'hôte does, or as a separate course mixed by the host like the Americans.

The Christmas versions simply included the conventional centre-pieces in this model. A huge roast turkey at lunch (I abhorred the stuffing). A Christmas pudding aflame with brandy included silver charms and threepenny bits, all carefully wrapped in paper by mother so that they should not be swallowed. (I did not like Christmas pudding so I cheated and peered for a glimpse of white corner before spooning out a share I should be pledged to eat.) I did not like mince pies either, and twelve of these had to be consumed, one each day starting with Christmas dinner, before Twelfth Night if one wanted to earn twelve happy months in the year to follow. Looking back, I seem to have enjoyed all the ceremonics without faith in any of them or a taste for the eatables that went with them.

In less than a week came New Year's Eve and with it the Servants' Ball. Everyone had to take part. Guests and family stood along one wall. Staff and their families along another. It was for the master's family to break the ice. I cannot remember whether my mother led off with the butler or the head gardener. My father's figure was not suited to dancing, so it must have been Stuart who followed with the housekeeper or Mrs. Hynes. (Did I say that the latter was unmarried? But in those days a "Mrs." was attached, out of courtesy, to her high office.) Everyone else had to pair off and follow.

I may as well say here that I have never liked balls or dancing. Certainly I started by having dancing lessons at the right age—5 or 6—and was taught the conventional dances of the period, complex formation affairs like the Lancers and Sir Roger de Coverley, and the twirling ones, like the waltz and polka, both of which were apt to make me giddy. I was not deft enough for the sword dance or the Highland Fling, which I should have liked to be able to do, and this touched my Scottish pride. When I did have to go to parties I ate my share of meringues and jellies and played my part in the games. But I never took pleasure in dancing with a child of my own age—save one little girl at a party in Elvaston Place when I was 6, whose name I still remember.

I did not like to be touched by either sex. I hated kissing. I could barely stand still to have my hair brushed and my mother was for ever reproaching me—to a point where eventually it affected my relations with her—in public and in private for not looking sufficiently tidy. It was not a matter of dirt—I was not a dirty child and anyway Nanny and Mabel saw to that—but of buttons forgotten and left undone, a crumpled shirt or ruffled hair, and I gave her plenty of scope. (To this day I cannot always manage to look in the glass to see my tie is safe under my collar.) Even well into adulthood and beyond my marriage, when I would pay a rare visit to my mother after infinite precaution under my wife's eagle-eyed control, my mother would ever—to my total confusion—step forward to remove an imaginary speck or straighten something fractionally out of line before all the other guests.

I hated the preparations for parties and I hated the physical contacts. Perhaps, with hindsight, I should now guess this latter aversion to have been some kind of infantile sexual response, for at adolescence dancing was much too deep an affair with me to be taken as a pastime. If I found a girl attractive, to embrace her signified too much, the music nothing. To clasp one, however distantly and fingertiply, whom I did not like, made me shrink inside.

There was much dancing to be got through at every Townhill New Year's Eve ball. It would never have done not to have had one's programme card filled out on every line. Or to have run off to bed before, at midnight, one of my brothers, impersonating the dark man who to bring luck must be first across the threshold, went out to return with his face blacked and carrying a bottle of whisky, and we could at last link arms, sing Auld Lang Syne and be released. The only engagements I looked forward to were the barn-dance and the valeta with Mabel and the senior parlourmaid.

As we have already seen earlier, I was of exploring, scientific bent. One New Year's Eve morning I picked up a large rock, as heavy as I could hold, and solemnly, enquiringly, dropped it from about waist high on my big toe, just to see what it would feel like. This earned me an invalid's exemption from duty, a small walking-stick, and an interesting bandaged foot throughout the evening and for some time afterwards. I assure the reader that, at least consciously, my design of research was perfectly sincere. And at that time I had not even heard of Freud.

§ 4

I DIFFERED from my brothers, though not, doubtless from many other children, in a particular interest in natural history.

Better said, perhaps, zoology. Plants were dull compared with things that moved.

A parental attempt to interest us in horticulture was not successful. We were each given small plots of Townhill kitchen garden. I was too small to work properly in mine, so I had to be helped. It became a flourishing business. The head gardener provided seeds. Under-gardeners planted them, thinned them and watered them when I forgot. I had the fun of picking the flowers, pulling out the lettuces and gathering the peas. The flowers I sold direct to mother, the vegetables to the kitchen. What was eatable when cooked was served to me eventually, and I ate it. My lavender bush grew enormous—my mother bought the lavender. I dried it, stripped it, sewed it into muslin bags with Nanny's help—my pay for this work was *6d.* an hour—and the finished product was still mine to perfume the handkerchiefs in my own drawer or give away. Not even this excellent subsidies system, however, awoke my interest in either gardening or commerce.

Animals had personalities.

Tame things seemed tame. Stuart had a spaniel, Ewen a fox-terrier. I mooned a bit over Caesar, the dog that followed King Edward the VIIth's coffin at his funeral, but had to put up with a white Angora rabbit that I called, hopefully perhaps, Ferocity. It failed to live up to its name and its owner combed it so irregularly that it soon developed tangled side-flaps like broad hairy wings. I wanted a fox but could not find one. I lost my heart to two red pandas and a jerboa in Gamage's pet department. I compromised with a hedgehog. Something in this sturdy animal's prickliness and defensive confidence appealed to me. Alas, when Ewen's fox-terrier found it in the loft above the stables and, rolling it down the stairs, forced it to open, the animal's spherical defence turned out its death.

I started as a hunter and killer. I found the birds' nests and blew the eggs myself; captured the butterflies and moths and put them in the cyanide bottle to die—"painlessly" we supposed. I would be up at first light to see which mole-traps had their iron framework crossed and point out to the mole-catcher new hillocks raised amid the dewy grass. My aim against the wasps was genocide. I learned to crush the thorax with impunity as the insect struggled for liberty against the windowpane. I scored my victims like an enemy's horse-chestnuts broken at conkers. When I accompanied the gardeners to a hole in the ground, helped push in the poison and seal it with plaster of Paris, as I listened to the buzzing in the nest below grow still, how many hundreds might I fairly add?

Suddenly, the very next summer, all this was reversed. I do not know what influenced this reformation. My father had always forbidden us to take from a bird's nest more eggs than one in three (the birds were not supposed to be able to count), and my mother would not wear egret plumes, but I do not think this made much impression. It could have been something I read; *Black Beauty* and *Beautiful Joe* did not impress me as much as had Thompson Seton and a remarkable pink-covered tuppeny paperback I got in the "Books for the Bairns" series called *Rambles of a Rat*. But if it was anything of the sort it is more likely to have been some motive utilitarian and egotistical: I had noticed in my fairy stories that the youngest son nearly always overcomes his brothers and wins half the kingdom as a result of showing compassion to some miracle-worker disguised as bird or beast.

Anyway, so far as wasps were concerned, now I was as eager to save as formerly to destroy. When guests flapped at intruding wasps at mealtimes, I lectured them on the benefits these insects conferred on mankind by killing flies, asking as toll not fresh fruit but only such as had fallen and bruised. I would explain that people endangered themselves only by sudden, careless movements, and proved my point by gently enveloping the window-trapped wasps in a handkerchief and putting them outside, preaching my theory the while. I even developed a special skill at catching them live at table under inverted wineglasses, transferring them all together into one to save glasses, and leaving that one with perhaps a dozen or more exploring the tablecloth angrily throughout lunchtime. The visitors were terrified.

I knew no moderation in my crusade and even went so far as to fight my eldest brother in the games-room to save a wasp. I grappled, we slipped, a heavy-framed picture came down and landed on our heads. As we continued our struggle on the floor I felt my fingers, tightening round his throat sticky with blood. Even then I did not stop until someone cried out that it was I who was bleeding. Then, scared at once, I halted for the usual stitches, this time in my scalp.

From now on I resolved to take the life of no animal for pleasure. For "science" was different. Or for food, if need were proved.

These qualifications enabled me largely to have the best of all worlds. I never shot for entertainment and, as will appear, have very seldom used a firearm even as collector. But in a few years' time I did a good deal of trapping of small mammals, no doubt exaggerating to myself the advantages to mankind of the knowledge so gained. For a time at least I went on fishing, consoling myself with the doctrine that fish do not feel pain, they are not like you and me. I would catch fish, and then put them back. It is one thing to renounce taking the life of a fellow-creature for selfish amusement, quite another to let it off a bit of discomfort. There is of course something in this convenient doctrine of unfeeling fish. Sharks, for instance, will go on snapping at a lump of bait even after being cut in half. But then injured men, too, sometimes are unaware of wounds in the heat of battle, and Tommy Parker, the Southampton right-back, played one of his best games after he had been concussed. Young as I was I began, however, to realise the fallacy of this hunter's argument: whatever the sensations of the victim, the harm is in the indifference to suffering that develops in the claimed superior. It is too easy to extend this complacency to humanity. One year when we were driving to Wimbledon, my mother was praising the admirable court manners of the Japanese. An English diplomat who was on his way with us to see the Lawn Tennis and who had spent some time in the Far East corrected her: "You should remember, my dear, these little men are different, they do not feel emotion as you and I." At least I did transfer my main interest from pinning out butterflies and moths to rearing them; and bowls of sucked-out meat fragments and tadpoles, white-wood breeding boxes of larvae smelling of insect excreta and decaying cabbage leaves, replaced the neat cabinets in the lesson room. If I did, at eight years old, take to going round the golf course with driver, iron, niblick and putter it was mainly because there was also a butterfly net in the golf bag, the insects captured while others drove through were identified and then usually set free.

I became pretty well a vegetarian for about ten years. I was never a very great one for meat. The youngest at house-party time is made to stay up for dinner or sent to bed early for the convenience of the household, according to whether he is needed to make a fourteen or must be got rid of to keep the numbers down to twelve. I was perfectly happy to eat curled up in the blankets in my own bedroom, so long as I could have sent up my favourite dinner: kippers—which somehow I never thought of as having been animate—followed by fried onions and mashed potatoes, and these followed by any sort of cheese. Like my mother I drank neither tea nor coffee, and it was impossible to punish me with dry bread and water for I particularly enjoyed both.

This bout of at least partial vegetarianism lasted until, as a teenager, I was first asked to lunch in their Adelphi flat by Mr. and Mrs. Bernard Shaw. I was the only guest and at the main course a covered dish was placed before me and the cover removed to disclose a solitary cutlet specially ordered by Charlotte so that the visitor should not be discommoded by the principles of G.B.S. I was much too embarrassed to explain this was unnecessary, and in my supposed position as carnivore heard G.B.S. explain how disgusting it was to incorporate into one's own body the dead flesh of other animals. To show spirit, I had to answer that by choice of words one could make anything sound disgusting, and that it was just as unpleasant to incorporate in the body, as he was willing to, decaying discards from the sex organs of hens. Charlotte applauded and he won my heart by taking it very well. When I got home I found that my devil's advocacy had convinced myself, and my vegetarianism was thenceforth at an end.

§ 5

Before I go on to school life and leave this stage of my infancy, I must write a little more here about games, because it was through these that in childhood I developed so many relationships both with adults and those of my own age.

Looking back, I think their special attraction was the opportunity for self-assertion, perhaps particularly important for a young boy. I did not at all like exercise for exercise's sake. The tag "*mens sana in corpore sano*" so beloved of headmasters, I found only boring, and when I went to school I hated all gym exercises that were merely repetitive. I have been sorry about this since, for I never developed the strength in my arms that could get me up a rope or enable me to do setting-up exercises, and I think that if the child knew how much the development of muscles depended upon practice with them he would never make my mistake. There is a photograph on record of what must have been the smallest Boy Scout troop on record: Stuart as troop-leader, Ewen and myself as rank and file, but this did not last more than a few weeks. Apart from swimming, which I have always enjoyed any time, anywhere—Ewen and I used to go in to Southampton open air baths as soon as we could cycle as far as the trams at Bitterne, even before we were allowed to go by ourselves on wheels right into the town—I needed the element of competition to be interested.

They say team games teach you to play for your side. Maybe, but only if they are not compulsory. A child of spirit will resent an obligation placed upon him by *force majeure* as a duty; he will scrimshank and get out of it as he may. If he volunteers, it is a different matter. It becomes an obligation of honour in such case not to let down your colleagues. Cricket is supreme in this respect: there is no other sport in which an instant's inattention or cowardice at batting or fielding may destroy your self-regard and lose everything, without any opportunity of second chance. At games the child is always being able to test himself. I was dead keen to win, or at least do well, and may have been unpleasantly gloating when I did. But we were none of us bad losers and none of us ever cheated or wished to cheat. This was not virtue but because we early realised that the whole essence of a "game" is acceptance of its conventions; if you do not operate within its arbitrary limits you might just as well not play at all.

I had a certain adroitness at Spillikins. My memory was good—I did well at Pelmanism and "I sent my Aunt to China". I could be quick amid the noise at "Pit" and "Racing Demon". Simple reasoning games I could master: I knew the trick of always winning with the Geese at "Fox and Geese" and of beating those who did not know it with the Fox. Nanny and I won prizes together at whist drives. But I think the most important training we had was in being allowed to gamble at games like Vingt-et-Un, Poker, Roulette and our favourite, a Japanese card game called Hana-awasi. (By the way, there is an extremely useful table of probabilities for all hands and draws at Poker in the *Encyclopaedia Britannica* 11th edition, but it was not much use to me for I have always been a poor bluffer.)

Hana-awasi was brought home by my father from his Japanese visit and was played also by some of his friends who especially admired oriental art, like the connoisseur Oscar Raphael. It was taught to us children by one of those closest in our family circle, Lady Tama Arnold, the beautiful young Japanese widow of the Victorian author of *The Light of Asia*, who eventually lived to a great age and died only a few years ago. It appears to be rather a disreputable game in Japan. Once when the Mikado's hereditary chamberlain, the Marquis Nakonomikado, came to spend the week-end at Townhill, my mother asked his wife if her husband played and she replied "Certainly not!" in rather a shocked tone of voice. But when he saw us children take out the cards and counters, it turned out that he certainly did. He joined in and trimmed us all.

The name means "Game of Flowers". It is not difficult but complicated and each pack includes forty-eight cards, representing four values and twelve months, each characterised by flowers, animals, weather and sun or moon. Special baskets contain your counters, and when you lose the capital you started with you borrow more, taking with the extra cash a symbol of the debt incurred, a Dharma, a fierce-looking bodhisatva with no legs or arms; this sinister holy man sat in one place so long he lost the use of them and therefore will never leave you for he cannot walk away.

The designs are beautiful, the wooden parts of the box for it and its compartments smell deliciously of sandalwood. I still have a set and remembered the game well enough to "take" the whole Japanese table tennis team during a railway journey to Leeds more than forty years later.

It may be wondered why we were allowed to gamble. In fact we were encouraged to. We nearly always played cards for money. The point is: it had to be small money. At roulette, poker or Hana-awasi or such games it would never exceed tenth of a penny points. Our pocket-money when we were small was not liberal—far less than it is usual to give children of £1,000 to £2,000-a-year-income families today. The losses were rarely crippling, but if we played recklessly and without regard for sense and probabilities they could easily become so. This taught us two valuable lessons: first, to play games seriously and fairly; second, that gambling can be fun and not dangerous if you remain aware that you are paying for amusement whatever you decide to afford, but that as a means of profit it is *out*.

As we grew older my father reinforced this practical lesson by a rigid moral one from his own example. Among those he knew, he was accounted an even better Bridge player than his brothers. Yet he would never play for a higher stake than 1*s*. a hundred. His argument was: most of those cutting to play against him were likely to be worse players than he; his profession was not cards but banking, he played for his amusement, not to rob. So, if his companions wanted to play high, the wealthy Lord Swaythling must be carried by his partner; he would not share in spoliation of the sheep. My translation of this ethic was to make 6*d*. my own top when I grew up.

Learning the value of money is no doubt difficult for children of rich parents. For one thing, every necessity was there, provided for us, as in the ideal society that Communism implies. Such money as we received regularly for ourselves sufficed and was intended to suffice, only for trivialities. For purchases we might aspire to beyond these, we had to cadge and beg. This form of training is more liable to produce pauperisation than a solid relation to finance. When we grew old enough to go out alone we would get advances and have to produce accounts—which we called "swindle-sheets"—detailing every penny of expense. I found it impossible to note such details—to do so takes your entire attention and enjoyment away from relaxation, observation, companionship, absorption in everything you may happen to do. Hence I would make up approximations afterwards and, being at least what Shakespeare called "indifferent honest", have scrupulously all my life undercharged my expenses and must, in its course. have robbed myself of hundreds of pounds that were my due.

Among the children on the estate, there were in our play at first no barriers of class. In outdoor games, we were one gang with the coachman's children, the gardeners' and upper servants' children, all the juniors of the village formed by the outbuildings of the estate. There were never more than eight or ten of us, but I remember some varieties of game we played that deserve to go down in Norman Douglas's book of those of London's streets.

Particularly two. One was a variant of Hide and Seek called "Dab the Monkey". You choose a Monkey; ours was a big black post between the barn doors. The "he" hides his eyes against it and counts up to a hundred. As he completes the count he calls it out as warning and then turns round to search. If the "he" spies you, he rushes back to the post and dabs it before you can, shouting "One, two three—Dab the Monkey!" with your name. Then you are Out and take his place. If you think the "he" has seen you or if he is looking in the opposite direction, your best chance is to come out of hiding and have a furious race to the post to dab first.

The other was "Monday, Tuesday, Wednesday." Here each participant accepts the name of a day of the week. The "he" has to throw a ball high up against a wall calling out a day; the one so named has to catch it as it comes down and, if he fails, throw it at one of the others all of whom run away instantly as fast as they can. A hit makes the struck one "he", a miss means it is the misser's turn now to throw against the wall. When the old lawn tennis ball we used in this game got lodged in a gutter, we would fetch a ladder and I would always be the one to go up on to the roof. At that age I was quite fearless of heights and never fell. Sometime in my teens, I do not know why and I do not know exactly when, quite suddenly this became completely altered. Usually I can force myself to face a drop nowadays, but only slowly and with ludicrous caution.

But an escapade turned out ill. I have not concealed that I was a spoiled brat. One day, feeling a yen for apples, I led the younger children to the orchard without a second thought. The head gardener reported the incident to my father. I was merely admonished; the children who had followed me were punished by their parents. My especial friend, Dick Aldis, the coachman's younger son, was beaten by his father and mine would not intervene. This was my first real lesson in property relations. I have neither forgotten nor forgiven it. Shall we call it: the end of innocence?

§ 6

IN DUE course we boys finished with governesses and tutors and went outside the family. This did not happen to my sister. My father had always wanted a daughter and the family increased until she came. He was very sentimental about his womenfolk. My sister was deliberately called Joy(ce) to make a pair with my mother whose name was Glad(ys). And when I wanted to share my knowledge of the alphabet with her and tried to teach her, he punished me, saying that he wished her to remain innocent as long as possible and not to learn to read until she was seven years old. From then to eleven she went to a family school in the house of an aunt, and afterwards to one only a quarter of a mile away. Even for this small distance in civilised Kensington she was invariably escorted both ways until she was seventeen. I suppose this sort of segregation does not happen to many girls nowadays. In those days it could be quite dreadful. An intimate of Joyce's, who got married in her teens, told Joyce that, on the eve of her wedding, her mother had confided the facts of life to her with the comment: "Your father has been very good to me. Fortunately he has not bothered me much." Fortunately there was common sense and none of this nonsensical prurience about Mother, and in the end Joyce grew up normally.

However, at the time when I went to my first preparatory school, this was still in the future. We had not been long at Townhill. I was seven and she was only two. Stuart had already gone on to public school. For him my parents chose Clifton, where there was a special house for Orthodox Jewish boarders run by a Mr. Polack. Stuart was quite a big man now, all of twelve, and tried to persuade Ewen and me that the "thing" at Clifton was to eat sardines with strawberry jam. Neither of us was tempted to emulate this fashion.

The school was in Sloane Street, so I must have been taken there each day; it was too far for me to have gone by myself in London traffic at that age. As I have since learned, it was one of a network linked by the Parents' National Educational Union (the P.N.E.U.), of which my father's eldest sister, Netta Franklin, was the animating figure. The headmaster was a Mr. Gibbs, a good-looking man with a stubby moustache and a likeable way with children. I do not remember much about the life there—except that I must have been happy because I was not miserable; or about the lessons—except that I must have been well-tutored at home because I found most of them easy.

The history date I shall never forget is Magna Carta 1215, because that is the time we used to break for lunch.

The only subjects I disliked were: Gym—I have already noted my resentment of ordered, repetitive exercise; Singing—I always followed a note behind and still do when ceremonial obliges me to join a chorus (incidentally, this allergy has not saved me, during my film career, from having to produce musicals); and Handwriting.

At the first examinations at this school, the mothers sat at the desks to write the answers dictated by their sons, who stood beside them. This was a big advantage for me. I hate the discipline of pothooks and found the regularity of such figures quite inappropriate to embody my disorderly rush of thought. (My father was no exemplar here: he once received a letter addressed "Signature Illegible, Esq.".) As late as the age of 20 I suffered the humiliation of having a fortune-teller, during a weekend away from home when I particularly wanted to make an impression on the daughter of the house, declare herself powerless before a sample of my handwriting as my "character was not formed yet".

This has been a particular handicap to me as a writer, because I cannot type or dictate the simplest letter; I cannot think consecutively without a pen or pencil in my hand. I make notes industriously for public speeches, but there are always bits I cannot myself make out when I come to them. It is not least of my good luck in marriage that my wife, an expert in such matters, can read my writing more efficiently than I.

Extra-curricularly I was generally a good pupil. I soon picked up all the first schoolboy jokes—the riddle about the hen crossing the road and the national anthem "Wa-ta-na-Siam". Much else besides. After a Saturday tea at Aunt Netta's, my Uncle Ernest rang up my father to complain that I had spent the afternoon in the garden teaching his son Michael to swear. I thought the complaint unfair, considering that Michael was a year older than I and had been longer at the school.

I was at Mr. Gibbs' for two years. One thing I liked very much. Each Wednesday afternoon a special visiting expert—explorer, ornithologist, chemist, electromagnetician—would give a lecture in his subject illustrated by lantern slides or simple experiments. It should be remembered that in those days there were no educational films or schools TV. I do not know whether every pupil's reaction was like mine, but for me it was as an opening of windows.

After two years I was already at the top and it was decided I should go on to Mr. Barton's.

This private school was at 43 Rosary Gardens, about half a mile up the back streets south of Kensington Court, just beyond Gloucester Road underground station. When I arrived the school was run by two headmasters in partnership. Fully unfolded from his chair Mr. Quilter was enormously long—about 6 ft. 6 ins., and rather slow and languid. He died in my first term, so I knew him little. Mr. Barton on the other hand was small and bustling. He had a high forehead and looked at you sternly through pince-nez but was usually fair. Discipline was exceedingly strict and schooling much more rigid than at Mr. Gibbs's. Latin was taught here—no airy-fairy outside lectures. Mr. Barton took the upper classes himself. We were a bit afraid of him but did not dislike him.

Here a digression. Sex intrudes. I was now 9. At that age I knew something about it, certainly, but, consciously at least, had no desires. I knew about babies and reproduction, but how I came to know I cannot be sure. I read natural history, lived in the country among animals, searched for the usual bits in the Bible, and my mother would certainly not have evaded simple questions. Quite early, a Japanese boy from a family that lived near ours in Kensington had come to play in the nursery and used the phrase: "When I was in Tokyo." Nanny and Mabel had caught him up in this, because they had been told his personal name meant "Born in London". He replied "I mean before I was born." We then learned that Japanese count their age from approximate conception, adding one year to the date of birth. This was sufficiently explicit.

In deciding to send me to board at Mr. Barton's, my parents certainly had no thoughts of any such matters, simply intending to avoid the risk for their son constituted by the underground journey or the daily crossing of Cromwell Road. There was a dormitory for a very few boys, two older and two younger, of which latter I was one. Immediately on lights out we two novices were ordered out of bed and each bidden to tickle one of our older companions in strange places, to our no small resentment. I did not connect the business in any way with procreation and saw no reason not to describe it with distaste when, at the week's end, I was naturally asked at home how I had enjoyed my new school. The result was as might have been anticipated. Mr. Barton interviewed the four concerned in his study, in sequence. When my turn came he as good as told me he suspected I was "as responsible as the others". I was indignant, first of all I did not know what I was responsible for, second I knew I was not responsible for anything. With hindsight I can see Mr. Barton's problem. I saw him then as an unfair judge, but he was obliged to act also as examining counsel and to me he was speaking as a barrister would in cross-examination: "I put it to you, sir," hoping from the demeanour of each boy thus challenged to be able to ascertain the truth.

But at the time it was a traumatic experience. Up to then I had been a natural truth-teller, if not always, at least confident when I was in the right. Now I learned that not only sin, but innocence, could be suspected. This taught me caution and was, I suppose, what is called "experience of the world", part of the process of natural growing-up. Anyway, my parents ended the boarding experiment immediately. Thenceforward I remained a day boy everywhere until I went to Cambridge.

Apart from this one incident I had no clash with Mr. Barton. He showed no animus against me for what had happened and I soon settled down. Mathematics and most other subjects I still found easy. I had to work hard at Latin to catch up, but did not find it difficult, only tedious. I resented it because I thought it useless. Here I was wrong. Of course I never learned it well enough to read, but it is undoubtedly true that the discipline of a grammar detached from current speech does help to disclose more clearly the grammar inherent in other languages, especially usefully with English as it is so little inflected, and make all easier to learn. There is a fall-out too, in apt literary tags and, for a systematist, in providing a clue through the labyrinth of Linnean nomenclature. Whether all this compensates sufficiently for the energy expended is another question.

The school had a peculiar system of sorting sheep from goats. It was called "Stars and Stripes". A huge wall chart listed the name of every boy. Against his name two horizontal lines advanced towards the right: an upper, of red "stars", to represent the merits earned during the week by classwork or behaviour, a lower of blue "stripes" to register the bad deeds. I was nearly always the farthest ahead in red. Alas, I was also conspicuous for my line of blue. It never reached, fortunately, the dimensions that automatically entailed a painful visit to the headmaster's study. I was never reported for my worst act, which therefore did not reach the chart. The war came soon after I joined the school, and the younger masters left, to be replaced by women "for the duration". These often had a hard time trying to control the adolescent boys. I was a thorough "show-off" and, in a geography lesson, kept correcting the teacher, a middle-aged lady, who burst into tears. I wish I could forget this, but I cannot.

Years later, in the twenties, my wife took on a job checking a questionnaire addressed to patrons of the Granada cinema chain. Greta Garbo, indisputably the biggest box-office draw of the day, was top of the favourite stars in the answers, but near top of the "most disliked" ones as well. Perhaps it is no disadvantage, therefore, to excite both love and hate. Anyway my blue line did not prevent me from soon sharing the top place in the uppermost class with a boy of my own age, Stanhope Joel. We alternated with each week's count of "stars". For all my last year we were amicable rivals. It suddenly strikes me as odd that afterwards we never made the slightest effort to communicate with one another.

We read so often in school stories of "crushes" of one boy or girl for another that they must be common. I had no such passionate friendships, and the only homosexual tendency I have descried in myself—if indeed it can be identified as such—is the fact that I think my wife looks nicest with an Eton crop. Yet, as I look back, it is just possible that there was some element of suppressed jealousy in the indignation with which, in this last year at Rosary Gardens, I discovered the bullying of a pretty junior from Australia and, taking my duties as head seriously, set about his rescue. His two tormentors, Irish and French, pinched him, twisted his fingers, made him run everywhere at their beck and call. The whole episode was very Beetle, Stalky and M'Turk, not to say Billy Bunter, and highly cloak and dagger. Convinced I was Sir Galahad, I recruited aid from other seniors, we secreted ourselves behind glass cases in the bird gallery at the Natural History Museum in South Kensington, and at a crucial moment sprang out to catch the miscreants red-handed. Using our evidence as blackmail we forced them to sign confessions and promises to desist, a device which, strange to say, proved effective.

I remember very few of the boys at either of these schools. Two were musical: one, Dick Addinsell, a close friend whom I never saw again; another, Solomon, a big gentle creature who was already on tour as a child prodigy and attended only occasionally, to stand, a rather bewildered figure in bows and velvet, amid schoolfellows who could not be real companions on such terms.

Only one became an associate in after life: Anthony Asquith, who turned up at Gibbs with an immense aureole of Struwwelpeter-like fair hair, and played Amyas Leigh from *Westward Ho* in the school play and, later, either Ariel or Puck. He asked me to tea at No. 10 and we spent all afternoon with one of those model aeroplanes that worked by twisted rubber propulsion; we launched it repeatedly over the garden wall and sent the policeman standing outside across Horse Guards Parade to fetch it back. I did not meet Asquith again until he followed me into films about fifteen years later. Eventually our trade union work made us close colleagues as long as he lived.

Two others reappeared after a much longer interval in distinct circumstances that only had their oddity in common. One recurred just before the war, the other just after.

In the late thirties, when I was already married and working with Gaumont-British at Shepherd's Bush, my mother telephoned to say she had a visitor from South Africa who had been at school at Gibbs's with me and said he must see me again, we had been such friends. I did not recognise the name—which we shall write here as A—but my wife and I duly made one of our rare visits to No. 28 for lunch. A was a small man, very affable. I racked my brains, and then suddenly recognised him as a boy called B—a name similar to A which clearly must have been adapted from it—of whom all that I could remember was an occasion when we had quarrelled about a ball in the schoolyard and I, not out of courage but because he was so much smaller than I, had taken him by the throat and shaken him like a rat. I forbore to recall the incident and he very warmly pressed my wife and me to come to the Oaks the following Friday as his guests.

Michael Balcon, my studio boss, knows South Africa well and had just negotiated a deal with the millionaire Schlesinger, whose virtual cinema monopoly there enabled him to drive hard bargains with everyone. I asked his advice. "You must go," he said. "A is immensely rich. In fact, your millionaire is much richer than my millionaire." I answered, "I can go to Moss Bros.—[I always do for Chaplin first nights]—But Hell—[that is my wife's name]—what will she do? She has no Oaks clothes." "Bring her here," said Mick enthusiastically. "She shall have the run of the studio wardrobe." And so it was. We waited for Friday suitably prepared. But that summer was terribly hot. In the middle of the night, Hell woke up and went downstairs for a glass of water. She fainted and broke her scalp on the tile flooring of our cottage kitchen. She had to be stitched, I had to ring up and make apologies to Mr. A.

He was effusively sympathetic. "Never mind," he said, "we shall go next year." But before next year I read of the arrest of Mr. A in Capetown and, subsequently, of the trial. The charge was of extracting twelve, or perhaps seven, millions from the public by means clear only to financiers and the sentence seven, or perhaps twelve, years in jail. We have still not seen the Oaks.

The second was a meeting *manqué*. One day I brought home to tea from Barton's a boy who was son of the then Serbian Ambassador; the father later on became for a short time one of the long line of inter-war Yugoslav Prime Ministers. My mother approved, saying: always be friendly to strangers, you yourself may want friends in a strange land one day. She enlarged on the usefulness of knowing foreign languages for the purpose: she herself was adequately fluent in French and German, with smatterings of Hebrew, Spanish and Italian and, when well over 40, started to take lessons in Japanese. I took her injunction to heart and, though clumsy in every language and with small vocabulary and no grammar, I can manage a bit in several and this ability has very much influenced my life. Nearly forty years on I was in Belgrade on an entirely non-political errand, leading an English table tennis team. We feasted on sucking-pig and joined in a student sing-song on plum-brandy. Back in the hotel I found a note in the message rack, signed by the name of my former schoolfellow and asking me to ring him at the U.S. Embassy. What could I do? The McCarthy witch-hunts were then at their height, I did not wish him to think me too snooty to communicate with him, but I felt certain a call from me must compromise his career. In the end I tore up his note and burnt it. If he sees this narrative I hope he will forgive me.

Extra-curricular education can be more important even than schooling. There was little of this at Barton's, but two episodes stand out. Once down at the school sports ground at Acton the Head entertained at the long trestle tea-table a friend of his, thin, gaunt, yellow and balding. This turned out to be Elliot O'Donnell, the famous ghost hunter, whose entirely fictitious stories of meeting spectres in almost every English street, village or country house thenceforward gave me an agreeable shiver however sceptical I might remain. Another time, it was announced to the school assembled in its hall that the conjurer expected to give the entertainment traditional at the end of Christmas term could not turn up. Instead a few tricks would be done by the geography master, Mr. Marks, a tall saturnine person in whom no pupil had hitherto suspected hidden talent. It turned out that in this other character he was a professional, a member of the Magic Circle, appearing at Maskelyne and Devant's in holiday time as "Douglas Dexter"; this enormously increased the respect in which his pupils held him.

"Culture", therefore, at this time came mostly outside the school. I practically grew up with cinema. We had had a toy praxinoscope to play with, kept in a stair cupboard just below the nursery landing. Already when I was four Mabel had taken me to Hale's Tours opposite Barker's, and later on the south side of High Street, beyond Lorberg's toyshop, to a fleapit where I saw John Bunny, Pimple in *Napoleon Crossing the Alps*, and Mr. and Mrs. Sidney Drew. My mother took me to the colour film novelties at the Scala off Tottenham Court Road: *The Panama Canal*, very brown and green; *The Opening of a Rose* in red and yellow slow motion; *The Delhi Durbar*—what a scandal it caused when the Gaekwar of Baroda involuntarily turned his back on the King-Emperor; and, a good deal later, *The Birth of a Nation*, with the real villains, whom Griffith the Southerner presented as heroes in it, to the rescue tinted rosy-pink. My theatre experience at this time was more sketchy. Our regular Japonaiserie took us to *The Mousmée* and Herbert Tree in *The Darling of the Gods*, and of course I saw all three of the famous farces: *Charley's Aunt* ("I'm Charley's Aunt from Brazil where the nuts come from"); *The Private Secretary* ("If you are discovered, you are lost." "On the contrary, if I am discovered I am found."); and James Welch in *When Knights were Bold*.

My taste in art was elementary, confined to the great ultranaturalistic battle pieces in the *Illustrated London News* or *Graphic* by Fortunino Matania, R. Caton Woodville and Norman Wilkinson; the heroics of Bernard Partridge in *Punch*; the comics Heath Robinson, H. M. Bateman, Harry Rountree and that appalling snob George Belcher in the *Sketch* and *Tatler*. Higher things here were represented by sittings, which all of us four children bitterly grudged, to an Hungarian who sculpted our busts in pairs, and a visit to the studio of a lady artist, Flora Lion, who was painting a portrait of my mother.

This last, thanks to the artist, provided a useful object lesson. There sat the painter, a substantial lady, brush in hand. Before her was the canvas, already a passable likeness, and our opinions were invited regarding finishing touches. Stuart wanted the mouth altered, Ewen the nose, I an eyebrow and father something else. As each improvement was proposed, the lady complied. In the end, of course, the picture was completely altered, all likeness disappeared. Don't speak to the artist at the wheel.

My allergical resistance to music remained. I still had to be dragged to Granny's box at the Albert Hall and was still bored, no matter whether it was a choral society or Kreisler, Kubelik, Melba or Clara Butt. The only artistes I found at all diverting were Willy Ferrero, conducting the orchestra as apparently an even younger child than I; Pachmann the pianist, because he was reputed mad and would unexpectedly stop in mid-flight to grin and mumble at the audience; and the diva Agnes Nicholls, whom the family knew and who came to Kensington Court and ate lunch in the nursery before afternoon concerts. I had never seen anybody consume such vast quantities of roast beef, roast vegetables and Yorkshire, or with such relish. It must have been to put strength into her voice. The only gramophone records I enjoyed, and these I played again and again, were the 1812 overture, the Ride of the Valkyries, Harry Lauder's "Roamin' in the Gloamin'" and "It's nice to get up in the Morning", and one in which a German gentleman, a supposedly imperfect speaker of English, tries by telephone to persuade someone to come and mend his damaged shutter. ("No, not 'shut up', 'shutter'! No, I'm not svearing at you.")

My reading, by contrast, was voracious. All of Henty, Brereton, and Staff-Surgeon Jeans—these boys' adventure stories are where much of my geography and history came from—but of Ballantyne only two: *Coral Island* and *The Gorilla Hunters* (the latter a most misleading work). The more grown-up adventure writers: Rider Haggard, Baroness Orczy, Cutcliffe Hyne (his Captain Kettle) and William le Queux. (*Not* E. Phillips Oppenheim—I could not get on with him although Uncle Lionel told me he was his favourite author.) Plenty of detective stories: on top of Conan Doyle, "Raffles", Edgar Wallace, Austin Freeman, Freeman Wills Crofts and my favourite, "Arsène Lupin". Neither Thackeray nor Dickens could I abide (except for *A Tale of Two Cities*), but as I had a habit of following up all the books of an author I liked, I worked my way steadily through all the blue, then four-and-sixpenny, pocket Kiplings and was enthusiastically lapping up H. G. Wells' scientific romances in the sixpenny and ninepenny Nelson or Heinemann hardbacks, snatching the opportunity to read paragraphs in the underground on my way to school. I was given Darwin's *Voyage of the Beagle* one Christmas and at once got hold of and read, with more excitement if less full comprehension, *The Origin of Species* and *The Expression of the Emotions. The Descent of Man* I found too stiff.

By this time, as can be seen, I was saving pennies to buy books, as well as begging and receiving them. My regular bookshops were W. H. Smith's, then at the corner of High Street Kensington and Church Street, and Gilbert's in Southampton, Above Bar. I found a second-hand bookshop in South Kensington underground station arcade and promptly made the usual stupid purchase of beginners, *Dr. Syntax*; then went on to a book auction, bid for and acquired, but could not pay for, a complete run of the *P.Z.S.* (*Proceedings of the Zoological Society*), and had it sent home giving my parents' names as guarantors. My mother paid, it was only a matter of a few pounds, but was disgusted, not so much at my unauthorised pledging of the family credit, but at the torn and dusty condition of the yellow covers, held on by spiders' webs. She soon had them destroyed. This full set of volumes would, of course, fetch hundreds, even unrepaired, today.

Earls Court, the White City and Olympia were local stamping grounds, and we were taken there to exhibitions from the start. The Naval and Military tournament was a regular, we specially enjoyed the races dismantling and reassembling mountain guns over obstacles, the tug-of-war and, above all, the musical ride of the Royal Horse Artillery.

The Science Museum I most liked, as I suppose do all children who are unmechanical, for the machinery one can animate by turning handles or pressing buttons; but the Natural History Museum in Cromwell Road became a second home. We had school visits there in crocodile; whenever rain stopped us going to games at Acton we would be marshalled to set out. Immediately we arrived I would break away from the others and soon knew every gallery, case and public exhibit: stones, bones, stuffed animals and insects pinned in drawers. I could find my way at once to the huge whales and articulated dinosaur skeletons, the great menacing plaster octopus and giant squid; past the elephant and pigmy shrew contrasted in the entrance hall, to the Big Tree Section with its dated rings taking history way back for centuries, or up the stairs past Huxley's and Owen's statues to the optical refraction in a block of felspar on the upper floor.

But this part of the story would not be complete if I did not note two acts of extraordinary kindness to me, a young child, on the part of elder relations. My uncle Ernest Franklin, Netta's husband, upset at hearing I liked nature and was indifferent to art, spent a whole afternoon taking me round the Victoria and Albert Museum and explaining to me the delights I was missing. All that happened was that we both became exhausted and he incredulous that such a small person could remain so obtuse. My cousin Herbert Samuel took me to a lecture he gave on statistics, and also to a meeting of the Young Liberal Association in the dim marble of the National Liberal Club. I suppose I must have had a reputation for precocity. I was extremely flattered. But I found it hard to understand the lecture, even when, at my request, he kindly sent me on a proof of it afterwards, and I was disappointed with the Young Liberals because, believe it or not, every one of those on the platform was between fifty and eighty years old.

It is now time to turn to the First World War. 1914-18 overlapped my stay at Mr. Barton's. I was 10 when it began, 14 when it finished. I suppose I am in a sense a product of it. I grew from dependence of mind to independence behind the thunder of its guns.

§ 7

WE CHILDREN were steeped in politics much earlier than we could understand them.

One of my earliest memories is of accompanying my mother when she went to sign the book during Campbell-Bannerman's last illness. We had to walk the last bit, for the carriage stopped a little way away. It seems to me that, outside, the straw lay thick to muffle the klip-klop of passing hooves, though this may only be confusion with some other deathbed.

With Uncle Edwin and Cousin Herbert rising meteors of the Liberal Party, with my mother active in Society and on the fringes of the Court, with the potentates and ministers who needed entertaining as part of my father's financial routine, politics was never far from the talk that floated around our heads. We knew what all the politicians looked like, for Sir Henry Lucy, "Toby M.P." of *Punch*, with his tiny stature and white cockatoo quiff was a favourite house-guest; each week we looked out for his caricatures.

General Elections in the early part of the century were an occasion of great sporting excitement. The constituencies did not then all poll on one day. This was an innovation that followed the First War—the Great War as we called it then, knowing nothing of what was to follow. Nowadays children only have maps of the constituencies to pore over and colour after the event. Then you had ladders with symbolic human figures; they would be fixed up huge upon the façades of buildings, or appear smaller in newspapers to cut out and pin up at home; these mounted rung by rung for several days as the result from each constituency was declared. I think there were only two such symbols, both with striped trousers and top-hat. Labour then probably counted with the Liberals. I cannot imagine what we did with the Irish Nationalists.

We were taken when quite small to see all public funerals and processions. The suffragettes were often spoken of. My mother disapproved of them. Though strong for women's activity and social rights, she accepted my father's Asquithian rejection of their need to vote.

With all this background contact with public affairs, it may be understood how my family, unlike so many others, did at least notice in that summer of 1914 the double assassination in Serajevo. I cut out pictures of it, to put in the scrapbook beside the wreck of the *Titanic*.

The curious thing is that, the week-end of the ultimatums, the Austrian and Serbian ambassadors with their families were *both* due to spend Friday to Monday with us at Townhill. The Austrian cried off. The Serbian came, and joined our usual voyage down Southampton Water with the picnic baskets. Serbia was in dire need of friends.

The papers were full of bemedalled generals and parades. My favourite soldier was the lanky Grand Duke Nicholas, with his long cloak to his heels. The talk was all the same: "It could never last." Night came and there were too many guests that week-end for me to go down to dinner. I sat up in bed and prayed—although already I had not overmuch faith in prayer: "Oh, God, do not let all this go to nothing. Let there be a war, even if it is only a little one."

Remember, I was 10. Should the child be blamed? What could be expected of us in those days, brought up with no knowledge of suffering, ancient generals on our walls, current colonels in the family, the king admired in uniform, the Naval and Military tournament our most delicious treat, lead soldiers in our stockings and battles the chief matter of our history lessons? If I am ashamed of this prayer, it is without guilt. But I cannot escape being shocked at it.

Almost at once we stuck up maps of the fronts and bought the pins with little coloured flags.

The summer was excessively hot. My brother Ewen and I were allowed to make up our beds on the terrace. The trees were still in full leaf. The summer lightning played, outlining their formidable blackness against the pale grey sky. All night long we could hear the rumble of the trains—afar off in the valley down beyond South Stoneham. The British Expeditionary Force was being carried into France.

Very soon changes came into the pattern of our lives at Townhill.

First arrived a family of refugees from Belgium. The mother was plump. There was a plump daughter too, "Bouky", and her two soldier brothers, Pierre and Albert, who came and went as their service alternated with leave. The father, Monsieur le Commandant Cartuyvels du Collaert, was wounded and sat in a wheel-chair. He had fierce moustaches like the Kaiser and, although older, reminded me of the Brigadier Gerard; still more so when he taught me to play Écarté. We became special friends and used to sit playing it for hours, marking the king and the other points with matchsticks; it was very good for my French.

Big houses in the neighbourhood became adapted for wounded; Belgian to start with, then our own. I had discovered, and adored, Charlie Chaplin. When the wounded were entertained, they had to put up with my imitations of the master: bowler hat, baggy trousers, cane and scrap-of-crêpe-hair moustache. Apart from the infant-prodigy recitations at a still earlier age—the Light Brigade, Horatio on the Bridge, and Sir Richard Grenville—this is the only public performance I ever attempted. Fearless at first—as with rooftop climbing—I soon became self-conscious, and with good reason. Acting is not one of my talents.

Later a wounded officer named Archie came to live permanently with us. He had a terribly wasted leg that kept being operated on, promising betterment and then relapsing. I could not understand how his leg had been made bad by gas. I now realise that the trouble was gas gangrene.

Over the other side of the Itchen valley, beyond North Stoneham, a remount depot was established. We often went there, splashing amid the mud and duckboards, and the officers came regularly to lunch. Major Armour, whose comic drawings so often dealt with horses, was one of them and this gave us a further interest in *Punch*. We competed for it to see if this week it had in it "one of his". There was also another gallant major who, invited by telephone, fell for the unusually musical voice of my mother's secretary and, after proclaiming his devotion, was crestfallen to discover our beloved, but elderly and arid Beanie.

Later still, when at last the Americans came in, my mother made a speciality of helping them to feel at home. She shared in founding the English-Speaking Union (referred to by us cynical children as the English-Slobbering Union) and made open house for the U.S. Naval station at Eastleigh. It was remembering this that Franklin Roosevelt, who had then been Assistant Secretary of the Navy, invited me fifteen years on to week-end at the Governor's Mansion in Albany.

Relatives went off to war. Blobs (my Uncle Campbell), the professional, was first to be wounded. I have already mentioned that he was in Netley Hospital. More name-dropping here—but the coincidence is curious. Prince Victor Napoleon and his wife came with us from Townhill to Netley, and the former who always signed himself grandly "Napoleon", found the preceding signature on the same page of the visitor's book that day "Wellington", so that the two are recorded in anachronistic juxtaposition.

Uncle Lionel volunteered for the army and was refused; he was very short-sighted. He pulled strings and got into the Royal Naval Division, saw service at Antwerp, later in Gallipoli and finally in France. He was wounded and won the D.S.O. He *said* it was for taking the *pâté-de-foie-gras* up to the front line for Freyberg, who was disabled and could not be moved back to base, the time the latter won the V.C. Who knows? Perhaps it was true. Now his own injury had affected Uncle Lionel's larynx and made him almost inaudible. When I visited him I soon found myself whispering as low as he did. This was ridiculous, and rather like a farce. But of course I did not mean to mock him.

Right at the start of the war, Aunt Carmel went off to Flanders and ran a hospital. I must digress here to tell the sort of person she was—earlier I only mentioned her in passing—although I was still much too young really to know her. We did not become friends and comrades until a great deal later. She was modest and unambitious for herself, but full of courage and totally ready to plunge into any and every adventure she thought righteous. As a young girl still in her teens she had been at a finishing school in Hamburg in the early part of the century, and read of the pogroms against the Jews. Leaving behind her with a trusted friend letters describing everyday events and dated appropriately in series, to be sent one a week to her mamma in order to conceal her absence, she quit the school and set out for South Russia. Here she stayed in inns as a travelling English young lady while officers who had just been out murdering with the Black Hundreds would stand cleaning their revolvers by the fireplace in the public room, boasting of the Jewish victims they had shot.

From this she next gravitated to Theodore Herzl and the Zionists. Then to her djibbahs, harp, Theosophy and Socialism, which naturally meant the Fabian Society, where she became an appreciated, if slightly flibbertigibbet, friend of both H. G. Wells and Bernard Shaw. She married, as his second wife, Leslie Haden Guest, of whom contemporary memoirs mention the rumour that he was a natural son of G.B.S.; this certainly was erroneous and based on no firmer foundation than my Uncle Leslie's red hair. Carmel became an authoress in her own right. Her first novel was her most successful; it was about the East End of London and was called *Children of the Fog*. A second, *The Yellow Pigeon*, was about her war hospital at Knocke, in Belgium. What she believed her best was never published. It was written during the Second World War after she had parted from her husband, whose apostasy from the Labour Party to the Conservatives in the late twenties, on the ground that Ramsay MacDonald was letting down the Empire in Hong Kong, she could not stomach. This novel was called *The Biography of Mr. Duck* and dealt with Labour caucuses and renegades and careerists; it even reached print, but while she was staying with Hell and me in our cottage—she made her home there during the worst period of the bombing—a bomb struck her publisher's offices and every copy, as well as the manuscript, was destroyed. Before she and her husband parted they had three children; the eldest, David, was a better Communist than I can hope to be and gave his life in Spain; the second, Angela, sent out as a child by her father to stay "out of mischief" with the Governor-General of South Africa, was as soon sent home again, for sitting down, arms crossed, on the Black side of a reception in Government House—she earned the nickname "Angel" nursing wounded, also in Republican Spain, later married and acquired a son while in Siam for the W.H.O., and was killed in a motor accident, again on health work, in Tanzania; the third and youngest began as a ballet dancer and is now a respected employee of U.N. In these early days of the First World War, Carmel, driven from Knocke by the German advance along the Channel coast, next busied herself with a Belgian relief fund; she launched one of those war-time gift-books to which everyone contributes, the *Marie-José*, from a reception at the Kensington Court drawing-room. No one could refuse her anything when she set her mind to it.

In 1914 Stuart was just below officer age. Soon, however, he was allowed in the O.T.C., very much the big brother to his two juniors. After training he was accepted for the Grenadier Guards and wore his 2nd Lieutenant's uniform and spoke of "Buck House" with tremendous pride. He carried a swagger stick and grew a small moustache, "extending to the corners of the lips", as King's Regulations then enjoined. Later he did his stint in the terrible trenches around the Amiens–Arras salient, finally falling ill with pleurisy and being invalided home.

Not so curiously, I suppose, because of our age, the First World War experience for Ewen and me was totally unmilitary. When the next holidays came round we were got out of the way with Joyce and Nanny and Mabel, being sent up to the Lancashire coast to keep company with the children of the Talbot-Cliftons, a wealthy and peculiar couple who had an immense and lumbering mansion at Lytham St. Anne's. The parents were there to receive us: the father, an explorer, lying full length on an immense sofa; the mother, a sort of poetess, all drooping skirts and necklaces. But they immediately went away and the stay was a feuding and unhappy one. The baby was found full of beer wandering in the courtyard in the small hours, and the two girls took the part of their brother when he hit Ewen on the head with his driver because Ewen outdistanced the brother on the latter's first shot off the tee. The only thing I enjoyed was using my putter to split open the salmon tins cast up on the beach from torpedoed ships: if they did not fizz you might eat the contents, if they bubbled they were bad.

Ewen, too, soon got into O.T.C. khaki at Westminster School. He was only 17 when the war ended so did not reach the army proper. I was young into Westminster, so eventually just had uniform at the very end, but I never managed to roll my puttees on properly.

My father did not talk to us about the war, but then, indeed, he was not in the habit of talking to us much about anything. At second-hand I picked up an account of his resourcefulness soon after war broke out when, motoring down to Townhill, he had needed to pass under a bridge guarded by one of the soldiers posted everywhere in the instant spy-scare that accompanied its beginning. He had produced his passport—a document possessed by very few in those bygone days (pre-1914 one could travel passportless to nearly every country). The sentry, who had certainly never seen one, took the request in it by His Britannic Majesty's Principal Secretary of State for Foreign Affairs to "allow the bearer to pass freely without let or hindrance in the name of His Majesty" more seriously than anyone needs to, and presented arms before standing aside.

I do remember, though, his head-shakings when Haldane was discarded from the War Office under attack. Thenceforward the pink *Globe*, the Tory evening paper that had hounded him, was never allowed into the house; my father stuck rigidly to his green *Westminster Gazette*. Though never wavering as an Asquithian—he could not reconcile himself later to his brother Edwin's accepting office under Lloyd George—he growled, with a foreboding later amply justified, criticism of Asquith for having yielded to the pack: "Never be disloyal to your colleagues. You will have to pay for it one day when others are disloyal to you."

What I learned about the war I picked up chiefly from interpreting scraps of dinner-table conversation and an omnivorous extension of my reading. I begged pocket money to subscribe to *War Illustrated* and every new special magazine. In politics I added to *Answers*, *Titbits* and *Pearson's Weekly*, the *Passing Show* and later also *John Bull*.

In imagination at least I lived all the technique of trench warfare, for

I read every word of Sapper and Boyd Cable. I knew the spindrift and peril as destroyers sped by night through mine-laden seas, and the anguish of the stabbing searchlights discovering you at night, for I learned these through Bartimeus and Taffrail. When Kipling went to France and wrote about it, I added his pamphlet to the blue cloth works I already treasured. It added to my worship of H. G. Wells, when I learned, from a reprint in yet another gift book, that he had long ago foretold the tanks.

For some reason, I especially admired the shape of the early tanks. They reminded me of a sort of tumble-over toy in some game we had, that rolled slowly but inevitably forward as you sloped the board on which it stood. When the first actual real tank to be seen by the public was set up in Trafalgar Square to sell Savings Certificates, I rushed to this spot. Unfortunately I had also obeyed earlier a savings campaign slogan that had called on everyone to "save farthings", and I remember the old-fashioned looks of the clerk in the gun-turret and of those behind me in the queue when I emptied out a bag of 744 farthings that required counting.

Saving and knitting were my first contributions to the war. I could put up at last with the music in the Albert Hall if I were allowed to knit there, and during concerts interminably made khaki-coloured scarves. I did not drop many stitches but could not cast on or off, so if Nanny was too busy to finish and start one, the scarves all came out much too long.

The feats of aviation aces fascinated me, from whatever country they might come. Cobblers are traditionally atheists because they sit and think and do not work with others; taxi-drivers are supposed to be independent in spirit because they cruise alone; the single-seater fighter of those days was the nearest thing modern war had to the knight errant. Now everything goes so fast his senses cannot cope and all must be computerised—there is no space for spiritual self-examination, only for automation and butchery. Then it was different. I read avidly of Bishop, McCudden, Guynemer—which I stumbled through in French—and, best of all, Richthofen. I have no idea why I was so impartial. I am sure that, at the outset, I did not doubt the current myths about the war. Who knew of the equivocations of Sir Edward Grey about the secret treaty with the French Government? We had come to the aid of "brave little Belgium". That much was clear. Had not Mr. Asquith said right at the beginning at the Guildhall: "We shall not sheathe the sword until Belgium has recovered all, and more than all, that she has sacrificed"? I knew all about the deeds of the Hun. My father had passed me the Parliamentary papers on German atrocities in Belgium and I was an especial admirer of the war cartoons of the Dutchman Louis Raemaekers (I did not then know he was paid for them by British Intelligence). But, as a devotee of truth, I saw no reason to withhold from an enemy admiration of his personal merits, if he seemed to have any. I did not think much of the British Generals; French was no hero to me, nor Kitchener, nor—I am glad to say—Haig. The only one I approved was Sir William Robertson, doubtless because of his bluff, friendly manner when he came to dinner. But Hindenburg and Ludendorff both also seemed disagreeable figures to me; for some odd reason the most dramatic seemed the bristling, unattractive Falkenhayn.

Anyway, Richthofen won my allegiance and I was thrilled when Cousin Hugh gave me as keepsake one of thousands of little paper strips dropped by British planes over the German lines as propaganda, bearing the words: "*Freiherr von und zu Richthofen ist heute auf der Ehrenfelde gefallen.*"

A child, I believe, does not know fear until it is taught. It does not seem to react instinctively to certain situations, as a chick does to the neckless silhouette of a hawk flying overhead. Dread, whether of spiders, ghosts or other creepy-crawlies is an infection from adults. In the late twenties or early thirties I received a card of invitation to the premiere of *King Kong*, stamped by the distributors, for publicity effect: NOT SUITABLE FOR CHILDREN. Of course, as a sceptic on these matters and for experiment, I took Hell's daughter Rowna, then around 8 years old. We took a forward seat and when, with Fay Wray bound and helpless on the stockade walls, thousands of savage extras dancing and beating tom-toms, the giant ape appears and grabs her, Row burst out laughing and exclaimed: "Why, Ivor, he looks just like the milkman!" I was 10 myself when the war broke out and never through it had a sense of fear. How can a child imagine being ended, any more than can an animal? Even when it sees death this is something that happens to others, not itself. Air-raids in the First World War delighted me. I liked nothing better than to be wakened, wrapped in my dressing-gown and hurried down to the basement, while the crackle of Ack-Ack accompanied the criss-crossing searchlights one had glimpsed overhead and could still visualise, and one strained one's ears for the dull thud-thud of the bombs.

Father and mother joined us in the basement during raids and my poor father, having no others to make up a four, had to teach Bridge to Ewen and me, to pass the time under the flimsy structure of the house until the sounding of All-Clear. Woe betide us if we failed to remember every card out in every suit or made a call on principles other than those he held as axiomatic. I was far more frightened of him than of the Zeppelins as I sat trying to make my mind up on a lead and he coldly remarked: "Make your mistakes quickly".

The first daylight raid over London is etched in memory. I was late abed for some reason and, as soon as the "Take Cover" warning sounded, seized my Brownie camera and rushed out into the street. Fragments of Ack-Ack shrapnel were falling round me, but I paid them not the slightest attention and manoeuvred until I could get the raiders into the viewfinder above a recognisable corner of the Court. There the Gothas were, about twenty to thirty of them I should estimate, with splendid and unhurrying deliberation crossing the London sky. The brown puffs of the ineffective anti-aircraft fire burst far below them. They did not even show as specks in the viewfinder or, for that matter, on the finished print, but, as I proudly explained when showing off the photograph afterwards, they must *be* there, for they had been just above the angle of those roofs.

One week-end at Townhill a small monoplane appeared, circling and in apparent difficulties. After some indecision it landed in a big field beside the Beech Copse on the back drive about half a mile away. The young airman who got out of it was good-looking and pleasant. He was made welcome and won golden opinions, exchanging with us children addresses and promises to write, promises that he never kept. On the Monday the commander of his squadron came for him, landing alongside and giving his pupil much encouragement before the latter seemed to feel sure enough of himself to fly away. Much later I read in wartime reminiscences of pilots that it used to be quite a "thing" to choose soft-looking propositions from the air for week-end entertainment; the sport even had a name: "Hunting Jew palaces". I have no means of knowing, of course, whether in this case the engine-trouble accused of responsibility for the landing was assumed or real.

At this time I studiously read airmen's poetry, the R.F.C. official instruction manual, and a splendid simple and clear book called *Practical Flying*. I was bent on learning to be a pilot, but as will appear later, found this only a dream when I did start air travel and turned out always airsick.

It was in Naval Warfare that I specialised and, oddly enough, came nearest to making a practical contribution. The grey silhouettes of naval vessels attracted me in the same way as the rhomboid outline of the tank. Even before the war I had cadged small Bassett-Lowke scale models of warships as presents. After its outbreak I never missed a year of Jane's *Fighting Ships* or its rival *Fleets of the World.* At the seaside I always carried a Jane's *Naval Recognition Book* and on a wartime summer holiday we spent in the Isle of Wight at Bembridge had field-days spotting the classes of all the ships I saw as now others do with aeroplanes and I try to do with birds. Mother got me Brassey's *Annual* and some of Mahon from the London Library. I knew all about the theoretical role of the capital ship for a navy (pre-air-power and pre-atomic) that would control the seas, and thus fully understood Jellicoe's strategy: the theory of the Ace that must not be played, the Queen at chess that must not be drawn out too early, the responsibility that lay upon him from the fact that, so long as the Navy remained in being and preponderant, the Germans could not win the war. So, in the controversy, I was always a Jellicoe man, not a partisan of the newspapers' darling, dashing but all-risking Beatty. My father gave me also the Parliamentary Command papers of the Jutland battle and I went through all the maps and dates and saw in them nothing to alter my opinion but only what recent disclosures in the matter have thoroughly confirmed.

So far this is preface. One of the servants' flats at Townhill had become vacant as the footmen went to war, and Ewen and I were allowed the floors of its various rooms to deploy our lead soldiers. With Ewen off to public school, I soon packed them up and instead worked out in the floor a means of moving various ships by mathematical reduction of their speeds and distance.

This developed, and presently an indulgent mother was helping me acquire huge areas of plain white linoleum from Selfridge's to spread out on the floor of Kensington Court's vast drawing-room. I carefully pencilled this off in squares by means of ruled straight lines and reproduced upon it, exact on the reduced scale, the simpler naval battles such as those of Coronel and then the Falkland Islands. When I had the results as well as the tactics in close correspondence with the actual course of each engagement I knew my reductions of scale and method of expressing the fighting must both be correct, not only for movement of ships but for offensive and defensive potential as well.

From Townhill we were friendly with Sir Hedworth Meux, then in command at Portsmouth, and had often visited him in the dockyard there. Perhaps to indulge my parents, he came up to London to our drawing-room but, having come, evidently liked what he saw. He must have said something to Jellicoe, because after the latter's retirement from command of the Grand Fleet following the Jutland row, Jellicoe himself came to Kensington Court too and spent several hours on hands and knees with the small boy, the latter's flags and innumerable pencil squares, until he too was satisfied. The result was: an invitation to the by now 13-year-old to lecture on his war game to the Naval Staff College.

This may be, and of course is, absurd but the explanation is as follows. The Staff College had, as I knew, long used an instructional war game. The method of this employed a scale reduction of speeds and distances, mathematically based, quite obvious and similar to my own. But it had no exact means of expressing the fighting. Unable to find one the College had comforted itself with the thought that naval engagements invariably contain elements of chance, based on incomplete knowledge by any commander of all the factors involved at any given moment, and had fallen back on a device of chance, or near chance, for settling the issues. When the vessels in the "game" came within range, the budding commanders would take poles each with a decentralised pin set in the end and strike at silhouettes of ships they were supposed to be firing at set on the wall. This required skill, and the decentralisation of the pin introduced the chance.

I disliked this system as too approximate and worked out a method of giving each ship an offensive value according to the number of guns capable of being brought to bear at a given range in a given direction, and a defensive value according to its armour and angle to the antagonist. Of course my indices (based on the freely published material) were wholly arbitrary, but they seemed to work.

This invitation now seems to me, and must seem to anyone, remarkable. At the time, such is the complacency and self-confidence (unkind people as old as I now am would say "conceit") of youth, I was not surprised at all. I set about preparing the lecture. Because my handwriting was so awful, my mother undertook to write it out and I have part of her manuscript somewhere still.

However, a few days before the date fixed, I called the whole thing off. In the meantime I had become a socialist and decided I was against war.

§ 8

BEFORE I explain this transformation, however, it is necessary to put it in its context.

The years of 1917 to 1919 were years of profound change. If any date may be said to be the watershed of the modern period, the explosive moment of the great break through to a world beset by our contemporary issues and problems, this was it. Classical historians, and those with their minds set in conventional blinkers, often date the breakdown of the old world to 1914, the outbreak of the First World War. But this is to hanker after the impossible, to visualise things as though the old order could have continued. "Had it not been for . . ." etc. Had it not been for the shots at Serajevo, the temperament of the Kaiser, the duplicity of Sir Edward Grey or some other millimetrage of Cleopatra's nose, all could have gone on as before, the rich luxuriating in their castles, the poor man in his preordained stance outside the gate.

But it was not so and could not have been so. In the first years of war the rich and powerful and privileged remained just as rich and commanding and privileged as ever before. As Bruce Forsyth puts it, they were still "in charge". Up to then the war cost them nothing but their sons, who had to set an example, and for whose loss we were supposed to praise and pity the parents. The great divide began in 1917, when all the accumulated strains and tensions of the century before, the anomalies and distortions underlying the complacent surface of progress "wider still and wider", burst like a boil to present the world with new perspectives and launch it on fresh struggles.

One moment the Captains and the Kings who had strutted in peacetime were still the figureheads, the next they were cut down to size. This did not make the problems more simple. In some ways they were to prove more complex. But it made them different.

1914 was not the cause of this great divide. It merely increased the strains and so accelerated its arrival.

These three years were my own years aged 13 to 15. In those three years the beliefs and moral principles were established in me by which I have lived since.

In orthodox Jewish families, 13 is the year of a son's Barmitzvah. This is a sort of turning point in the life of the young boy. Whether the moment is chosen as the supposed age of physical maturity in the Mediterranean region or of understanding I do not know, but now is the time when he stands forth before the full congregation in the synagogue, shawled and fringed and capped in velvet, to read in Hebrew his portion of the Holy Torah, the sacred scroll of law unrolled after being borne from the Ark in which it is kept. He helps to remove and replace the tops on the rolls of Torah, decorated with little silver bells, as his father watches from his seat below and his mother trembles with anxiety in the gallery for womenfolk above. Before the ceremony a child, henceforth he is a member of the community with full adult rights.

The characters of written Hebrew are all consonants. The vowels are small diacritical marks, omitted from many Jewish documents such as the Torah, since the words are supposed to be familiar and the consonants merely reminders. My knowledge was not extensive enough to read Hebrew in this form, my part had therefore to be brushed up by coaching.

Now the curious thing is that, although this ceremony is, after all, a sort of religious initiation or confirmation, and I never questioned that, following my brothers, I should go through with it, I had long since ceased to have any sort of religious faith at all.

I had been brought up in Orthodoxy—with reservations. My mother had not failed in her duty to teach us the Old Testament and pride in Judaism. We ate Kosher and generally observed the rule about walking on the Sabbath. No ham or shellfish of course. The one dietary exception: strict orthodox Jews do not eat milk products and meat at the same meal in accordance with the Biblical text: "Thou shalt not seethe the kid in its mother's milk." My father disobeyed this injunction for he had noticed another passage where Lot in Sodom is visited by angels; the host here entertains his guests with flesh and milk and my father said that what was good enough for an angel was good enough for him. Also, my brothers and I rode bicycles down the hill from Townhill on Saturdays, although we were careful not to obtrude this on my Grandmamma's attention. We respected her feelings. We were allowed this exception because the prohibition against riding or driving on the Sabbath is supposed to be to save animals from labouring on the day of rest and we could not see how this applied to bicycles. In London, where we were not allowed to bicycle for safety reasons, our observance was rigid, and I walked from Kensington to the West End and back for all Saturday matinées, three times each to *Chu Chin Chow* and Robert Loraine's *Cyrano* (of both these I was an addict) and once to the Bing Boys. Every Sabbath morning in London also we walked to Synagogue and of course we spent the day there fasting the full twenty-five hours every Day of Atonement. (My father used to complain that the Rabbi had only two sermons each year that this came round, neither calculated to encourage the crowds who pack synagogues only on that day: "Why is today the only day you come?" and "Give me money.") We were supposed to follow the service which was in Hebrew, and our prayer books were in both English and Hebrew so that we could do so. But when the service was long we were also allowed to read books carefully covered in brown paper, so long as they were serious books suitable for the occasion, not novels or such. I mostly sat and daydreamed about benefiting humanity, although one year I did get through Karl Pearson's *The Grammar of Science*. My father ploughed through the many volumes of Graetz's *History of the Jews*.

But the more I reflected in synagogue or out, the more impossible I found it to believe in or even approve of God, or accept all the manifold barbarities I read about. It was not secular study that made me an infidel, it was religious study. I had inculcated in me a deep sense of justice. All Jewish teaching lays great stress on justice, which it calls righteousness, and which perhaps in common parlance we might call fair dealing. The 'catch' absurdities of the Bible did not bother me—like classing a bat as a bird or describing a measure as three cubits round and one cubit across; these could readily be dismissed as myth or ignorance, though they did deprive the Bible of all possible claim to infallibility. What stuck in my gullet were the obvious wickednesses the Bible clearly approved of: Jacob's trickery, David's carryings-on, Sarah's behaviour to Hagar, the mass destruction of the enemy after pretending to accept their conversion and cutting off their prepuces, and what right had God got to give the Jews the land that belonged to the Canaanites anyway? It was all very well for my mother to stress that the Lord was a Lord of Lovingkindness and Mercy, but what did He say Himself about His character in the commandments? "I, the Lord thy God, am a jealous God. Thou shalt have no other Gods before me." The image emerged of a monster in pettiness, who kept insisting on his tribute of burnt flesh, blasted people wholesale for mere disbelieving in Him (when I got thus far with my reasoning I naturally tried out a few blasphemies as an experiment but without noticeable result), and rewarded sycophants like Abraham for being ready to kill their offspring to curry favour with Him. I know that there are Freudians who say that one's attitude to God is dictated by identification of Him with one's father. This, in some cases, may indeed be a possibility. But not in my case . . . I might have my differences with my parent, and he might when I was younger have seemed to me arbitrary and awesome, but a "Father" like the "God" of the Bible, if he really existed, could only be contemptible.

Decisive, however, I am quite sure, was the problem of Evil. I could not swallow the combination in one Being of Omnipotence and His sanction for the existence of suffering among the innocent. If Evil took place despite God's will, He was not omnipotent. If He willed it, there must be something wrong with Him. I was not in the least satisfied with the explanation that suffering is a reward of sin—this was quite obviously not so, too often the wholly innocent catch it worst. Or that it is sent to try us. My parents had early taught me that it is wrong to leave money around and that, if anyone places temptation in the way of the poor, he is as much responsible for the theft as the thief himself. This apportionment of responsibility seemed to me obviously sensible. Why should the same criterion not apply to God? In any case, if God were all-knowing, what did He need suffering or temptation for in order to prove to Himself something about the potentialities of the tempted that, by definition, He must already know? It seemed an oddly, a wholly unacceptable, complicated way of going about things. As for the explanation "the ways of God are unfathomable", this seemed to me the last despairing refuge of the unreasoning bereft of argument to account for the unjustifiable. Man might just as well shut up shop as be content with that sort of abasement.

My religion foundered on one image above all: the caterpillar with the ichneumon fly grubs eating it from inside. A scheme of creation that did that on purpose could only be diabolical.

It will be understood therefore that the great materialists were in no sense *agents* contributing to my scepticism. Rather did they provide paths to explain phenomena and relationships whose religious interpretation I had *already* for myself found theologically unacceptable.

I was never credulous enough to believe that science at any stage had all the answers. I think I always approached it with the commonsense attitude that the whole of science can never be more than an approximation, with its temporary conclusions constantly extended as more and more aspects of the universe are disclosed by ever more refined methods of investigation and experiment. Lenin's *Materialism and Empirio-Criticism* (which I did not, indeed, encounter until my late twenties), with its conception of everything being knowable but never capable of being completely known, wholly fitted my own attitude; and J. B. S. Haldane's definition of science, not as providing answers but as disclosing ever more exactly the questions it is useful to ask, was not a flash of new illumination to me so much as a brilliantly epigrammatic statement of the obvious.

From this standpoint, I was never bothered by the questions which are supposed to obsess so many youngsters, the so-called ultimates: How did the world come into being if it were not created? What is life? What happens to us after death? What is it all for? For the first two mankind will find adequate enough explanations if it survives long enough. The fourth is silly. It *is*, is that not enough? The third seemed inherently absurd. We were dead, what else? And why on earth should anyone wish to be otherwise?

By definition, an organism that is dead has no means of regretting anything. It is obvious enough that no evolutionary mechanism is conceivable to develop survival of organisms after their reproductive capacity is exhausted, and that without limited duration of reproductive capacity in individuals, species could not adapt to changing conditions and therefore life itself would not survive. In any case, what does "we" mean in such questions since nobody can pin down an "I"; since no John Doe can be the same thing—except nominally—when a baby and when eighty. (It will be seen I was quite ready for the monistic and dialectical understanding of reality inherent in Marxism when eventually I found it, i.e. the reality of processes rather than things—which latter are simply arbitrary convenient abstractions—and the only basic reality that of the entire changing universe as a whole.) I was not in the least dismayed when ideas that might have satisfied me provisionally turned out juvenile in the light of later-acquired detail. The one thing I was quite certain about was that the teachings presented to me as religion could not be right.

With this mood upon me, it will be understood why the Rabbi assigned to prepare me, linguistically and theologically, for my Barmitzvah, after a few futile Paleyisms about how everything must have a beginning, every watch has a maker—how much the more so therefore each infinitely more complex living being—the kind of reasoning that has been called (the phrase I learned later from Lancelot Hogben) "seeing the finger of God in the eye of a cockroach", and the like, gave me up as a bad job and simply sought to keep me amused by giving me cigarettes and tips for races. It was my music teacher and lead soldiers over again.

The tips did not come off and I was not interested in smoking. My father early promised each of his children free smokes for the rest of their lives if they did not begin until they were 21. I do not know how this worked with my brothers, but I know I promptly (I was about 10 at the time) tried out both cigarettes and cigars in the lavatory (not at home, but away; obviously at home it would have been indiscreet to leave the lingering scent), found nothing pleasurable in either, and since then have never had the slightest inclination towards tobacco in any form. Indeed, if I have ever smoked at all, it has been for purposes objective not subjective, that is, out of doors when there are mosquitoes about.

Soon I was looking at other faiths and finding no more in them. With youth being cut down everywhere, spiritualism flourished. These were the days of Asquith's *Raymond* and the Max Beerbohm cartoon of Lodge and Lankester (naturally my sympathies lay with the latter). My mother read books by F. W. H. Myers, a wiseacre in this field; his sons Harold, a pleasant dilettante, and the tall brother Leo, an intelligent author of philosophic novels, were frequent house guests. These modish bumblings seemed to me so many hot air balloons sustained by wish-fulfilment. Christianity scandalised me, for the precepts of its founder appeared in no way to have influenced for the better the conduct of its most prominent professors, either in past times or the present. I could pass the miracles as ordinary credulity and false report, and the virgin birth as well-meant propaganda based on a mistranslation of the Isaiah prophecy, but heaven as a conception seemed to me wholly immoral: the limbo for the unchristened innocents and the idea of blessed saints, good in their lifetime not for goodness sake but because confident of reward, now sitting up there rejoicing while the sinners—whom, after all, God must have allowed to be tempted or they would not have fallen—roasted eternally in hell was as foul and barbaric as any Judaic tradition. I pitied those who practised Holy Communion and yet thought themselves superior to the cannibals to whom they sent missions. Above all, the central "happening", the crucifixion, was an outrage upon reason. Certainly the voluntary acceptance of His passion by Jesus for mankind's sake parallelled in noble symbolism, though it must be less than, the sacrifice of every mortal martyr to a cause; but the God who exacted such an agony from His Son as the price of granting redemption of sin to those who had not earned it otherwise was simply a continuation in worse form of the Old Testament monster and, if one could arrive at any meaning for the obscure *oneness* of the Trinity, this could only turn the whole purported "sacrifice" into a gruesome masquerade.

About this time I met a priest in a camp on Salisbury Plain where I had gone to visit a Jewish schoolboy friend, older than I, recently conscripted and undergoing training. The little round Yorkshireman, who was popular with the soldiers because he used to do card tricks in the mess as a warning to them not to play with strangers for money, had befriended him but could do nothing with me. I brought him to Townhill and was embarrassed to hear him tell my parents that I reminded him of the infant Jesus who put questions to the wise men in the Temple and could not get answers. This was not at all how I saw myself. (Although I did once again hear the same comparison, on very different grounds, ten years later from Renee Houston; she used to comb my hair down the middle and then say that it made me look like pictures of the Holy Infant.)

In my arguments with the priest, I cited Buddhism against him as a really compassionate faith, considerate of all living things (possibly I was confusing it with Jainism). It happened, luckily, that he had been in Central Asia and insisted that, had I ever seen Tibet, I should know Buddhism as little guaranteed its adherents against degraded superstition and inconsistent conduct as any other faith. I had not at that time seen, as I have since, a lorry-load of steel-helmeted Thai soldiers armed with U.S. tommy-guns jump down from their vehicle, form up on command and march to join the congregation at a Bangkok temple, but I took the warning. Someone has justly remarked that there is a great deal of difference between a religion as practised by a persecuted minority in a society, and the practice of the same religion in a community where its adherents have assumed responsibilities of state.

Why, since I had already reached such definite convictions of irreligion, or at least agnosticism, at that time, did I proceed with the Barmitzvah, and why did the Rabbi, to whom I was always ready to expound my views, permit it? It is curious that, until these recollections forced me to confront it, the question never occurred to me. Of one thing I am sure. I am certain that on my side it was not simply that, on a base material level, it was to my advantage to conform. I have never been morally dishonest. (Not that I am exceptionally upright; it has been my luck never to be under pressure strong enough to constitute a test.) I have no superstitious objection in principle to a lie where it is obviously unharmful or else necessary to defend others, e.g. a white lie to comfort a dying person or to protect associates against unjust force. But even in a petty case, my scientific aspiration towards exact description has made truth so much a habit—even to the point of risking boring others—that I cannot convincingly maintain deceit; and I do not think that, short of pressure by torture, anything would make me lie about my own beliefs. It was certainly not to please the family—whom I was so ready to irritate—that I went through with the ceremony, nor for any fear of missing the Barmitzvah boy's post-ceremony reception, to which all afterward bring gifts.

I think it must simply have been that I had become convinced religious beliefs were so untenable that I was no exception other than in candour, and that all intelligent persons who professed to hold them were just pretending for convention's sake. Since those days I have come to recognise that not everyone who professes a supernatural belief is necessarily stupid or a hypocrite, although I still half wonder how this can be so. To obtrude my disbelief or to make a fuss would simply have been to insult others by implication, embarrassing them by forcing exposure of a common secret. Judaism is so much a matter of ritual and good works, as well as faith, and its holy are so much revered for their example—which is apparent—as well as for what they may have thought inwardly, which must be taken on trust, that it does lend itself to that possibility. Of course now I understand a good deal more about religion than I did then, especially in its historical and sociological aspects. At the time, however, at 13, I simply resolved that if I was to do as others and wear the label of Jew, honesty demanded that I should at least maintain the observances of a Jew. And long after I had ceased to believe in any reason for this, right into adulthood, I continued to practice the dietary laws, sporadic synagogue attendance, the fasts and so forth. I told myself that I wanted to be quite sure my disbelief was not a rationalisation to fit my convenience. Indeed I was 27 and in Hollywood before, being asked by Eisenstein why on the Day of Atonement I proposed to fast for the twenty-five hours, and, on explaining, being faced by a second question: "Wasn't I quite sure?" that I at last realised I was being a fool and packed it up.

Anyway, I did proceed successfully with the carefully rehearsed rites of my Barmitzvah at synagogue. The drawing-room at Kensington Court was once more filled with tables laden down with presents; it was clear that there were advantages after all in being a member of a numerous clan. My library was refreshed abundantly. Several aunts who asked what I wanted were given names of books by Freud and anxiously asked my mother if this was all right. (He had not yet become the foundation pillar of contemporary U.S. "thought".) In such matters my parents had no prohibitions. My mother believed in all possible enlightenment in the field of sex. Conventional as she later showed herself in politics, proper as was her own outward and, I am sure, inner life, she never showed herself narrow-minded in respect to others' morals or prudish towards her children. About that time in the war, so high a percentage of British troops bored with trench warfare were out of the line with syphilis acquired on leave, that Brieux's V.D. plays were put on in London, the government persuading the Lord Chamberlain to remove his ban. My mother, who immediately took my two elder brothers, did not dare take me because I was so obviously young, but came up to my room as soon as they got back from the performance to tell me all about it. She joined the pious "Combating" organisation of the establishment, which mainly went in for moral exhortation, but I am glad to say switched to the "Prevention" one, which called for prophylaxis, after I introduced her to the book of Archdall Reid—who tried out supplying kits to one whole unit and treating infection as neglect of duty; his statistics made his case.

One envelope I rightly appreciated above all other gifts. It was a Life Fellowship of the Zoo from my father. At that time it cost only forty-five pounds. It was accompanied by the condition that until I was 21 I should give the Sunday tickets to him. Evidently he thought this bargain good business, as I was likely to live longer than he. I did not mind this condition in the least and many times of desperate hard-upness found those two "freedoms" he had conferred on me—the other being life membership of the Hampshire County Cricket Club—a boon I could never have afforded to keep up. They have already lasted me more than fifty years.

§ 9

THIS SAME period, 1917–19 was my time at public school. I entered at 13 and left at 15 and I did not enjoy any part of it.

The school, as I have already noted, was Westminster. Ewen had preceded me there, to Rigaud's. As he left, I came in to the next door house, Grant's, of which Mr. Tanner was then head.

Westminster consists (or did in my day) of several houses of day boys, and one of residents all holding scholarships. My parents wished, and I no less, that I should be a day boy, and so I was, travelling each day by underground from High Street Kensington to St. James' Park. As the school uniform—Eton suit and top hat—seemed to me absurd, I used to disguise myself for travel, wearing a light coat and cloth cap and parking these at the left luggage office at the school end of the underground journey, where I would take out my top-hat left there overnight.

As a non-resident scholar later on, I felt even more ridiculous in cap and gown.

There were very few scholarships granted to non-residents. To become a non-resident scholar—and, in fact to become a scholar at Westminster at all I had to be a non-resident one because the resident scholarship "House" was restricted to Christians—I therefore had to come very high on the examination list.

My first try from Mr. Barton's did not succeed. I do not know how high I came but I won an Exhibition. I sat again and got a non-resident Scholarship at the second attempt.

Examinations still came, or perhaps, in view of what I shall presently have to admit, better said "seemed to come", easy to me. So easy, in fact, that in this first try I made my own difficulties. Perhaps the reader knows that some even quite serious exams have catch questions. The examination for cadetships at Dartmouth Naval College, for example, used to be especially full of them. The type of question: "If the such-and-such-a-time train from Glasgow to London travels at so many miles an hour and starts punctually, and the such-and-such-a-time train from London to Glasgow travels at so many miles an hour and starts forty minutes late, the distance between Glasgow and London being so many miles, how far apart will they be when they meet?" The answer, of course, should be: "The distance between the up rails and the down rails" and it does not need much mathematical calculation to arrive at it. However, examinees are supposed to read a question to the end and understand it before they begin answering it, and if they do not, but begin covering their paper with figures before they have understood what they are asked, this shows a want of mental discipline. I, alas, fell into a trap that was not even set. The question involved a time-table of two persons walking between two consecutive milestones H and K. I answered it by rather clever and complicated algebraic reasoning in terms of the distance HK, and added at the end the observation that, if this distance had only been known, the question would have been quite simple. Since the question was No. 1 on the arithmetic paper, and the questions listed usually start with the simple ones and increase in complexity as a paper proceeds, I was being double-stupid.

I do not wish to blame Westminster at all for my unhappiness. If a child is unhappy at school, the disharmony is like a marriage, it may be the fault of one or other or just the incompatibility of both.

Of course the war laid a great handicap on the teaching. Good young teachers were snatched up for the holocaust, the old had to continue or return beyond their best. There was one very fat old mathematics master who caused great schoolboy amusement in geometry one day by drawing a freehand circle on the blackboard (he was complaining of the irregularity of everyone else's diagrams) and saying: "This is my figure." On the other hand, when I got moved up a class, there was a superb languages master, Mr. Etheridge, far above the usual standard of languages in England, who taught French and German. He pounced scathingly on one's mistakes, and I owe to him any facility (I have no accuracy, but that is my fault) I possess in those languages. He used to stand the class in line, give each of us in turn a brief speech to make, and send us down one place for every error. I remember a dreadful one I had failed to prepare, beginning: "*Içi se vendent des livres d'occasion*" that took me, in my tattered gown, right from top to bottom of the class. There was also a drawing-master, Mr. Kneene, whom I shall always remember with gratitude. He found me incapable and bored with the usual exercises of shading cylinders and pyramids, and woke my interest by letting me do pictures of rats and woodcock and copy things like Blake's *Ghost of a Flea.* Not even this, however, increased my capacity; I have found the inability to draw any but hesitant and clumsy lines a handicap and nuisance in many fields.

In my first term I had a useful experience. The form master was Mr. Mitchell, an elderly individual whom I much admired because he had huge tufts of hair growing out of his ears and I had never seen the like before. He was otherwise rather a messer. The book we used for French was very easy. He used to set a certain amount to be read in advance as homework and then go over the prepared passage in class. As he asked the class again and again: "Who has gone further than this?' I would jump up each time with a prompt, "I have." I was not boasting or being goody-goody, I just had, because reading French came easy to me and I'd found the story interesting. The result was, not at all surprisingly, that after class one day my classmates made a dead set at me and beat me up.

Shortly afterwards the probing doctor found several tender places around my belly and I had to have an appendicitis operation. I bore no grudge. I could see things from their point of view and even then, the moment I reflected on the situation, realised that they were in the right. The more I showed I could prepare, the more it would be calculated they ought to prepare and this would have been totally unfair, for they had not had my advantages—French tutoring, contact with Belgian refugees, etc. It is the same problem that makes it necessary for factory workers to ensure that no one indulges in excess production for fear this will be made a pretext for the boss to raise the norm.

I had a good operation. They say the first twenty-four hours have a lot to do with your speed of recovery and my first night after the cutting-up was a real thriller, an air-raid with bombs close to the nursing home, searchlights you could see easily out of the windows and a motor-chassis-mounted AA gun banging away just outside in the street. I had no time for sleeplessness or self-pity. I was up and eating mashed potato in seven days, out in a fortnight, and back at school after three weeks. My only disappointment was about the appendix itself. This had specially been put in a bottle for me to take home and show off to my friends, but someone had undone the bottle and given it to the cat.

When I came back to Westminster I found myself less keen on work, and examinations less of a cakewalk than before. At the time I put this down to having learned my lesson in compulsory solidarity, but since then I have realised that it may only have been adolescence, that youngsters who have been advanced before maturity do often, as they grow up, slow down.

Why did I dislike Westminster so much? I did not lack friends. I have "got on" with people, and found companions or at least sparring partners in all surroundings. One, from a stationery-making family called Delgado, used to take me home to bridge (by now I could myself win regularly at levels below the best); another, Jack Gielgud, showed me his model theatres; a third, a rather melancholy type, was a son of the editor of my beloved *News of the World*—we used to stay out of Abbey services (I as a Jew; I do not know why he did) and argue in cloisters about the course of the war, betting on events from the inside gossip we had respectively picked up. I always bet on disaster, not because I wanted defeat but because the opposite. It is a useful principle to lay *against* what you want to happen; then, if it doesn't, the cash should be consolation. However, this rather macabre reasoning lost me a packet in half-crowns towards the end of 1918.

I think my resentment was not against this particular school, but against what was then called the "public school system". Better men than I had found themselves odd man out in it, e.g. Shelley. Before and after this period, also, there was much argument about reforming it: Alec Waugh's *Loom of Youth* was being talked of, and H. G. Wells's search for proper schooling for his sons resulted in his writing up of *Sanderson of Oundle*.

For the better part of a hundred years the public school had been designed to separate out and train an élite class, destined to form part of a ruling apparatus as principals or subordinates, to have charge, at home and in the Empire. The method: unreasoning acceptance of a medley of traditional customs (the absurd and insanitary clothing was an example), and an apprenticeship at ruling and being ruled that required loyalty to an arbitrary hierarchy of elders constituted by the monitor system.

I had not chosen the school. I did not approve its objectives. I had not been consulted over appointment of those who expected me to obey, or at at least conform. I would not be loyal.

I do not claim to have been any "better" than those who did not rebel against the system. Maybe a little old for my years, that only. There is a stage in growing when the young, or at least some of them, are beginning to feel independent mental muscles, to resent forms and authorities they find "over" them, usages sanctioned rather by custom than by reason, choices in which they have no opportunity to share. With some who go through the usual middle-class educational mill this comes relatively painlessly, when the bonds are partly loosened at university. Those for whom it comes earlier must quite naturally prove misfits.

My great consolation at Westminster was that I would use every pretext and excuse, bolstered where necessary by medical certificates, to scrimshank out of compulsory games and O.T.C. parades, and stop half-way home by underground to haunt the British Museum (Natural History), to give it now its formal title.

I had by this time penetrated behind the scenes in the Mammal Gallery. My first friends were the brothers Sherrin: Tom, the tall, lean taxidermist upstairs who taught me to trap, measure, skin, cure and label, so that I was already sending specimens from Townhill back to the collection; Will, who had a shock of greying hair, glasses through which he blinked amiably at children, and a black moustache that would have been walrus if he had let it grow. Will Sherrin knew everything in every cabinet and exactly where in every drawer. He showed me all the preciosities and the tricks; the skin of the first Giant Panda known and one of a Tiger with long fur and white stripes instead of black; how to distinguish skulls of alligators from those of crocodiles, of lions from tigers, of wild cats from tame ones. (The first have teeth half-way along the lower jaw that in one species fits into a hole in the upper jaw in the other doesn't; the underside of the lower jaw of one of the next pair fits tight on a flat surface, while, if you put your head down you can see daylight under the other's; and, with the last pair, in one the hypophyses of the lower jaw are so level that it will stand up on its end, in the other they aren't and it falls over). He showed me how to keep the skins safe from clothes moths, in addition to putting camphor in all the drawers. You leave an unwanted old skin out near the cases to distract the moths, destroy it when it is full of eggs and caterpillars and then put out another one for decoy duty. He let me into the secret of the collector who had asked the B.M. to save carefully all the sawdust he had sent back his specimens in; much to the dismay of the department it proved to be finest tobacco that thus got in uncustomed. Curiously enough, with all this mammal love and love of the department, Will Sherrin's own speciality was mosses. He found some splendid fruiting specimens of rare species at low tide in the South Stoneham salmon pool when he visited us at Townhill.

My special patron was M. A. C. Hinton, whose great field was rodents, and with whom I did much work, as will appear, in the years that followed. Head of the department was Oldfield Thomas, a handsome white-haired old gentleman in a black velvet jacket, with a moustache exactly like the white bristles of a paste-brush. He wisely used me as a path to acquisitions. When the new Air Ministry office was opened in Kingsway, family introductions procured me an interview with Brancker and "Boom" Trenchard, and they consented to ask Air Force stations in East Africa to try to get us Colobus skins, which duly reached South Kensington. Under his blandishments my father put up money to finance an expedition by H. M. Loveridge to the same area, and the latter rewarded us by calling a mongoose after me and a rat after my father, a subtle distinction I appreciated though it surely cannot have been deliberate. I had an immense and justified respect for Thomas, who had a house in St. Petersburg Place almost opposite our synagogue. I thought his lot ideal and have no idea why one day he shot himself through the head.

I envied my brothers who were by now at Cambridge (Stuart left just before I came up), and I wished to follow them as soon as possible. I started to prepare for a first try at the University entrance examination ("Little-Go", it is called) at the age of 14. At that time one compulsory paper was in Greek, which I had never studied. I had to have a coach at home, extra to my school-hours and homework; he was an elderly man with glasses and a shrivelled neck, very conscientious and rather like a cockroach. We began on the *Alkestis* but I was bad at assimilating it and, fortunately for me, suddenly compulsory Greek was abolished and the candidate could take two Latin papers instead. Nevertheless I failed. It was my own fault.

The candidates go up to Cambridge and take the exam in the spring when term is over. They live in college and dine in hall. The rooms were cold, or were in those days if you did not know how to keep alight the fire lit by the college servant ("gyp"); the air was cold, shivery and damp. Baths were across an open-air courtyard and you had to wash in cold water out of jugs. The Little-Go is (was?) in two parts. Part One, which included the mathematics, I got through all right. Part Two, the languages, was the stumbling block. I was told I had got eighty-odd in unseen French Translation, sixty-odd in unseen German Translation, fifty-odd in unseen Latin Translation, thirty-three in prepared Latin Translation (a passage from Caesar) and that, as thirty-four was the general pass mark, I had failed.

I was furious. It seemed to me totally unfair, a veto only because I was so young. How could any examining board discriminate so exactly as to know that a candidate had failed by but a single mark? This was a sound point, so far as it went, but of course I could, and should, have put the matter beyond doubt by more application to the set Caesar passages. As it was I did not even look at them to refresh my memory the night before the paper. I had been distracted by examining all the books in the shelves of the college room I stayed in, reflecting on the taste and character of its rightful occupant. I always do this in a strange room.

Anyway, I hated Westminster more than ever and lived only to get away. I passed the Part Two of the Little-Go the following year and was now qualified, at 15, to go up to Cambridge. Now the college for which I had been put down and where both my brothers were, Trinity, refused to take me at that age. I must wait till 17, they said.

I became angrier than ever and said that if Trinity would not have me at 15, I would not go at all. I must have been very disagreeable and provocative during my remaining time at Westminster.

During this time I was made, as every boy was, to attend the annual school cricket match against Surrey Club and ground. The school captain went in first and was out first ball. I clapped him all his slow way back from Oval wicket to Oval pavilion. Expecting to be hauled up before the school authorities for disrespect, I prepared a neat argument: what one should applaud was not mere success but sincere effort, and I presumed the captain had tried just as hard as if he had made a hundred. Perhaps wind of this awkward defence got abroad, for when the Grant's monitors did summon me it was for a crime I had never imagined and therefore had failed to guard against. As a scholar I had to wear not only a gown with my Eton suit but also a white bow-tie. My quick-changes of costume had made it more convenient to use a made-up one, and the monitors beat me because it was not hand-tied. This was the only time I was ever caught offending against an ordinance, if indeed there was such an ordinance.

Towards the end of my last school term Mr. Tanner called me into his study and told me he did not know what to make of me. He then added an incautious remark. "We thought," he said, "that when we gave you the scholarship it might make you interested in the school, but it has not worked."

I knew already that whenever I won an exhibition or scholarship or any other prize award my father made up its value privately to be accorded to some other candidate. He did not wish any success by his child to deprive another, possibly of less well-off parents, of an academic success or opportunity the latter might have gained had I not been in the field. This was a cruel act to me, because I could never know whether I had won on merit or received the announced award simply as an act of policy that cost the school nothing. Mr. Tanner's remark was presumably intended to take me down a peg by reminding me of this situation. On the contrary, by reminding me of the lengths the school authorities were prepared to go by compromising their own standards for an ulterior purpose, it left me a firmer rebel than before.

§ 10

WHY AND how, directly I began to think for myself and find a political orientation of my own, did I come to Socialism? This is a question I have often asked myself.

Certainly there must have been some contributory factor in the air of the times. Of my four grandparents' twenty-six grandchildren, five, including myself, eventually became members of the Communist Party. This is a very high proportion for children of parents of whom only one (out of 16) was even a socialist.

All the five were quite different in their characters, had different upbringings, and only this in common: that in no case had economic interest or industrial experience, either in ourselves or our immediate families, anything to do with it.

For others I cannot answer. Save for my brothers and sisters I did not know any of my generation of the family at all intimately. I can only try to answer for myself.

The problem raises as preface deeper questions. How does anyone develop independence of mind and a social conscience? Again, I can only give a personal answer.

Of one thing I am sure: none of it was due to schooling. All the influences on my character were extra-curricular.

Much, very much, came from parental influences and standards. But from my interpretation of my parents' behaviour and example, rather than any precepts. I was always allergic to precept.

My mother told me to be kind, polite, thoughtful of others. She was all these things herself. I did not take much notice of this. I was not unkind or intentionally rude. But I was preoccupied, self-centred, thoughtless; I suppose many children are. I could be repentant afterwards; that is, if I noticed that I had unintentionally hurt anyone's feelings. I was also inclined to equate politeness with hypocrisy. It was only when I was much older that I realised that acts of courtesy and kindness, which often cost the doer so little, can sometimes mean so much to the recipient that the potential doer can have no excuse for not remembering to do them. Indeed, even for purely selfish reasons they are worth while, for their regular omission must lead to callousness.

Incidentally, being waited on is not only corrupting to the character but destructive of the most elementary abilities. As a child I never cooked, washed up, made the beds, mended or tidied my clothes, cleaned my shoes. If I left my things in a heap on the floor, this would lead to recrimination, but in the end they would be picked up and put away by others. I never washed or dried dirty crockery and cutlery until, in my late twenties, I spoke at a Young Communist League summer school at Worthing and would have been ashamed not to try to do my share. To this day, apart from boiling eggs and hotting-up tinned soup the only dish I can cook is kippers in the oven. (This I do by ear, judging "doneness" by their crackling and spitting.) What my poor wife must have suffered during our more than forty years marriage I can hardly estimate, although she does now occasionally let me wash up (seldom) and make the beds (almost never), and bringing her tea in bed every morning is possibly the chore that pays for all.

I have noted that Judaism lays stress upon equity and justice. Goodness, social service were inculcated as having a religious sanction. I saw them practised. I was not old enough to calculate that a wealthy life such as ours necessarily, by simple arithmetic, must deny to others the privileges and advantages that we children accepted as a part of natural order; or that the tithe of income my father insisted must be distributed to charity could not possibly suffice to restore the balance. Sufficient that the duty of concern for others' problems, both individual and on a world scale, was taken for granted. Cain's reply was not acceptable.

This duty seemed to me no less a *sine qua non* when it lost in my eyes its supernatural authority. It was sufficient that it was the only possible logical basis on which a human society could be maintained. What possible claim can you have upon others to worry about you and your affairs unless you are ready to worry about theirs? "Do as you would be done by" need not be the voice of God. It is plain common sense, as much in your own interest as in that of others.

This thought, and the various injunctions against selfishness—a sin to which I knew myself particularly inclined—were crucial, I think, in determining my direction.

There is one scene that stands out as decisive in my memory. In her lifetime, I never dared recall it to my mother—she who was so upset by my socialism, which she could never understand or sympathise with, would have been upset to distraction if she had ever thought herself, however unintentionally, responsible for my path towards it, even in the smallest degree.

It must have occurred just after we went to stay at Townhill. I was about 7 years old. My paternal grandfather had just died, and my mother, to whom the court dresses and the new "ladyship" must have meant quite a novelty in her own life, called us three boys together for a talk under the mulberry tree. I do not know what it meant to the others, but I extracted from it above all the stress she laid upon the words "*noblesse oblige*". From now on we were to have the prefix "Hon." in front of our names and this meant a corresponding obligation to act more nobly and unselfishly than other people, to think of others and our duties to them before thinking of ourselves and what was ours.

Did she really mean it? Surely. What did it mean to her as a rule of life's conduct? I have no idea, or rather, I can make a shrewd guess: it meant to think of others but strictly within the framework of what was normal to one's class and time.

I took it seriously. And without limitation. I do not in the least mean that I ceased to act selfishly. How often is the Old Adam, or even only thoughtlessness, too strong for what one should be aware one ought to do. But thenceforward it was by this standard that, when I thought about them, I measured my deeds and those of others.

I was perfectly logical. When it later came to the problem of what to do in life, I dismissed any occupation involving a profit motive as so much dishonesty and stealing, incompatible with any pure idea of service. The only motive for work that one could be capable of living with must be that it was something one could do ably and which would be useful to others. And the word "others" could not be logically limited. If it was wrong to work for oneself, what right had one to work for one's family, unless one could satisfy oneself that their benefit did not diminish in any degree the welfare of any other family? The same criterion must apply to kin and nation, no goal could be adequate that did not embrace the whole of mankind, with no discrimination of nationality, race or colour.

The interest of every individual must supplement, not run counter to, that of his neighbour, the highest interest of each people and nation become recognised as bound indissolubly to the advance of all.

The only political and economic system of society that made sense in this context was, when I met it, Socialism; the only plausible explanation of man's history and the processes of the universe, Marxism; the only hopeful road that took account of this ethical problem and these facts, Communism. It followed that to devote my life to advancing Communism has been necessary simply as a mere honest act of gratitude for life.

But such conclusions were, at that time, as yet far in the future.

At present we are still trying to decipher the past. Why should I have sought independent conclusions, and what accidents of circumstance decided their form?

In respect to the first part, my father's role was important. Independence and scrupulousness of mind were as much a part of our family atmosphere as social responsibility. I grew up without any contamination by the notion that conformity can be a proper substitute for deciding on one's own ideas. Everything tended towards this: Judaism itself is a minority religion in Britain; the history books presented Protestantism as an intellectual and ethical advance; it was admirable to die at the stake for conscience sake and craven to disavow conscience; with the Governments consisting of familiars like Uncle this or Cousin that and the Opposition of their rivals and quite probably inferiors, how could one renounce criticism, deify state policy, or assume that patriotism consisted in endorsing blindly whatever might be done or said by men who were obviously not divine or exceptional, but simply coeval humans who happened to be in office?

One's duty to serve society included putting at its service one's critical faculty and thinking, and judging society, for oneself. This was not in any absurdly arrogant spirit, believing one's judgement necessarily to be right, but because it was one's duty to bring all oneself had to bear and, if it was one's own judgement, made in all prudence and sincerity, to abdicate from it would be cowardly abdication of duty.

This was so ingrained in me from earliest days, it became so much second nature, that I have simply pitied—without understanding—the suburban conformity of keeping up with the Joneses; and found at first incomprehensible, then a sort of betrayal of youth, the tendency described as existing commonly among many young Americans as an unhappiness if they discover they are "different", kept out of Phi Beta Kappa, prevented from running with the crowd, etc. In most company, I should have truculently rejoiced at being different and would either have dismissed a Fraternity as easily as the fox the grapes or, more likely, never have wished to join.

The ultimate evil and oppression to me was being expected to accept standards ready made, without right of challenge to them. Therein lay my hatred of the public school, and later, when I understood the loyalties they demanded and bred, of the O.T.C. or army life. I could be loyal enough to a symbol if I chose it myself, but I rejected every symbol that might be mine by such accident as birth and refused to endorse assumptions I could not intellectually accept. It astonished me to read in Rebecca West's book on spies and traitors, written at the height of the Cold War, the charge that nonconformity of judgement of what is best for one's country is an arrogance to be condemned. The right of exercising one's own conscientious judgement is frequently enough praised as one of the chief gains and glories of "Western" civilisation until it is taken seriously by Westerners opposed to the Cold War.

My father's attitude supported this general conception. Certainly we children were expected to conform in certain minimum aspects of behaviour: elementary honesty and truth-telling, washing our faces and being at least minimally tidy, wearing evening dress for dinner. But opinions conscientiously held my father seemed to honour as a private right. He himself was ready enough to express views against the stream—he was constantly a target of denigration by Jewish community journals for opposition, from his own assimilationist standpoint, to the concept of a Jewish state in Palestine, for example.

I will not attempt to answer for my brothers and sister—I have no mandate—but I myself never accepted without thinking my parents' ways, in small things or big, just because they were those of my family. It is true that I followed my mother, in, for example, not drinking tea. But this was only because I did not like it myself, any more than I liked beer or spirits or coffee, used by everyone around me. If I followed my mother in anything in the tea matter it was in her defiance of convention in following her own taste. We were taught that taking things for granted was liable to be silly. My mother never lived it down and was teased by all of us for ever after, because once, on recommending some new biscuits to us as "four times the food value of meat" and being challenged on how she knew, she had replied: "It says so on the tin."

At 9 years old, before I wore spectacles, I was several times obliged to defend myself in boxing matches at Mr. Barton's, and very fierce ones too, to rebuff persecution by bigger boys as a "little Liberal". In those days and in such a social setting, as in that described by W. S. Gilbert, no one had yet thought of anything more "left". But by 11 and 12 I was already beginning to explore other scriptures. And my father's sententious remarks when he saw where my inclinations tended—that he, too, believed in equality, but in levelling up, not levelling down—I could already see as nonsense, postponing until Doomsday the necessity for any sacrifice of privilege by the rich.

The point where I wish to pay tribute to my father—by hindsight if at the time I could not recognise it—is in his liberality and generosity, I may say "respect for the personality" of his children. He had no form of communication with them. His prejudices—religious, political, of knowledge or of taste—were not for discussion. He would declare right and wrong so rigidly as to brook no discussion, whether it was a matter of the "correct" number of children for a family ("about four", of course) or condemnation of the Impressionists as worthless and unable to paint or draw. Nothing that he had laid down could be disputed and this made intercourse impossible.

At University one of my friends was S. M. Hadi, the Indian Davis Cup player. Our companionship at the time was in sport only; I did not know he had any interest in politics until one day he was attacked by "hearties" when leaving rooms where he had listened to an address by a well-known Leftist. The self-syled patriots waited for him with hockey sticks and broke his shins. Meeting him again some years after we had both gone down and learning that he and his brother now had a job tutoring the children of the Nizam of Hyderabad, I was surprised and asked him how such a feudal ruler could possibly entrust the upbringing of his children to liberal-thinking mentors. "The Nizam", replied Hadi, "no more considers the political views of his servants than he would those of his horses or his dogs."

My father was like that so far as considering seriously any views of his children was concerned. I am sure he loved his children and his hopes were that any views they arrived at would be the right ones, that is, exactly identical with his own. All honour to him then that, disdaining to such a degree any value judgements on which they might differ from him, he yet respected them as people enough not to coerce them. I am sure that, as with *his* father before him, his ideal for all his children was that they should join the Bank. When the time came, only Stuart took it on, with the impetus of his strong urge to continue the line of patriarchs. It is an irony that even Stuart soon dropped it and retired to the more socially commendable occupation of cattle farming, and that the only enthusiastic banker in the family, by yet a new contrary reaction in the next generation, proved to be his own son David. To Ewen and me the Bank was also open. We were each lunched there and shown around, but no pressure was put upon us.

I can see, then, how social responsibility, conscience, the duty of a judgement independent of received authority, arose in me as natural. The particular forms that their expression takes are of course no more independent in anybody than the winds, formed each day by the complex of influences known and unknown, temperature, moisture, pressure, rotation of the earth, influence of heavenly bodies, rain of extra-terrestrial particles, that make up or falsify the patterns of the weather chart.

War and revolution were the influences of these few formative years. They made the boy.

How could I not respond to the slaughter? I knew what was going on all right. From the child who prayed for "if only a little one", the youngster who devoured and was thrilled by the tales of fighting in trenches, at sea and in the air, I passed to the young man who pondered Barbusse, Stephen Graham, Siegfried Sassoon, Robert Nichols, Robert Graves, Osbert Sitwell.

How could the boy who listened to the table-conversation of generals, politicians, diplomats be left with any illusions? When, eventually, I read Lloyd George's memoirs there was nothing that surprised me, nothing I had not already guessed.

Once Owen Seamen's patriotic verses had delighted me. Now I read Shaw's *Peace Conference Hints*.

I have mentioned that I was always a follow-upper as a child; sometimes this led to discoveries I never anticipated. I have mentioned how when D. W. Griffith's *Birth of a Nation* came to the Scala, I failed to recognise it for what it was and was delighted when the knights of the Ku Klux Klan rode to the rescue clad in robes of pink. But I urged my mother to get me a book with their real history from America, and when it arrived, fully documented, I was so shocked I at once presented the book to the London Library.

One of my favourite Raemakers' cartoons had been an heroic depiction of "Luther-Liebknecht in the Reichstag" denouncing the war credits. Now I found Karl Liebknecht's own *Militarism and Anti-Militarism* at the Bomb Shop in Charing Cross Road (where Collett's now stands), read it on the top of a bus and learned what he really stood for.

How could I miss what happened in Ireland? My cousin Hugh might joke about the old lady in the sweetshop who said: "Sure and I cannot serve you unless you point your revolver at me," but I read in the newspapers what Connolly said, and about Casement, and knew what was done to Sheehy Skeffington.

Each day as I walked from St. James's Park underground station to Westminster School in Little Dean's Yard I passed the old offices of the Fabian Society in Tothill Street, In the window two pamphlets by Bernard Shaw caught my eye. I blush to admit it but I thought them appropriate to me. One was entitled: *Socialism for Millionaires*, the other: *Socialism and Superior Brains*. I admit further that they did not mean much to me when I tried to understand them, but I found another, *This Misery of Boots* by H. G. Wells, which is the best socialist propaganda pamphlet I have ever read.

It was this pamphlet and the Liebknecht, I think, which made me call off my lecture to the Naval Staff College.

§ 11

SOON I had joined the Fabians.

I knew Jack London, of course, if only because of *White Fang* and *The Call of the Wild.* Now I found *The Iron Heel* and *People of the Abyss.* I saw the reverse of the bright coin of Edwardian London, whose glitter the child had taken at its face value.

The February revolution in Russia had been only one event among others. Mr. Barton had called the boys together in the school hall and told us that something had happened which was startling but not dismaying. It should turn out good for the Allies, and for the world too. Russia had been a country of much darkness, long disapproved by thinking people in Britain. The new changes must make it better and also a more efficient partner in the war.

The October Revolution was something else again. New, mysterious names appeared. It was obvious that the papers knew nothing—much of what they wrote was incredible—and, besides that, they were afraid. Who were Lenin and Trotsky? There must be some good in them if the papers and the politicians were so upset.

I went back to the Bomb Shop but, at first, only found books by the terrorists—a novel by Ropshin, Stepniak (who is fascinating), as well as an excellent pamphlet on intraspecific cooperation in nature by Kropotkin. I ate up every first-hand account that came from "over there"—Phillips Price, Alexander Wicksteed, Arthur Ransome. But these were not forthcoming until later. My sharp eyes discerned an advertisement—an address by an English artisan who had been employed in Russia and just got back safely. Was his name Keeling? He had actually seen the great men of whom everyone was talking. The meeting was to be in Hammersmith. It was a small room on the first floor, on the left on the way to Chiswick beyond the Broadway. It was fairly crowded. He was not an accustomed speaker. His account was factual, it did not pretend to interpretation. But here was a real live witness. Soon I had arranged for him to speak to the Fabian Society.

The Americans came. Chaplin made *Shoulder Arms*. The bands played "Over There" and Pershing and Sims became new guests at Kensington Court. The giant armies swayed to and fro for the last time. At last the German soldiers broke and the German navy refused to sail out to certain destruction. Liebknecht had won, not the Kaiser. The Bolsheviks were justified.

Until late at night we jumped over the bonfires and out of the way of the firecrackers in Hyde Park. Rockets lit the sky.

Then came the Khaki election. Lloyd George hastened an election to consolidate his coalition majority and smash Asquith before the people had time to think. His certified followers, conservative or liberal, were given a coupon, a sort of testimonial that they had contributed to victory. All others, Asquithians or Labour, were by implication near-traitors; men like Keir Hardie, Ramsay MacDonald, "left" labour, were worse denigrated still—they were Bolsheviks before they had ceased to be German spies. Carmel and her husband, Leslie Haden Guest, came to dinner. I did not know then that he was asking my father for a substantial contribution to his election expenses. My father, no doubt with memories of Lib–Lab collaboration and in his Asquithian hatred of Lloyd George and the Coupon, consented. All I knew was that Uncle Leslie was a Labour candidate and here, ostensibly at least, was a standard-bearer of socialism. I volunteered to help.

Each day after school I put my top hat and white tie in the underground luggage office, took out a cap and a red tie and went off to Southwark. I folded addresses and wrote envelopes. Sometimes I tried canvassing. I am not good at canvassing. I am too shy and, however illogically, feel it an intrusion to call on people I do not know. Uncle Leslie was fighting the three Southwark constituencies with two colleagues, Isaacs of the Printing Trades and Naylor, also a trade unionist. They held a joint meeting. It was packed and exciting. Suddenly the meeting was thrown into confusion by a man dressed as a sergeant. He was burly and handsome and wore many medals, including the V.C. He had a tremendous voice. He denounced the cowering Naylor, accusing him of having neglected to secure justice for him over some wound he had suffered. Denials were of no avail. The platform was rushed, the meeting shattered.

A week or so later there was a picture in the papers showing the sergeant in hospital. He had been beaten up when it turned out that he was not a sergeant at all, and had no medals; he was merely an impostor supporting the coupon candidates. This was my first introduction to electioneering.

At another meeting Shaw made one of his rare appearances on an election platform. He could not refuse Carmel. I thought his speech the most witty and convincing I had ever heard. It made no impression whatever on the voting figures.

The Southwark Labour candidates were not successful. Lloyd George swept the country. He fought the election on two promises—of course not fulfilled—"Hang the Kaiser" and "Make Germany pay until the pips squeak". Even Asquith lost his seat and my father was very angry. But Lloyd George's victory was a Pyrrhic one. Henceforward he was a prisoner of the Conservatives.

Waves of unsettlement passed over Europe and the world. The Allied Victory Parade, which I watched from a flat high above Trafalgar Square that belonged to a Japanese financial counsellor in London, Mr. Mori—we played Hana-awasi all day waiting for the procession to pass—provided a circus but settled nothing. The Guards marched on Whitehall, impatient to be demobilised. Discharged and demobilised soldiers and sailors marched on the Commons, discontented at being out of the army without work or houses. I emerged one evening from Westminster as this march was passing Dean's Yard and the Abbey, and became caught up, top hat and all, in a charge of police breaking up demonstrators and knocked to the ground. One of the policemen attacked a banner bearer and seized his banner just in front of me. I always carried an ebony silver-headed loaded cane and, still on the ground, reached out and struck the policeman on the ankle, bringing him down and rescuing the banner. It is the only copper I have ever scored.

Soon the coppers themselves were on strike and marching in Hyde Park. They had formed a police union which demanded recognition. Their organiser was a big man, named Hayes I think. By the time the first Labour Government was formed, he had become respectable and was appointed an officer of the Royal Household.

I began to take part in politics more seriously. I discovered that one advantage of being a scholar at Westminster was that, provided I wore cap and gown, I had a traditional right of access at any time to the Public Gallery of the House of Commons without waiting in the queue. I was already entitled, as a younger son of a peer, to listen to any debate in the House of Lords standing at the Bar.

I used these privileges at once but found myself, like Omar Khayyam, ever coming "out by the same Door as in I went". I did not like the Lords, where the style, then at least, was for nobody to seem interested in what he or anyone else was saying. The Commons was worse:

it disappointed for the opposite reason. The debates were exciting, the points raised in the Opposition speeches seemed unanswerable: but on the next day some other subject would be under discussion and no one appear to care a scrap that what had been said yesterday had not been answered and nothing was being done about it.

Albert Hall meetings were better. Every seat was packed and hundreds stood. Outside, I bought the *Worker's Dreadnought* and inside we cheered Soermus when he played the violin and Cedar Paul, dazzling in electric blue with red-gold hair, sang "The International" in a translation by her gangling, greying husband Eden. People cared, passion burned on the platform. Zangwill spoke, his epigrams bit with acid. I do not think he belonged to any party. Frederick Soddy, whose pioneering books on nuclear physics I had tried to understand, was another unexpected speaker. The great hero, who was in his tragic, unstable phase, having just come out of jail, and almost frothed upon the platform, was John Maclean. I did my stint of joining in Labour hymns, Blake, Ebenezer Elliot and "The Red Flag". It was exciting when a manifesto with hundreds of signatures came out, calling for Home Rule for Scotland. The first name on the list was the Hon. Robert Erskine of Marr, monarch by descent from the Bruce; the second, John Maclean, Bolshevik Consul in Glasgow. It was more exciting still when the Albert Hall management tried to stop further meetings and had to yield when the electricians simply removed the fuses from the main. I still have the old weekly *Herald*, edited by George Lansbury, with a first cover page consisting of the outline of an electric light bulb and the words: "The Light that Failed."

In my thirst for "further Argument" I found the Central London branch of the old British Socialist Party, one ancestor and part-founder of the Communist Party. I wrote to Albert Inkpin, then the National Secretary, and asked to join. The branch met in the Minerva Café, a haunt run by women anarchists in High Holborn. We met fortnightly, for speeches and discussions. The secretary of the branch was, I think, called Alexander. Our meeting date was Wednesday. One evening Comrade Alexander told us that, ten days previously, he had received an appeal from Moscow asking all sympathisers to take part in a one-day worldwide strike against intervention and blockade. As we met on Wednesdays, Comrade Alexander explained, and the date of the demonstration had been set for the day before, the Tuesday, there had been no means of telling us, but he himself had closed his own shop in sympathy.

Later I was able to help in something more effective. The branch received parcels full of Lenin's famous booklet *State and Revolution* in English translation. Despite the ferment, there was by no means a revolutionary situation in Britain at that time (or since, for that matter), but Scotland Yard was said to be in search of the pamphlet. I offered to take the packages home with me and store them until they could be distributed. No one would look for them there, I averred. And so I did, and piled them without any concealment on the upstairs landing at Kensington Court until they were ready to go out.

All good things come to an end, however. After a few more meetings I offered to take one side in debate. The theme of the debate was to have been "Revolutionary Action versus Parliamentary Action" and I was to prepare the speech defending parliamentary action.

I wrote out my arguments carefully and left the document containing them openly in my room on the desk beside the window. I returned from school that night to encounter melodrama. The butler himself met me in the outer lobby and, as he took my cap and coat, grimly indicated upstairs with an attitude that thunder lay ahead. On the first floor I was called straight into the library. My mother had come up into my room for some reason, seen the speech lying on the desk and immediately read it. My father had the document in front of him. He had not yet read it. He said it was private and he must therefore await my permission. I could not appear ashamed or lacking in courage so I had no alternative but to give it. We waited while he turned the pages. Then the fat was truly in the fire. My parents could not take exception to the viewpoint, of course. What was inadmissable to them was that I should be associating with people who could even consider the matter appropriate for discussion.

My mother asked me to leave the B.S.P. My father ordered me to desist from politics. I rejected the plea and made clear my determination to disobey the order. Tears and anger on my side. Anguish and frustration tempered by my father's principles and sense of justice on the other. My father insisted that it was not fair to use his money for purposes of which he disapproved. I insisted equally that it could not be his intention that his son should be untrue to principles in which he believed. Finally a minimum compromise was reached. I was to promise faithfully that, whatever I did politically in the future, I should not, until I was 21, spend more of my allowance upon politics than I was spending now.

The problem of family relations is insoluble by any universal formula.

I have often been puzzled by the folk-tales and novels which take it for granted that brother invariably loves brother, children honour parents and so on. If you search, I suppose, you will find just as many real life families in which siblings are rivals, parents cruel to children, or children callous towards old parents, etc. The reality is that every permutation is possible and that varying periods, varying economic relations and social stresses must at different times make one pattern more common than another. In my generation, towards the end of the Edwardian and the opening of the new Georgian periods, we were reacting against the Victorian horror—morally fortified by Biblical injunction and precedent—whereby the paterfamilias considered it not only his right but duty to expect absolute obedience from his children and unlimited gratitude. After all, had it not been his deliberate effort which had endowed them with the priceless gift of life? Now children were replying with a counterblast: on the contrary the parents owed everything to them—the children had not asked to be born and they knew well that, in many cases, they had been the incidental outcome of a parent's self-indulgence. It seemed to me then, and it still seems to me now, that, in this exchange of logic-chopping, the child's case is unanswerable. On the other hand, as it is easier now to realise than when one's own juvenility put one in the van of battle, this dispute is not the whole case, and it is a better foundation for family affection for all concerned, of whatever age, to treat each other without presuming on claims of any kind but with the kindness and mutual respect that should oil the rub of every human contact.

Special trouble arises when the structure of society, the property relations affecting the economic group to which the family belongs, place it in the parents' power to determine the whole opportunity and future of the child. It is to this problem that Shaw refers in his aphorism that parents are the last people in the world who should have children. How can any child of spirit not react against the subjection involved in such a relation? He is like a worker without a union. No matter what generosity or tolerance is shown by the parent, how can the child show gratitude without self-consciously feeling that a base motive may be read into, or even actually inhere in, his display of affection?

Cordelia had my full sympathy. Henceforth I was a stranger. Gone was the confidence that had made my parents my rock, their house my home. They did not abate their love, but I, no longer expecting understanding, repaid with wariness. I would not be a hypocrite to pretend, but neither would I be a fool to provoke. On these terms the armistice was concluded and amiable coexistence outwardly resumed. For the next six years I must keep the promise on which they insisted.

More or less, I did.

§ 12

THE YEARS 1919–21—my years from 15 to 17 years old—were a sort of suspense so far as my relations with my family were concerned. I looked forward to University as a setting-up, if only term-time and therefore half-and-half, of an establishment on my own. But the Cambridge age block was insuperable. My parents tried to pull strings with Sir J. J. Thomson, the Master of Trinity, and I waited on him in the hall of the Athenaeum. The old man rumbled more graciously than I deserved in the circumstances, and questioned me, but nothing came of it. Then they tried the head of the Imperial College of Science and Technology, a small and lively Irishman called Sir Alfred Keogh. Sir Alfred had been at King's and advised me to try there. King's is choosy; it does not accept the Little Go—this general University Examination "does" for most Cambridge colleges—but insists on an examination of its own. I survived it, but when King's too proved reluctant to take anyone under 17, Sir Alfred suggested I should put in the waiting-time taking the Zoology and Botany courses at the Royal College of Science. The R.C.S.—one of the three constituent colleges of the I.C.S.—is a part of London University and here too there was an age limit, so I was allowed only to attend the lectures and sit for the examinations as a courtesy. I could not qualify for the degree. But I jumped at the chance.

For the next two years I should at least be able to put public school behind me and learn what I wanted so much to learn, even if I should still be staying at Kensington Court, punctuated by Townhill.

Precisely these same two years 1919–21 were the years of the peace-making and the new war to crush the Russian Revolution. The Great War had ended. Now the hopes and illusions that had mounted together with its sacrifices were to be ended too.

The shambles of Versailles capped the butchery of the fighting.

Promises were broken abroad and at home.

The War to end War was replaced by a barrage of lesser conflicts.

The late enemies cooperated against the Bolsheviks even before they signed peace between themselves. Churchill spent 100 million pounds—it seemed a big sum then—and led a crusade of fourteen interventionist armies to replace the Tsar upon his throne. Fighting broke out even between Allies. D'Annunzio raided Fiume and Italy held on to it. Lloyd George launched the Greeks into their disaster against the Turks.

The U.S. President Wilson, with his top hat, lantern jaw and black statesman's suit contrasting so dramatically with the bemedalled uniforms and sashes of the kings and generals who sat beside him, rolled through the capitals to the cheers of the thousands he was so speedily to betray.

"Liberation" and "Self-determination" plainly did not apply to any territory which a powerful claimant coveted. The British continued to hold Ireland and India by force. They used the pretext of a Jewish "National Home" to dish their allies the French and their dupes the Arabs in the Middle East.

The diplomats spoke of "humanity" while maintaining blockade against the Central European powers despite the armistice. They urged "relief", and then, through Hoover, used food as a weapon to starve the recalcitrants into renouncing rebellion. They claimed to be returning "civilisation" to Russia, and found it possible to back insane murderers and bandits, as well as deny not only food but medicines to the areas they had paid mercenaries to devastate.

The League of Nations, sole relic of the Utopias dangled before suffering millions in the last years of the war effort, was repudiated by the U.S. Senate, and Wilson, its originator and peddler, conveniently evaded reproach by lapsing into personal breakdown.

Lloyd George's piecrust was just as fragile. The Kaiser remained unhanged, acquiring a comfortable new wife in his Dutch refuge. Germany not only failed to "pay"—as Keynes had warned it could not —but received huge credits, and was enabled to use them for re-armament on the advice of the very military commissions designated to control its disarmament. The "Homes for Heroes", promised to returning soldiers, remained unbuilt. Many of the heroes themselves, despatched to Archangel, Central Asia and Vladivostok in pursuit of dividends, were even denied return until they mutinied; when they got back they found only poverty and unemployment, a parliament of "hard-faced men who looked as if they had done very well out of the war". Soon Lloyd George too was gone, the Tories, returned by the 1918 election with an absolute majority whenever they chose to drop the coupon, no longer needed any radical mask.

This was not a world likely to instil in an observant teenager faith in his elders or respect for betters. They impressed me as possessing neither honesty nor superior knowledge.

I might not know everything of Russia but I knew that Lenin was not as Churchill described him: "a tyrant grinning on a heap of skulls". It did not escape me that Lloyd George, paying tribute in the Commons to "our gallant Allies, Denikin and Kharkov", on being interrupted and reminded that the second name was that not of a man but of a city, turned angrily to rebuke a subordinate with the exclamation, "Why wasn't I told?" How could I continue to take my mother seriously as a mentor when Mrs. Nesta Webster was allowed to lecture on "The Hidden Hand" in our drawing-room to gaping imbeciles frightened for their comforts and possessions? The bumbling stupidity of the late Petersburg Ambassador of Britain, Buchanan, was apparent to me at the Townhill dinner-table. I heard my father's friend Urquhart speculating over the cigars and port on the prospects of his recovering the Lena goldfields. The link between Balfour's liking for lawn tennis on the courts at Sir Arthur Crosfield's home on Highgate West Hill, and the cabinet's disastrous Smyrna adventure, was apparent in the passionate support for Venizelos of Domini, Sir Arthur's fascinating and energetic lawn tennis playing wife.

I think that what astonished me most in this world I did not like and was determined to do my best to amend was the fact that the statesmen and politicians, high-placed or modest M.P. alike, with whom I had such plentiful opportunity to talk, seemed to have no interest in long-term prediction. They were indifferent to the question whether misery and exploitation might not be inherent in the current form of society; its moral aspects were equally irrelevant. Either they were totally sceptical about the possibilities of social analysis, or clearly content with any solution that would 'last their time'—that is, preserve the structure of privilege for the length of their life span and active enjoyment. Neither of these approaches had any appeal for me.

For me the moral aspect was primary, and science the means to identifying the strategy and tactics necessary for making morals work. Socialism was the key, and knowledge of it must lead to progress.

It is true that there were unencouraging signs: I was naïf enough to try to canvass the cottages at Townhill, only to be told by the head gardener's wife, as she refused her vote, that she had no doubt the Labour man meant very well and would do his best if he got in but "what could he do for anybody? he hadn't any money" (a view that, in terms of British politics, seems much less unreasonable to me now than it did at the time). On the other hand there were signs that not all the people were all the time being altogether taken in.

My Uncle Leslie, turning to the L.C.C. and standing for a seat in the two-member constituency of Woolwich, was again faced by typical Tory tactics right on the eve of the poll. At the last moment Woolwich was plastered with great posters;

IF YOU WANT THE
NATIONALISATION
OF
WOMEN
VOTE FOR
LESLIE HADEN GUEST
AND
HARRY SNELL
THE LABOUR CANDIDATES

This time the trick backfired. The pair got in with the biggest majorities in London.

Anyway, it was one's duty to make the world better to the best of one's judgement and ability, so it seemed to me. Nothing else could give one a right to live and enjoy, or even to self-respect. But, less of a man no doubt than my Aunt Carmel had been in her youth, it never occurred to me to break away before my majority. Till that target, I would carry on and go though the motions.

§ 13

THE Royal College of Science is (was?) in a big red building in Cromwell Road, next to the Victoria and Albert and nearly opposite the Science Museum. Here I was on home ground. For two years in term-time I lunched at a small restaurant beside South Kensington station where a dark-haired Italian waitress served minestrone and wobbly pink blancmange with a sauce made out of raspberry jam. Between the station and the college stood a street bookmaker who took my sixpences until the police chased him away. Then I opened a credit account with Douglas Stuart ("Duggie never owes"), whom I wrongly imagined to be a Scotsman, but he would not accept bets of less than half-a-crown, and this led to losses I could not afford, so I had to give it up.

The Zoology Department was on the top floors. There was a lift, but only staff members were allowed to have keys; students were supposed to be young and vigorous enough to walk up. We soon learned to open the lock with a knife.

In a way the atmosphere of the class was much like that described by H. G. Wells in *A Slip under the Microcope*. This is not extraordinary since it was here a generation earlier that H.G. had been first student, then pupil-teacher. Yet there was an important difference. As at all universities at that time, many of the students were older men, whose conscription had caused them to miss their turn of schooling and who were taking it now, belatedly, after demobilisation. They were ex-officers. Some were uncongenial, but this did not obtrude at first. The great thing was that our little class, not more than ten or a dozen at most including two women and H.G.'s elder son Gyp, was so very small. When there are so few of you, each can receive individual attention and you learn wonderfully.

I became intensely absorbed in the work. We went through the usual gamut of the animal orders: Amoeba and Paramecium; Hydra; flatworm, threadworm and earthworm; crayfish and dogfish; frog and rabbit—does anyone who has dissected the dogfish ever get the smell of formalin out of his nostrils? I swotted the Botany too but still found it less romantic. Incidentally, ill for a week, I missed the dissection of the bird and so funked it when the examination came; I regret this blank in my education, for to this day I can carve a chicken only by trial and error.

I made copious notes, drawings and diagrams. My draughtsmanship was still poor, the notes nearly illegible. But it did not matter too much that unless I transcribed my notes immediately I could not make them out; I found the act of note-taking helped me to remember a little. In general I found my memory less reliable than when I had been a child; I suppose everybody does. What stuck were not so much facts, as my conclusions from them and where to look up the facts. This faculty, useful in life, does not help much in examinations.

Our Professor was E. W. MacBride, a rounded hump-shouldered man of middle age, with a large head and bulging brow. He was a good, clear teacher of elementary Zoology, very affable and cheerful but also a little pompous. We were delighted once when, saying for some reason, "I am an Irishman", he happened involuntarily to scratch his nose with a piece of green chalk he was holding for blackboard demonstration, leaving a huge mark. He asked me to tea at his home one day and there I was astonished to find that his son was a classical scholar. I could not imagine how a young man with the opportunity to imbibe zoology from the cradle, so to speak, should drift to the classics. The further conversation gave me an inkling. On the son happening to ask MacBride a question about the descent of man, the father gave him a perfectly sound answer necessarily qualified with so many "ifs" and "maybes" that it could not possibly appear an answer at all to any non-specialist. Correct enough, it was yet such as only an expert could unravel and led me to reflect from a new angle on the difficulties of communication between the generations.

Incidentally, on this special subject; I remember a gala evening at one of the Zoo's Tuesday scientific meetings. A new fossil skull, called at the time *Homo rhodesiensis* but since classified as a less distinct category, had just been sent in by the Broken Hill mining corporation, and the bigwigs were there to argue its implications. Among them were Sir Arthur Keith, a lean debunking kind of man, Ray Lankester and all the star contemporaries. Professor Smith Woodward, a more effusive type, was introducing the specimen with others ranged before him for purposes of comparison. "This is Swanscombe Man," he said, "this is Neanderthal Man. Here is a Cro-Magnon Man. This is a gorilla, and this is my old friend Professor X of Chicago University."

The principal demonstrator was Lancelot Hogben. He was slight, handsome, with an unruly quiff that kept falling over one side of his forehead. *Ariel* had just been published then, and I cannot think why he always made me think of Shelley for really he was not like him in the least. His mind was acute and brilliant, his verbal expression exceptionally lucid, his manner dry and acid, broken every now and then by a smile that had less of amiability than fleeting derision in it.

His sarcasm was cutting. At the Natural History Museum, one of our two rather floppity women asked him one day whether certain holes in a giant coral were its "pores", but without precisely articulating the "r". He looked blandly back at her: "Paws? I thought the only organs of grasping the animal possessed were its tentacles." In the lab we used to have to identify and mark the apertures of our preparations. Hogben admonished the class. "Would you kindly not confuse your genitives. During the dissection of the earthworm yesterday one of you exclaimed, 'My heart is broken', and today with the nematode a lady asked me to please help her poke a bristle up her vagina." Our two women students non-reacted like Queen Victoria.

Hogben's first wife was as dark as he was fair, and wore long, loose-fitting garments and necklaces. He insisted, disconcertingly, on pronouncing her name Enn-id, instead of Ee-nid, but he would also say Eng-land and Eng-lish as they are spelled, refusing them the usual Ing. She was as brilliant as he, having come out above the Senior Wranglers in her examinations, though in vain so far as recognition is concerned, for in the Cambridge of her day women were not allowed to take degrees. The two had a child, crawling about the cottage floor; they had been so young when it was born that Hogben used to say they were an example of neoteny, a zoological term for reproduction in the larval state.

I owe him an immense debt. This is not because I blindly accepted his precepts—I argued with him obstinately—but because of his precise and lucid methods of presentation. We would trudge along the muddy lanes of Chesham Bois, where the young couple had their cottage. I would grow hot under the collar as I heard my ideas refuted and feel humiliated when Lance pointed out that my infinitives were split. Maliciously he would ascribe to imperfect consciousness of logic grammatical slips that really were caused by being out of breath. But the point is that this dialogue forced me to examine and revise for myself my own too facile "progressive" assumptions. For example, I realised for the first time that equality, e.g. of the sexes, is a mere empty slogan: there are so many anatomical, functional and associated differences that equality is a non-starter—what women require for emancipation is a social pattern, including prerogatives and differential legal protections, which ensures equal opportunity and equal reward for service. Likewise I learned to foresee that progress cannot be a continuous automatic process resulting from the smooth spread of enlightenment, and that the breakthrough of revolution in Russia did not just mean that there would be automatic emulation by other societies as soon as this success was understood, but might well—on the basis of historical precedent—lead on the contrary to increasedly rigid repression in other societies to prevent imitation of the breakthrough.

It will be remembered that accident rather than revolutionary conviction had led me to the old B.S.P. It was the rain-sodden walks in Buckinghamshire that now led me to serious thinking and took me beyond the Second International to look carefully at the Third.

Hogben had fought his way forward with scholarships from one of those backgrounds where parents had to face harsh sacrifice if a child, however brilliant, was to reach university. His mother was shocked by her son's materialist philosophy and, when he showed her slides through the microscope, would ask him how, in face of such marvels, he could doubt divine creation. He had had a promising academic career before him, but had been so angered by the maltreatment of University friends who became conscientious objectors that he had torn up the exemption certificates he held as a research worker and gone to join them in Dartmoor. He had scarifying tales to tell of brutal treatment there, including water torture, recalcitrant men in detention fixed motionless under a perpetual drip from a holed bucket suspended above their heads. Now, with one group of young scientists he was doing teaching work for the Plebs League and writing anonymously in its journal; with another group, including Crewe of Edinburgh, he was founding the *Journal of Experimental Biology*.

In my second year I joined Lancelot in research. He taught me to use a microtome and look for a cavity in the developing tadpole that we never found. We importuned my Uncle Gerald, who by that time was running a large-scale poultry farm at Great Fosters near Egham, and persuaded him to let us do experimental feeding of a group of chickens. We kept axolotls and fed them thyroid to turn them into the salamanders of which they are an evolutionarily arrested larval form. In Biology as in politics, Hogben taught me by example to take nothing for granted, to be rigorous in challenge of every proof. He dismissed the current statistics of human hair colour inheritance as useless, pointing out that, with Victorian prudery, the current Galtonians and eugenists had dealt only with head hair; and he was quite ready to demonstrate on his own person, even be the occasion a dinner party, that in man like other mammals it is the whole bodily pattern that requires study. He reversed the then popularly-taught theory of recapitulation—according to which the life history of each animal tends to repeat what is assumed to be the evolutionary history of its descent—supporting the then heretics who pointed out what is now universally accepted, namely that larval and even embryonic structures are often as much adaptations to the special environment of the particular stage as are those of the adult. He teased with the stimulating paradox of Clifford Dobell, his contemporary at Cambridge, that single-celled (he preferred to call them acellular) animals and plants should not be thought of as simpler than many-celled ones, but as more complex, since in their single cell, or better said without cells, they must achieve all the processes of life and reproduction for which others require numerous organs and innumerable cells. In particular, and of course in this schools teaching soon supported him, he disagreed with his Professor on the question of the possibility of inheritance of acquired characters.

Since those days we have had the battles around Lysenko, which have spilled over into politics and public attention, and about which there will be something in this story later. At that time MacBride was almost solitary among zoologists in still preaching Lamarckism, as evolution by inheritance of acquired characters is called. The trouble of this school is that, plausible as this may be as a conjecture, experiment can find little, and no unchallenged, warrant for it. And to MacBride the work of Kammerer appeared as a godsend.

The story is a real-life melodrama. Paul Kammerer was an Austrian, a slight and quiet man who set out to try to prove Lamarckism. It is obvious that an effect perceptible only over several generations must, unless the species investigated be particularly short-lived, take years of patience to become evident. Kammerer worked with amphibians—toads and salamanders—at a famous experimental institute in Vienna. A certain species of marsh toad, whose habit is to mate in water, has horny pads at the base of the fingers the better to grip the female during the slippery act of copulation. An allied species that mates on land has not. About the end of the Great War, Kammerer, after years of trying, thought he had evidence that his second species, after years of laboratory breeding in watery conditions, had developed a pad. At MacBride's invitation he brought over to show in London his microscope slides purporting to show this pad on sectioned toad-fingers.

Hogben and nearly everyone else were scornful and cocksure that the visitor must be a fake. The puzzle remained for a few years, until Kammerer justified the sceptics by committing suicide, the sceptics said "to avoid exposure". In Moscow, where even then there was a hankering to find Lamarckism true, a feature film was produced in which Kammerer was shown as the victim of a capitalist plot to discredit his ideas. The truth, it seems, was more subtle and more romantic. Kammerer had a lab assistant, an old man who could not bear to see Kammerer so long disappointed. Unknown to Kammerer he had injected ink under the toad's skin to humour his master and produce the effect that Kammerer wanted to find. It was when he discovered this that Kammerer killed himself.

Incidentally, I should note here that, before this exposure—I think it was in 1923 or 1924—I went to Vienna to check up on the Kammerer experiments and also on others, at that time sensational though now familiar, in which, at the same institute, insects had, by grafting, had their heads exchanged, with the result that sexual and feeding behaviour followed the head of the new chimera, not the body. On this occasion Dr. Przibram, the Institute's chief, whose reputation was never challenged, vouched to me for Kammerer's integrity, which chimes with the romantic version that I have cited here as exculpating him.

When Kammerer came as MacBride's guest, he was only the second scientist of "ex-enemy" nationality—Einstein being the first—to visit Britain after the 1914–18 War. I asked him down to Townhill and pressed him to say if there were anything he specially wished to do or see before he left the country. He had two wishes: to eat a kipper and—as subsequent experience was to show me was a yen of all Central European intellectuals—to meet Bernard Shaw. He explained the first by saying that an old English lady, whom the war years had trapped in Vienna, had above all missed during her exile the taste of kipper and made him promise to eat one for her. The second was as easy to satisfy, for by then I had met G.B.S. and knew he had absurd ideas on evolution. He believed in the inheritance of acquired characters himself—not altogether unforgivable because in his generation, before the publication of Mendel's work and the foundation of genetics as a science, it was hard to see any other mechanism by which natural selection could operate. Only Shaw's variant was not Lamarckism, which supposes the fresh characters inherited to be developed by use, but Samuel Butlerism, which holds they are developed as an act of will. (Sometimes, as certainly was the case with Shaw's verbal flirtations with fascism, you could not tell for sure whether G.B.S. really believed such nonsense or was advancing it simply to force others into re-examining views they had accepted as axioms without having themselves thought seriously about them.)

Something unpleasant happened before I left R.C.S. Conscientious objection to military service seems to me rarely the most effective way to oppose war. None but fools or knaves, however, equate this stand with cowardice. Absolute refusal to participate required in 1914–18 as great a courage and could be as hazardous as the trenches. Hogben himself had his constitution ruined at Dartmoor. Some of the ex-officer group, now that exams were safely past and their careers, thanks to his help and teaching, safely assured, started to persecute him. White feathers were left around, and scraps of paper with scurrilous messages in carefully disguised capital letters.

I, of course, was fiercely on Hogben's side. The battle was inconclusive, like Peer Gynt's against the Boyg. After I left we remained in touch for a while and our paths crossed once more, as will presently be described. Eventually he got a professorship elsewhere. I look back on the period spent under his instruction as among the most fruitful of my life. But it was a surprise to me when he became a best-seller not in Biology but with his popularisations of mathematics and linguistics. It should not have been, of course, because their great virtue was his exceptional lucidity.

At this time I fully expected to become a professional zoologist. I was at home in the B.M. (N.H.) by now and even occasionally had a table there for my odd jobs and bits and pieces. Another home was the Zoo, where I had taken advantage of my father's gift to become an assiduous attendant at the Tuesday afternoon scientific meetings, and to get on good terms with Sir Peter Chalmers Mitchell. Chalmers Mitchell, the Zoo secretary and dictator, was a tall man in glasses with a gentle manner of speaking who ruled with a rod of iron. His book *The Childhood of Animals* had long ago been a cherished Christmas gift from someone and even before I left Westminster and while I was still 14, I persuaded him to allow me to spend a night at the Zoo to listen to the sounds made by the nocturnal animals. The lions and wolves, for example, though feeding times and visitors' importunities had made them ordinarily exchange night activity for day, would often wake up in the dark and start one another roaring or howling in chorus. I must admit to having been after a time extremely scared and convinced that something was surreptitiously on my trail. I turned round at the end of a path and faced the unknown, gripping my cane by the end, but all that emerged into the moonlight was a night watchman whom Chalmers Mitchell had forgotten to warn of my presence.

Chalmers Mitchell took part as an observer in one of the first big flights to be arranged, Cairo to Cape, and thereafter for a time developed a habit of prefacing his remarks at meetings with: "To one who has flown over Africa . . ." or "As I was flying over Africa . . ." It became so predictable that, if anyone had dared, Mitchell's leg would certainly have been pulled about it, but of course this flight, the first in the area by any trained zoologist, had indeed disclosed remarkable patterns of movement and composition in the then still abundant herds of African big game. I got to know him far more intimately after his retirement, in the days of the Spanish war. Our relations at the Zoo only rarely trespassed beyond the borders of the official. At one dinner after a scientific meeting, Chalmers Mitchell grew reminiscent and started to tell us of a curious incident of the 1914 War. He had been a scientific adviser to the War Office and he described how the Admiralty had suddenly come up with a ridiculous idea for spotting submarines. "Some idiot had put it up to them," he said. "Their idea was that seals must have long-distance underwater hearing and that it should be possible to train them to react to the sound of submarine engines. They got several seals and stuck them in a lough in Ireland together with a submerged engine and gave them a special feed of fish whenever the engine started up. This part went all right, but as soon as they took the seals into the open ocean, the damn things just swam away. Anyone could have told them that would happen." Some years later I was dining at High Table in Trinity as a guest, with S. M. Eisenstein, of Peter Kapitza. (I have described the dinner-party elsewhere, in a book called *Film World*.) The Master was holding forth. "Good ideas always seem to get sat on in wartime," said Sir J. J. Thomson. "There was a good instance while I was Scientific Adviser at the Admiralty. Somebody had the splendid notion of using seals to spot submarines. Of course the beasts must be sensitive to sounds under the surface, and we trained them in an Irish lough. The first experiment didn't come off right, I'm not quite sure why, because it was a very sensible idea, but some ass at the War Office poured cold water on the whole thing and they didn't go on with it." It was a rare privilege to have heard both sides.

Just at this time, my Uncle Edwin made me a rather strange request. At least I thought it strange. Remember, I must then have been only 15 years of age, give or take a few months. He told me that as a boy he had two life's ambitions: one was to become one of the trustees of the B.M. (N.H.)—that one he had been able to realise thanks to the fact that the appointments were in the hands of the government and he was a Minister: but the other—to be elected a member of the Council of the Zoological Society of London—he could in no wise achieve. He was always put off, he could not discover why. The elections of Council at the Zoo were, and still are, the nearest thing possible to a formality. Joe Stalin himself never thought up anything like them. Each year three members of Council retire, three replace them. The elector attending the appropriate meeting is handed a printed paper bearing the three names recommended by the old Council as replacements, nothing else, and this, unaltered, he folds and places in the ballot-box. I put the matter very tentatively to Chalmers Mitchell. He heard me out, his wise old grey head on one side. "Quite impossible," he said finally. "The members of Council look on your uncle as a Bolshevik." As my uncle's entire political career had been spent as a lieutenant first of Asquith, then of Lloyd George, and as he had just passed from Financial Secretaryship to the Treasury to Minister of Munitions in the wartime cabinet and finally to being His Majesty's Principal Secretary of State for India, it will be understood to what an extent the Zoo Council of those days was toffee-nose and High Tory. Since, at the moment of writing, I have now become, to my intense astonishment, a member of the Zoo Council myself, and since affairs of Council are, of course, confidential, it would be highly improper for me to reveal whether its social composition and outlook does or does not remain the same. Sufficient to observe: "times have changed".

§ 14

BEFORE I continue the consecutive narrative, and arrive at last at Cambridge, I must find place for two further digressions. The second will be to speak of the changes of emphasis in our life at Townhill. The first should need no excuse; it is a sketch of my relations with Shaw and Wells, both of whom I met during this period and with whom I remained on good terms until they died. Rather is the excuse for this book, if indeed anything can be sufficient justification, the recollection I can assemble of persons of such general interest.

The present reader should recall what both these writers meant to young people of my type and generation. I don't mean while we were still children, and their names just echoed in our ears as those of lions. There was a time, just after the war began, when a Scots girl called Nowell Maclagan came to stay with us—I rather think her father was at the remount camp. She was a fine tomboy and companion, and among the scandals we got up to together was to try to collar the autographs of famous lions by writing con letters asking if we might call my hedgehog after them. Some she would draft, some Ewen or I. It was surprising how easily the great fell, even those reputed difficult like G.B.S. We would enclose a stamped card with replies "You may/may not call your hedgehog after me" ready made out, so as to make things simpler for them. Harry Lauder filled his in and added: "A quaint idea for a wee lassie." H.G. said "yes" at once. Shaw crossed out the "may" and explained: "Certainly not, its ideas may be quite different from mine."

But I am referring to a later time, when we grew up able to understand their work and purpose. Shaw was not to us primarily the playwright whose skill in presentation of argument and character on the stage has now survived the period of eclipse that followed the death of its author to delight anew, as it will probably long continue to delight, fresh audiences of playgoers. Wells was not primarily the polymath and novelist of contemporary manners and innovations whose permanent contribution to literature, if any, is condescendingly argued nowadays in courses of Eng. Lit. These were to us above all the pioneers whose work challenged and overthrew the accepted canons of

Victorian and Edwardian conventional society, morality, religion, ethics, marriage, the family, children and all the rest. The measure in which their ideas now seem unshocking and old hat is precisely the measure of their success in liberating not only us but the generations which have followed us and not known the restraints that tied us down. It may be easy, I do not know, to show that they were not the creators and discoverers of these ideas; what is certain is that it was the skill of one as a playwright and his genius as a public persona—what would nowadays be called the "image" he created without benefits of P.R.O.—and the popularity as a novelist and the unceasing publicistic energy of the other, which broke a path through for these ideas and made it impossible for our guardian elder generation to smother them.

We young ones did not have to agree with everything they said, or abdicate our critical sense and worship them as idols, to feel at least a boundless gratitude and admiration towards them, as paladins *on our side*.

I have already noted that I first started reading H. G. Wells when I was 9 and going to Mr. Barton's. The first books of his I read were *The War of the Worlds* and *War in the Air*. Then on to the novels. I ploughed with more difficulty through the early sociological books. By war-time I was cycling all the way from Townhill to Southampton to get *Mr. Britling* and later *Joan and Peter* from the bookseller on their publication dates. I was disappointed with *God the Invisible King* and not at all sure what the author was driving at. The successive parts of *The Outline of History*, though they did not contain all that much previously unknown to me, delighted me with its sweep and the universality of its view. I collected first editions of everything H.G. wrote and have most of them still, though they have largely been rendered valueless as marketable goods by a stroke of bad luck. When my wife and I went to Hollywood in the twenties, Sidney Bernstein let me have harbourage for them on his bookshelves—a lot of space for a friend to claim of anyone—and, alas, his valet left the bathwater tap running and it overflowed through the ceiling to ruin the covers only a few days before the three of us came back.

Shaw I came to a little later, through seeing the plays staged, mostly at the Everyman in Hampstead, and then reading the prefaces in father's first editions, where they stood on locked shelves next to those of Oscar Wilde. I have already explained how these locks were never locked to me.

Anyway I was steeped in both authors by this time. As far as I remember it was through Carmel that I first met each of them.

My first lunch with G.B.S. and Charlotte on their invitation I have already described. After that I lunched with them very often, at Ayot St. Lawrence and in London, first at the Adelphi, later at Whitehall Court; first alone, later, when I was married, Hell and I would go together.

Shaw, although he liked to pretend otherwise, was kind and gentle. He was well-organised and made an art of not getting involved with anyone because he did not want to be distracted. But he also made it such a principle to be considerate and encouraging to everyone, especially the young, that being so became second-nature and he could not be rude except at pen's length. It is for that reason he set up so many defences, through Charlotte and his secretary Blanche Patch and his well-known printed postcards; only so could he possibly have time for his own work. Once these defences were penetrated he was as naked as a hermit-crab's tail. He could not repress his good nature and, if he liked you, you were welcome again and again.

Charlotte missed warmth and was always looking for it. If she liked you, she too was always on your side.

I do not want to exaggerate our acquaintance with G.B.S., or with H.G. either for that matter. We saw G.B.S. regularly once or twice a year. Either he would ring up and ask us, or we would ring up because we had something to talk about and he would make a date for the following week. I am rather shy and do not like to presume on friendships. At first I used to communicate through his secretary, Blanche Patch, with whom I got on rather well. But once I must have inadvertently addressed my letter to her "Blanche Sweet", which was the name of a film star of that day, only to get a card back from G.B.S. asking me in future to address my letters to him, as "your variations on my secretary's name indicate the poet rather than the man of affairs". When next we met he said that women were much more sensible than men. When women wanted anything they went straight to the point and came straight to him, whereas men beat about the bush and tried all kinds of roundabout ways to get round him. Be that as it may, he never refused me anything—perhaps because if one uses common sense one does not ask friends to do anything one does not know they will be glad and willing to do.

As also I have already recorded, Central European intellectuals always wished to see the Shaws. Thanks to his translator into German, the Austrian, Siegfried Trebitsch, G.B.S. was gaining royalties from his plays in Germany before he could earn a living from them out of British receipts. He never forgot this, and when Trebitsch at last himself wrote a play he "translated" it himself in order to get it a showing on the English stage, defending his conversion of it from tragedy into howling farce as a simple change to maintain unaltered the impact of the play upon the different audience, accustomed over here to see its theme—a matrimonial triangle—treated in this style rather than by the gloom no less conventional for it in Mittel Europa. (How Trebitsch took this I have no idea.)

Naturally I used discretion and passed on only those visitors I was sure could safely be relied on to intrigue him, but one of those I sent was nearly his end. This was Elisabeth Bergner, his Berlin St. Joan, who was so desperate not to miss her appointment that she came with a heavy cold. He caught it and, being over 80 already, took many weeks to recover. This taught me how vulnerable age is to our common ills.

My bringing of Eisenstein has been related in another book. One day still in the twenties Walther Ruttmann rang me up. He was in London to make one of the world's first sound films *Melodie des Welts*, a picture of the sights and sounds of every country produced by Tobis-Klang. It was backed by some German tea corporation, and at a given moment everywhere in the world people were to be shown drinking tea. G.B.S. was obviously a characteristic sight and sound of Britain. Ruttmann could not possibly leave without getting him in the film.

Shaw was willing. He had no objection to tea drinking. But he was going down to Ayot St. Lawrence. We must come and find a location in Whitehall right away. We took the van and Shaw into a side street but reckoned without the police. A bobby approached heavily and asked to see our permit; it appeared that the whole cul-de-sac was property of the Office of Works. A crowd was collecting and, rather than lose time, I suggested we should do the shots at Elstree, which is on the way to Ayot St. Lawrence and where we could be sure to be undisturbed. I telephoned to the studio manager, Joe Grossman, and he agreed to let us do it on the lot but, instead of making this leave a courtesy, astonished me by asking for £25 as a hire.

When we arrived at Elstree, there was Grossman, a small bustling man who peered around at each of us and asked which was Bernard Shaw. He really did. Then he asked G.B.S. if he would stay after our shots so that he could also be filmed for studio publicity. This was too much and, having paid the hire of the lot, I sent him packing. But then a problem arose. G.B.S. refused to appear unless I did also. I was willing but had come so quickly when Ruttmann rang that I had had no time to change, and my old grey flannel trousers had a big hole in the seat through which my shirt projected. Obviously the only solution was for me to sit throughout the scene on a handy pile of bricks. Shaw had in mind what I had said, that he was to appear as a characteristic sight and sound, so he devised a scene in which he approached me, sitting on my bricks as it were at the roadside, and asked me the way to some village. I was to reply and he would then say: "My name is Bernard Shaw," and begin an agreed *spiel*. This was all very well, but even with the recent spectacle of Mr. Grossman fresh before me, I did not feel very competent to act someone who needed to be told the name of G.B.S.

This however, is how the scene appears on the film. Shaw had a most harmonious voice, as everyone has noted, but for the first time I discovered the difference between one's own voice, as one hears it every day through the bones of the skull, and its impact spoken by a machine and heard through the air. I found my tone disconcerting, affected and unexpectedly Cambridge.

Until Eisenstein came, I never asked for film rights of any of Shaw's plays. I knew G.B.S. was supposed not to wish them to be filmed and in any case would not allow them to be cut or altered. This I regarded as fatal. It was still silent days, remember. As a matter of fact *The Devil's Disciple* was the one I had an eye on, but even that would have needed altering. One day he himself proposed that I should film a short story of his: *Aerial Football*. One of his *jeux d'esprit*, it is right enough in print, but the sort of fanciful imagery that so many non-experts think suitable for cinema although this is not necessarily so at all. I thought it would have made a very bad, if not impossible, film. I realised what a concession from his fixed rule this offer was, and I suspected that Charlotte in the goodness of her heart had been on at him to make the gesture. It was a temptation, for the first film of any of Shaw's works would have been a novelty for which the capital would assuredly have been forthcoming, but I put it behind me. I was terribly embarrassed, but managed to get out of it without, I think, offending.

I believed firmly that any play, including his or even especially his, requires adaptation to be made into film, even talkie film. Arguing with him that this would be necessary with *St. Joan*, which at one time he was keen to see done, to prove it I took the script home to our flat—then in Chiswick—and spent the whole night mock-acting the action and reading the dialogue out loud to a stopwatch. The woman in the flat below banged on the ceiling and then got on to the police. She said the man above had gone mad and was reading the Bible.

I am certain I know why Gabriel Pascal appealed to him when he turned up and borrowed carfare after asking for the rights of *Pygmalion* and *Caesar and Cleopatra*. A lot of people in professions which Shaw did not know really well he saw as stereotypes. These stereotypes were not wide of the mark, they had plenty of the essence in them—you can see traces of the idiot reporter of *The Doctor's Dilemma* among B.B.C. interviewers every day—but knowalls like us and the critics would often tell him that he was wrong. When he met someone who really fitted his notion—and Pascal was 200 per cent his preconception of a film man—he was immediately delighted and felt somehow justified.

Some pieces of advice that he gave me almost as soon as we met I have always acted on. For example, he said, "Never contribute to or pay for the cost of publication of one of your own works." He explained that a young man can destroy all objective sense of his value that way; it is much better to wait until someone else has faith enough in you to publish, even if you have to be patient a long time. Also: "Do not ask for or allow an introduction to the book by a public figure." If the book is a success, it is his name that will be connected with it, not that of the author. He also refused to give a donation to the *Labour Monthly*, telling me that he did not believe it worth keeping alive a left publication that could not sell enough copies to keep itself going, but that he would always be ready to write an article free if the editor, R. P. Dutt, wanted one. I don't know about that dictum. It may have been true when he started in the mid-nineteenth century, but costs have increased so much since that no *Daily Worker*—or *Labour Monthly* either for that matter, and it has kept going fifty years—could have been possible without its Readers' Fund.

He told us how his famous trip to the U.S.S.R. came about. Lord Lothian (formerly Lloyd George's secretary as Philip Kerr) had inherited with the title considerable landed property. He saw Philip Snowden, who was then Chancellor, and suggested to him that as he, the new Lord Lothian, had not enough cash to pay death duties, in preference to selling off part of the estate it would be better for the Treasury to take it over and let the Ministry of Agriculture run it as an experiment. Snowden had shuddered and said this would be quite impossible as it would be against public policy. Lothian was intrigued by this socialist chancellor who refused to socialise any part of the land when the capitalist came to him and asked to be dispossessed, so he came to Shaw and told him the story. Shaw commented: "These socialists are not socialists at all," and advised him to go and look at Soviet Russia. Lothian went to Lady Astor to persuade her to go. She said she would if Shaw would, and that is how it all happened.

He was full of amusing stories of their adventures and particularly of how Lady Astor, reproving Stalin for some harshness of policy (this was before the purges), had been disconcerted by Uncle Joe replying: "In England you beat children, don't you?"

When he came back he made a radio speech to U.S.A. I asked his permission for the Russia Today Society to print it as a pamphlet. I had a few copies done on special paper and numbered, and sold all these to Bumpus for a figure that easily covered the costs of our ordinary public print.

It was when the fascists attacked Abyssinia that Shaw deliberately provoked liberals with good words for Mussolini. This was simply using a stick to debunk too-facile liberal assumptions, but in any case it was irresponsible. More than once Charlotte, asking us round, said: "I do hope you will tell G.B.S. off," and sat delighted while we went at it.

Shaw's slowness to see Hitler for what he was was due to a quite different cause. He discounted Nazi atrocities because of his vivid memory of the lies of the British propaganda machine in the 1914–18 war. "Wolf!" called once was once too often for him. But I was able to convince him, by adducing examples of who was making the charges and who was covering up, as well as by showing him chapter and verse for the crimes charged, that the case was very different this time, and any illusions that he may have entertained on this point he abandoned long before 1939.

Since there has been a lot of conjecture about the relations between T. E. Lawrence and the Shaws, and some too wise conclusion-drawing, I will give our own impressions—these are Hell's as well as my own—though they clash with a good deal that has been written. I never met Lawrence to speak to, though he was pointed out to me once at a Schneider Cup Trophy race in the Isle of Wight, in N.C.O. uniform but giving orders to everyone.

Shaw first mentioned Lawrence to me soon after he had first read the manuscript of *Seven Pillars*. He knew how much I admired Doughty's *Arabia Deserta* and insisted there were passages in Lawrence as vivid, accurate and complete. This I doubted, although, not having read the

MS myself, I could not say much. He was amused, later, at Lawrence's trick of sending to the recipients of author's copies volumes with particular plates abstracted, so that if they ever put them on the market he, Lawrence, could identify them. (This ungenerous trick was played on Cousin Herbert, for example; though it should be recorded for Lawrence that when Herbert sent him the hundred pounds or so it was known that Lawrence was asking for copies, he sent the cheque back with the volume saying he could not possibly sting Herbert for it.) Our quite clear impression was that Shaw was encouraging Lawrence as much as he could, partly because he always did encourage young writers and partly because of his delight in the non-professional who had succeeded as soldier and was now about to beat at their own game authors as well. Also we felt that Charlotte favoured Lawrence because of her general warmth and because at first she liked him; she did not need to push him with G.B.S., he had already decided his attitude which was quite impersonal.

So far this chimes partly with the legend. Some months later, however, the atmosphere had changed. Charlotte no longer spoke of Lawrence with the same enthusiasm. It was as though he had disappointed her as a person. And G.B.S. seemed satisfied by the fact that a breach had occurred without his becoming in any way involved.

Towards the end Shaw was restricted, more or less, to Ayot St. Lawrence. In these last years he could never see films any more. The last time I saw him in London was at the time of Dunkirk. He was striding down the top of Lower Regent Street when I ran into him. It was a time when many were panicking or pessimistic. Not Shaw. Quite the contrary. Firstly: "You do not push over an institution like the British Empire so easily, just a shove at one corner." He was right. Second: "Britain is certain to win this war." The reason? "Because she has not prepared for it. By the time the fighting really starts all the British weapons will be up-to-date, the ones they're making now, whereas the weapons the Germans have made in preparation for it will be out of date." This was not so silly either.

I watched him grow old. Young people do not understand about old age. Death, when they do get beyond infancy, is something they perhaps can visualise happening to them by either accident or illness. But age is too far off, too far to be worth bothering about. It was for me, then.

Tass rang me from Moscow with the news of Gorky's death asking me to get a comment from G.B.S. The first thing he did after I told him was to take up the telephone and ring H. G. Wells. He said to me: "The trouble about age is not yourself dying; it is all the people you know going, leaving you more and more alone like a peak above the flood."

Charlotte broke a leg and was chair-ridden for some time. When she could move a bit, she naturally favoured that leg and strained the other one, so that still left her in her chair.

Presently she died. Much has been said about how their marriage was not a love match. Perhaps. But you do not live, a span longer than many people's lifetimes, together in peaceful coexistence without at least getting used to one another. However, G.B.S. put on an air of cheerfulness. He said that being alone again had given him a new lease of life. Charlotte used to make him go to bed punctually at 11 o'clock. Now he could stay up till the B.B.C. shut down at midnight and join in, by singing the words, while they played "God Save the King".

I tried to get the film company I was then working for to send a unit down to Ayot to record this—his voice was always good. He was quite willing, but nothing came of it.

He was very frail now, but no matter how frail he would always accompany you, and without a stick, as far as the gate to open it for you and shut it behind you.

You could see his face behind the wispy white beard. It was the face of a friend, a twinkling, kind old man, but not Shaw. I remembered that when my shaving had begun I had resolved to grow neither beard nor moustache. The face is the index of the person; it is the shape of the potential he starts with, modified by experiences as the character is modified. To wear facial hair seemed to me to hide, to be afraid of one's personality. But I could now see Shaw had made his beard to suit the personality he chose; it might have changed from red to white but, unless you looked beneath it, he could remain the same figure he had chosen.

Bill Rust, editor of the *Daily Worker*, asked him for an article. He sent it at once in an old-fashioned shorthand, saying that he hoped someone could read it, but he doubted if any would be able to, and he had no one at Ayot who could transcribe it.

An old printer on the staff could read the unusual marks. But when the transcription was laid on the desk, we could see it was impossible to publish. It was not properly coherent, it did not hang together. A paper like ours is always in a delicate situation in such a case. The invited contributor may take umbrage if the article is returned. We are always vulnerable to the suspicion of having refused because of political disagreement. And on the other hand a G.B.S. article, however rough, would have been a feather in our caps.

But to use it would not have been fair. We sent it back, explaining as gently as we could. We would not have caused offence or hurt him for the world. He wrote straight back, this time in longhand, thanking us and saying he fully understood. After all, he was 94.

Hell and I just missed him at the end. We had rung him and he fixed the date as usual. Then came the news that he had been up a ladder pruning and fallen off and broken his thigh. Still, he improved so much in hospital he was able to come back to Ayot and, with the press news that he was getting better, we rang to ask if visitors might call. His faithful housekeeper answered the phone and came back with the message, yes, he would like to see us. But he did not live through the night. He is reported to have said: "I am tired and, when death comes, he will not be an unwelcome visitor."

§ 15

My first meeting with H. G. Wells was quite different. It was not arranged but accidental. There was some affair, some educational reception or other, at some South Kensington address. I went and there was H.G. I was hesitating at one side of the room and he came straight across and shook me by the hand: "I am so pleased to meet you," he said. "I have heard so much about you."

This was absurd. It was preposterous. It was what *I* should have been saying to *him*, had not such words been by convention out of place from a youngster to an oldster. It would have come more aptly from me anyway. I suppose Carmel must have spoken to him sometime. You can imagine the glow and the encouragement that such an initiative from him gave to a boy of 15.

Just as he was quite a different person from G.B.S., so his kindness was different. G.B.S. was kind to everyone he met, and so had to be protected behind fences from the consequences of encountering too many people. H.G. was kind only to those he liked. He could be quite fierce and disagreeable towards, and quarrel with, anyone he didn't like. And so he was accessible to everyone. Any barriers needed he would set up himself when he had had a look.

There are so many photographs extant of the two men that it is unnecessary to insist too much on the physical differences between them. The tall, graceful, deliberation of Shaw, the personally designed sculpture of the portrait—diabolic, it is said, in his youth, patriarchal when I knew him—the sonorous Irish voice of which any sentence made music. And the bustling, round eagerness of Wells above the neat bow tie, the high squeak, so startling on first encounter but which one speedily accepted.

Wells was the most eager person I ever saw. It was not just the kind way he sprang on me. He sprang on everyone and everything like that. *Nihil humanum mihi alienum est* goes the tag—"nothing human is outside my range". Wells went further, his passion was everything in the universe. In the 1880s H.G. had been an assistant in the drapery business. Forty years on Hell had been an assistant in the drapery business. Directly he discovered this he pounced upon her and did not let go until between them the two had drained the subject of every possible comparison between then and now.

Visiting G.B.S. was a staid experience, not cold at all but slightly formal. The rooms in his house or flat were not dark, but cool and quiet, with a Victorian profusion of oddments—art nouveau or picked up on their latest voyage—chosen not for beauty but rather as mementos, portraits, prizes, gifts accumulated in one clime or another. Shaw did patronise and push artists, but they were mostly naturalists he liked personally, for example Rodin and Topolski. Visiting H.G. was to plunge instantly into an animated family life. The two sons, Gyp and Frank, in and out; doors and windows flung open, neighbours and visitors turning up, sides being recruited for games, conversations started and interrupted. Wells was no aesthete, the reverse, but every here and there your eye would be caught by some object beautiful in itself, like his Ming horses. The only thing that saved the whole from chaos was the presidency of his wife, Catherine, far-gone in illness and pale, but ruling everything gently from her wheel-chair throne, and the efficiency of Marjorie, H.G.'s secretary and Catherine's adjutant, whose favourite garb was severe black surmounted by a sort of conical, wide-brimmed, anarchist's black felt hat.

It would be quite incorrect to give the impression that the Shaw's life was a sort of uppish hermitry isolated from their neighbours, contrasting with cordiality in the Wellses. As has now been abundantly recorded, Shaw, a unique and self-constructed image in the public eye and to all the "media", was in Ayot St. Lawrence a modest and dutiful village neighbour, on good and unassuming terms with everyone. Next door to him lived a real hermit, Cherry-Garrard, who for half a lifetime fled contacts in the totally unjustified gnawing self-reproach that, if only he had gone one march further, he might have saved Scott and his companions from dying in their tent. To see this unhappy man enter Shaw's garden as to a haven, or Shaw with shears exchanging greetings over the hedge with a passing labourer in the lane, was to glimpse a house at ease, humane and unpretentious. But the society into which it fitted was *village*, closed, limited, self-sufficient. The Wells country and household had Dunmow a stone's throw away, it was at once more populous and the boundaries more nebulous. People flooded in, the family burst out. Everything was more haphazard and was coped with as it might come.

Shaw's attitude to games and exercise was not quite as severe as that of his He-ancients and She-ancients in *Back to Methuselah.* He was very partial to swimming and motoring, as he had once been to walking and cycling; and late in life he discovered that lawn tennis was all right if you played it the wrong way. That is, you should play gently, cooperatively, and lose the point if your opponent failed in his return. At H.G.'s you could be swept into a bridge four with Cyril Edward Marmaduke Joad (whom I did not like at all but who was very popular with Gyp and his father), rushed into the garden for some home-made exercise between showers, or dragged to Lady Warwick's hard courts for a four with some shy, bearded Greville, all according to the weather. Lady Warwick, by this time a legend, was then so stout as to seem almost as broad as tall. Now that I have escaped that fate only by being much taller than she, I only wish I could emulate the swift, eagle grace with which she would jack-knife down and up in a single movement to sweep her Pekingese off the ground and into her embrace. When you got back to Easton Glebe you would find H.G. locked in battle over the draught-board with Hell, the only guest he could not beat easily; she had been taught by her father.

About the quietest—but hardest—exercise was arguing with Kot (S. S. Koteliansky), whom I did like very much and got to know much better later.

Shaw's handwriting was fine and neat, with a craftsmanship Morris would not have disdained. H.G.'s manuscripts are an outrage, an imposition on those obliged to reduce them to order. He could no more have composed upon a typewriter or dictated than I can, and for the same reason. His pages are devastated by afterthoughts; scratching-outs, amendments and balloons.

One of the casual guests it most thrilled me to meet at Easton was Granville Bantock. I knew that "The Red Flag" was supposed to have been written to be sung to the music of his "White Cockade" and not to "Tannenbaum", which Shaw described as "The Funeral March of a Stewed Eel", but I did not dare to ask him to play it and I have not heard it to this day.

My special friend at first was Gyp, who was older than I and whose last terms at R.C.S. coincided with my first. I much envied him his trip to Russia with his father and, later, his partnership with H.G. and Julian Huxley on *The Science of Life*. Both Gyp and Frank were planning to follow their father at that time if only as zoologists. Gyp was still at Cambridge (Trinity) when I went up and Frank, the younger, followed afterwards. Gyp remained a zoologist and became a Professor specialising in worms. Frank, as I did, diverted subsequently to cinema, so that we came together again and in the end I knew him much better than I did Gyp. Both Gyp and Frank married young. Gyp married Marjorie and Frank a neighbour's daughter. H.G. had nothing against Gyp's marriage but he was disquieted by Frank's choice. It seemed he thought she had not been long enough at school. Parents are nearly always wrong about their children. If they are not, there is usually something wrong with the children. Frank's marriage was extremely happy and successful, and when his Peggy died she left him two children one of whom is a third generation zoologist and good to boot.

H.G. was very well pleased that Frank went into the cinema and pleased also that we were working together. He encouraged us in every way. One day he had a serious talk with me and told me that he hoped we would stick together in our careers and that he thought it would be good for both of us. We did for quite a time but it did not in the end work out that way. I should have liked nothing better. Frank is a splendid companion; we laugh at the same things and so does Hell—that is essential. There has never been a quarrel or a cloud between us. But because our difference was not a thing you can argue about it never became explicit. The point is: both Gyp and Frank grew up wholly unpolitical. It always astonished me that this should be the case, with H.G.'s whole being and output stressing social responsibility with every breath, but this circumstance was perhaps the reason. I have a suspicion, founded only on guess and nothing more solid than her tolerance, that both caught a deep but quietistic liberalism from their mother. When Frank and I were partners and needed a telegraphic address for our firm, this happened just as the world struggle to save Sacco and Vanzetti was reaching its climax in their execution. I have never known anything like that emotion. The crowds in the streets. A sort of mass shudder ran through the world. It even exceeded the later anguish for the Rosenbergs. I wanted to perpetuate this moment and hoist a flag by registering "SACANZETTI" as our address. But Frank would not have it. We "compromised" in the end on "CEPHALOPOD". This was a pun; the zoological term means, literally, a head-footed animal; we intended it to signify something that would progress by its brains. (Curious that Frank's son, Martin, should have done his major work on the behaviour of *Octopus*.) This was a triviality, but when our film technicians' trade union came into being to transform conditions in this disgracefully casualised industry and I naturally threw myself into helping establish it, it turned out that for some reason or other Frank would not join a union. I worked for a closed shop, he escaped conflict by taking a job as boss, in its quiet way a much more socially useful employment than any mine in cinema turned out to be, successfully making films for children. We did not part or anything drastic, but our ways just went on differently.

H.G. did not at all look forward to growing old. It was rumoured that he had had a rejuvenation operation. Not Voronoff's, of course; this, the kidnapping of testicular material from an ape, the so-called monkey-gland operation, may, it seems, have an effect from the added hormones for a time but, as one would naturally expect, the graft does not take. The other one, it was so said—Steinach's. This is different, a simple ligature of the *vas deferens*, that carries the semen from testis to penis. The *vas deferens* is paired, and severance of both branches is recommended nowadays for sterilisation of the male. It can be done by a mere snip, and in favourable circumstances the sterility can later be repaired by reuniting the *vas*, though this is more difficult. In the thirties Steinach showed that severing even one *vas* much increased vigour of all sorts, including potency, in old rats. The trouble was, he popularised the treatment for humans without waiting long enough, and soon it became evident that it did not lengthen his rats' lives but merely changed their quality; they soon began to decline, perhaps more quickly than if they had been untreated. This decline could only be arrested by cutting the second *vas*, and of course the trick could not be repeated more than once. It now seems probable, however, that this result is not indeed a necessary consequence in humans, and anyway many old men would settle for a shorter life if a merrier one.

Whether the rumour was true or false, H.G. himself showed no signs whatever of decline. He was over 60 when he rang me up to join him in a game of badminton at a Norwegian club in the basement of a church in Marylebone. With the boys married, he set up successive new households of his own, the first in a flat above Baker Street station, the second a house in one of the Nash Terraces on the West side of Regents Park.

His appetite for knowledge remained no less insatiable. Another telephone call and he picked me up and dashed me at short notice to see one of the first functioning helicopters. The pilot brought it down and kept it a few feet from the earth while we shouted a conversation to him above the engine noise.

The last invitation came not long before the Second War. It was to a sort of dinner-party while he was still at the Baker Street flat. Apart from H. N. Brailsford, none of the rest of us was beyond his thirties. He knew how to order a good dinner, the table was polished, its surface and the silver reflected gleaming candlelight. When the meal was finished, H.G.—plumper now—leaned back in his chair. "I understand all you young folk have been criticising me," he said. "Now, come on, what have you against me?" Full of his food, melted by his wine, smoking his cigars and drinking his port, what could any of us say? How could any of us abuse such hospitality, especially with such mellowing inside? Punches were pulled by anyone still capable of saying anything. I stayed silent and glowered. "So you don't seem to have so much to complain about, after all," H.G. observed wickedly. When I got him aside I told the old scoundrel what I thought of him, but he only giggled. It had, of course, been a quite deliberate plot.

We met once more still, on neutral ground. He responded to an invitation to lunch with Hell and me, and chose the Escargot. It was in 1942 and I wanted to take up with him his support of the French Socialists against de Gaulle and the Communists, in which I thought he had been led up the garden path. The French Socialists always mistake the hour. During the war, when unity was essential, they denounced de Gaulle as a Catholic reactionary and the Communist support for him as kowtowing to reaction. After the war, when it was necessary to oppose him, they joined de Gaulle in chucking the Communists out of the cabinet. H.G., who wore a flower, was affectionate to us both—he always had a soft spot for Hell—but there was no discussion. It was not that he would not argue, but he could not any more and said so. He laughed but was very unhappy. There was nothing to do but cheer him up and talk of old times.

I went to the cremation, J. B. Priestley read the tribute. I wore my trade union button, not to spite Frank, but out of respect for H.G.

§ 16

In this second digression before the end of my schooldays, the Townhill one, a great deal must be about sport. This is unavoidable, for it has occupied so much of my lifetime. I must apologise to the reader; this life story must necessarily hare off into so many directions, I cannot fairly expect anyone so have the same variety of tastes as I and so find all the quarries we pursue rewarding.

I saw a lot more of Ewen, now and for the two years we eventually overlapped at Cambridge. He took over from me for a time the role of accident-prone one. Twice he nearly lost his face and each time I was with him. Once it was nearly scraped off, once burned off. On the first occasion we were going at a great lick down the drive on our bicycles to catch a boat for the Isle of Wight and he skidded and shot a great way along the surface, face down. I did about the best thing I could; left him there and ran as fast as I could back up the hill for help. The second was more spectacular. He was trying to start a car that father had given him, in the garage my father now rented for the chauffeur and his family behind Kensington Court. Ewen took it into his head to look into the radiator and did so with a match. Unluckily he must have filled it with water from an old petrol tin. The result was rather like the firework Brock calls "Vesuvius" bursting straight on to his nose. His beauty survived both ordeals, however, his eyebrows—which always met—growing even thicker than before.

It should be mentioned that my father promised all three of us a car when we should arrive at 21. Stuart and Ewen both became ardent drivers. When my turn came, I was not on good terms with my father—as will later be related—and did not want to dun him for so expensive a present. I asked him instead for a sculpture I had seen at the Leicester Galleries, a bronze of Gaudier-Brzeska's sleeping fawn. As it only cost £25 he was agreeable, but as it still survives and their cars have long reached the junk-pile, perhaps my quixotry was prudence after all. Incidentally, neither of my brothers drives much nowadays—they have reached the chauffeur-driven class. I, who have never in my life owned anything but a second-hand car, drive nearly everywhere until the old faithful fails its test or falls to bits.

After Cambridge Ewen went for a year to Harvard Law School and then was the first of us to marry. His bride, Iris, a daughter of Solomon J. Solomon the painter, is small and bright. He is a Chairman of Sessions and they have two useful children, one an expert on old musical instruments, the other on bronzes. Stuart married for the first time soon afterwards. Mary, his first wife, is a grand person; she was a daughter of Shell Oil. I visited her mother, whose connoisseurship in porcelain I admired, and took a younger sister to the theatre. Years have passed and so I am sure my charge will not mind me noting that when I discovered she had been brought up so strictly she had never been allowed to see a play by Bernard Shaw, I decided that social obligations acquired in-law were too strenuous; they were not for me. Stuart presently left the bank and took to cattle farming. He and Mary had three children—one became a lady doctor, another turned out to be *the* banker to make father's and grandfather's hearts glow, the third I remember nothing about. Eventually Stuart and Mary parted. Mary happily married Henry and Stuart happily married Jean. At the time I now speak of Joyce was still overtaking us. The nurseries at Townhill had by now become her apartments and Mabel her personal maid. She was at this time around 11. When she grew up she married Oliver, an expert in trade, photography and bellringing and their son is a young computer-wizard. Mabel is still with them. But all this is their story and not mine; they will only occasionally come further into this one.

The only major change in our household just after the war had been the arrival of Woolven. Up to now there has in this account been nothing about butlers. This is because the one we now acquired bulks so large in my memory—and I dare say also for all us siblings—that he effaces every one who preceded him in that office. In personal bulk he was not large, indeed he was undersize. But he made up for this by adroit dignity, a mastery of every person and situation that was not only capable of controlling routine but equal to every quiddity and emergency—a butler in the tradition of the Admirable Crichton rather than of Jeeves, with perhaps (though this may be hindsight for at the time his deference made everyone unaware) just a touch of the evil genius in *The Turn of the Screw*.

We all, the whole family in the largest sense, knew him before he came to us, for Woolven had earlier managed my Grandmamma's household, operating there just as efficiently and unobtrusively. Not one subsidiary household but must have coveted him. Grandmamma, my father's mother, died in 1919. All the male relatives were at the cemetery. (In the Jewish custom, the womenfolk are absent.) I remember the scene at the graveside. After the coffin has been lowered, each mourner in turn takes up the spade that has been provided and drops earth into the grave. As he straightened up after this exercise my Uncle Ernest, the eldest sister's husband, said as though casually to my father: "You don't happen to know what Woolven is planning, do you?" My father replied at once: "You are too late. It's all arranged. He's coming to us." And so he did. From then on, until my father's death and long beyond, the whole domestic organisation revolved around him. My mother depended on him absolutely. His competence and his respectful demeanour with our parents and their guests was flawless. Only we children, of whose adolescence he was the confidant, knew that he was human.

The kaleidoscope of diplomats and bankers, singers and other musicians, lions and parasites at Kensington Court and Townhill continued as before, an ever-changing pattern with some recognisable pieces. Some I specially liked: the Swedish Minister, a great joker with youngsters, Baron Palmstierna; a small, clipped man called Beneš, who came up to my black and yellow room at Kensington Court, gave me an autographed book on Czechoslovakia which I soon lost and told me he had once been a footballer; a benign and jovial old gentleman whose bridge fitted what was now Townhill's lowest table, with Granny—a Law Lord named Shaw of Dunfermline who taught me that the nine of diamonds is called "the curse of Scotland" because on it was written confirmation of the order for the massacre of Glencoe, and who, whenever he overcalled and went down, used to say cheerily: "There were waur losses at Flodden."

Some were beautiful and strange, like Edwina Ashley, who afterwards married Mountbatten and whom we young ones gazed on with awe because we were told she was an heiress; or the ringletted Elissa Landi, about our own age, who afterwards became a film star and excited in us the same wonderment because we were told she was a natural daughter of the Emperor Franz-Joszef of Austria, although this was nonsense because the dates make it quite impossible. Some were just strange, like an American financier, Clarence W. Barron, who ran his own newspaper and was so monstrously fat that when he telephoned he balanced the instrument stably on the belly that stuck out horizontally in front of him: and a dried-up little Canadian called Grant, closely resembling Lob in *Dear Brutus*, who told my mother that she really must take a trip on the steamer that goes down the West Coast from Vancouver to South America: "The cabins are so comfortable and the food is so good that you'd never know you'd left home." Rather a long way to travel, would it not be, for that sensation?

A favourite with Ewen and me was an ebullient young Croat violinist named Zladko Balòkovič. He was a perpetual bundle of energy and excitement. I can see his big eyes widening now as he watched me pour sugar instead of salt on a soft-boiled egg in Lyon's Corner House, explaining, *after* I had tasted it and spluttered, that he had said nothing because he supposed it was an English custom. One evening at Townhill he had a bad headache and did not want to play. Lady Mond, also a guest that week-end, unforgivably boasted that "he will for me", and dragged him by main force from the sofa where he was resting with us into the garden room and forced him to give his performance. Ever after, when her name came up, he would speak of her as: "Our old friend—more old than friend—Lady Mond."

During this time Queen Mary paid her only visit to Townhill.

She remained always a close friend of my mother and sent her every year an expensive present, not always to our taste. One day in London my mother was showing her round the boudoir and said, with her usual lack of premeditation: "Here is where I keep all the things I do not know what to do with." She realised just too late the Royal provenance of some of the ornaments on the various tables and cupboards and some of the pictures on the walls and hastily tried to cover up with: "Of course some of them are the most precious to me of all." Mary forgave even that gaffe and arrived one summer from Cowes with an enormous train, including one girl who startled me by the bleached whiteness of her face. I enquired who she was and learned that she was a shipowner's daughter who was about, a few weeks later, to try the then fashionable sport of attempting to fly the Atlantic. All honour to her as a pioneer, for she never came back.

Queen Mary had the reputation of being a domineering woman. The Australian cartoonist on the *Sunday Worker* (not yet the *Daily Worker* as it afterwards became, but a weekly)—Will Hope, who signed himself "Espoir"—used to draw a highly irreverent series "George the Fifth and Mary the Four-Fifths", but really the boot was on the other foot. Every year my uncle Lionel ran a book among his cronies on the colour of the toque that she would wear each day at Ascot. Browns and greys would be favourites and sombre purple a possible outsider. You could have got any price for a scarlet or a yellow. These drab colours were thought to be her own choices. On the contrary, the King made the selection, for though smaller and brighter-looking than his mate, as are males among birds of prey, he ruled his whole family. It was the grandeur of the Queen's demeanour that earned her the "four-fifths" reputation.

Before the visit I had been obliged to undergo hours of preparation, to become presentable in cleanliness and clothes. I grudged it all, for I was staunchly anti-monarchist—H.G.'s words, right across the head of an *Express* article, had been stirring: "I am a Republican in the tradition of Milton and Cromwell"—but I must admit that I admired the royal devotion to duty. Queen Mary sat on the edge of her chair, feet as wide apart as the skirt would let her, gingerly exhaling from a cigarette held in the tips of her fingers. It was obvious that she did not relish smoking, but knew that etiquette would prevent anyone else from lighting up before she set the example.

On that occasion I incurred no disgrace, but did blot the family copy-book a few week-ends later, when left, as family *responsable*, to put the lights out when the guests were ready to retire. My father had gone to bed early, the next morning being Monday, and the train to the city before eight. Everyone was off except one bridge four. Two experienced players, an elderly nobleman who, I had been told, was Britain's, England's or Scotland's premier marquis and a younger, but sophisticated, regular visitor, were partnered against two beginners. The latter hardly knew one card from another. About one in the morning it suddenly dawned on me that the men, who kept their partnership throughout, were steadily rooking their opponents, two gooey-eyed American girls, who followed the bad advice they received and went down hand after hand. I do not know what decided me to rescue those who may not have wanted to be rescued; it might have been romance, it might have been pure selfishness, for I was already half-asleep and due also to catch the early train the next morning. (I had a young green woodpecker to take up to the zoo.) It should have been perfectly apparent to me that the scene was no melodrama, for the stakes were small and the two jokers were only seeing how long it could go on. At first I tried hinting it was time for bed, but, when this failed, I ordered them to go, turning the light out when they would not budge. This little jape cost my parents a return visit to the Marquis's Scottish seat and my father the prospective slaughter of at least several grouse.

I became a boxing fan because there was a champion on the spot.

It was entirely due to Joe Beckett being a Southampton man. Some sports one enjoys watching because one has practised them enough oneself to appreciate their art—to be able to understand what the contestants are getting at. Others because they afford opportunity for the expression of personality. After Joe's first debacle against Carpentier, the article G.B.S. wrote comparing the latter to Charles XII caught my eye. I managed to get Joe's address and cycled over to call. His mother opened the door. She was a rugged woman who had managed a fair-booth, and was reputed to have fought Joe as a spectacle there when he was a boy and challengers to the regulars were few. She told me a time to come back and thus our acquaintance began.

To follow him, I became at last a willing habitué of Granny's Albert Hall box, not indeed for concerts but whenever good fights were on the bill. I saw Jimmy Wilde and Pete Herman, Johnny Basham and Kid Lewis. But these were distant heroes. Joe became a friend—the "Swaythling Champion", as the Earl of Athlone called him (his wife, Princess Alice, was one of my mother's special royal pets), because I had taken him one day to Joe's training quarters. Joe was tolerant of the importunate youngster who hung around his dressing-room at big fights. Once, a few years later, he came to my rescue at Newmarket. I used to go out there two or three times a year from Cambridge—I saw Mumtaz Mahal's career end when she stopped fantastically in her tracks with a ten-length lead, and another time enjoyed the excitement of seeing my choice, Leighton, backed only to win of course, beaten a short head at 66 to 1. Anyway, on this occasion I had got into a foolish row with a bookmaker because I thought he was paying me sixpence too little on a dead heat. Stubborn and full of temper I ran into Joe and poured out my woes. "Lead me to him," said Joe grimly. The offender still expostulated: "Do you think I would do you for sixpence?" he demanded. "You have done me for sixpence," I replied remorselessly. The bookmaker took one more look at Joe and paid without another word. When I got home to pencil and paper I found, of course, that he had been in the right. Is there any benevolent fund for bookmakers to which I could remit conscience money?

Mother liked Joe too. I do not know what the truth was about the booth story and his own mother, but I fixed up for him to play a table tennis match with mine, for charity, at the Town Hall. I coached Joe. "This is a game you could get angry at," he said with set teeth, as for the twentieth time he pushed the bat forward several inches north or south of the passage of the ball.

His trouble was that, with all his hardened exterior, he was extremely unsure and nervous inwardly, and also extremely sensitive, and this no one could suppose. The British boxing public could never forgive him for having won the heavyweight title by knocking out their darling Bombardier Billy Wells, whom they forgave every defeat. Joe was so overwhelmingly anxious to prove himself in their eyes, that before his big fights he could not sleep a wink and hence the fiascos of his two fights with Carpentier, the first, knocked out after 73 seconds, the second, even quicker. All the more honour to Joe, that, with such a temperament, he managed often to pull himself off the floor and fight his way back to win against men who had put him down or beaten him the first time.

Added to this disadvantage he was also inarticulate. Expression did not come easily to him. Once he brought an action against a sporting writer who had incautiously described him as "the undisputed champion of England". Joe's contention was that the adjective belittled him; "*the* champion" was the only correct description. I know exactly what he meant and how he felt and, moreover, from the strictly logical point of view, he was in the right although it appeared impossible for him to explain. Two stories illustrate this difficulty. Once, returning from Newmarket to London he came to supper in my rooms at Cambridge. I invited him to meet Paul Deraniyagala, the Ceylonese scientist and scholar, then, under the name Paul Pieris, a University boxing blue as lightweight. Joe was in a particularly good mood. I had shown him the trick whereby you press the back of your hand against the wall for a short time, and then stand away and leave the arm loose, so that it rises to the horizontal by itself. (The pressure results in a temporary tetanus of the inhibiting nerve.) Joe's face beamed as he tried it and it worked. Seeing him in a good mood, Paul put the question he was so anxious to ask: "At infighting, how do you force your way in?" (At this aspect of his game, Joe was particularly effective.) Joe was quite willing to give the answer—if he could. He stood in the middle of the the room, hunting for words, his brow puckered, his fists up, slowly fumbling forward like pistons, first one and then the other. At last: "It's easy when you're there," he got out.

The other occasion was at the Albert Hall. Joe was not fighting that night, but had accepted my invitation to see the programme from the box. With me was a film colleague, J. O. C. (Jock) Orton, of whom more later. Jock had been in the R.F.C. during the 1914–18 war and asked Joe if it were true that he had been in the same service. "Oh yes," said Joe, "I was the best—best—." Again he was at a loss. "Gunner . . . Artificer . . . Leading Aircraftman . . ." Jock prompted, trying to be helpful. "No," said Joe, his face lighting up in triumph as the name came back to him, "the best leadswinger in the corps. That's the word."

Football is a messy game I had not liked at school. Again it was the "local interest" that started me, more reluctantly at first this time, as what in Russian is aptly called a "*bolelchik*"—"sufferer". "Whom do you suffer for?" is the question in that language that we would render more prosaically, "Who's your team?"

Somebody argued that football is so much "faster" than cricket. I disbelieved this but agreed to give watching it a try by going to Loftus Road to see the Saints (this is the nickname of the Southampton Football and Athletic Club; they started as a church boy's club called Southampton St. Mary's) play Queen's Park Rangers. Southampton was high in the old Southern League that year. Score, nevertheless, 0–0. Ninety minutes in which, to my eyes, nothing happened. A muddy bore. I was unconverted.

I should not judge on one game, I was told. Try again. This time I saw a home match at the Dell. The Saints versus Northampton. Score 8–0. They were right! I was hooked.

From then on till this day I have worn the cherry-stripes: ties, scarves and rosettes. And I used a rattle. Also a megaphone, which eventually came in handy for film direction before the days of talkies.

Except for Ewen, no one at Townhill shared my enthusiasm. Soccer seemed to be looked on as rather "common". Stuart supported Rugby Union. We did, however, arrange a yearly cricket match with the football team—Phil Mead was in business partnership with an ex-Saint Walter Toomer, running a sports shop the family patronised, and that helped make peaceful coexistence—but the Saints nearly always had a first- or second-class county cricketer on their staff and this was too much for our bowlers.

Father was President of the Hants C.C.C. I became at 16 the first President, Ewen Vice-President, of the Saints Supporters' Club. I continued in this office for several years. When at last I resigned it was partly because I found it embarrassing to call for the loyal toast at dinners, partly because Southampton had been beaten in two F.A. Cup semi-finals and I felt it to be a president's duty to bring the club more luck.

Only on the first occasion, however, could I be held responsible. We were drawn to play Sheffield United at Stamford Bridge and on our way to Walham Green pressed close against our Yorkshire enemies in the underground train compartment. I trailed the tail of my coat before them, boasting that never had the Saints lost a cup-tie while I had worn the red and white rose now proudly in my buttonhole. The cunning tykes were too shrewd for me, however, and it was only when I was on the top of the mound that formed three side of Stamford Brook's great bowl that I clapped my hand to my lapel and found the stem alone, the flower itself had been surreptitiously snipped off. It was a terrible feeling to be in that 60,000 crowd and see, late in the game, Tommy Parker, our rock-of-Gibraltar back, advance to take the penalty that would have levelled the score and be the only one who knew—knew with certainty—that he must inevitably miss. For the second semi-final I had an alibi. I was in a nursing-home with jaundice after my return with Hell from Sicily in early 1927. The radio commentary was insupportable. "Rawlings" (that was our centre-forward) "is through. The Arsenal goalkeeper has come out. Surely Rawlings must score. He's going to shoot. Oh! Now he's been brought down from behind. The referee's looking at the spot. He's going to give a penalty. No, he's not. Yes, he is—No, he hasn't, he's waving play on." Patients who are fans should not be allowed radios, at least for live cup-ties.

In those days all this playing at superstition and fierce local loyalties had an element of humorous make-believe about it. It was an outing to relieve the otherwise humdrum. Sport is often blamed for violence, among crowds or players. Rather, when it does approach violence, is it an occasion for release of passions and resentments that could take other forms. My *News of the World* reported the case of a woman living in Wolverhampton who complained to the magistrate that every Saturday her husband set out to support the local team, and that whenever it failed to win, but lost or even drew, he beat her afterwards. "Go home, woman," the magistrate bade her, "and be thankful that you don't live in Middlesbrough." (The bottom club in the division.) The causes of violence now, in the field and around it, are to be sought in present-day social factors, not in the game itself. The characteristic of football crowds in the twenties—apart from the traditional enmity between Celtic and Rangers which has always had a basis of racial and religious incitement—was that they cooperated for all their carry-on. Without the supporters of *both* sides there would be no game and everyone knew it then whatever they pretended. Ewen, imposing doubtless deserved sentences nowadays on fan offenders, surely remembers the time when the wife of a Fulham director in the box just in front of us observed: "No wonder the Southampton team foul like this if all its supporters are like the man behind with the trumpet." (He had my megaphone.) Or when, the visitors (Notts County) having played a particularly uncompromising and frustrating game, and one of their full-backs getting a cinder in his eye, our captain, Arthur Dominy, advanced to the rescue with screwed-up handkerchief at the ready, and a clear voice rang out from the crowd: "Shove it further in, Arthur!" Ha, a humorist. But good, clean fun or so we claimed.

Something of this I tried to write in my first published essay, appearing, not in English, but in translation in a between-wars German youth magazine, dignified by the title *Fussballbegeisterung*. Well, how I did live through that last twenty minutes in 1966 trying to *will* the Saints to keep out Clapton Orient, the bottom club, and earn the point they needed to take them up out of the Second Division after forty years hovering between Third and First I shall never know.

§ 17

LAWN TENNIS was quite a different matter. It engulfed post-war Townhill. My mother took it up when already over 40.

It had been played in a desultory fashion before the war, secondary on the lawns to bowls and croquet. My father's two maiden sisters, especially Mamie, had, I was told, been pioneers in the nineties, and my father under great pressure had very occasionally been prevailed upon to show his prowess with a rare stabbing sideways volley in doubles at the net. But my mother had never played.

I have recalled the Mishus as guests of ours. I was asked to a young people's party at their embassy, got up to amuse Prince Nicholas, whom I thought so spoiled and rowdy that I detested him at sight. The Mishus' children, however, I much liked: the daughter Lilli, a dark beauty, whom I met again briefly as the wife of a bourgeois-party politician, a decent-seeming man, in post-Second-War Bucharest when I was *Daily Worker* correspondent there (I have never learned what became of them); and her elder brother Nicholas, who was at one time a first-class player, though eccentric, and always a friend. I can remember, but I cannot exactly date, a single he played on our top court with one of the Tatas, in black beard and coloured turban, and the two elegant young men lying panting with exhaustion on the verandah afterwards, swilling lemonade.

But what turned the Townhill sports world topsy-turvy was the incursion of two Canadian officers who had served in France: Colonel H. G. Mayes, who had represented Canada in the Davis Cup, and his doubles partner, Leslie Kirk-Greene. The latter was much the younger man, shy, modest and a teetotaller. The only time I ever saw him touch alcohol was after the pair had won the doubles at the Southampton Open one year, and the cup was filled with champagne. To protect his subsequent shakiness, we coaxed him into a safe bridge four. At the inevitable inquest after he had gone down, he beamed around and observed that his king had been "almost a singleton".

Colonel Mayes himself, already middle-aged, was dark, short and prone to repeat catch-phrases to himself, such as one from a parody of the smith under the spreading chestnut tree: "The muscles of his brawny arms stood out like sparrow's knees." He made a fetish of physical fitness. So did my mother, for that matter. When she was over 70 years old and beginning to be crippled with rheumatism, she would still take a running jump on to her bed to show visitors that she could do it.

Colonel Mayes' own bodily health was perfect, his skin was bronzed and silken, in play he was tireless. He had no strong strokes, but his placing was so accurate, his tactics so sound, that he could beat the best on the hard courts of the winter circuit in the South of France, where he appeared for some reason always under a pseudonym: "Overseas" or "Philathlete". I have seen him take Cochet to four sets even on the grass at Wimbledon. The women stars of the day loved to practice against him because of his accuracy. It is an interesting fact that although there could be no question that the other women—Kitty McKane, Mrs. Peacock, Elizabeth Ryan—were far inferior to Lenglen, they could all get a game or two against him in practice at the odds he gave, by stringing a few brilliant strokes together; Lenglen herself could never win one game because the strengths and weaknesses of her own style were so alike to his.

All at Townhill of an age to do so, except one, now took up lawn tennis. The existing grass court was perfected and became very good indeed. A croquet lawn was converted as a stand-by; moss made it rather slow. An *en-tout-cas* hard court was laid down. House parties were made up with the week-end handicap mixed doubles tournament in mind. In autumn when the scheduled home matches at Southampton had been ended, the County Cricket ground was adapted for an annual Open, at which each prominent local family sought to wipe its neighbour's eye. The strongest of the stars around were the Tuckey family—Mrs. on the court always seemed to bully Mr. mercilessly but they were an effective pair none the less—Dr. Zorab, a Parsee oculist, and Sir George Thomas, who was even better at badminton, better still at chess. The foremost rivals of our household were the Pleydell-Bouveries, a numerous clan, and the massive Lady Wavertree, a stout *grande dame* who brought F. M. B. Fisher of New Zealand to counter Colonel Mayes. Later, my Indian and Ceylonese friends from Cambridge, all Davis Cup players eventually: C. Ramaswami, U. Kramet, S. M. Hadi and Donald Rutnam, gave us an unbeatable hand.

My mother served a simple dolly underhand service—always into court, never a double—and never attempted a volley, but she was a keen pupil and had learned to execute her ground strokes correctly, returning any that came to the middle of her racket and were not out of her reach or too fast for her to see. This made her a quite adequate partner for easy handicap mixed; she usually played, of course, in handicaps with Colonel Mayes and there was another Colonel in the household, Ramsay, an elderly man we called "Father William", who partnered her when "Overseas" was away. In the open "Overseas" played with Lady Crosfield; she was very good-looking, and a very good player too until she broke her arm in a car accident on the Riviera. Her husband, Sir Arthur, was much older than she, rather a rickety poor fish in a way, who played with underhand service right from the back of the court and was not really in her class. Their house in Highgate became for many years the site of the famous eve-of-Wimbledon party and charity gathering of all the stars.

I said: all the household with one exception. I stood aloof. Cricket was still my enthusiasm in summer and I was loyal to it. I thus missed the unforgotten final at Wimbledon between Lenglen and Mrs. Lambert Chambers, which I was pressed to see, preferring the Oval match where on the same day Hampshire beat Surrey after my hero Brown had miraculously caught Hitch.

What eventually began it for me was that, in my last year at Westminster, a boy I had never noticed much asked in the cloakroom when we were changing shoes and hanging up coats whether there was anyone present who could play lawn tennis. Apparently there was a tournament coming up shortly at Queen's—it was the first Schoolboy Championships, an annual event since—and he wanted a partner. By the rules it had to be someone from the same school. I was the only one who said "yes". It seemed a soppy game to me but, after all, I had seen it played at Townhill and held a racket in my hand. He took me home to Bayswater, where there was a crude court in the square, lent me a racket and tried me out. First set he won 6-0. Then he gave me 15 and won 6-0. Then he gave me 30, still 6-0. Then 40 and at last it was 6-2. But what could he do? He was lumbered. There was no one else.

I brought him back to Townhill and when Colonel Mayes discovered that I was to burden so brilliant a boy player, he was horrified. He made me go out on the court and fed me with soft ones. "Bite the ball," he kept commanding and insisted that my first rule must be to hit at it with all my might. He explained that if it went over the net it could at least be in or out. It was bound to be a lost point if it did not even reach the net.

At Queen's my partner, whose name was Charles Weinberg, easily won the singles. In doubles he poached as much as he could and carried me to the final, but there we met two fairly competent Etonians and, although I brought off one or two flukes, they were too much for us as a pair, or rather, I was too much for my partner.

After that, Charles became for the next few years my closest contemporary friend. We were inseparable in summer. He spent nearly all the time at Townhill and we did the tournaments together, picking out the ones that had good junior events. We also watched all the great, seeing W. M. Johnston—my favourite—as well as Tilden on their first trip here.

Charles was a year older than I. He had a natural genius for match play and tactics, a command of placing by volley and off the ground, but no great severity of stroke. He was stocky and very small, and lacked confidence in his ability to remedy this in service and overhead. As a boy he won everything in singles—not only Queen's but the national title twice running. (The L.T.A. could not make up its mind about the best age for juniors and raised it several times in successive years, giving him extra chances as oldest.) I had no genius for anything, but practised hard.

Fired by the Mayes fetish for fitness, I took to running the Townhill mile drive downhill before breakfast. It is a short mile and as it is downhill I could do it in around 4.45 and made myself unpopular recruiting guests to come with me. Neither the mile on land nor in the water was difficult for me—not because I have ever been an athlete but because my blood-pressure has been unusually low and so I used not to get tired; the 100 yards was quite a different story.

I became a schoolboy member of Queen's and my mother and I would set out to play on the covered courts at 7 in the morning. The bare boards were nearly as inviting to her singing voice as a bare bathroom, and she would sing odd arias as we waited for our ball-boy partners, she playing with Dan Maskell, I with the younger Pearce. I practised ground-strokes against a marked wall—the forehand drive was fair, but curiously enough I could only rely on chop, lobs or drop-shots on the backhand. (I say "curiously", because at table tennis later I could not play a forehand stroke at all, while at squash I could play readily on either side.)

Anyhow I made myself a fair enough player to shine a bit at country house level and induce Stuart and Ewen gradually to lay off the game for fear of invidious comparisons with their junior. On the tournament circuit I never had a year of success, because, the season I had looked forward to being the oldest of the juniors, the L.T.A. changed the age again, this time dropping down a twelvemonth, so that I was never top-dog in years at all.

Charles and I played doubles together regularly, perhaps because no one else much liked playing with either of us, and in the end we began to dovetail fairly well. He insisted on serving with the sun behind him and so I took pride in not being disturbed by having to serve into it. We usually reached semi-finals of juniors and handicaps, but never pulled any off. The reason is simple. We quarrelled a lot during play. Usually we kept it to undertones but afterward it took some time to simmer down. The early rounds of a tournament event are usually spaced out at one a day, which allowed time to cool before each next round, but towards the end of the week survivors have to play successive rounds with tiny intervals. It *was* known for one or other of us at that stage to serve at the back of the head of his partner standing at the net.

One day I had a lucky break. At the national junior the authorities suddenly decided to introduce a mixed event—not played hitherto—as a social "extra" to melt the ice for the competitors. Partners were fixed by drawing from those present, put all together in a hat. My portion was an anonymous puddeny-looking sort of a girl, 11 years old I think, who to my surprise began to pull me through round after round. I later had reason to recall her name, for it was Betty Nuthall. Alas, even here I did not succeed; Charles and I had one of our spats and, at the crucial stage in the mixed, he stood behind the back-stop netting and booed whenever I shaped up to hit the ball.

Charles Weinberg had an unfortunate fate. It was not his fault that he was deeply insecure and furiously bit his nails. His father was quite a well-off man with Boudins on his walls. But he had spent his last years investing in such currencies as marks and rubles under the impression that they were bound to rise, so that all at once his children faced disaster. Charles clearly felt he had no talent other than the lawn-tennis that made him a good companion and welcome country guest. Yet he wanted to give up the game, for he had no confidence in his ability to remedy the handicap of his short stature when he reached senior level. He preferred to be a famous has-been, rather than a current mediocrity. He tried many escapes in vain: Antwerp, New York, Granada Cinemas and an assistant managership in the West End. Just after the Second War he shot himself. Long before that day our paths had separated.

I should have gladly gone on playing seriously beyond adolescence. Hard courts I found hard work but, as at cricket, I loved the feeling of turf beneath my feet, and I liked the fast, springy boards of the wooden courts at Queen's, which suited my drives and service. I even played some games that fed my hopes—a single against old C. P. Dixon at Dulwich, scoring 3-6 3-6 with a ridiculous experimental paddle, as broad as it was long, with taut metal strings; and a good doubles with Colonel Mayes against one of the best pairs, Doust and Hunt, in the Covered Court Championships. But it was not to be.

Let there be no mistake. I have no illusions that principle deprived the nation and sport of any noticeable talent when these lost my services at lawn tennis. Indeed, the three matches I most clearly remember from my short career all ended with perfect blanks on my side of the score sheet. One was as a conceited junior against an unknown-to-me Captain J. G. Smyth on the perfect grass at Winchester. One as a rather humbler young man, readier to be surprised, against an unknown 14-year-old in his first junior championship, H. W. Austin. And the third as a rather older and desperate perpetual trier who drew Donald Budge in the latter's first game in this country at the London Championships at Queen's. I strove ferociously to break the duck and was several times at 40-15, managing to get in a lovely going-away service on each game-ball, but he saw no reason to make any presents. Budge finished off my ordeal with one of his immortal backhands down the line, at least a yard and a half out. As the umpire called "game, set and match", Budge came hurrying up to the net to exclaim "Wasn't that one out?" What can A do in such circumstances? I hastily replied: "Yes, but please don't mention it". You cannot very well ask the umpire to allow a point to be replayed at 0-6 0-5 0-40.

The end of my career as lawn tennis aspirant is an unpleasant story, but perhaps not inappropriate to its period. As a biologist I knew colour prejudice to be based on ignorance; as a sociologist I knew discrimination to be based on competition and colonialism; as a young man at least half-way honest I could never have faced myself if for a moment I had tolerated the practice of either. I despised any Jew foolish enough or base enough, as I saw it, to try to run for shelter from one side of a line to the other. Fortunately, indeed, there was no trace of either prejudice or discrimination in my home or upbringing. My father did sometimes speak of Indians as "my brother Edwin's black subjects", but I am certain this heavy attempt at humour would never have been uttered in the presence of anyone who could possibly have failed to recognise that it was intended(!) to be funny. Only Stuart brought back infection from the Brigade of Guards. One picks up odd ideas there. At this stage he was the sort of person who would knock the hat off a neighbour who did not stand for the playing of "God Save the King" and he once did this very thing at the end of a film performance, only for it to turn out that the victim was stone-deaf, had not the slightest idea why he had been assaulted, and followed the embarrassed Stuart out of the theatre, tapping his forehead and muttering "Mad! Mad!" to the growing crowd. One dreadful night Stuart flounced from the ballroom at Townhill and betook himself to bed because he could not induce my mother to refuse dances to our Indian guests. When I visited Cambridge for my King's entrance examination, Stuart was still "up" and I had gone to lunch with him in his rooms. He had with him at University his army batman, named Sollis. Talk had sprung up about the row at Townhill, and I had hotly pointed out that many Indians of the north, the only true Aryans, are closer in culture and race to many Englishmen than are most Jews (as either Semites or Khazars from Central Asia). Stuart grew livid and waited till Sollis had left the room. Then he burst out: "How dare you say in front of the servants that we have a dash of the tar-brush too?" This incident was wholly foreign to the atmosphere of our household or to my brother's own native decency of character. Moloch twists its victims early, and it should be remembered that, though a War veteran, he was only 22 years old. Fortunately, and the roll-call of votes in the House of Lords is proof of this, the disease wore off and Stuart has long since reverted to his slightly stiff, affectionate self.

One rainy summer Charles Weinberg and I had had to wait for a fourth round handicap match throughout the day, the court at Hendon Country Club being playable only after dark. It was a hard game, with candles at each corner where the lines joined and players and umpire together trying to guess, with torchlight thrown on to the dust of the hard court, exactly where the ball had fallen. All day we had passed the hours of drizzle playing bridge with Ethel Levey—whose husband Graham White was the club's proprietor—and Mohammed Sleem. That is how I had made the acquaintance of a remarkable man, then Indian Davis Cup player and captain. Sleem was a man of theories. He smoked incessantly, but claimed he was not victim of habit. "I am accustomed to make my will prevail," he would say, entirely unconscious of any humour. "If I wish to give up smoking I do. It is quite easy. And then, after I have proved to myself that I can, and have no desire to smoke any more, there is no reason why I should not resume, and so I smoke again."

He played bridge. He was a brilliant player of the cards, but for calling Sleem had a unique system. My father had taught me the orthodox Auction conventions: one club or diamond as an invitation to no trumps, never to bid one of a suit initially without the king or ace of it, length without strength to be indicated by an initial two, etc., etc. Sleem was simpler but more subtle. Your hand should *never* be given away by calling. As you have two opponents and only one partner it *must* be only half as valuable to identify your cards as to keep them obscure. Therefore a call should never mean more than it exactly offers, namely that you will make the bid you declare, given a normal distribution of the cards invisible to you. My fidelity from then on to this logical rule led to my exile from the Townhill top bridge table, but to a harvest of sixpences at lower level.

At lawn tennis the conception behind his theory was equally hard to controvert, but it would destroy the game at once if everyone practised it. He held that you should always hit the ball back to exactly where it came from. If your opponent had not been able to score a winner from that position with his stroke to you—and that he had not was evidenced by the fact that you were now hitting it back—it was unlikely that a second attempt would lead to any result more favourable to him. If you had sufficient patience and accuracy you could thus stalemate him, until he gave up or did something foolish in his despair. To prove this theory against all and sundry he would play not only in open events but handicaps, winning the latter from absurd odds, such as owe 40 against plus 30.4. More astonishing, it brought him successes in high company, one of his Davis Cup victims being that brilliant stroke player, André Gobert, in a tie played on a French hard court.

As result of this meeting we became good friends and one day a few years later Sleem asked me if I would put him up for Queen's Club. I did, of course, and nothing happened. In the bar I questioned E. B. Noel, the Secretary, one of the "greats" of Tennis and Rackets history. He replied that membership for Sleem was out of the question. "But he is an Honorary Member here already," I pointed out, for visiting Davis Club players were by rule accorded the privileges of membership throughout the period of the competition. "Yes, that is all right," replied Noel, "but it would never do for a native in India to be wearing the same club colours as our members over there."

I resigned at once.

There is no other place in the country where a lawn tennis player can find play at almost any ball game of the Tennis or Rackets family in any weather, where he can ring and find a professional opponent at short notice, in short where a busy man can rely on exercise and not on wasted hours waiting, in company with an equally disgruntled friend, for rain to clear and courts to dry. I tried other clubs here and there, but could never manage to use them much.

I did ask Colonel Mayes to put me up for the All-England in its new Wimbledon premises. But it seemed that somehow he never got round to it. He caught a light cold while staying at Lady Crosfield's and died very quickly. The man of perfect physique and health was so unused to illness that he was like a lost child, without resistance. I went to see him during his last hours and he kissed me on the forehead. My mother astonished me by telling me later that he had been in deep distress because he really loved me but could not bring himself to put up a socialist for the All-England club. From Lady Crosfield I received a gold match-case he had asked her to give me. I cherished it for years, but one day, when we were very hard up, it went.

III

GILDED YOUTH

Sighing like furnace—W.S.

§ 1

WHEN I went up to Cambridge at 17, Ewen was still at Trinity, only one year ahead. Stuart had just left. The degree course is three years, so Ewen was there throughout my first two. These three years were 1921 to 1924.

I do not know how far the Cambridge rules and regulations have changed since my day. Therefore, what I say about the University then must not be understood as necessarily applying to the University now. But some things may broadly be the same, just as others as certainly are not.

There was, and I believe still is, a sharp difference of setting between Oxford and Cambridge. Both consist of beautiful and ancient colleges around a lovely river. The colleges are distinct, separately organised social units and the university a federation of them, much as the U.S.A. is made up of its (in some respects) separate sovereign states. Oxford had a supreme reputation for the classics and humanities, Cambridge for modernities and science. This is not of course to suggest that, in any discipline, Oxford had not researchers and Cambridge scholars of eminence equal to its rival's, but this was the general aura. It was precisely for this reason I had chosen to go to Cambridge, despite my loyalty to dark blue as the prettier colour from my days as childhood boat race fan.

I was to find a much bigger difference: life at the two Universities is much affected by their respective settings. Oxford is in a biggish city, overbalanced by the industrial development of the Morris motor interests. Cambridge is a market town set in fen country; its working-class area, though grown since the twenties, still plays a lesser role. Economically, Cambridge is much more dependent on its University.

Each college has a different tradition. All the older ones have been in being long enough for their lists of distinguished members through the centuries to give them snobbery. Some of those more distant from the centre and most recent were, at least in my day, looked down upon. Trinity, the largest, is so big it is nearly amorphous. King's, where I went, prides itself on its intellectuality and is inclined to disdain all the others. In my day King's was at peak in economics—with Keynes and

Pigou in residence—and in classics: Montague James had just ceased to be provost and Sheppard was soon to follow him. The greatest scientist there was the physiologist Adrian, who had interviewed me when I came up for the entrance examination (I am particularly weak in physiology). The outstanding zoologist was the Dean, Gray, a comparatively young man against whom I was unfairly prejudiced. My tutor—the various students are allotted to "tutors", who are supposed to keep a paternal eye on them and their studies and to whom they can go for advice—was an agreeable and an extremely able man, J. H. Clapham, whose speciality, Economic History, was one which I respected.

King's, as an architectural structure, has several features of exceptional beauty: the pierced wall and main gate fronting the street; the famous chapel with its glorious roof and windows—rudely described as looking from the outside like a sow on its back, with all four legs and dugs in the air; the lawn—whose perfection of surface gave rise to the legend of the American millionaire who asked the gardener to advise him how he, on his estate, could attain such a smoothness, only to receive the reply, "First you water it and roll it for three hundred years . . ."; and lastly the backs, the sets of rooms, near and far, giving on the river.

The student at Cambridge or Oxford is known as an "undergraduate" until he passes his examinations. Thereafter his status is "postgraduate"—unless he become one of the few elected "Fellows", exceptional young men who may receive one of the historic grants within the college gift and remain for life, or until resignation, a "don", i.e. a part of the teaching or research apparatus of the university. In his first year as an undergraduate the student is called a "freshman". Undergraduates are equipped with a traditional mortar-board cap and gown to wear (as were scholars at Westminster). But at Cambridge in my day no self-respecting undergraduate wore his properly. It was sufficient to wear your wrinkled and tousled gown draped somehow about your shoulders in the evening, and have your cap in hand, to pass muster by the proctor, a disciplinary authority among the dons who, attended by two top-hatted toughs called "bulldogs", stalked the streets to see that such rules were paid a modicum of respect and that you were not outdoors after permitted hours.

The first and most important persons the freshmen met were none of these, however, but the porters of his college. Chief porter in my day at King's was the famous Nightingale, rotund, bustling, small yet oozing authority. All the porters in my experience were, beneath their official exteriors, pleasant, helpful, even rescuers where need arose.

It should be understood that most colleges do not have nearly enough accommodation for all their members to be found rooms "in college", that is, inside the more or less ancient structures that bear their name, and are sealed—save to adventurous climbers—from midnight to 6 a.m. Each college disposes of lodgings scattered outside its walls. The undergraduate is expected to spend one year, perhaps two, in college; but unless he is a scholar or an exhibitioner he has little chance of gaining access as a freshman. At this decisive stage of his university life, his active contact with the college, apart from sessions with his tutor, is attained chiefly by use of a junior common room, membership of various college societies and, above all, by attendance each term at so many compulsory meals "in Hall", the giant refectory in which all take lunch and dinner in common, undergraduates at benches running its length, dons at a "high table" set across the top. The hall at King's has its walls lined with superb paintings of provosts and other eminences of the past, by masters of English portraiture, selected with taste and enterprise by generations of dons.

In my first year I was put into lodgings rather distant in the suburbs. In my second I was offered lodgings nearer the centre, in St. Edward's Passage, close to where the Arts theatre was built a few years later and just opposite the college gates. My new landlady was a handsome young woman with a young handsome husband and a pretty new baby. I found myself extremely comfortable there and well-situated. In my third year I asked to be, and was, allowed by the college to stay. I never lived "in".

Behold me then, at last on my own, at least in term-time. I was helped from home to acquire furniture to suit me, an arm-chair, settee, and roll-top desk which I still used for many years after; some pieces have survived to this day. I was given an allowance: £500 a year. All academic expenses were already separately paid, this sum was for my own expenditure.

§2

NOWADAYS, IF I understand things right, a high proportion of University places, including those at Oxbridge, are state subsidised, however insufficiently. This leads to the outside demand that students should be assiduous, should not "waste their time", and that they owe a duty of thorough attention to their studies.

This was not yet true in my day.

Oxbridge was essentially the place where the young man was on his own, tasted freedom, had to support himself morally by his own wings.

The public school "educated" a ruling class. Young imperialists were taught discipline and to exercise it, to be beaten and inflict beating. Conformity was imposed and, with it, groundless arrogance. The individualist was, and was made to feel, a misfit. Learning depended on chance, the accident of personality and ability in a teacher.

The University was something entirely different. The undergraduate was thrown into the sea of responsibility, to discover his identity, to sink or swim. Everything was available, first-class teachers in every faculty, culture in all its facets, a social life each could construct for himself. All depended entirely on the undergraduate himself—what he learned, whether he worked or slacked. And, mostly, he could afford to choose. Scholarships and exhibitions were few; many of those on offer were restricted to competitors from particular historic schools, so that the bulk of the undergraduates enjoyed the privilege of a time at university through paying parents, owing obligation to study only to their own consciences. The bulk of their companions were an intake from the public schools and some of these sought to prolong the uniformity of behaviour imposed there, but here any youth of spirit could much more easily resist.

On the academic side, tutorial supervision was light. Discipline was rigid but only minimal; it could be an irritant, but only because it concerned trivialities, like the obligations to eat in hall and to be in your rooms from midnight to 6 a.m. for so many nights each term in order to qualify for a degree. The examination time provided a reckoning for the neglectful, but here the standards of the colleges varied; some of the larger or more distant colleges were quite contented if their students gained no honours but only the relatively easy pass.

One other distinction from present Oxbridge must be mentioned. Monasticism, the cult of the exclusive male society, still prevailed. This is not to say that homosexuality was common. It was, perhaps, not altogether uncommon. Oscar Browning was still up when I came to Cambridge. Two of my very good undergraduate friends used often to sit in my rooms, moaning that the pretty youngster they both fancied was ungratefully betraying them with a third, and that same youngster—afterwards a clergyman—used to receive an advance insight into the English Literature papers from A. E. Housman. What was more far-reaching was that woman was still kept beyond arm's length, treated as a cultural inferior, excluded from the "Greek ideal".

Boys came up from the unnatural hothouse world of the segregated residential public schools, their passions and their rivalries diverted to each other, knowing intimately no females but their mothers and sisters, with others simply mythical sex objects. They entered a world where still their class were males, their fellow-undergraduates males, the most highly reputed scholarship the classics, religion served by male priests, the worshipped sports stars males—those of rowing, rugby, cricket, football, boxing, athletics—and women's aspects of sport, e.g. in athletics itself, hockey, lawn tennis unBlued, unchronicled and despised. The women's colleges were far in the outer suburbs, their charges further protected from sexual intercourse by rules and hours of visiting more suited to a hospital or a prison. Their inmates were denied degrees—this only altered several years later; the traditional common meeting-ground of undergraduates, the Union Society, was closed to female membership (it remained so for yet another generation). Both the dramatic societies excluded university women; that at Oxford (the O.U.D.S.) brought in, when need be, professional actresses; that at Cambridge (the A.D.C.), as well as the more frivolous "Footlights", used, as in Shakespeare's day, baby-faced young men in the female roles.

It is astonishing indeed, that so many undergraduates remained normal. Actual bed relations between students and studentesses were no doubt uncommon, at any rate in term-time, and when they occurred were a subject for gossip and envy or, if too obvious, sending down. Male students who sought it had to find heterosexual practice elsewhere, traditionally with girls of the town or even further afield. The last train back from London in the evening, arriving before midnight in Cambridge, left Liverpool Street at 10.20 p.m., too early for a visit to the London theatre beforehand—so that it was known as the "Fornicator", there being no other exercise in the big city that could be adjusted to the time.

The greater harm caused by this segregation probably occurred in arresting the normal adolescence of the younger men and delaying their coming to terms with a real world in which both halves of humanity are needed, not merely for procreation or indulgence but to make a spiritually and intellectually fertile whole. There is nothing wrong with voluntary segregation where tastes are different—a London-Scottish or a London-Irish or a mothers' meeting or a sewing bee—but where segregation is compulsory it implies inferiority, not merely difference, either in sex or race. There was even in my day one don who, forced to allow women to attend his lectures, seated them carefully in the front rows and kept them meticulously behind at the end after the others had left, to ask benevolently: "Was there anything, my dears, that you didn't understand?"

One pioneer hostess stood out against this barren tradition. This was Lella Sargant Florence, born Lella Secor, a freckled American redhead who had been belle of the campus and a spirited battler against the violence with which the U.S. authorities assailed pacifist protest towards the close of the 1918 war and, vindictively, afterward. She had sailed on Henry Ford's ill-fated peace ship. Her husband, a thickset and amiable young British economics don, looked stolid as a rock; but he had hidden depths, for he had kidnapped her in face of fierce competittion from her native admirers, rescued her from arrest and brought her with him back to England. Dear Lella! she found Cambridge a backwater that could not possibly be permitted to go on benighted. She set up a salon that attracted young people of both sexes by her political glamour and held them by her effervescence and charm. Here she set out to introduce them to one another. The old-fashioned Establishment regarded her as some sort of transatlantic modernistic bawd come to disturb their peace of centuries. Really she was just a respectable if broad-minded matchmaker, crusading to bring their fossil society up to date at least with Jane Austen's Bath. I believe that this couple, whom I have not met since those days, still flourish as worthy philanthropists in Selly Oak. They did us all a very great deal of good.

§ 3

FROM WHAT I have said in these previous two sections, it may seem—and this I guess corresponds to reality—that my time at University occurred near the end of a several-centuries-long interregnum. In medieval days the two great Universities had been *the* seat of learning, perhaps the only place in the country where learning could be acquired. Their students would have the arrogance of knowing themselves on the way to become scholars, superior in knowledge to the aristocracy who wielded power in society and state, and would further know that this scholarship would be their sole asset in achieving for themselves a dependent niche among their ignorant betters. Today the multiplication of Redbricks and the universalisation of the rat race combine to make education, or at least training and qualifying, important once again for most at Oxbridge.

But in between, the big University was not primarily a school. It could be, if the undergraduate wanted to make it so. All the opportunity was there. But this was not supposed to be its chief function. It was mainly a sort of adjunct to, or cheap substitute for, the European Grand Tour—an experience in between school and adulthood through which, by making friends, acquiring contacts that might be useful in after life, picking up a general smattering of culture, experimenting with activities that were a miniature model of, but themselves unimportant to, the fully grown-up world, the boy could turn into the *gentleman*. Except in the disciplines of teaching and the sciences, the fact that you had "been to University" counted for more in the general post-university world than what degree you took. A future doctor would still have to follow Oxbridge technically with a medical school, a future lawyer to prepare in chambers. In commerce, indeed, and industry the fact that you had been to university was, by an inverted snobbery and perhaps correct appreciation, positively a disadvantage, which a good degree made worse. In this atmosphere, except for the special demands made by certain colleges, it did not so much matter what you did academically at university, your extra-curricular activity was quite frankly the determining factor in enabling judgement on whether your stay was a success.

This was soil in which I expanded like a flower.

Academically I did nothing, learned nothing, achieved nothing, during my three years at Cambridge, and in this field my status was at the last moment, as will appear, rescued by a fluke. Yet I was as far as could possibly be from the undergraduate who idles or luxuriates away his time. I was as incessantly busy in every other direction—perhaps too many directions—as I have been ever since.

I wished to be a Zoologist. To get a degree after the minimum nine terms you must take the Tripos examination, so called because it reposes on three feet, your own specialist subject and two cognate ones. My supplementary two were agreed to be Botany and Chemistry. But these three were all fields in which I had studied already. I had no great interest in once more going through the rigmarole of attending lectures on elementary aspects, or performing dissections and experiments, all of which I had been through before and mostly under more favourable circumstances. I tried out one or two visits to lectures and labs, but found myself one of a crowd that seemed four or five times as numerous as the corresponding class had been at R.C.S. Whatever the quality of the teaching, it would have been impossible for the teachers to give the same amount of individual attention as I had already received. By comparison, at R.C.S. I had been spoiled and featherbedded. I decided to skip the elementary course altogether and never went to regular faculty lecture-room or lab again.

The result was, of course, that, when examination time came, I fell flat on my face. The Tripos is in two parts: the three subjects at the end of the second year, your speciality in some more advanced aspect at the third. As will eventually appear, I failed in the first part and never reached the second.

What I did, or rather didn't, do appeared obviously sensible at the time, but I learned the hard way that you cannot flout with impunity the proved essential preparations—however otiose and unattractive these may appear. I did attend certain lectures outside the elementary courses on aspects of Zoology I was specially interested in, e.g. Borradaile on Zoogeography; and also I took special coaching in some subjects my previous training had missed out altogether, such as Organic Chemistry and Biochemistry, but this minimum gesture was hopelessly inadequate. When examinations came I was all rust; I ought to have known everything, but could remember next to nothing. Data on most of the questions were fully set out long ago in my own notes and diagrams made in South Kensington, but these notebooks were not with me in the examination room.

Of course I had expected to be able to rub up this knowledge by cramming in the last few days before examination. The thing is impossible. Generations of neglectful undergraduates must have shared my experience of frantically poring over their books at the last moment to the frightful tintinnabulation of the Cambridge bells. Cambridge has, or seems to have, innumerable churches at such moments. Pre-revolution Moscow with its hundred churches can have set up no more hellish din. Each peal has a different note, each starts just as you are hoping another is going to end. Concentration is impossible. The voices of doom ring in every clang: "Faustus, thy soul is lost." The case resembles his, repentance is too late.

Enough, for the moment, of these unpleasant reflections. The devil I sold my soul to was still extra-curricular. Politics, art, sport, new friends and old enthusiasms were the temptations I went a-whoring after.

My new contemporaries *in stat. pup.* included: among Conservatives, R. A. B. Butler, Geoffrey Lloyd and S. V. T. Adams; in the Labour ranks, young Arthur Henderson (whom we called Cousin Arthur, to distinguish him from his father, known to everyone as Uncle Arthur—his brother, who had just gone down, equally had to be Cousin Willie); in the arts, George Rylands, Cecil Beaton and Dennis Arundel. I list these names, not to suggest personal acquaintance with those who bore them, but to identify the period and its intellectual temptations precisely.

I do not know what would be the equivalent today of my allowance. Then at any rate it was enough for me to yield to most of such temptations. I still cannot plan out a proper budget and keep to it. The only way I can manage is to work to a rough scale of living that should cost much less than the prospective income, pay every bill at once as it comes in, and so have something left over for books and emergencies and deserving causes—three vague enough categories in all conscience—without running into the red. I cannot save. But at least I never had to go back to my father with debts to be repaid.

§ 4

Is it possible for me to detach myself sufficiently from the author of 60-plus to depict truthfully and without anachronism the ideas and principles he brought with him to Cambridge at the age of 17? This must be tried, for without that picture there can be no body or background to the incidents and feelings that the subject now recalls.

I was a Socialist for moral and intellectual reasons. These were not entirely separate, as of course they should not be. I had never been called on to experience poverty. I had been surrounded by every affection and indulgence. I did not know in my own person any of the miseries of frustration, deprivation, unattended illness or undernourishment for oneself or one's dear ones which afflict, at one time or another, the vast majority of mankind. All these ills I knew only through literature, at second-hand.

What repelled me about society as it existed was its unfairness, the hypocrisy or complacency of its supporters, who either denied its ills or accepted them as irremediable, and saw nothing incongruous in their ready acceptance of its inherent advantages for themselves. What attracted me about Socialism was its reasonableness and morality, its insistence on the feasibility of just realisation for all of inalienably equal rights and opportunities. I regarded my attitudes on this fundamental matter as only a logical consequence of what I long called my "scientific training", though—heaven help me—my own professional science then and later was little more than mammalian systematics, which real scientists despise as "stamp-collecting"; and my own self-education has been little more than acquisition of a sceptical and analytical habit of thinking, based on childish aptitude for mathematics, prolific reading, delight in reflecting upon paradoxes, and lucky encounter and argument with intelligent seniors. Flaws in socialist argument could not shake me, just as disappointments in socialist experience recognised in after life have not been able to. It has seemed to me that they demonstrate only the necessity of finding out and planning better so that factors previously unrecognised may be allowed for. The only cardinal sin of the human spirit is to deny the possibility of solutions to human problems and abandon search for them. This is a betrayal of the faculties one is born endowed with, and of the obligations associated with being a member of a social animal species: the ultimate treason—a surrender before the complexities of life.

How do these obligations affect one's behaviour? One's judgement must be independent. Of course it cannot be this in the sense of being independent of the real world, the traditions of the past, the human contacts of the present. It is independent only in the sense of being a unique personal combination of one's own nature with these external processes but, whatever it turns out to be in result, it is dishonest and a failing in one's duty of contribution to society not to recognise it as ultimate guide. This, I think, is what is less precisely in more usual terminology called conscience.

I had no very mean opinion of myself and my capacities. I expected to be equal to any call I might encounter. (Not until my thirties, under test in Spain, did I realise that I might fall short.) On the other hand—and this is perhaps a small claimable virtue among all the egotisms—I had no ambitions at all for personal glory or distinction. The *job* has always attracted me, the opportunity to do things I considered right or useful, not the title, fame or office. I have felt as fulfilled helping, however anonymously, in work that needed doing, either as a personal adjutant or as a member of a group, as I could have felt on my own. I have no lust to command, and if I have sometimes been fated to lead a little this has only been because a gap appeared that clearly needed filling.

I was prepared to be a revolutionary. I am still, but I admit that matters seemed simpler to me then than they do now. I could see the self-interest or self-deception of those who denounced revolution. But I have not often enough allowed for the fact that hypocrisy or ignorance in a witness, though a useful warning, is not *proof* that all he says is false. Also that an insincere or inadequate objection to a proposal does not necessarily mean that other snags, unmentioned and unanticipated, may not lie in wait on the path towards its realisation. It was sufficient then for me to be repelled by those who prated of the sins of revolution while they had themselves induced them by their complicity in repression and counter-revolution; who blamed famine and breakdown on the new society while themselves imposing intervention and blockade; who condemned "class-war" and pitied those who had had to sell some of their jewels to reach their bank accounts in Paris, while themselves remaining totally indifferent to the exploitation and suffering by which their friends' wealth had in the first place been collected.

It is not that I was callous. I think the reverse. Disregard of the detail of individual human suffering is the surest descent to Hell—the individual, not a statistical total, is the unit that feels joy and sorrow—but to be disproportionately emotive about detail is to betray truth. Nor is it a matter of believing that the end justifies the means. That is a denigratory charge that has been used by all manner of opponent-traducers, against Jesuits long before Communists. It is a matter of understanding that means and ends cannot be separated and weighing both together.

No revolutionist in his right mind, however benevolent, would be arrogant enough to seek to change society merely according to *his* will and judgement, or to subject others, by a choice not theirs but his, to an anguishing and chancey process of change from one static form of society, bad, to one *he* supposes may be good or at least potentially better. But that is not the problem at all. Nothing is static. Society is rapidly changing anyway, as everything else is. It is an affair of using your God-given loaf to try to understand the processes and the "laws of movement", and help turn fate in a better direction rather than a worse. Unless man does this, he is as every other animal, object not subject.

All this is a sort of instinctive materialist dialectic outlook. I knew little of Marxism at the time but was not afraid of it. I did not study its philosophy until several years later. What I understood of its theory of history seemed plausible; its interpretation of current events struck home as accurate, according with everything I noticed at first hand. Trotsky I found exciting in his graphic *My Escape from Siberia*. I liked the liveliness of his polemic in *In Defence of Terrorism* and *Between Red and White*. Of Lenin I knew only *State and Revolution* and *Imperialism, the last stage of Capitalism*; I found the reasoning of these two books incontrovertible—an incomparable key to understanding of contemporary affairs. I knew that I should try to found politics on economics. In Cambridge one is allowed to gatecrash any course of lectures to taste them. I tried both Pigou and Keynes—the latter's lectures were so full one had to stand, but all the categories of orthodox economics seemed so remote from reality that his crowded room reminded me only of a witches' sabbath. I ploughed earnestly through *Capital*, finding parts especially hard going, other parts, especially the diatribes on gold and on the Highland Clearances, pure poetry, and no flaws in the argument.

What all this added up to, in sum, was that in search of the greatest

GRANDPAPA

GRANDMAMMA

Front Row (*L. to R.*)*:* MOTHER (aged 20), WITH STUART, GRANNY, CARMEL (aged 18). *Standing:* FATHER (aged 30), GRANDBERTIE, GRANNY'S FATHER (MR. F. HENDRIKS)

FATHER, THE SOLOMON J. SOLOMON PORTRAIT

FOR PRESENTATION AT COURT, MOTHER

28 KENSINGTON COURT, W.8

TOWNHILL AT WAR—THE CARTUYVELS DU COLLAERT

TOWNHILL, THE WEST FRONT

BATH CLUB MEDAL

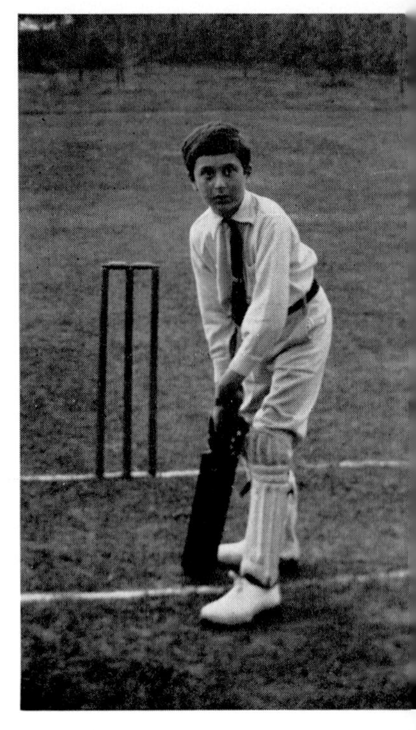

STRAIGHT

QUEEN'S CLUB JUNIOR

"WHAT HAVE I DONE?"
I.M. *v.* BRONSTEIN

CAMBRIDGE *v.* OXFORD, 1923
Front row (*L. to R.*)*:* D. L. T. Lee-Elliott (Magdalene), A. E. Evans (Christ's), F. B. Kipping (Trinity), F. Crawford (Magdalene). *Standing:* B. N. Mookerjee (Trinity), I.M. (King's)

AT EASTON GLEBE (S. S. KOTELIANSKY AND G. P. WELLS)

AT TOWNHILL PARK: "A FOUR-LETTER WORD?"

THE PALMYRA OF THE NORTH
(LENINGRAD, 1925)

IN SEARCH OF *SPALAX*

ACADEMY OF SCIENCES BUILDING IN LENINGRAD, 1925

THE GEORGIAN MILITARY ROAD

"THE FROSTY CAUCASUS", 1925

PROMETHEOMYS BURROW

AT 7,000 FT.—THE KRESTOVY PEREVAL

OUR TEAM CELEBRATES

HALT IN THE FOOTHILLS

THE DUSTY PLAIN

TIFLIS: TO MEET THE GERMAN DELEGATION

THE SUN-HATS I
BANCROFT CLARK

HUNTING MELONS

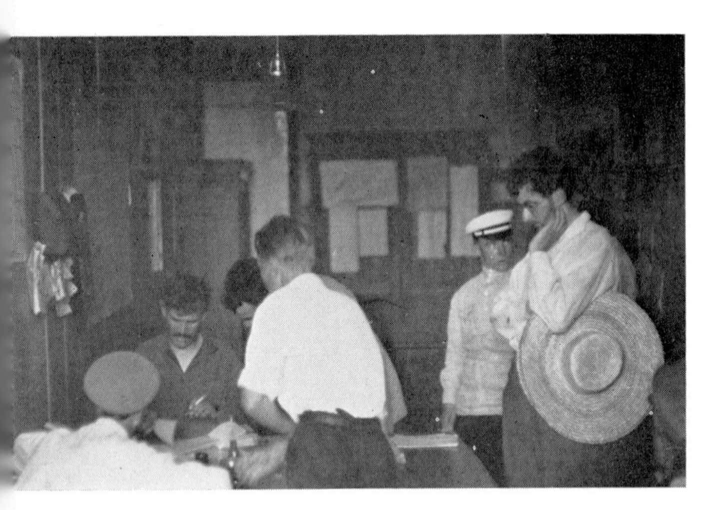

QUEUE FOR STATION-MASTER

THE SUN-HATS II I. M.

THE BOLSHOI THEATRE, 1925

MOSKVA EMBANKMENT AND KREMLIN WALL, 1925

WEDDED PAIR

good of the greatest number, I rejected the system that had resulted in war and was unfair in peace, supported that whose only advocates to gain a breakthrough had initiated peace and were trying with their people to make society more moral and effectively improvable. This meant, in Britain, that I must be active in Labour politics.

The students of today, or at any rate many of them, reject the existing political parties and find in organising *qua* students an outlet for feelings to which these deny expression, not only a means of defending their interests in their teaching establishments—which my generation never found necessary—but also a hope that they may overcome frustration by becoming an independent political force. I will not discuss here whether this last hope can lead anywhere or is a mere evasion—my opinion, as that of an old square, is anyway not the one that most matters on the subject—but only note that in those days youth did not feel such frustration; any student who wanted to be political gravitated at once to the appropriate University political party.

And this was linked directly with its adult national centre, not grouped in a student federation of its own. Even the National Union of Students, if known at all, was so only as a tourist agency for holidays. Youth was not yet disillusioned and self-segregated, but then, much had not yet happened that has since encouraged disillusionment. Those who know the Labour Party only today, after more than a generation of right-wing domination during which its leaders have sedulously inculcated a disbelief in its socialist principles as thorough as the disregard in the Church of England for the wording of the Thirty-nine Articles, will not know that at that time it was a *coalition*, uniting all willing organisations of workers by trade or industry (the trade unions it was particularly founded to represent) with *all* willing groups and societies of socialists, whatever their particular shade. It was not until much later that the right wing, annexing for themselves the name of "social democrats" (which meant something quite different on the Continent, where it came from), and dismissing the constitutional clause about nationalisation as cavalierly as they ignore all inconvenient conference decisions, began to convert the Labour Party to a uniformity and obedience in which only their own heresy was recognised as orthodoxy, and dissenting socialists—beginning with Communists and continuing with individuals such as Pritt, Cripps and Bevan—were driven into outer darkness, to be re-embraced only if and when they had abjured.

G

In those days the Labour Party was still a hodge-podge, in which all of us could find a home, to work for change by and in the interest of a working class, which was ultimately destined, through socialism, to become the whole community. So far as I was concerned, to work how? With all my heart of course. But it was not immediately apparent to the young man in what precise direction, with what associates.

There are still naïve people who ask why a convinced socialist does not obey the injunction of Christ to sell all that he hath and give to the poor. Indeed my sister is worried by this and has only recently given up expressing surprise to me about it every time we happen to meet. (My father and mother were obviously a bit afraid of it, too, for they carefully placed the capital of any bequests made to me outside my reach.) I am sure private charity, if given without hope of heaven (but only then, of course), is good for the soul of the giver; but it is clearly an uneconomic way of devoting the whole of the giver's resources to improving the lot of the receiver. At least a part of the same expenditure, devoted to advancing beneficial change in society, is likely to be more far-reachingly successful in this aim.

Such income as I received in Cambridge days was an unearned, conditional allowance, not my own for free disposition. It was easy, and seductive, to argue to myself that all acquisitions, e.g. books, and purchased experience were fitting me more completely as an effective social being. Nearly as easily, that all congenial exercise was necessary relaxation, contributory to more efficiency, all intercourse with fellow human-beings learning and practise in communication. This kind of reasoning, undoubtedly containing a kernel of truth, cannot but be a trap for self-indulgence too.

Seeing something that plainly needs to be done, it is not hard to give up all else and do it. So far, owing less to nobility of character than to ease of circumstance, I have never had to hesitate in such a situation. But, alas, there are other times when need and usefulness are less obvious and there is always the devil whispering at one's shoulder that one cannot forever be at full stretch—it is not only in Jack's interest but in that of his efficiency to work for others that he should not always be a dull boy.

Ostrovsky, not the nineteenth-century playwright Alexander, but the young Nikolai who died as result of wounds suffered in the revolutionary struggle, wrote in *How the Steel was Tempered* a passage often quoted: 'Man's dearest possession is life, and it is given him to live but once. He must so live as to feel no torturing regrets for years without purpose, nor ever know the burning shame of a petty and a wasted past; so live that, dying, he may say: all my life, all my strength were given to the finest cause in all the world—the struggle for the liberation of mankind.' I first came across it at the time of the Spanish War and kept it a long time in my pocket book, so that I should not forget it however much in my day I have fallen short of it.

In Cambridge, while I was up, Cecil B. de Mille's super-colossal Biblical epic was shown at a cinema in Market Square. As, at the beginning, a title displaying the Ten Commandments was thrown upon the screen in place of a splurge, a hollow voice from the audience rang out with the examination formula: "Only six need be attempted".

I did not yet know the Ostrovsky quotation when I was at Cambridge but I would certainly have accepted it. Shaw had set up a target at once more moderate and more comfortable in the sense of being easier of attainment: "A gentleman is one who puts more into the common stock than he takes out."

I suppose the rest of this autobiography will be in a sense a book-keeping account of how this balance worked out in my case and I hope the reader will not judge it too severely.

§ 5

FOR POLITICS of my colour there was the Union, the University Labour Club and the Spillikins. The last we invented.

My first port of call was the rooms of M. H. Dobb, then a recent graduate at Pembroke; since, an economics don at Trinity; all his life a student of Marxism with a deserved world-wide respect and reputation for common-sense analysis and clear unjargonised exposition. Maurice Dobb was then a slim, extremely elegant young man with fair hair and perfect pink complexion, of modest, almost diffident manners. He was a bachelor in those days; he afterwards married an attractive red-haired woman who wrote one of the best books of its kind, wrongfully neglected, describing her experiences as a warden in the London blitz. Yet even then he was so neat, in contrast to the rather scruffy appearance of most of us, that the saying was that if we ever wanted to print underground leaflets we should be able to do so in Dobb's trouser-press.

Already arrived at the small meeting in Dobb's rooms was a brilliant young man, a biochemist if I remember rightly, called B. ("Woggy") Woolf. Woggy was short, eager, nervous, humorous. He had dark curly hair, glasses and what is called—I know not why, because Jews are neither a race nor in the least homogeneous in appearance—a "typically Jewish" cast of countenance. Woggy handed us postcards on which were depicted a crowd of raggedy children sketched in black and white, advancing, not so much towards as away from, a crimson dawn. I gathered that these postcards had something to do with the Young Communist League, but, if they constituted us formally members and our ensemble a branch, it was the last we heard of it, for we never had any formal business to transact, communications to report, or dues to pay. I liked and admired Woggy without reserve. He was a fine comrade and companion throughout the three years at University. He had a scholarship and no money resources behind him. I do not know what became of him afterwards, for in spite of being one of those rare geniuses who can combine political conscience and activity with good examination results he found it hard to get a job. I fear whatever happened cannot have been good or I should have met him again.

We did, however, form a group and, because we did not really know what we were, we called ourselves—at my suggestion—the Spillikins. I cannot truthfully call us Communists, even though I should like thus to be able to claim early membership, because we did not discuss Communism or, most of us, know then properly what it was. We included some very intelligent, even exceptional people. Allen Hutt, the typographical expert who, as chief sub, turned the *Daily Worker* into a prize-winning, even more, a readably-laid-out newspaper; Philip Spratt, one of the defendants in the Meerut Conspiracy Case, who later drifted off into Hinduism; A. L. Morton, the historian; and Desmond Bernal, already so engrossed in crystallography that he only visited us marginally, were among our number.

What we really were was a ginger group, or—to make it sound less like a "fraction" and more like its real essence, one with nothing remotely conspiratorial but everything traditionally collegiate about it—a caucus of like-minded radicals providing a backbone to the Labour Club.

As such, we influenced the latter throughout my three years' University stint, drummed up speakers for the Union debates, planned subjects for meetings and speakers to be invited, rallied to the support of Labour candidates for the town and country constituencies at general election and by-election times, made ourselves generally useful busybodies at whatever crisis might come up.

We put my brother Ewen forward as University Labour Club chairman after Cousin Arthur had gone down. Our zeal nearly got him elected as secretary of the Union—there had never been a Labour Party secretary—against the Tory paladin S. V. T. Adams. The first result was a tie, but on a re-run, as always happened with a Union voting issue at a crunch, Tory parsons, whose membership dated from the year dot but who had taken out life membership for economy's sake when they were up and so were still technically eligible to vote, responded to the emergency canvass and descended from their far-flung benefices in great black-clad droves, to swamp the interloper. Sam Adams embodied Tory reaction to us in those days, the ideas he expounded so vehemently came from the Ark, so Ewen created precedent by standing again the following year, this time to oppose Sam for the Vice-Presidency. Unlike Oxford, where at the Union the three posts of Secretary, Treasurer and President are contested separately and success in winning one is by no means followed by automatic succession to another, in Cambridge the tradition is—or was

—that an aspirant once elected to Secretary should be allowed safely to proceed unopposed to Vice-President and President in the succeeding years. Our innovation was thought unsportsmanlike, Ewen's second defeat was therefore by a wider margin. Sam was so upset he would not speak to any of us. I knew him then only as a bogy. I did not meet him personally until years later in the Commons corridors, and found him an humane, decent man whose rigidity had simply been a reflection of sincerity. His early death by accident may well have been a loss to politics.

The Union nowadays, both at Redbrick and Oxbridge, seems to have a function at University quite different from that traditional at Oxford and Cambridge in my youth. The Unions today coordinate the social pleasures as well as the politics of their members, serve as the one place in which students have elbow room to manage their own affairs, and even represent the students in clashes with the administration. The Unions of my day, though they did provide reading-rooms and dining-room, were principally, as they had been for generations, all-party political clubs centred around debates in mock-parliamentary style, where ambitious junior politicians could try out their speaking ability and which officers of the national political parties could comb for promising recruits. The Cambridge Union had even a sort of parody of House of Commons "question time", at which questions could be put to the current President before debate. One horrible story tells of a President who, wanting to be thought a wit, arranged with an intimate for the latter to put two questions he himself had drafted and for each of which he had prepared a crushing repartee. The friend agreed, on condition he might afterwards put a third of his own choosing. The first part of the programme went well, and the applause and laughter after the second question were just dying away as the friend rose, to put the last, his own: "And what, sir, was the third question you asked me to ask you?"

Oxford had a facetious speaking tradition, with a primacy of gags over matter. Cambridge, though it also had plenty of facetious debates—the final choice of subjects is the President's—could also be earnest. The Spillikins tried hard, amid the welter of catchers of the President's eye who followed the prearranged list of speakers printed on the order paper, to put their leftist point of view. The other Cambridge parliament in which university Labour supporters sat was the Trades Council. Here the C.U. Labour club had six seats, but the only regular attenders among the appointed delegates were Woggy Woolf and I. Here I spoke less and learned more.

I remember no demonstrations from the left—another difference from today. The only violence emanated from the right, from bone-headed athletic members of the Conservative social clubs, and was usually avoidable by tactical care. Once the Spillikins brought off a coup by subtlety. Black Friday, the collapse of the Triple Alliance of miners, transport workers and railwaymen, through betrayal of the former by Bevin and Thomas leaving the miner's union to fight alone, was fresh. So was the libel trial of the then weekly *Worker* for its comment upon it. A fierce fight within the C.U. Labour Club on whether J. H. Thomas should be invited to come down was won by the right wing. We managed to get out some hundreds of leaflets on coloured paper with the *Worker's* famous cartoon of the case. Another of Will Hope's, it shows a giant zany Thomas in the witness box, pointing to a tiny defiant defendant at his feet and complaining (as he did) to the judge: "Please, sir, he called me Jimmy." With these we distributed and pasted up quantities of yellow streamers with the date and place of the prospective meeting and a wording I devised in heavy black: "THE RT. HON. J. H. THOMAS, P.C., B.F., WILL ADDRESS THE LABOUR PARTY. ALL MEMBERS ARE REQUESTED TO BE ON THEIR BEST BEHAVIOUR." The hint was enough. A wire came to call it off.

My Uncle Edwin had been dismissed from the Lloyd George Cabinet not long before this time. Documents that have since come to light make it plain that the immediate cause was what the Prime Minister regarded as Edwin's disloyalty in voicing at the Versailles Peace Conference the Indian Government's objections to the "Jewish National Home" project in Palestine. Lloyd George considered, no doubt with constitutional correctness, that a British Secretary of State must speak only for his cabinet's policy; Edwin that, whatever the strict constitutional position, having been assigned the role of speaking for India at the Peace Conference, it was his moral obligation to express her views. But this behind-the-scenes clash was not at the time apparent. What was clear to everyone was the virulence of the Tory attack upon the man whom they looked on as responsible for risking the "brightest jewel in the British crown" under the guise of Dyarchy, the initiator of the Montagu–Chelmsford reforms. The abuse of Edwin, particularly in the columns of the *Morning Post*, was unmeasured and the hunters were especially enraged by a phrase he used in a big Commons debate; he had spoken of the "pathetic contentment" of the Indian peasant, reduced at famine time to eating cow-dung from the walls of his hut. This was incitement to rebellion, shouted the Tory publicists; how could a man's state be pathetic if he were contented?

Edwin had been a leading light at the Union himself and he accepted an invitation to come down to a debate in which the *Morning Post* editor pursued the vendetta as his chief opponent. Edwin listened to the insults in his usual "front-bench" position, slouched with his long legs far in front of him and a sardonic expression behind his single eyeglass. When it came to his turn he, I thought, did well. I did not manage to get into the debate, but I sat far forward and several times caught his glance.

My approval for him in this context, however, did not in the least prevent me from speaking for the Labour candidate against him in the next election. Edwin sat for Cambridgeshire. Ewen, if I remember rightly, supported Hugh Dalton in his candidature for Cambridge Town, but I disliked and mistrusted Dalton whom I thought patently a careerist. I saw no personal dilemma in working in the County constituency. Stubbs, the local organiser of the Transport & General Workers' Union, stood for Labour and had an eloquent stock speech in which he analysed the agriculture labourer's wages and outgoings for a family of five, the rent and every item of necessary expenditure on food, clothing, boots, etc. leaving at the end of each week "two copper coins", which Stubbs would hold aloft to the meeting with great effect. We followed him around and canvassed for him and strove, as is the duty of lesser speakers, to hold audiences in outlying villages till the candidate arrived. I tried to imitate his matter at villages he could not reach but soon found that the "two copper coins" argument was far emptier when it sprang not from direct knowledge and personal experience but only from the arithmetic of an outsider. Stubbs' meetings were crowded, his reception enthusiastic. We thought we were well away and concentrated our fire on the sitting member. The Tory, a young captain, did the same. Edwin, as sitting member, correspondingly saw in us his chief opponent and his campaign devoted itself to rebutting Labour. We both ignored the Tory. Result, which astonished everyone, for Edwin had long been a good member in the constituency and was well-liked: Edwin far to the bottom of the poll and the Tory scraping in just ahead of Stubbs.

I think Edwin's heart was broken at losing his position in public life. His story is one of the usual sycophancy and manœuvring that came in those days into the career of every bright young politician trying to climb the ladder of a traditional party on the British parliamentary scene. Asquith liked him, but called him, in the language disdainful of

Jews that in the days before Hitler was careless small-talk even for those not really anti-Semitic, "the Assyrian", and he married Venetia Stanley, one of Asquith's young women friends from a great Liberal family. But there is no doubt that at the end he found a cause, and was in despair at being separated from India before the process the reforms had begun had reached its logical completion in self-government and independence. I was not altogether surprised when he died soon after; though a comparatively young man, he put up no resistance to the most virulent of the big post-First-War epidemics, encephalitis. He never seemed to bear any grudge against me for the by-election, however, taking it for granted that I should support my own principles.

The Indian Majlis—the social and political club of Indians at Cambridge—asked him up to a dinner of honour after his retirement. This time he certainly did feel "Solomon's" eye upon him, from the lower end of the table, and he watched to see my reaction as he conjectured—to my surprise—in his after-dinner speech that India, once free, might find the way from feudalism to socialism without the intervening phase of capitalism. At this, some of the more far gone in wine of his hosts shouted "Bolshie!" If his prediction has so far remained unfulfilled, this is not without first British, then U.S., neo-imperialism having had a hand in preventing it.

I only saw him once more before his death, at the big house in Norfolk he bought so as to watch birds on its mere—both he and Viscount Grey were fanatical bird enthusiasts. I had then my first and only sight of Edwin's baby daughter in her pram, but I did have a peculiar encounter once in the late twenties with his widow. Out of the blue she asked me to lunch at her house in Grosvenor Crescent. I found myself the only guest and she came straight to the point. She had engaged a pilot and she wanted to fly with him in a two-seater across the deserts and mountains of the Central Asian Soviet Republics which few Britishers had ever visited before, none—certainly—since the Civil War in U.S.S.R., at any rate as tourists. How could she get the necessary visas? I promised to make enquiries of the then Soviet Ambassador—I think it was Bogomolov. He heard me out and then asked: Was my aunt a spy? I replied: "Almost certainly." And explained: if he meant, in the professional sense, then probably not; if he meant, would a woman like herself, with her social and cabinet connections, clear such a project before it was undertaken, keep her eyes open and answer any questions that might be put to her when she returned, then undoubtedly yes. I went on to say that my opinion was, if the U.S.S.R. had anything in these regions to hide, it should not let her go; if it had not, then it had nothing to lose and indeed might gain something by admitting her. She got her visas.

My other political uncle, Leslie, was a member of the first Labour and Trade Union delegation to go to Russia. It came back with an optimistic report. Through my aunt Carmel I met Sir George Young, one of the few Englishmen, if not the only one, who could speak Georgian. He was an ex-member of the consular service or the diplomatic service, I forget which. He had been with the delegation when it had been much exercised to find at Baku the memorial to the twenty-six commissars, "executed by the British". The delegates had wanted the inscription removed but had politely been told that it happened to be true. I was much interested in Georgia. I had read Trotsky's polemic *Between Red and White*, and Oliver Baldwin, Stanley's pink son, who had been much upset—not unnaturally—in Georgia to enter the prison and find various friends butchered during a brief period of the swaying struggle of revolution and counter-revolution there, and had been up to Cambridge to talk about it to the Labour Club.

Sir George Young was now helping to entertain the return delegation to Britain from the Soviet trade unions. This numbered four: a giant with a huge black beard from the Ukraine, called Radchenko; a small round man with close-cropped bullet head who was head of the U.S.S.R. trade union movement and a member of the Soviet Union Communist Party Central Committee, called Tomsky; a pale economist, called Lyubimov; and a smiling functionary in the Soviet trade union foreign department, called Yarotsky, who spoke excellent English, was a most cheery companion and gave me pamphlets about England that he had written himself but which I could not then make head or tail of because they were in Russian. Their trade union opposite numbers in Britain did their best to repay the hospitality received on the original visit with equal entertainment. Among these hosts I remember especially Fred Bramley, of the Locomotive Engineers and Firemen, and a huge Yorkshireman named Swales with an imperial stomach, who would lie back in the hotel armchair and sing ancient music-hall songs in a deep voice.

I had my eye above all on a possible future zoological visit to Russia and invited all four down to Cambridge. They came and stood in King's College by the lawn as I pointed out Keynes's room to them. They had been particularly interested to see where he lived, for his was a name of power in Europe in consequence of his differences with

Lloyd George summed up in *The Economic Consequences of the Peace*. It is an ironic sidelight on the diagnosis of "failure to communicate" as an essentially modern disease, that my father one day complained to me that Keynes's predictions in this book had been totally misunderstood by the "practical" financial world when it appeared. Apparently some of the terms of economists had been used in it in exactly the sense opposite to that in which they were customarily employed by bankers, so that the latter had dismissed it as typical amateur rubbish instead of paying attention to its warnings eventually justified by the event. My father seemed to think this was Keynes's fault, that the "City" was entitled therefore to a grudge.

I had the utmost difficulty in explaining to my guests why Keynes was not a Professor. Abroad, anybody who is anybody in the teaching world is called a Professor; it is rather disgraceful not to be one, just as anyone who has been to University in Germany emerges as "Herr Doktor". They could not grasp my explanation that in England each University faculty has only one "chair", with its occupant called "Professor", just as each ship at sea has one captain; that he may at any time be a quite dingy and outmoded old man while younger teachers in the same faculty may be far more brilliant and world-famous but can never be more than assistants, lecturers and "Readers".

But, before they left, Tomsky, at Yarotsky's instance, had promised me I should be able to make the British Museum trip to the Soviet Union that I planned. It would be quite easy to fix, he said, for he himself was President of the Hunters' Union.

§ 6

MY FATHER would be invincibly opposed to the Soviet trip, so I knew it was a target I could not hope to reach till I was 21. Meanwhile I began to make regular B.M. (N.H.) journeys to more accessible places, both while at, and after I had left, Cambridge, continuing them annually for several years.

Accident, the various occupations I have fallen into, have made me a great traveller. It would be ungracious to say I have had more than enough of foreign travel; let us put it—more than my share.

I have been to every European country but four—Portugal, San Marino, Andorra and Luxembourg. I have been to eleven Asian countries, to U.S.A. and Canada, in Africa only to Egypt, and not to Australasia or South America. So there is a good deal of the world I have not seen yet. But the parts I have visited amount to quite a lot.

My first trip abroad was to Belgium when I was still 14, soon after the ending of the 1914 war. I went on the invitation of the refugee family who had been our guests, and especially their paterfamilias, my old écarté partner, then Commandant, now Baron, Cartuyvels du Collaert. I ate Couques de Rheims and Couques de Dinant and stayed in their old mansion in Namur, which had not been destroyed. The Baron, whose leg was now well enough for him to walk with a stick, took me on a motor ride, during which I had an experience quite extraordinary for an English schoolboy—we called at La Ferme de la Haie Sainte, scene of the crucial defence all day at Waterloo by British redcoats, with the musket bullets still embedded in its old timber, *to collect the rent.*

I had an introduction to the Musée d'Histoire Naturelle in Brussels and goggled at the rich group of iguanodons there, discovered almost intact. Next I went on Sunday to the Zoo. A lion and a lioness on heat were confined in adjacent cages of a quite small house. A staid suburban paterfamilias, thoroughly Rousseau le Douanier, tipped the keeper to raise the wooden partition that stood between the beasts, leaving only bars, through which the animals could smell and see each other. The female arched her back and roared, the huge-maned male, whom bitter experience had probably taught any attempt to rush the barrier would be in vain, lay on his side and roared, his long pink penis exposed and working vainly back and forth. Papa in his bowler and pince-nez watched, Mamma in bodice and bun watched, two little girls in their manifold petticoats and son with his sailor suit and hoop also watched. All were far too serious to be anything but deadpan, and from the matter-of-fact way the father presented his tip it was clear that this somewhat surrealist scene was a usual Sunday treat.

The journey home was by air. Passenger air travel was only beginning in those days and the plane was an open two-seater. This, my first flight, led to my disappointing discovery that I was a bad air sailor. No provision had been made of brown-paper bags, and to keep the aeroplane clean I had to use my cap and throw it overboard. The cap was held in the slipstream against the tail-plane and, whenever I looked out, there the accusing object hung, like the albatross round the neck of the Ancient Mariner. Goodbye, if not to my cap, at least to my boyhood dreams of becoming a pilot.

My second trip abroad was to Paris a year or two later. This time I was taken by mother, to the hotel she and father always stayed at on the Place Vendôme, broadening out of the rue de la Paix. On our first morning a card was sent in from Herriot. I cannot remember if it was his first premiership or if he was only Minister of Finance, but he brought with him a great bouquet of flowers; he was engaged in some government credit transaction with my father. My mother initiated me into the delights of Paris: the expensive shops, where she bought clothes; the Louvre, where, after the usual tributes to the Winged Victory, the Venus de Milo and the Gioconde, she alarmed me by setting me down before a Boucher portrait and saying that was the sort of daughter-in-law she had always hoped for; Boissier, where she bought me *petits pois sucrés*, *dominos moux caramelisés*, and *sucre d'orge* sticks flavoured with apple; the restaurant of Prosper Montagné, who was, she told me, the best cook in the world and who served us a salmon in self-coloured sauce so tender you had only to wait for it to melt in the mouth, and a chocolate mayonnaise with stiff sour cream; and the Moulin Rouge, where for the first time I beheld female breasts, in the flesh and not just pictured.

But from Cambridge and from now on I ventured on my own. The spring sally of 1922 was not a distant one; it was to the Marine Biological Laboratory at Plymouth, to a special course for university zoological students. This was a splendid fortnight. I discovered the full riches of the fauna I had hitherto only scraped the edge of with my child's shrimping net in the rock-pools of the shore. I also learned that you (or at least I) need never be sea-sick, toss the boat never so high, if you watch the waves and adjust to their ups and downs, but that the moment you begin writing notes, or examining the specimens in the bottom of the boat, you feel queasy and have to stop. Here in Plymouth I was popular with my landlady, who found me no trouble to her so long as she gave me kippers for every meal, and I played lawn tennis with her daughter,

The first B.M. (N.H.) trip took place in the Long Vacation that summer. The entomologist Balfour-Browne gathered a group of undergraduates for the Hebrides and he included me to gather the Small Mammals. Many of the Scottish islands have peculiar forms of mice, voles and the like; the isolation of the islands has promoted development, or preservation, of their peculiar characteristics. Hot argument has raged about which; whether, that is, they represent new races or survivors of an older fauna. There is also among zoologists a long-standing quarrel between the splitters and the lumpers. Should such local varieties be dubbed "races" or dignified with a Latin scientific trinomial as special subspecies? At one time the argument was of such fierceness that an American detective story was plausibly written about a murder whose motive was this squabble. Nowadays the "lumpers" have won hands down, for more is known about the ways such differences come into being and their relationships, their mathematics and genetics, and most of the work my generation and our predecessors did has been shown as deplorably slipshod, based on too few specimens taken from one place at one date, without allowing for variation due to age, sex, state (i.e. pregnancy), season, habitat, temporarily prevailing food supply and similar factors liable to influence the characters supposed diagnostic. Further studies are always liable to disclose once-unsuspected overlaps. Still, at the stage systematics had then reached, I don't suppose we "splitters" did much harm by overemphasizing distinctions. At least it indexed odd appearances for our successors to look into. My revered senior at the Museum, M. A. C. Hinton, was a splitter, as Oldfield Thomas before him, and I must say I enjoyed the sensation of naming the animals I collected. One felt oneself a member of a great chain whose first link was not even Linnaeus but Adam in the Garden of Eden.

We spent some weeks in the Inner Hebrides, on Islay and Jura; the first is flat and treeless, the second a double mountain with an inhabited shore. I cannot remember that any of the small mammal specimens there turned out to be inventable new species, but a vole on the smaller island of Gigha, caught by some of my colleagues who landed there after I had left the main party, I dubbed *M.a. fiona*, why I have now forgotten but I *think* it was because of its unusual shagginess and the fact that somewhere I had read a translation of a Gaelic poem about Fiona of the beautiful long hair. There was one remarkable, possibly unique, find, however. This was a grandfather among Common Shrews. It is pretty well established that the shrew is an annual, being born in the spring and dying of old age, if it survives so long, in the autumn of the following year. Our exceptional specimen bore a grizzled coat and its teeth were worn right down, presumably by age. I do not think a like example has been encountered anywhere to this day. Anyway the specimen itself is still in the B.M. and the facts were all set down in my first scientific paper, which appeared in *P.Z.S.* (the *Proceedings of the Zoological Society* of London) a few months later.

I learned to be a good trapper, using break-back mouse-traps and making my regular round of them, to measure the bag and to skin, cure and label it, all according to Hoyle, or rather, the B.M. leaflets. I carried the necessary scalpels and labels and acquired a sports coat with huge poachers' pockets, to be filled in the following order: first outer, mice; first inner, traps; second inner, bait (usually cheese); second outside, cartridges. For now that I was a full-fledged researcher my conscience was at rest and I could go to the family gunsmith, Churchill of Leicester Square, and get me a ·410. I did not do much execution with this weapon, however. I am not a bad shot, but it was not often fired. Once at a rabbit, killed; and many times at bats, in vain.

These bats were a tantalising mystery. Each evening they appeared at dusk and flew around. I knew something about collecting bats, but obviously not enough. A fellow Kingsman was studying their parasites at the time and used to fly-fish for them successfully, from the window of his rooms giving on the river at the Backs. Sometimes they got themselves foul-hooked. I had been out with him on the roof of Ely Cathedral, using forceps to pluck protesting pipistrelles out from the crevices of the carved stonework where they slept by day. But what species were these in Islay and where did they come from? Did they fly over from the Scottish mainland and return, each evening and morning? (Bats do not fly by night, only at dusk and dawn.) Where did they sleep if resident on Islay? I tramped the wide grassland, looking in vain for trees, of which there were none; I searched every ruin, especially one old distillery full of cosy-looking holes bound to have been occupied had the bats been such as roost in buildings. I tried to shoot one, my cartridges included spreading dust-shot which should have been deadly against bats, but how on earth do you aim when, as soon as you raise your weapon, the quarry dives towards it, and dances exactly round and round the end until you grow tired and put the weapon down? The mystery still remains. I still do not know the identity or provenance of the Islay bats.

On both islands we stayed in farm houses and learned to greet passing crofters with a lilting "Blowy dee!" Each home had a now-vanished way of life, in each we were treated with limitless hospitality, in each the cooking was done on open fires under a great chimney. Oatcakes were the delicacy of one, girdle-cakes and syrup of the other. On Jura were guests in the same big house, an extraordinary pair, man and wife, well over 80, retired and on holiday from Glasgow, a Clydeside shipowner from the early days of industrialism, when the employer still knew his every man by name. This one told of paternal relationships more unbelievable to nowadays than tales of fairyland: of how to save his men money he had picked up a mite of dentistry and pulled their teeth himself; of how, when he and his wife had got married, they had not wanted to enjoy themselves alone, so they had stopped work at the yard and every man jack of them, employees, their wives and families, had joined them on shipboard for the honeymoon. Through these old bodies, painfully limping about the garden, the wife smiling and nodding in confirmation of her long-time partner, one could glimpse a quite unexpected past.

When the next term started some of us young zoologists—I use the word "us" though most were much more entitled to that name than I—got together to form the Zoological Tea Club, which met in a café at weekly intervals to talk shop. The chairman was Omer-Cooper, who made a speciality of woodlice. One of the most distinguished in after-life was W. S. Bristowe—amateur in the strict sense, for his work is not zoology; spiders are his passion not his profession, and he has written better about them than anyone in his field. There was Evelyn Hutchinson, now a Professor in U.S.A. so elevated I find his works unintelligible, and his first wife Grace Pickford, a small, keen girl with soft hair and pebble spectacles, who brought back shrews from a Guernsey holiday. I wrote them up jointly with her for a new P.Z.S. paper, hoping to immortalise our names together by thus attaching them to a new subspecies (she was especially glamorous in my eyes for she was the daughter of a Vice-President of the Football Association).

Alas, everyone has rejected that new subspecies since. When eventually the news of my marriage leaked, Hell and I received from the still-existing Tea Club almost our only wedding present, a glass water jug. I was so touched I never could bring myself to use it; it is still preserved as precious, and intact.

At the Tea Club we planned some of our further Long Vacation expeditions. My programme, concerted with the B.M., went thus: Inner Hebrides 1922 (finished); Yugoslavia 1923; the Carpathians 1924; the Caucasus.

The B.M. proposed Yugoslavia for 1923 because a retired English major had written from Ljubljana offering to help conduct an expedition round the area. This time I was to be in charge. The Tea Club were all fixed elsewhere on their own specialities and none were mammalogists. I sought in Hall at King's someone, not necessarily a zoologist, who, being at a loose end for the vacation, might care for the trip and not mind helping on the job. I broached the matter with a tall and quiet young man of my own year named Cotton, whose large head was surmounted by hair en brosse, who wore glasses, and seemed patient enough to be a good companion. His Tripos was History, but he readily agreed.

Our preparations were thorough. I got sheets of maps of Slovenia and Croatia so detailed and complete that, years later, I was able to pass them to Tito's representative in London, General Velebit, for they were fuller than anything at that time at the disposal of the Partisans. I got letters from both the Yugoslav and Italian Ambassadors in London "to whom it may concern", to cover the carriage of cartridges and my good ·410. Cotton practised skinning. We got letters of credit to cover expenses including the hire of a car.

The journey each way was by rail. All went well outward until we reached the Italian frontier. The officials who came on board the train were Fascists; the new dispensation had just taken over and they were zealous with new-blown authority. They seized the gun and cartridges as soon as I declared them and pooh-poohed my letter. "Who is the Ambassador? We spit upon the Ambassador!" Disarmed, we continued the long pull round past Gorizia.

The major was amiable and efficient, and soon had us on the way to Bled, our first collecting-place. Bled was not then what I understand it has since become, a place of holiday-palaces and sophistication, a Presidential resort. It was almost empty and a jewel set amidst mountains. There was a string of simple boarding houses round the edge of the lake, strung like widely-separated beads upon a necklace. No one lived at that time of year in these primitive hotels; the partitions of their rooms were oiled wood, the furniture spare, the linen clean, the bedcovers in dazzling zigzag patterns. A French engineer we met was supposed to be building something more luxurious; he spent most of his time collecting edible snails to send home to his wife. We had our meals in the gardens at the edge of the transparent waters of the lake, and trout, clearly visible beneath the surface, waited like cats or dogs for table-scraps. Around towered the mountains, cool and glowing.

We were sad when we had to tear ourselves from Slovenia and go on, as planned, to two Croat villages, Kupjak and Skrad. Here the conditions were more primitive. We stayed mostly in farms and ate peasant-style. This was lucky for me. There is nothing better to dispel crotchets about food than having, after a hard day's work, to eat what is before you or else go without. At home I had always disdained soup and omelettes. Here, if I rejected these, I must eat worse. I got used to both and henceforth had no trouble with my finicalities anywhere in Europe. For trapping small mammals *is* hard exercise. First you must walk, several miles maybe, laying out your traps, trying to guess runways, for those are the best places. Then you must walk round them again at least twice a day in case something else gets there first and eats your booty before you find it.

We had a scare one night in our Kupjak farmhouse. We had been offered at supper *palatchinka* (I write it phonetically)—a sort of giant eggy pancake, wrapped round cream cheese and jam. There was nothing wrong with it at all, it was excellent; only it was much too big. Hungry as we were, we were full long before we came to the end. But we had learned already that to refuse anything in a farmhouse is to offend your hosts, and not to finish it a proof that you dislike it. By rapid prestidigitation, we hid it in a newspaper and put the package on top of the wardrobe in the bedroom Cotton and I shared. We might get rid of it more easily later. In the middle of the night I was woken by a terrific weight falling on my head, a violent scratching, screaming and spitting and a crash, as of the devil jumping through the window. When candles were lit we discovered that the cat, which must have approved of *palatchinka,* had contrived to get up on the wardrobe and found no route down but on to the bed. In its panic it had dropped its prize which was now all mixed up in the bedclothes. Fortunately the animal appeared uninjured in the morning, but I was sorry it had lost its banquet; we had to scrub mightily by candle-light to remove the traces.

To go from Kupjak to Skrad we struck off into the mountains. It was soon evident that, despite our detailed map, we were hopelessly lost. The map was, in fact, too detailed, for it marked every tiny pathway, whether accessible to car or not. The township in the area was called Ogulin and whenever we came to a crossroads every arm of the signpost, whether forward, sideways or back, said Ogulin. It was still worse when there was no signpost. We would wait for a peasant and, when he came by, ask "Ogulin?" and point. He would nod his head and sometimes reply what we understood to be "12 kilometres". We would then point down another branch, he would nod again and again say "Ogulin", but this time perhaps "15 kilometres". Everywhere led to Ogulin, but as like as not we would find as we proceeded that the road narrowed as it approached some valley, or ran into some roaring stream, or got lost among the boulders as it approached a peak. Countless times we had to reverse with a precipice on one side, and the night began to fall. There was a mist that turned into cold rain. It dawned on us in the end that in the mountains every road did lead to Ogulin, because, being the only town, it was the only place anyone would want to end up in sooner or later, and so everything led to it by different routes. And how could peasants who had never ridden in a motor car, perhaps never even seen one before, gauge the limits of its travelling capacity and warn us that any particular route would be impassable? We were cold, wet, starving, thirsty and miserable. The nightmare was dissolved only by more or less kidnapping a peasant to come with us, and he eventually did get us to Ogulin which turned out to be a place with a big square and railway station and a comfortable ancient inn with great tall rooms. Our mistake had been that the railway to Skrad did run through Ogulin though no proper road routes did. We ought to have left the mountains alone and stayed far away from Ogulin on a wide Napoleonic road adapted for motor traffic and skirting them on the north.

In the end we got back to Ljubljana with fair collections. We acquired other specimens beside small mammal skins and skulls. Near the last I crawled down a damp cold rocky passage set into the clay of a hill. On all fours I shone the torch above me and saw some longlegged creatures clinging to the roof. As the light hit them they seemed to jump down on me. I was scared but grabbed some and they turned out to be harmless cavernicolous grasshoppers with enormous waving antennae adapted to the dark. Back in South Kensington, B. Uvarov, the great expert on the Orthoptera, later wizard of locust control, was glad of them. There were also some small scorpions I put alive into an ink bottle. At Ljubljana a schoolmistress with whom we had made friends, called Ljubica Tomljenovic (Louisa Tomlinson in English), had gifts waiting for us: twenty-six *Proteus* in jars and a baby wolf cub. The former were for Lancelot Hogben. *Proteus* is a pale pink amphibian with red gills, much thinner than Axolotl but related to it. It is not uncommon in underground waters in southern Europe; this batch came from the famous Dalmatian caves that have nowadays become a show place for tourists to visit in lighted boats. Axolotl, *Proteus* and *Typhlomolge* (which is found in artesian wells in Texas) are three forms that reproduce as larvae and never pass the equivalent of the tadpole stage. The last two live underground in the dark. There are Axolotl stocks that do in some places turn into a dry land adult salamander, *Amblystoma*; but in its characteristic Mexican lake habitats it does not, perhaps because the animals have for generations been cut off from land by salt-poisoned lake margins. In its place I have mentioned how we at R.C.S., as other experiments elsewhere, had made them metamorphose by feeding them on thyroid. Now Hogben wanted to try the same diet on *Proteus*. What might it turn into? The experiment has been carried out since he thought of it and does not work, but then this result was not yet known. The wolf cub was a sweetie-pie in a basket.

It saved us on our journey back through Italy. When the Fascists opened the basket and saw the cub they exclaimed: "*Il poco lopo!*", held up their hands in admiration and let everything pass. At Paris we had to change trains. To avoid trouble we had booked first-class. We disposed our precious baggage in the compartment and put the basket carefully on the seat. The only other occupant of the carriage was an Englishman in morning-suited splendour who sat behind an open *Times*. (Somebody told us he was an M.P.) Shortly after the train started, weird and heart-rending howls began to emanate from the basket. The M.P. put down his newspaper and said crossly: "If you must bring a dog on the train you might at least let the poor brute out." I undid the straps and, as I did so, naturally replied: "It isn't a dog, it's a wolf." The M.P. screamed, jumped up on to his seat and tried to protect himself with flapping movements of the *Times*. When the basket lid was raised, the tiny cub sat up and stopped howling immediately, its pointed ears cocked and its head endearingly on one side. The M.P. was rather crestfallen but we became reconciled.

At Dover the wolf cub was taken away for the Zoo to arrange its quarantine. Then I had trouble because the railway refused to carry the *Proteus* in their jars. The official went through all the categories of livestock in his regulations and maintained that nothing resembling them was listed. I asked to see the regulations and then declared that I was a great zoologist and that on my oath they ranked as fish. The official looked suspiciously at their legs but that hurdle was overcome.

A further hitch occurred at the last moment when we were leaving the customs hall. As every traveller knows, an extra officer is seated at the exit and if you excite his suspicions in any way he can make you turn out your pockets. He caught sight of a bulge in my outside breast pocket and ordered me to take out the ink-bottle I was carrying there to keep it the right way up. "Open it," he said. I refused. "I have the authority to make you open it," he said. "You have not," I replied, "but if you wish to take the responsibility for opening it yourself, you may do so." He took the ink-bottle from me and started to pull out the cork. Before he had it quite out, I told him what was inside, and he hastily gave it back. Perhaps in these days when so many are engaged in drug traffic one would not get away with it, but it might be an idea for would-be smugglers to try keeping scorpions in their tubes of pills.

In London I said good-bye to Cotton. I still had the *Proteus* on my hands. They were to go to Edinburgh, where Hogben was now working with F. A. E. Crewe, and they could not catch a train until the following day. I took them to the Zoo and arranged with E. G. Boulenger for them to stay in the old Reptile House overnight. In consideration for this favour, I proposed, only twenty would go on to Edinburgh, six I would present to the Zoo. That night was the hottest of the year, the hottest for many years, super-hot. The next day the weather broke, it was the day the famous cloudburst threw water on the Zoo so quickly the drains would not carry it away, and in a few seconds such volumes had rushed down the old tunnel which runs under the road, connecting the north and south parts for visitors, that they flooded it to ten feet deep. Fortunately no one was drowned. When I went to the Reptile House that morning, however, Boulenger was full of excuses. The night had been so hot, he said, that even the cooling apparatus had not been sufficient and many of the *Proteus* had died. "The twenty that died were yours," he explained. "The six that survived happened to be ours." He was very sorry. Lancelot and Crewe had to wait for the experiments to be tried, eventually, by someone else.

The story of the wolf cub ends more fortunately. It survived to reach the Zoo and became quite tame. The keepers named it "Loppity" and it would allow those it knew into its cage and then make much of them. It was a she, and bred well when later it was one of the first wolves to be removed to Whipsnade. Indeed there was a time when the keepers would point out all the wolves in the old Wolf Wood as children and grandchildren and further-generation-descendants of Loppity.

I thought of this suddenly and burst out laughing when years later the family all gathered ceremonially round Stuart's dining table to celebrate my mother's eightieth birthday. I could not count how many of us there were. It reminded me of Loppity. But, fortunately, when I explained nobody seemed to mind.

I went back to Ljubljana in 1965, but now there are no wolves left in the surrounding hills.

§ 7

If I had supposed that I should earn athlete's glory at Cambridge in any field I should have been mistaken.

Soon after coming up I put my name on a sheet posted in the college Junior Combination Room asking for the names of any freshmen interested in playing football. This led to a question in what position I could play—more difficult to answer. I answered that when I went to a football match I considered myself qualified to shout advice to any player on the field, irrespective of position, so that I ought to be able to play anywhere. I was told this did not follow, so raked around and remembered that I *had*, at preparatory school, played alternately goal-keeper and centre-forward. I duly found myself assigned as goalkeeper in a trial match between scratch sides, and bought myself sweater, shorts and football boots.

The match was a disaster. Five-nil was the score we lost by, but I still decline to believe that it was all my fault. We played on a rugby football ground and I discovered to my alarm that rugger goalposts are far higher than those at soccer. The five opposing forwards would charge down the field and if I pushed the ensuing shot up it was still well beneath the bar; if I saved it by repelling it to the side plenty of opponents would be on the spot to pass it to one another until they put it in. It was no good my shouting "offside!", as I had learned to do from the public stands. The referee, a member of the college club committee, coldly informed me that "offside was not played in practice matches".

This was my last essay at college level but, unwilling to sacrifice my gear so emptily, I next joined the Y.M.C.A. and volunteered to play for them. It was with some misgiving that I learned my position this time was to be right-half, for I remembered that Andy Ducat, doubly an English international having his cap at both soccer and cricket, had told me in the Surrey dressing-room that in his opinion—he was a half-back himself, of course—the wing half has to run more than any other player on the field.

I found that he was quite right. The pitch was muddy and a foothold difficult. I had had no idea how hard it is to run and yet keep your balance so that the proper foot is there at the moment of arrival of the ball. Still, I must have played well enough, since, if I never managed to kick the ball itself I always stopped the man, and the only time the ball did hit me it bounced off my instep to one of our forwards who promptly scored the only goal. Result, however: in spite of a bath as hot as I could stand it, an agony that bound me immovable for two days and sent me to my biochemistry crammer's textbooks to discover all about sarcolactic acid, its accummulation and dispersal. And a retirement, honourable but prompt, for my new boots.

At university level lawn tennis I had no prospect at all. There were veritable giants at Cambridge in my time; I should think the Freshmen's tournament at Fenner's has never been so strong. Besides the outstanding Indian players I have already mentioned there was a young South African humorist who had also already played in the Davis Cup, Lezard, and a brilliant American, Jimmy van Alen. Not in my wildest dreams could I hope to compete with such an array of excelllence. Rather did I stand gaping with the beginners during a rest period as Lezard held forth on tactical ethics from the wisdom of experience: "Never argue with the umpire. Insist on every point in doubt being given to your opponent. Never cheat, until five all."

My level was to play regularly as top pair in the College second team. I learned why my first team appearances were few through a friend at Magdalen who questioned our captain about it one day while playing a match against King's. The reply was to the point: "Montagu? How can we play him in the first team? You know how he behaves on the court." In fairness to myself I should explain to the reader that this sentence did not in any way imply impropriety or even unfair conduct on the part of the present author; it only expressed revulsion at my tactics, for at that time I was much taken with the style of Nicholas Mishu, my acquaintance with whom I have mentioned earlier and whom I played with and against often, sometimes even in tournaments. Mishu had a habit of mixing his numerous orthodox services with occasional squiggly underhand ones, or even turning his back altogether on his opponent and serving over his shoulder to tempt the latter to overhit, as well as standing up on the service line when receiver, in order to half-volley the server's aces. The purpose, of course, was to upset his opponent's rhythm and temper, and it was effective in every context but the highest class. I thought it all an excellent idea but apparently it did not fit what at college level was considered "DONE".

It was passing Gray's sports equipment shop so regularly on the way to the Union or the Real Tennis courts that made me think of ping pong. There was an 8′ × 4′ Queen Anne table in the outer hall at Townhill Park, and on wet days, when even after we had ourselves rolled the courts and rewhitened their lines they were not fit for play, Charles Weinberg and I used to have long sessions at ping pong. According to legend, my Uncle Edwin and Sir Edward Grey had played bridge against each other for some fantastic sum a point all through the 1914–18 war and had been so well matched that almost nothing changed hands at the end. It was something of the same order at ping pong with Charles and me. The hard, polished surface of the priceless table gave a fast game and a true bounce. We knew only the half-volley, but *6d.* a point made us accurate and any margin between us wiped itself out over the weeks. I thought I was good. It suddenly occurred to me that if I got Gray's to make two tournament-size tables to order and put them up at the Real Tennis courts, I could get out notices, start a club among those interested and, for a change, this time I would shine!

I confess that it was this ignoble ambition, not a disinterested sense of public service, that started me off. Once more I was disappointed. More than 140 undergraduates entered this first tournament. This always happens with a game new, or newly revived after an interval; everyone thinks themselves good because they have never competed outside the family circle. After standards establish themselves, and all *aficionados* become organised, everyone who is anyone knows everyone, and the weaker stand off because they now know they have no chance. That is why newspaper sports competitions among the public usually decline and settle down to a small number of contestants a few years after their initiation. Here the number entered at the beginning was quite sufficient to disclose unknown talents and produce surprises. I whispered to a running blue just as he was changing that he must be gentle with his opponent, a young cripple whose wheel-chair was carried to the table and wedged there with chocks. The blue looked at me strangely afterwards, for he was beaten out of sight. I survived only a few rounds. In the final Evans, a Chess Blue, got home against Ramaswami, the Lawn Tennis Blue. So the sports establishment emerged triumphant after all.

The reader deserves a reassurance that this book is not going to be made into a pretext to shove down his throat a dissertation on the history, art and development of table tennis. He shall have that promise.

I shall try to keep off everything of a specialist character connected with the game. Perhaps, if the government ever establishes in this country a museum of sport there will be room in its archives for an MS monograph on such themes. Here references must necessarily intrude from time to time but I shall try to limit them to what is either of general interest or unavoidable because of its relevance to the eponymous hero.

I became Chairman and President of the national Association before my eighteenth birthday. It happened like this. We got our University club going. The tie was Cambridge blue of course, with a thin double stripe of green and white—the colours of the table. (The Spillikins had a tie too, by the way—black with small red spots.) Eventually we played Oxford, who had a Cricket Blue, G. T. S. Stevens, on their side. We were six a side and each played all opponents. Cambridge won 31–5 and (hush) I lost the only matches for our side. But before that we had got in touch with and played matches against the newly-formed "All-England Club" that the papers were beginning to talk about.

It should be explained that "Ping Pong" had been virtually dead for nearly twenty years, surviving organised in England during that time in two provincial towns—north in Sunderland, west in Plymouth—and otherwise only as a parlour game. The motive force in its revival was a short but active wealthy Manchester business man, A. F. Carris, who fancied his chances just as I had done and came to London with big ideas to put the game once more on the map. He would have ping pong teas, ping pong toys, he would even buy a racehorse and call it Ping Pong. He found two survivors of the old days, Percival Bromfield, the last English Champion before the game had folded (in 1904), and J. J. Payne, the last secretary of the old Association. Together they started up in St. Bride's Institute, a club for business men in the area of Fleet Street, and in a café in the Strand. These welcomed me on the committee, I suppose because they saw in this contact a symbol of the extension of the revival to renowned Oxbridge. They had already staged their first championship, at the National Sporting Club. Carris, also like me, had been disappointed, losing in the final to Andrew Donaldson, a determined Sunderland schoolmaster. He had objected to the noise made by the schoolmaster, who wore an ordinary dark suit and simply took off his detachable collar; his boots had made a heavy stamping noise every time he moved. The schoolmaster had countered by protesting against the flashing of the diamond shirt studs in the front of Carris's dress shirt.

At least one of the reasons that had led to the collapse of the game in the early 1900s had been the multiplicity of rival organisations with different names and confusingly different rival codes of rules. We determined not to make this mistake, and set up a group to codify one single set of laws and regulations. I was already a strict umpire at both cricket and lawn tennis (I had successfully survived the ordeal of a Wimbledon crack striding up to the umpire's chair of the local tournament he was ornamenting and glaring at the elevated schoolboy tormenting him, with the brusque demand: "Recite the footfault rule.") And in this group I fought for a logical order and legalistic phraseology that remained sufficient for all countries for more than forty years. All went swimmingly until our committee, endorsing applications to hold tournaments, approved one that was to be held *without* specifying equipment manufactured by Messrs. Jaques. Unknown to us, and I suppose to most of the world which employed in many languages the term "Ping Pong" either to designate the game or generally to denote any relatively futile to-and-fro movement, this name was the registered property of the London firm of John Jaques & Son; it had passed into common speech without realisation of its legal status as monopoly property, like "kodak" or "gramophone". Crisis: our committee felt the game could never develop unless independent, yet there could be no doubt of the legal rights of Jaques. An emergency meeting was called. Jaques' manager, a member of the committee, had equipped himself with countless proxies, gathered at high-speed from all the towns where dealers sold his firm's equipment. No one wanted to bell the cat and I—possibly as youngest—was made the fall guy. I was voted into the chair, ruled all the proxies out of order, accepted a motion to dissolve the "Ping Pong Association", and led a move into the next room of everyone but Jaques' manager, where we reformed ourselves, with identical rules, into the "Table Tennis Association". I record this incident to show that the name was altered not, as some suppose, out of a craving for dignity, but simply because "Table Tennis" happened to be earlier, unregistered, and hence free of legal restriction. Almost by accident, certainly by *force majeure*, the name was fixed under which the game subsequently became organised in a Federation of more than ninety national associations and I became lumbered with a responsibility more or less for life.

I became referee of English championships and World Championships, played (successfully) in the first match London against Paris, wholly unsuccessfully in more World Championships than any other player, served countless times as non-playing captain of England, wrote on this subject my first book;[1] and retired at last as "founder-president" of the International Table Tennis Federation, a crotchety old cross-patch at the age of 63. If anyone asks why I accepted this decree of fate in its initial phases the answer is absolutely clear. It was neither from illusions of grandeur nor (any longer) dreams of prowess as a player. My reason was political—simple, straightforward philanthropy. I saw in Table Tennis a sport particularly suited to the lower paid, above all—since it was played indoors—in crowded towns. Its equipment was relatively cheap, it did not require extensive or expensive special premises. Nor, at least in those days, could it be staged so as to accommodate great numbers as a spectacle. Hence, as I saw it, there could be little profit in it, no income to reward wide advertising, nothing therefore to attract the press. Yet its low cost meant that it could give pleasure and exercise indoors to youth of a class that, in towns and in those days of low wages and small public subsidy for sport, enjoyed little enough outdoors of either. I plunged into the game as a crusade. That, at least, was my conscious motive. How far this was rationalisation of the yet simpler fact that at that time I still enjoyed playing, it is not for me to guess.

Two incidents taught me such unexpected useful lessons that they should be set down.

At Kensington Court we set up a standard table on the nursery landing, added special lighting, and I would invite cracks from the All-England Club to play and practise with me under these ideal conditions and with refreshments available. Those in the house would sometimes watch them and it never occurred to me that anything could be wrong. One day Bromfield as spokesman sharply objected and told me that neither he nor his companions would ever come again. He resented my father and his guests coming upstairs after dinner and watching from the staircase before going on to the theatre, complete with dinner-jackets and cigars. They felt, with justice, that they were being made a show. It had never in the least occurred to me that my table tennis acquaintances would feel as a slight that they were not dinner-guests in this house, since I myself had grown up looking on evening-dress dinner as a chore and bore.

The second incident happened at Cambridge. A team from the Indian Students' Hostel in Gower Street, London, one of the pioneer influences in English table tennis, was coming up to play the Univer-

[1] *Table Tennis Today* (W. Heffer & Sons, Cambridge), 1924.

sity club on my invitation. Some emergency arose at the last moment; I could not go to the station to meet the visitors; I simply sent word of the hotel, the times and places of the match and welcoming meal. When I did reach them I found the guests had taken my absence for discourtesy and were in rebellious mood, refusing to play and ready to return on the first train. I was so innocent I was bewildered. That I, the abominator and abhorrer of all discrimination could be taken as one who practised it! I knew indeed of racialism in sporting circles at Cambridge. I once asked the then University club captain why a University lawn tennis team without Hadi and Rutnam had been selected to play a certain match in East Anglia and had been told: "The host club bars coloured players." It was an outrage that a University Club should accept an invitation on that basis, but I pointed out that nevertheless Ramaswami was in the team. "Oh, they do not count Ramaswami," was the reply. Of course I at once told Ramaswami, as I warned the captain I would, and the former withdrew from the team as he had been placed without his knowledge in an impossible position. But even with the clue of this incident, it had not in the least occurred to me how the omission of a station platform courtesy to which I should myself have been perfectly indifferent might appear to others.

Each of these two experiences was a salutary shock. They helped to open my eyes to the existence of feelings and ways of looking at things in other people that might be different from my own.

§ 8

SO FAR I have measured the progress made in several fields that were special to me before I went to Cambridge, but the effort expended in these fields was far less than that dispersed in others entirely fresh, and in making friends. To try to disentangle all this results in what is, from one viewpoint, the portrait of a typical Oxbridge idler, from another that of someone busy in at least one of the standard occupations, that of acquiring a wide, but shallow, cultural veneer.

The intellectual snob society of the day was the Heretics. It stemmed to some extent from the influence of C. K. Ogden and Ivor Richards (Basic English and *The Meaning of Meaning*). The outstanding senior supporter in my college was R. B. Braithwaite. A disciple was Alexander Tudor-Hart, a fellow-freshman, then quite unpolitical and studying history, now a doctor and enthusiast for Mao, who quite reasonably told me at the time of Wittgenstein's *Tractatus Logic-Philosophicus* that "though he did not understand it, it did him good". The Heretics managed to induce on to its lecture list an astonishing series of the intellectual lions of the day, who, after performance, would proceed to someone's rooms in college where we could interrogate them far into the night. If young people got on with the lecturers it might be a start of long-standing fertile friendships. It was there I met A. S. Neill, to hear of Summerhill, and Norman Haire, the gynaecologist and populariser of studies in sexual behaviour: what the Germans call *Sexualwissenschaft*. It was through him that I received a request from a Vienna practitioner for facilities to visit the Black Museum at Scotland Yard. The then police commissioner (could it have been Colonel Laurie?) was a guest at Kensington Court so my mother was able to arrange it, but I fear Norman Haire's friend must have been disappointed for the commissioner told us primly: "We did not have much to interest him. I am afraid we do not study so carefully here those matters they seem to be so interested in on the continent." At the Heretics, I think, rather than at the Labour Club, I first met R. Palme Dutt and Robin Page Arnot, the best and clearest expositors of Marxist socialism I had met up to that time, and started pupil-teacher relationships that led speedily to my joining them on the board of the *Labour Monthly*, where we still work together.

I did not take at all to Bertrand Russell, who came with his current wife, Dora; I got to know her much better afterwards when they were separated and she active in peace movements. He told fantastic stories about a visit to America and the peculiar consequences of state rights as you crossed the continent by train. At the border of one state they would search your luggage to take away your spirits, at that of another to take away your tobacco, at yet a third they would separate you and the lady you were travelling with—if you were not married—into distinct sleeping compartments. He had obviously been alarmed by his visit to U.S.S.R. for there, as he complained, they exalted work without realising that the aim of life must be enjoyment, and labour only acceptable in so far as it creates conditions needed for happiness. (There is possibly more in this than at the time I would allow, but it is a creed only for rich humanists in advanced countries, not for peoples in poverty trying to pull themselves up by their bootstraps.) His Chinese trip had convinced him that the warlord divisions would continue as they were then for at least another century.

Roger Fry, on the other hand, attracted me. Gaunt and shy, he set out a way of looking at the arts that was then novel enough to be refreshing but which we have since all learnt to name "formalism" and damn appropriately. The subject of a work of art was insignificant in appraising it, he declared. Everything lay in its composition. One had to train oneself to look with equal mind on a portrait of the Virgin and a picture of a bottle; he himself would, alas, never be able to know what sort of a piece of music *as music* was "God save the King", it was impossible to dissociate it from its overtones.

By now I was buying books in several languages hand over fist. First editions of *Arabia Deserta*, Swift's *Gulliver*, Walpole's *Castle of Otranto* and Lewis's *Monk*, a complete set of Herman Melville, Wegener's *Entstehung der Kontinenten* (of which I was a premature partisan), fine illustrated volumes. I must have become one of the best customers of Heffer's in Petty Cury and old David's barrow in the market, as well as of several of the exotic curiosity shops. Whenever I got an odd new volume I would check it at the B.M. Library. My taste in graphics was beginning to form. I visited the B.M. to admire the Lohan and the Egyptian cat depicted in *The Foundation of Aesthetics*, bought reproductions of Marc, Matisse and van Gogh for my walls, and visited the Leicester Galleries in London for Nevinson, the Nashes, Ethelbert White, John, Sickert and Epstein, Frank Dobson's bust of Lopokova (whom Keynes had just married), and—joy of joys—his "Concertina Man".

As centre in London I used the 1917 Club. This was Ramsay MacDonald's haunt before he became Prime Minister and earned duchesses' dinners. Kingsley Martin, whom I knew from Magdalen, turned out there to be a table tennis fan; a table of poor quality stood in the basement, and a fair performer among the members was Francis Meynell. The Stage Society frequently brought me to London on Sundays; I squired MacDonald's secretary Rose Rosenberg to Toller's *Masses and Man* in the translation by Meynell's wife Vera, with Sybil Thorndike in the chief part. I was constantly visiting London for one errand or another. Besides the Zoo scientific meetings, I used to go up also to those at the Royal Anthropological Institute. At Cambridge a family touring company had settled in a small hall in the railway district. Are there still such companies nowadays anywhere in England? The hall was bare and might hold 100, seats *6d.* to *2s.* The scenery consisted of a few props and pieces with backcloths that rang the changes on every clime and every period. The cast was mostly made up of old father, buxom mother, stalwart fair-haired son who did the sword-play, winsom daughter; only the dark-browed villain may have been unrelated. They had a repertory of about 200 plays and did four or five a week. The lines were given every ounce of dramatic ham, the audience hissed and cheered, the favourites were *The Shaughraun* and, better still, *Jane Shore*, but the villain was splendid also in *Maria Marten*. A bunch of us saw nearly every show. I managed to keep in touch with the family and, a few years later, tried to get the film company I then worked for to give a test to the hero son. I hope it did not disappoint him when not much came of it. Now, however, I was especially interested to see how the audience would take Shaw, and concluded that *The Showing-up of Blanco Posnet* would best suit their style. G.B.S. was as usual quite willing. Unlike some other authors who charged a minimum fee to save themselves trouble, often set beyond the possibilities of amateurs, G.B.S. made a practice of letting anyone do his plays on percentage. The play went down well but its performance disclosed an extraordinary fact. None of the cast could remember lines; indeed the villain was so incapable of doing so that he had to play the part of the sheriff seated at a slightly elevated table so that the audience could not easily see the 'book' spread out in front of him. The cast was glib in the plays they knew, but it was clear that there they were perfectly ready to gag and made up most of the text freely as they went along. So again we have an instance of the latest fashion in method proving old hat to those whose memories are long! Anyway we had the pleasure of sending G.B.S. a cheque for each of our two performances, the first I think was *7s. 4d.* the second *5s. 10d.*

One or two young men whom I had hardly known at Westminster became frequent companions at Cambridge. One of these was Arnold Haskell. I have barely spoken to him since and, curiously, although I was as ardent a ballet-goer as theatre-goer—my favourite ballerina being Lopokova and ballet "Tricorne"—I cannot remember that the subject was then of special interest to him. But another, Angus MacPhail, a red-haired and rather gauche Scot from Blackheath, became my closest companion in a number of the classical dissipations of University youth. We both played billiards badly; it would take one or other an hour to reach 100 and a 10 break was an event. I received my worst sports injury at billiards—once completely missing a sharp stroke played with the rest and taking off the skin of all my right-hand knuckles against the pocket. We both played auction bridge well and with Arthur Elton and Ian Dalrymple composed a regular four that exhausted so many combinations of the cards that eventually we became bored and, to revive interest, went astray after strange modifications, such as the Minus form, where every call that may be made plus may alternatively be made minus—an undertaking to lose, not win, that number of tricks—and ranks in the bidding just above the plus equivalent. One of the first of my articles printed outside "youth" journalism was a *Manchester Guardian* back-page column on this invention. It is a curious fact that the other three members of this four all followed me into the film business in the years after University.

It is also a curious fact that Angus and I should have been such relaxed and easy friends for so many years, for really we shared few interests, if these intensively. Eventually he became one of my wife's best friends too. Some jokes we shared, but these were limited to puns, Donald MacGill postcards, and inadvertently erotically-worded headlines in the papers. (The best in my collection of these ran right across the front page of the *Daily Express* at the time of the Empire Crusade: "LORD BEAVERBROOK REVEALS HIS GREAT OBJECT".) We were familiar with, and could speak of, the same literature, but our tastes here did not in the least coincide; I could not read Proust, he had no interest in Melville or Doughty. He was a Heretic, certainly, but totally blank as regards any form of politics or science; where, besides bridge, our interests did coincide was in the music hall and the fact that we endlessly played chess together.

Gilbert Seldes' *The Seven Lively Arts* was then a book of power, one of the first to deal learnedly with Charlie Chaplin and the comic strip as nowadays *The Times* music critic analyses the compositions of the Beatles. We not only revelled in the same English comic music hall stars—Billy Bennett, Monsewer Eddie Gray, Nelly Wallace and Lily Morris—but we studied Seldes and welcomed every American visitor he mentioned favourably, for instance Chaz Chase and above all Frank Tinney. The peak of course belonged to neither category; this was Grock. We made the important discovery that you could do the first house of a London music hall and still reach Liverpool Street in good time for the "Fornicator".

I never tire of reading about chess masters or of playing chess but my own playing is wholly ineffective. Sometimes I play badly, sometimes well. When I play badly I lose at the beginning, when I play well I lose at the end. I am ashamed to say that I have never had the industry for study of openings and therefore, with any player of even moderate skill, am lost almost as I start. Chess can be an embarrassing game. It is awkward to begin playing with a pocket set on an airplane and have Kmoch stand up in seats behind you over mid-channel, study the board, and remark: "Won game for black" almost before the journey has even started. I played in a simultaneous against Bronstein once and *knew* that my first four moves were sound, for it was only after the fifth that Bronstein started saying: "Tch! Tch!" and shaking his head. He soon had more power in the centre files than I previously knew existed on the chessboard. As a kibitzer at the great post-First-World-War London Congress at the Central Hall I went in for one of the lightning tournaments. I know others have lost by *zugzwang* (that is, for *non-afcionados*, a position in which the player whose turn it is to move cannot do so without whichever pawn or piece he chooses to move, being at once taken by the opponent), but it happened to me then against Wahltuch with every piece on both sides still on the board. Yet it was at the London Congress too that I received the greatest compliment ever paid to me in any field in all my life. I was standing on chairs with a friend, peering over the backs of other spectators in order to get a glimpse of Rubinstein versus Alekhine. An attendant came up to me and said: "Please do not make your remarks in an audible tone of voice as it might assist the players."

If only I can get past the opening it is sometimes not so bad. Angus and I joined a simultaneous against Reti at Cambridge and, after I had lost at the beginning as usual, we continued together in consultation on his board and at least survived as far as adjudication. My greatest weakness is that I am impatient and if I do manage to get the initiative my combinations are unsound. My best games are under pressure, when your opponent is attacking so hard you have each time somehow to find the best move in order to survive at all. The only really good game I ever managed to play was like this, and it took place at a Soviet sanatorium. My opponent was a shy young man who looked mild and inoffensive. If I had known he was U.S.S.R. Second Category I should have trembled and fallen through the floor. He mounted an attack so fierce I had no chance for frills or choice but to hold on, and after much sweating on my side it came out a draw. In the return game we exchanged everything off and of course he won easily. When I discovered his rank I made my excuses for having dared to take him on. He replied with a giggle that when we had drawn the first game he had become terrified lest I was a master and exchanged in worse panic than I to give himself a chance.

The trouble about chess and the reason I play so seldom is that it is difficult to get pleasure unless your opponent is an equal. If you are worse than he it is an impertinence to ask him for the game, if your opponent is much worse than you there is little pleasure for either. Angus and I were well-matched, although he was undoubtedly the steadier. We played several times a week all through my nine terms, and developed catchwords. I have said we used puns, but for the reader to grasp our full littleness it is necessary to cite one. Whenever either offered a gambit he would say: "Pawn up, poor hopeless nup."

Cubical chess was played by the mathematicians in Trinity in my time. They constructed a special three-dimensional board. I was never invited to try this, but one of them—a brilliant young Chinese named C. H. Hsu who died tragically soon afterwards in an aeroplane accident near Shanghai—taught me Wei-chi, the game called Go in Japan, that is at once so much simpler and deeper than chess. But his lessons were only kindness. Whatever odds he gave, he would presently be saying (the verb is a technical one): "I eat . . . I eat . . ." and you would be swallowed up.

I started new societies. One of the most absurd-sounding was the Cheese-Eaters' League. Instead of special ties, members wore miniature rosettes in the button-hole, like those of the Legion of Honour but yellow instead of red. The guest of honour was always the President of the Union—D. H. H. Smith, afterwards a Washington correspondent of *The Times*, and Denis Johnston, the Irish playwright and already a man of exceptional dignity, intelligence and humour, were among the first. Because precedents were always followed in Cambridge society and we could not remember which we had done at the first dinner, toasts had always to be drunk neither sitting nor standing but half-way up. Yet the league had the serious (?) purpose of biochemical research. We ate at our dinners not just *good* cheese, but *new* or at least hitherto little-known cheese. Our best were a huge cannon-ball from Roubaix, with red flesh and dusty outside, a great cylinder from Egypt made from camel's milk and so hard it creaked when you tried to saw it, and a delicate white soft thing from the Arabian desert, bottled in oil and imported by a friendly Kingsman whose brother was a sheikh. We were particularly anxious to try a whale's-milk cheese—whale's milk is reputed to taste of shrimps—and we did make enquiries of Sir Sidney Harmer, then director of the B.M. (N.H.) and a great cetologist, but these were fortunately unproductive. It is possible to get milk from a dead whale, but no whaler could admit to killing a nursing mother for these are supposed to (and should) be rigorously protected.

I plunged also into journalism and became film critic for the *Granta*, which Ian Dalrymple was editing. Incidentally, we were of course buying and binding all the "little" literary magazines by then: the *London Mercury*, the *Criterion*, the *Adelphi*, the *Dial* and the *Transatlantic Review*. Angus tried to pull Ford Madox Ford's leg by sending this last a cod poem entitled "Le Rouge et le Noir", but Ford got the better of him by heading it "Dear Sir" and tailing it "Yours truly" and printing it as a letter without paying him anything. I started a new paper, unillustrated and in newspaper format, the *Cambridge University Times* and was flattered when T. S. Eliot, a great god for us then because of "The Waste Land", praised an article in it I had entitled "A Communist approves of Compulsory Military Service". I think the argument was only the obvious one that it must be useful to a revolutionary to know how to operate a machine-gun; I did not then know Lenin's acute remark that Britain was the freest of all countries in bourgeois Europe because it did not have a background of conscription. Dissatisfied with this journal, however, I bought from Cedric Belfrage, who was going down, his *Cambridge Mercury*, and filled it not only with poems, short stories and articles but also with woodcuts by one of my University table tennis stars, Lee-Elliott, who afterwards became a professional artist, and caricatures by Woggy Woolf. But the magazine did not succeed, except in delighting its contributors. It cost me all my spare cash.

§ 9

AFTER THIS catalogue of activities the reader will be in a position to understand why I failed in my Tripos examination. The only surprise is that I got my degree at all. I made my unsuccessful bid at Part One after only two years but it was really megalomania for me to try for it at all. In Botany and Chemistry I drew blank. In Zoology the results announced "Montagu I. G. S." as having "attained the necessary pass standard". This result must have been generous. In a sort of truculent desperation I had answered the questions provocatively, basing myself on Dobell regarding the Protista for example, and writing (quite incorrectly) of mammalian descent that "the paucity of the evidence prevented properly cautious and competent persons from advancing any theory", but that "others had from time to time favoured the following views" and then outlining those being peddled by a zoologist I guessed would be one of the examiners. Whether this resulted in leniency towards me in order to avoid suspicion of prejudice, or whether my *P.Z.S.* papers were taken at all into account I do not know. But these latter possibly helped me at college. Unlike most Cambridge colleges, King's likes to keep on only undergraduates who intend to try for honours, which means firsts in the Tripos, and you cannot sit for Part Two in your third year if you have failed Part One in your second. At King's, even ordinary pass-degrees are normally not enough. An old hand whispered to me that King's also likes undergraduates who publish papers. They can circulate reprints among the appropriate faculties at other Universities and so look like a hive not only of learning but research. I do not know if this was a gross slander, but in any case the sending-down did not come.

I have already explained that the one unalterable requirement in getting a degree was to be in one's rooms between the prescribed hours of the night, for a prescribed number of days in a prescribed number of terms. I could no longer try for the Tripos but to get an "ordinary" (that is, "pass") degree I had still to take two more subjects and stay three more terms.

The examinations for the "ordinary" degree are held twice a year, at the end of each autumn term and then again in the summer term at the time of all the other examinations, including the Tripos. To have two strings to my bow I elected to try at once the examinations at the end of the first—the autumn—term of my last year; if unsuccessful I could sit once more in the summer. As subjects I chose what I presumed would be the two easiest for me without any study: English and French. Thus I should not need to interrupt any of my multifarious current occupations.

The English went according to plan. I duly sat and obtained an undistinguished Third. But a peculiar thing happened to me on my way to the French examination. At that time I was exceedingly busy with a by-election in Cambridgeshire county constituency; Stubbs stood once more and again did not get in. The day of the examination was the day after the poll. The examination was in the afternoon, the counting started in the morning. I went into the Town Hall without any idea that those present at an election count are not allowed out until the counting is completed. The voting was fairly close and the result was not arrived at until late in the day. As a consequence I missed the examination altogether. I waited for the inevitable thunder. But when the results came out, there was my name: "Montagu, I. G. S., First".

What could have happened? Again the old hand was ready with an explanation. If your papers are Fail, Third or Second, it appears you are entitled to demand to see them, in order to find out your mistakes with a view to sitting again and trying to do better, as is in such case your University right. It was known to the examiners that if unsuccessful I intended to sit again. As the invigilators had presumably failed to notice my absence and there was therefore no record of it, and as with any other result I might have asked to see my papers which could not be found and were therefore presumed "missing", the examiners had had no way out of their predicament but to give me a First.

I insist that I am not characteristically dishonest. But again what does A do? Providentially at that moment I overheard a conversation between two King's dons in Hall, just after one of them had returned from a meeting that morning of the University Senate.

The first said: "Interesting affair at the Senate this morning. Vice-Chancellor had a letter from a fellow in the Pacific. Said he was dying of blackwater fever and, before he died, wanted to get it off his chest. Said he cheated in the Tripos."

The other grunted and queried: "What did the Senate do?"

The first replied: "Didn't do anything, of course. How could we admit that our invigilators could make a mistake about anything?"

There is a much-quoted tag: "Thou shalt not kill, but needst not strive officiously to . . . etc." Especially, surely, when you have just heard that your confession will not be of any practical effect.

I had now overcome all the necessary examinations. My tutor explained to me that, to complete the formalities for a degree, during the remaining two terms of my obligatory period of residence, I must qualify for a "certificate of diligence". This should have been simple, it could be done simply by attending a minimum number of lectures during the period and signing my name each time on the attendance sheet. Simple? Perhaps. Not so simple, however, for me. One course was a delight. It was a series by a don who was an enthusiast for Marlowe. He interspersed his discourses with copious quotations from the verse and plays, and declaimed so splendidly with such a resounding voice, that the "mighty lines" thundered and the souls of his hearers opened to numerous hitherto undreamed of aspects of Elizabethan literature. But the other courses I put down for turned out impossible. Literally impossible, from the physical point of view. I discovered that, having missed lectures for more than two years, I had lost the faculty of being able to stay awake *when one and the same person is talking in his ordinary voice for a whole hour*. This is no joke. Often an even shorter period of monotone sends me to sleep. If I turn on the radio after waiting up for a talk I particularly want to hear, I fall immediately asleep. It is convenient to be able to sleep whenever you want to. This I can do pretty well. A few lines of print are effective in sending me to sleep in bed. I close my eyes and sleep immediately in any moving vehicle—plane, train or bus; this can be awesomely dangerous if you are tired and you yourself are driving; fortunately a pull in to the side of the road and even only ten minutes asleep refreshes me completely. But there is not only the danger to oneself and others in such cases, there is the embarrassment if this weakness attacks one when one ought by social obligation to be alert. I have had to stay out of plenary sessions at peace conferences when big speeches have been made, and suffered agonies in Sofia when, as a guest of honour there once, I had to sit in the limelight of the front row. I have asked a question in China and come to myself with the tea cold and a hole burned in the tablecloth and no more idea than the man in the moon what the answer had been. There is a photograph in existence of a British Communist Party Congress during one of my periods on the Executive with me fast asleep on the platform during the General Secretary's report. And that General Secretary my beloved Harry Pollitt, one of the best and most moving orators in the world. (Here I perhaps had the partial excuse that I had heard it all the previous week when the text had been agreed on at the E.C. meeting.) But at Cambridge I had no excuse. By now I knew most of the Zoology lecturers personally, the lecture-rooms I tried to attend were not large, and before I knew what was happening the lecturer would often innocently address some remark to me in an aside. I would start up, obviously unaware of what had been said, to the resulting embarrassment of us both.

This difficulty was confided to my long-suffering tutor. He suggested an alternative to lecture attendance; a piece of research would be accepted at the end of the two-term period as evidence of "diligence". I went my way rejoicing, resumed my usual occupations undeterred, only to be brought up sharp two weeks from the final date by a request from the tutor to see the research supposed by now to have been accomplished. I hared off to the Sidgwick (Geological) Museum, measured all the skulls of fossil fen beaver there, noting their every dimension with my specially-designed and specially-made B.M. micrometer that measured to a hundredth of a millimetre and, working night and day, produced a new *P.Z.S.* paper. Then I collapsed with a nervous breakdown: B.A. (Cantab.).

The M.A. followed in those days—I don't know if it still does—simply by one's father keeping up periodic payments for a given time. It was a purely automatic process, concluding with returning to Cambridge for an afternoon, hiring the appropriately-trimmed gown and cap, and kneeling before the Vice-Chancellor to place your hands in his.

I may be some kind of a squirt but, though it appears in some reference books, I have never used the degree either for glory or in applying for a job.

§ 10

TWO MORE digressions are due before we leave Cambridge for good.

J. B. S. Haldane was a big man. He was massive, towering, beside being as big in spirit and intellect as any man can be.

I first met him not through Biology but in Market Square, Cambridge, on General Election night. An illuminated screen was fitted up which announced constituency results on lantern slides as soon as they were declared. Conservative win after Conservative win came up, each differing only by the size of its majority, and as each appeared on the screen J. B. S. Haldane booed. The rowdies did not like the boos and, headed by one or two soldiers in uniform, they surrounded and tried to rush Haldane. He stood his ground, and such was his stability and mass that, as they approached, each successive wave fell back as from a cliff.

The second time, he came to a party in my rooms, fixed up to celebrate a showing of *The Cabinet of Dr. Caligari* that we had organised. There was a large bowl of pink "cup" of some kind on the table. Under its influence J.B.S. seated himself in the revolving chair of my roll-top desk, stuck Lella Sargant-Florence's floppity chiffon hat on his head, took my terrestrial globe in one hand as a sort of combined orb and sceptre, twirled himself round, and announced that he was descended from Hwulfdun and rightful King of Scotland.

This was the beginning of a friendship lasting many years.

Quite early I ran two banking accounts. One was opened for me at the family bank, Samuel Montagu & Co., and had a blue cheque book. The other, whose book is buff-coloured, I opened at Lloyds when later I went to live in Lincoln's Inn and decided I did not wish my father to know from the cheque forms what I was spending money on. Unpremeditatedly this arrangement turned out a convenience in another respect. Bankers do not mind an overdraft if you quickly cover it; a deficit that leads to an unpleasant interview is soon appeased so long as the account is kept in motion. When I ran short I had only to remember which was which and juggle the overdraft between the two to make both accounts seem "live" and get away quite well with more credit than the net balance justified.

It has so worked, again not by design, with my many interests in life generally. To zoologists I have been a film man, to the film world a politician, to politicians a sports specialist and so forth, in each domain receiving credit for rather more expertise than I was entitled to. J. B.S. (I never called him "Jack", though others did; I felt it somehow inappropriate) embarrassed me by gravely assuming, or pretending to assume, that my zoology was much less superficial than it really is. I was always in fear my bluff would be exploded, but it is highly possible of course that he was never deceived and only enjoyed teasing me.

At Cambridge in my day he was still quite a young man, not long out of the army. He was not yet a Professor, his status was that of "Reader". He already had a considerable reputation among his contemporaries for oddity and originality in his experiments. One story I had already heard from Hogben and A. L. Bacharach of the 1917 Club. At a meeting of the Biochemical Society Haldane had described some research in the course of which he had injected urea into his arm and produced in the latter symptoms resembling those of tetanus. This result had been quite unanticipated, and the chairman vainly asked those present for a comment. After a time a brother Scot had taken an extra puff at his pipe, removed it, and observed briefly: "Verra interresting, verra interresting, but I wud like to hae the experriments repeated on a norrmal subject."

Haldane would never brook the slightest hypocrisy in life. He was himself bold to challenge every preconceived notion—hence his originality in science—and he had no mercy on cherished restraints and sacred cows. At that time he had still an *enfant terrible*'s desire to shock. If a sudden silence fell on the noise of a Cambridge party, his great voice —who else's could it possibly have been?—might be caught booming out some such sentence as: "I have never gone in really seriously for bestial sodomy."

The trouble over his Readership was really somewhat his own fault, for his frankness before Charlotte's divorce and his marriage to her really amounted to trailing the tail of his coat. Before leaving High Table at Trinity he would exclaim: "I am going to sleep with my mistress tonight," and in those staider-seeming days this not unnaturally got up the nose of the stuffier dons. After the divorce case, in which he was adjudged to pay damages, he was hauled up before the disciplinary committee of the Senate, known as the Sex Viri, and dismissed from his Readership. (It should be noted that this romantic-sounding title has nothing to do with either sex or viruses but only indicates the number of members composing it.) Of course the most articulate and enterprising of us were up in arms for him. He fought the verdict and was reinstated on appeal, his contention being that to accept adverse judgement in a divorce case, the current laws on divorce being what they were, did not of itself necessarily imply turpitude, and that a co-respondent might have very good reasons not only for rescuing a woman from an unhappy marriage but for setting up no defence. His victory on this point was not only a personal triumph but a minor step towards improvement of the law. It did not prevent him from complaining that, thanks to his quixotism, Charlotte had cost him £1,000 more than he expected.

J.B.S. was the most utterly rational person I have ever known, completely regardless of his own safety or interest, almost a polymath in science, personally courageous without limit, possessed of wide scholarship and an extraordinary memory that allowed him to quote not only from the classics and the Bible abstruse passages apparently at will, but also from the sacred works of all manner of exotic religions and philosophies.

I lost sight of him for a time after leaving Cambridge, and ran into him again only after he started his *Daily Worker* contributions in the thirties. When I first knew him Haldane had not yet become a Marxist; he had seen the fallacies in what Marxists call "mechanical materialism" and been inclined to what they call "God-building". It was encountering Engels, whom he valued above Marx, that changed this attitude, and he found in dialectical materialism as outlined by Engels a view adequate to unify the disclosures of processes and reality achieved by science.

The thirties, with their sense of gathering storm and the patent incompetence of the course followed by the statesmen, intensified his sense of social responsibility—as they did that of so many other intellectual workers in the most diverse fields. He asked himself how he might best bring his special qualifications to participate in the fight against fascism and the coming war, and hit on the idea of offering the public, through a newspaper, a regular exposition of current scientific developments and a critical analysis of current events and controversies in the light of scientific knowledge and a scientific approach. He first broached this proposal with the *Daily Herald*. It would seem incredible, but that newspaper rejected it on the ground that science was not sufficiently important, and could not be made sufficiently interesting to the public, for a regular series.

Only then did he—with no prior connection with the Communist Party—try his idea on the *Daily Worker*. Bill Rust, its editor, jumped at the offer, and this began a friendship and trust between the two men, as well as the series of popular articles by Haldane—most of which have been collected in book form—that lasted over several years, and for clarity, accuracy and pungency of expression have been never equalled in the field of popular science exposition. It also began Haldane's association with the Communist Party, his chairmanship of the *Daily Worker* Editorial Board, and led to his activity in relation to Spain and in the pre-war campaigns for adequate A.R.P.

J.B.S. would come down to our cottage in the country near Kings Langley—he was almost too big for its shaky narrow staircase—and spend hours in the garden tanning vast pink expanses in the sunshine and working out notes on scraps of paper. He got on with Hell, and liked jotting down memoranda on bits of paper as soon as he thought of them; at peace conferences, as orators droned on, I have seen him utterly absorbed with a few tiny notebook scraps on his knee, covering them with small figures, which he afterwards mentioned as the working-out of a novel theory in cosmogony.

He had the same habit of pedantic precision of speech as Hogben. I do not ridicule it. I wish I could have exercised the mental self-discipline necessary to have acquired it myself. It is a tool priceless beyond rubies for self-inculcation of precision in thinking and writing. My own is so sloppy I cannot even follow Haldane's primary simple but severe rule: never write a sentence that makes an abstract noun the agent subject of a verb. Nevertheless, he could carry such verbal exactitude to absurd lengths—probably he did so deliberately as part of the self-disciplining process.

After his first marriage broke up and he began his association with a fellow-biologist, Dr. Helen Spurway, they would sometimes come down to the cottage together, and she could play the game of gravity every bit as pedantically as he. One day they came in to the cottage unexpectedly after collecting *Planorbis* (the pond snail) from the woods a few miles to the north, and it was preposterous to hear them courteously discussing their specimens as they ate their tea in the tiny, low-ceilinged room, he so huge, she so angular and slim. "Do you not think, Doctor . . .?" from the one, and, "Yes, but what is your opinion, Professor . . .?" from the other. During the Second World War I conceived the notion that a film debunking racialism from the scientific point of view might be useful. (As I recall, I found the cue for this in something said by Molotov.) The film was made for M.o.I. under the title "Man One Family", and both Julian Huxley and J. B. S. Haldane cooperated with the commentary. We disposed of Julian first, in a recording room in Wardour Street, and when J.B.S. was finished it was lunch-time. "Have you—er—any canine or anatine leanings?" was the formula with which he proposed adjournment after lunch to the neighbouring hostel which happened to be called "The Dog and Duck".

The experiments which he and Spurway conducted during the war, on the effects of breathing in concentrations of carbon dioxide, which cleared the way for use of midget submarines, were really dangerous. They brought the two even closer together and led to his second marriage, happier than the first and lasting till his death, for in their eccentricities—I use the term in its literal and not at all in any derogatory sense—they were well-matched. Spurway was one of his guinea-pigs. Others were men formerly of the International Brigade; one was a distinguished German anti-fascist whom he managed, by demanding him as indispensable for this purpose, to get back from detention overseas, whither obtuse authorities had deported many such in the sudden panic of 1940 after the German invasion of the low countries had been aided by a Fifth Column. So biased were the petty officials against the left they had no conception that such a man as Hans Kahle, heroic battalion commander of the Eleventh Brigade in Spain, whose sudden death soon after his return to Germany was a tragic loss to the G.D.R., was the last person in the world to suspect of being a menace in the war against Hitler.

The research cost at least one life, and Haldane, who made himself the chief guinea-pig as usual, sustained a severe back injury during the induced convulsions.

Spurway around this time worked, as Haldane did, at University College in Gower Street. Aside from his own research, he took a paternal interest in hers, which was chiefly on newts; they also interested themselves in the genetics of cats. We had a beloved Siamese female Natasha, whom we never restricted in her romances, and one of her sons—from an unknown sire—who displayed a pattern unlike any I have ever heard of—they accepted for breeding. This F_1 animal was a short-hair, silver-white with black markings; it showed no trace of cream or brown, but the black, in the form of clearer or fainter stripes, was restricted to *exactly* the same areas: face and head, tail, legs, line on back, as the seal points of the pure-bred mother, the rest being pure silver where a Siamese would be cream. I missed hearing what the f_2 or further results were.

A few years after the war our friendship was unluckily broken. Lysenko was the occasion. At this time Haldane's *Daily Worker* contributions had become irregular. He was irritable even with Bill Rust, and none of us liked to importune him, for we knew that he was not only suffering bad pain from his back, but deep distress at the accidents to some of the volunteer guinea-pigs. Without doubt the scruples of conscience were totally unwarranted, but he felt wrongly that somehow these casualties reflected on his care or competence, that *somehow* he should have foreseen and provided against them, and his own nagging pain reminded him of them. He never voiced these feelings, but we understood and deeply respected them. At one moment he declared that he could not possibly find time to write until the *Daily Worker* provided him with a charlady to do the housework. The postbag was accumulating queries about Lysenko which someone must deal with. If not J.B.S., who? Bill Rust overbore my objections and persuaded me to undertake an "open" answer in the paper. J.B.S. turned up immediately in a towering rage, declaring firstly that the answer was all wrong, secondly that he was offended at not having been asked to do it himself. (He had been asked, in the first place, of course.) I am still satisfied with what I wrote. The point at issue between us was not my explanation of the genetical problems involved, but my assertion that in Britain it was taught in many biological faculties that characters acquired in life are never, in any circumstances or group, inherited in the progeny. He said it wasn't. I knew better, for I had been to zoology classes more recently than he, and I knew what I had heard from Hogben. Haldane liked Darlington, who also occupied this extreme position, but when Haldane liked a colleague he was too generous-minded to recognise that the colleague really held views he himself thought erroneous, and so he would not accept this as true of Darlington at that time either.

I revered Haldane and would not quarrel with him, so I kept away.

It has been said that J.B.S. left the *Daily Worker* and broke off his association with the Communist Party because of his disbelief in Lysenkoism. That is not exactly right. Haldane himself was far from the conventional genetical schools' position of denying the inheritance of acquired characters absolutely. He adopted the much more scientific and sensible attitude, not indeed unorthodox nowadays, that different groups of organisms probably differ in their "plasticity" in differing degree, and that while there is no satisfactory evidence for such inheritance occurring in some groups (e.g. complex multi-celled animals like vertebrates), there is evidence, difficult to interpret otherwise, in other groups (e.g. *Protista*), and that therefore rigid *a priori* generalised positions should not be taken up. I heard him express precisely this view to a Soviet Academician at the lunch table during the Wroclaw Conference of Intellectuals for Peace in 1947, with the result that he was invited there and then to contribute an article expressing this view to one of the leading Soviet scientific journals. It never appeared, but then I do not know that it was ever written. What did upset him was learning, or suspecting, the administrative measures that had been taken against Vavilov, whom he respected, in the controversy and, still more, the general revelation that the Soviet state apparatus was prepared to take administrative measures to suppress one side in a scientific controversy. Certainly what had above all originally attracted him towards Marxism, and support for the U.S.S.R. as a state founded upon its basis, was its proper attitude towards science which he saw as the uninhibited search for greater and greater areas of truth.

He never said a public word against the Communist Party, nor for that matter one that might injure the U.S.S.R., for however imperfect they might be, he would not range himself with their enemies; but he was certainly shocked and disappointed. If he never wrote much about the Lysenko-genetics controversy this was, in my belief, because he saw himself in a trap, certain to be popularly used and misrepresented: the cold-war warriors would use his general scepticism about Lysenko for crude anti-Sovietism, and dismiss his qualifications respecting the possible plasticity of certain groups as proof of a sycophantic eagerness to excuse the U.S.S.R.

I need say nothing about his last days, for he has himself written of his own death in terms so cheerful, objective and clear-sighted as to match the noblest words on the subject in all philosophy. I will note only that, when at last I ventured to approach him during the final illness, I was welcomed as cordially as ever and as though not a day or shadow had ever parted us.

§11

NOW FOR the second digression.

Et ego in Arcadia. This, literally, means: "I, too, dwelt in Arcady", which, if still obscure to anyone, may be more freely translated as: "I, also, in my time chased girls." Alas, I was no less clumsy in this direction than at any other juvenile sport.

I knew by now everything about everything—and I mean *everything*. I began, as I suppose most boys do, with the Bible. My voracious approach to literature included the pages in the bookseller's catalogue labelled "Erotica" or "Curious", and I have yet to see an atom of evidence that pornography ever did anyone any harm. Its persecution, largely instigated by impotent old men incapable of distinguishing between prejudice and judgement, is far more meaningless than that of pot. I had read the whole of Havelock Ellis in the *Nouvelle Revue Française* edition and re-bound it in a strong coarse-grained brown linen. If I did not go on to Krafft-Ebbing and the other solemn Germans it was because I found them a bore. On obscurer matters my mother sometimes consulted me. I remember a conversation in the library after she had discovered the existence of female homosexuality. Males she could understand, she said, "but Lesbians . . . what do they *do*?"

The trouble was, my knowledge was totally and completely theoretical. Of practice I had none.

I remember firmly telling one of my mother's protegées—a middle-aged lady who preached "The Renaissance of the Greek Ideal" and illustrated it with "aesthetic" poses—that Mrs. Bloom was Every-woman, information that startled and possibly alarmed her when I showed her *Ulysses*' final chapter one day after lunch at Kensington Court. A rude aphorism says: "The boy scouts, the girl guides." No one had ever guided me. Casting my mind back I can remember in early teens only two cases of even slight friendships with older women. I do not now know how I met a widowed lady painter with children, who lived south of the river, in Battersea. I liked her paintings, which were delicate landscapes, and for long I cherished one she gave me, in misty lilac, of the Embankment and the power station. I visited her flat and invited her to Townhill, but my parents strongly disapproved. I thought at the time that this was just snobbery, for she was certainly very hard up. But it is possible that I misjudged their motive, for they were equally cautious when another widow, this one unattached, beautiful, rich, American, and the sister-in-law of a peer in the Cabinet, asked me to take her to the Zoo and call for her at her hotel room. I was strictly admonished not to go inside the door. I thought this was probably some aspect of etiquette I had never heard of, but now the "prudence" explanation seems to me more likely. After all, my parents would never have supposed anyone could value my company without some ulterior motive.

The first girl I ached for and whose attractions kept me desperately awake at nights came much later. She was a thin young woman I met at Oxford, with rather an elfin face and hair of that deep red mahogany with highlights in it which you see sometimes in furniture. I had gone over with the Cambridge University Labour Club to debate with our Oxford counterpart, whose leading light at that moment was Malcolm MacDonald. I do not remember much of that debate. I remember better a young Conservative named Charles Smyth whom we ran into before it and who told us he had spent the day at the Bodleian writing an essay on the Divine Right of Kings. "Defending it?" we supposed. "No," he replied superbly, "establishing it."

The young lady was clearly intelligent and spoke well in the discussion. I tried to meet her as often as possible, took her to the theatre in London, and to dinner with my brother Ewen, who had by now married and set up his own household. But to my mortification she obviously did not think of me "in that way" at all and very soon married a Unitarian minister.

There were several young women whom I met at Lella Sargant-Florence's and found attractive. I think now that the reason for my lack of success in romance at this time was the fact that I had no social graces whatever and that it never occurred to me to counterfeit an interest in them as persons with, perhaps, likes and dislikes of their own. I could be clean. I cannot claim to have been noticeably tidy. I was not impolite, but I was forgetful. If I walked along the pavement not beside but in front of them—as I tend to do even with Hell today—this was not rudeness but simply a practical deduction from the fact that we were both trying to get from point A to point B and I had the more weight and penetration in traffic. The trouble was that in my egotism I made the mistake of assuming, as I do with all people I like, that their tastes must be the same as mine. If I made them gifts, it was of things I thought beautiful, not after finding out what they thought beautiful. If I took them to the cinema or theatre it was as companions to see what I wanted to see, not after finding out whether they wanted to see it. This was not selfishness. In a way it was, from me, a sort of compliment.

But it is possible, all the same, that this was not appreciated; nor—for that matter—may it have been welcome that at the show itself I would pay the lady I escorted the same compliment of being more interested in the play or film while we were there, and supposing that she would be, than in the fact we were together. After all, would not the time for sociabilities come better when the play was over?

Towards the end of my stint at Cambridge I fell head over heels in love with one particular young woman up at Newnham. "Love" of course is a word with many connotations. Certainly it includes desire, that is, the conviction that sexual fulfilment with the loved one would be a supreme bliss; but, for the word to be appropriately used there must be more: an element of obsession, the belief that life with the loved one will suffice for happiness, life in her absence be but a bleak sour-tasting wilderness. *Love*, "true love" as the romances have it, requires also an element of luck, for it can only feed on reciprocity, and this eventually teaches many virtues—patience, restraint, mutual respect and at least enough unselfishness to seal a partnership. Blessed indeed are those pairs who share in addition a sense of humour.

But "being in love" requires nothing but the obsession and desire and can be purely selfish till, from lack of response, it withers. The problem for youth is that time only can distinguish one state from the other, and the lover of either sex, however dashed, cannot but persist, at least at first, hoping against all evidence for some alteration.

My inamorata might be assessed, with a certain measure of imagination, a Cambridge version of Zuleika Dobson. She had not by any means the staggering beauty or the Edwardian elegance of her Oxford prototype, but, at least among the intellectuals and would-be intellectuals of the day, in numerous coteries of art and science, she exercised the same bewitching and all-conquering attraction.

I stuck like a burr, unable to conceive that, in the long run, my qualities would not overcome resistance. She never gave me the slightest encouragement to believe so, but readily accepted me as a companion. In the story-books the lady in such circumstances dismisses the unwanted lover, obliged to "be cruel to be kind". According to my observation, young ladies in such embarrassing circumstances are often too kind to dismiss, and hence comes the cruelty. Pity the thwarted lover whose frustration is heightened by propinquity and prolonged by tolerance: his ecstasy is drowned in misery.

In my case, fortunately, the misfortunes were coloured with comedy. No matter how I tried to play the cavalier and the swain, all gestures were fated to misfire. Aboard the Poole Harbour ferry one day I boasted of my prowess as a swimmer and, reckless of unknown tide and current, responded to her dare by leaping overboard to finish the crossing in the water. Of course the steamer had to circle and put back, dragging me dripping to the deck and safety. Another time a group of us camping on the North Devon coast set out along the shore, where I hoped my marine biology would enable me to shine. Alas, instead we were cut off by the tide and had to clamber back clinging to the cliffs like flies. In the end we had all to remove our clothes and swim for it, holding them in bundles above our heads, and drying in the sun enough to put them on again when we reached uncovered sand. But not before we had come to a sheer bit, not high or dangerous but steep enough to wake the phobia that had grown on me and now forced me to a craven halt, while *she*, just ahead, had to come back and clamber round the corner half a dozen times before her example encouraged me sufficiently to dare to follow.

Indeed, my courtship was not only doomed from the start but maladroit. It spun itself out for several months beyond Cambridge, till it died naturally and became replaced by a peaceful elderly friendship which Hell shares as comfortably as I. I knew its vanity as romance well enough before the last sweet-sour University evening on the Backs. Parting from University is traditionally a sentimental moment. This occasion was made more so by the calm and serenity of its setting. The quiet river, the stone colleges barely illumined, the summer night languid and refreshing after the heat of the exhausting day. In the punt, besides the lady and me, two among the pleasantest of my college contemporaries, Clark and Morland, Quaker shoemakers from the West country, one of whom was to accompany me on my next B.M. hunting foray, and several precious bottles of Tokay.

§ 12

THERE IS nothing like the sort of travelling I went in for to establish a relationship of ease and acceptance in foreign parts however alien and remote. Come as a tourist, everyone is rapacious, for the resident's livelihood depends on the short season of opportunity to exploit the visitor. Come for business, everyone is on the defensive, for by its nature your livelihood must depend on taking advantage of *them*. But come as such as I, on foot with a bundle of mousetraps over your shoulder, and you are God's fool and everyone turns out to help you.

Indeed it is sometimes hard to convince your interlocutors that their underrated mice are really your objective and in the foothills of the Carpathians I once had a hard job preventing offence from being taken when I refused an offer from a passer-by to buy all the traps in my bundle.

The goal this time—as soon as I had shaken off the effects of the fen beaver—was a few weeks in the high hills to the east of Czechoslovakia, to be followed by a search for the rodent *Spalax* (of which more later) in the hot south Hungarian plain. I prepared for the journey by contacts with the national museums in the various countries, making the journey from Vienna to Budapest down the river. The steamer was full, there were no empty berths, I slept on the deck beside my Bergen rucksack, wrapped in a big waterproof silk quilted eiderdown of finest lightness (6′ × 5′ 6″ but it packs easily), a traveller's tip that Bancroft Clark taught me and still worth passing on today. I learned as useful a tip, too, from one of my fellow-travellers who saw me lying inexpertly, destined for aches and stiffness the next day if I did not alter. Never sleep on your back or side if you lie hard, as you must directly on a ship's deck, for that way your weight lies on your bones, which are thinly covered. Lie forwards, on your upholstered, stomach, surface; but not flat—which would press too heavily on the belly—just three-quarters, so that you get enough of the chest muscle and the soft to carry the weight and the side bones serve only to keep you steady.

During this journey I came to terms once and for all with the idea of suicide. It is a curious thing how many people I have met have killed themselves; but I do not know if the number is larger than to be expected by anyone with a large acquaintance. It was natural that the thought should come into my mind as I lay on the deck, for I was gloomy and, just before, had heard of the self-killing, reason unknown, of a north-country undergraduate whom I had liked for his cheery down-to-earthness and who had been as much a fan of Lincoln City as I was of Southampton. I came to the conclusion that while suicide is reasonable and common sense if you are suffering unbearable pain, or have good reason to anticipate pressures to betray your colleagues or your principles that you might not be able to withstand, the only other possible justification could be to annoy someone you dislike, "die on their doorstep" so to speak. Otherwise there can be no sufficient grounds for it, for the very reason that it can be done at any time if tomorrow is not an improvement and cannot be undone if you change your mind, and meanwhile, waiting for the better morrow, there are bound to be things of interest in the world if it be only the football results. As I did not sufficiently hate the lady who had failed to respond as I thought she should have done, and perhaps even more because I was pretty sure dying on her figurative doorstep would cause her no lasting qualm, I dismissed the idea as anyway purposeless and perhaps this was the beginning of my cure.

I was to return to Vienna, as I remember, and meet Bancroft Clark there. Stephen Morland, who had been holidaying with him, would return to England and Bancroft and I would go on up to the Tatras. Bancroft was a strongly-built young man, solid, reliable, quiet in speech and manner. Above all he was practical and never flapped. Like Cotton in not being a biologist—he read economics—he too tried out skinning under my attempted instruction and proved impressively good at stuffing tails. This requires an even spindle-effect winding of the cotton-wool on the wire, before smearing it with arsenical soap, that he said resembled some process of bootmaking he had already mastered in the factory. He was of liberal disposition and reading, we shared an interest in the Heretics and most of the cultural heroes of Bloomsbury; the expedition I think appealed to him by its promise of unfamiliar settings and techniques. I could not have tumbled on a more agreeable and invaluable companion.

Bancroft in those days wore as his working kit a rough short-sleeved khaki shirt, a coarse red—if any—tie, and bright blue linen trousers. He was as blond and pink as I was dark and sallow, blue-eyed to my brown. We did not talk a great deal—it is proverbial that friends at ease do not need to—and one day sitting silent in the car of a suspension railway in the Tatras we had the delight of hearing the doyenne of a group of English ladies, clearly identified as Lady Flinders Petrie by the conversation, point him out to her companions as a typical Slovak dressed in national peasant costume.

We trapped in the valleys and near the peaks, around the moss-covered shores, peppered with mouseholes, of a fir-forested lake; balked at climbing Gerlach—he in his brogues, I in black elastic-sided house slippers—when we came to a vertical rock-face set with easy iron hand-holds; but we did reach a high point on the frontier whence you could see, and, if need seized you, even pee, down into Poland. The collecting went extremely well. We spread our maps and made our plans for moving south to Hungary, when we noticed, projecting like a pimple of the Carpathians right down into the plain of Hungary, the hill of Tokay.

With the sentimental farewell to Cambridge so fresh on our palates, missing this was not to be thought of, and we worked out the time-table for a diversion that would give us a clear day there on our way.

Tokay is exactly what it seems from the map, a pimple tenuously linked with the hills to the north, a few hundred feet high only and entirely covered with vineyards. We wandered on its slopes, the sun beating down on a land devoid of shade; every so often we would pause to mop our sweat or pick a few of the small white tasteless grapes. Lunch in the one hotel was tasteless too; we ordered Tokay, of course, to help it down, but all that was served under that name was pale and raw.

It was only when we came out again into the parboiled streets that we were accosted by a little bent old man with a white beard and panama hat, walking with a crooked stick. He spoke to us in halting German, saying that in his youth he had been in America but not long enough to pick up more than a smattering of words. He told us he was the Duke of Windischgraetz's steward and, having heard our plaint, asked if we would like to see his master's cellars. (I was not at all clear then, and have not become so since, whether the Duke had been succeeded by, or only turned himself into, a limited company.) Any-way, limping before us, his steward led the way through a farm gate like all the other farm gates, into a yard as hot and dusty as all the other yards, and at his beck a short sturdy man in an apron came hurrying up and opened a trapdoor. Gratefully we went down into the cool. There, as far as the light of the minion's torch could reach, stood barrels ranged upon barrels, line upon line, receding far into the dark—more than a kilometre, we were told, of barrels.

We were each given strange glass vessels, something like egg-blowers only much bigger; from top and bottom of a distended spheroid ran an open-ended tube. The man in the apron would run forward, opening casks and drawing a little of the wine up into the swelling by sucking at the top tube with his lips. The knack was to take it from him, substituting your thumb for his above without letting more than a drop of the sample flow out to waste below, and then use your thumb to regulate the remainder pouring down into your mouth.

At every cask, it seemed, we would stop and the little old man would name the year. "*Ein gutes Jahr, nicht wahr?*" he would ask. But then a few steps on we must try again even if this time, with a headshake, he pronounced: "*Nicht ein gutes Jahr.*" We went on until we could no longer tell the difference. This is the one and only time in my life I have been thoroughly drunk. The old man saw us off at the station and helped us with rucksacks and packages up into the train, but not before giving us a card to Windischgraetz in Vienna and a list of dates when the "*Essenz*" was at its best and richest: 1908, I think, and 1889, and 1868, and even what he called the "*Wunderjahr*", 1812.

Thenceforward I used to call at this address on every visit to Vienna, to get the special bottles at a privilege price; the card even worked at an address in London. Though there came a day, after the Second War, in 1945, when those in the wineshop declared that all the "*Wunderjahrs*" and the rest were gone, "drunk by the Russian soldiers". This is what they said, but why indeed should the Nazis have left anything?

As the train drew off into the dusk, leaving the little old benefactor behind waving his kerchief, we dozed, and I took off my boots, for wine always goes to my feet as well as to my head. It settled there too, this time, for when the local train reached the junction where we had to change, waking us with a jerk, it was far too late to get them on again over my swollen feet before the train restarted, and it was all we could do to gather up our bundles, persuade the guard to stop specially a half-hour on, and climb down, boots in hand, to wait several hours, sitting sadly on our rucksacks level with the track, for another slow local in the opposite direction to come by and take us back to the junction and the south express.

Eventually we reached our destination in the southern plain, a provincial capital named Hódmezovašárhely. The first vowel is that sound no Englishman can pronounce—half-way between the German *ö* and *ü*. (Some Scots can, they do naturally; it is the *o* of every Glaswegian.) The *s* is aspirated and the last two syllables run together and sound simply "Hi!", and the whole word means just "Beaverbrook".

Here we were sure to find our target animal, *Spalax*. This is sometimes called in English the mole-rat, unimaginatively for it is quite unlike either verbal component. The Hungarian name is *földi kutya*, the earth dog; it is even less like a dog but it does live in earth. *Spalax* is about the size of the biggest of rats but thicker and heavier, with no neck or tail and a battering-ram head; it is yellowish in colour and it has not even the pin-point eyes of a mole. Wholly underground in habit, it has lost eyesight altogether, for the eyes are not functional and are covered with unbroken skin.

We did not, however, catch *Spalax*, but not because there were none around. Its digging powers are enormous, and extended far beyond ours. With the help of a specially engaged labourer we dug on and on in the hard clay earth of the field with the frightful sunshine beating down. In all we dug 200 yards with burrows constantly branching and running sometimes as much as four feet deep for twenty yards or more, sometimes rising to within a few inches of the surfaces to give the animal access to succulent root crops. When we did reach a nest or storehouse, of course the quarry had long had warning from our efforts and no hide or hair of it was to be seen.

The town was a small and green one, with pleasant roads, big granges, schools and a museum; the people were interested, especially one old man who had been a doctor in France and, when he retired, came back with his small garnered pile to live comfortably in old age and help his relatives. Everyone who could do so would come out into the fields, or make an evening date in the town to talk to us. The common idea is that to learn a language you should live in the country where it is spoken. This is all very well and is obviously a needed step to speak it accurately, but it depends very much on finding teachers or being able to spend enough time. I have a rather different recipe. In the countries that speak the language you want to learn, say: French in France or German in Germany, everybody speaks it too perfectly. The first thing the innocent abroad finds it hard to get used to is that the veriest infants in France speak better French than he and it is even more humiliating to go to the Moscow Zoo and be outshone in Russian by the parrots. The natives are inclined to be impatient with your stumbling efforts; they may even laugh at or be offended by your errors, or in too much of a hurry to wait while you find words for what you want to ask. Go to a remote corner of a country where the language you want to learn is a *second* or *third* language, however, and all is different. Some local bigwig, or a former migrant returned from somewhere, will be sure to have a reputation among neighbours as *the* citizen with mastery of tongues. To sustain this credit, he simply *must* show that he *can* talk with you. You will have plenty of practice in the second and third local languages and, better still, your interlocutor will probably speak as badly and as slowly, but as readily, as you. You will never learn, of course, well enough to pass an examination, or even "pass as a native" —as my teacher warned me I should never do years later when I was trying to learn Chinese and confessed my inability to get hold of the "Four Tones"—but you will gain confidence and become able to understand and be understood. It was so that I learned to be fluent in French and German in Central Europe and the Balkans and so, later as will be related, to get on in Russian without mastery of either grammar or vocabulary simply through a trip to Georgia.

We did not lack for helpfulness in this out-of-the-way spot in Southern Hungary and, if *Spalax* did elude us physically, ours was more than a moral victory in the end. We made maps and diagrams of our diggings and also a fascinating discovery: *Spalax* completes its burrows with its nose. Unlike the mole, that has forepaws transformed into powerful spades but a soft and sensitive nose to smell out worms, *Spalax* rasps away the clay with its powerful projecting rodent teeth and then packs everything that has been loosened tight into the wall with a toughened nosepad. It turned out that every wide-burrow wall was pocked and pitted by these nose-prints, so that it looked like the matrix of some gnarled and rugged tree-bole with a scaly bark. Only a few branches of narrow bore had their sides smoothed again by the constant passage of the fur. Two artisan brothers came out from the town and made casts for us. One set still reposes, or should do so, in Hódmezovašárhely Gymnasium Museum to which we gave it. Others are now scattered in various capitals; the negative itself lies in the B.M. One more paper for the *P.Z.S.*

§ 13

WHEN THE work at the B.M. was finished, tidying up the results of the expedition for the *P.Z.S.* paper, there was not much of the year left and I still had £35.

Early in the next year I should have to have an interview with my father and settle what was to be done. Of one thing I was certain: I could not go to U.S.S.R. in the year I went down—that is, 1924—for I was not yet 21 and my father could prevent me. As the law stood a minor could neither obtain nor, if he had one, retain a passport without parental permission. It was understood quite well that I would go as soon as I was 21—by hook or by crook, by fair means or foul, somehow—but what was to be my future otherwise? This was still all to fight for and meanwhile the armistice agreed between us had a few more weeks to run. I would spend my remaining money and get back to Townhill by 25 December. None of us children had ever voluntarily been away at Christmas yet.

Thirty-five pounds could take you quite a long way in those days, if you were content to travel hard and live cheap. I was thinking that perhaps I could make some kind of a living from translation. I set out for the continent to track down two playwrights. We had read about them in a vogue book of the time—Ashley Dukes' *The Youngest Drama*. One, Fernand Crommelynck, had written on the theme of jealousy but in a mood not of romantic tragedy, like *Othello*, but of fantastic comedy carried to the *n*th degree. The other, Ernst Toller, was to us youngsters an heroic symbol. I hunted Ashley Dukes down and got introductions.

The first port of call was to be Paris. I started off on the night crossing, via Le Havre, travelling third. It was cold on deck in the darkness. As I patrolled the ship I made friends with two English commercial travellers whom I had already noticed on the train. There was a pretty young girl on the deck, inclined to plumpness, who seemed to be having language trouble with the purser. As usual in such cases, with either sex, I took this as a cue to intervene. (Not long earlier, coming back by train through the Rhineland, I had found myself sitting opposite a hatless Englishman in the restaurant car who was having trouble with the menu. This had turned out to be Alan Cobham, making his way back from a forced landing incurred on one of his pioneer flights for the *Daily Mail*. He was very anxious not to miss Cologne, where he hoped to pick up a fresh plane, and before he stretched out exhausted on the whole of one side of our compartment made me promise to wake him when we arrived. I shook him as we drew up in the station, but all he did was to haul himself on to one elbow, gaze bleary-eyed at the huge notice hanging outside the window, grunt, "It's not Cologne, this, its AUSGANG" and try to go to sleep again.)

This time the girl in question knew no English and but little German, but I managed to sort things out and ascertain that she was a Czech who had been serving as nursemaid with an English family and was now trying to make her way through Paris—with no French—to her home on holiday. A little later my two new acquaintances, passing the seat on deck where, as good Samaritan, I was now sitting with the young woman beside the funnel, both of us wrapped in the voluminous eiderdown I had extracted from my rucksack, made pointed remarks about "cashing your Czechs while you can". However, like the three knight-errants we were, we helped her all the way to the Gare St. Lazare, escorted her across Paris by taxi to the Gare du Midi, and waved her farewell onto the right train. The only intimate nothings I had been able to say under the eiderdown were two I had culled in a Compagnie-Internationale-Wagon-Lit earlier that autumn: the Czech words for HOT and COLD engraved on the heater lever.

My companions took me to a cheap hotel in an alley behind the Galeries Lafayette. The rooms were tiny and one could not eat there, but it was central and suited me; from then on until it closed down I always used it whenever I visited Paris, at first alone and then later with Hell. I was grateful, for up to then I had known nowhere but my mother's far too expensive "palaces". My companions also took me to a dance hall called the Olympia near the Madeleine and I made my own way to the Cirque d'Hiver to see the Fratellini, who were more magical as clowns than even their reputation, and to Crommelynck's flat. He was amiable, gave me other plays to read and an option on *Le Cocu Magnifique* for the English language. It has been one of my disappointments in life that I could not find a publisher for this before the option expired—although I did get one performance by the Stage Society—and despite efforts I have never been able to make contact with Crommelynck again to renew it.

The next stage on the journey was to be Switzerland: Toller had been released from jail and was reported to be resting in Lugano. When, after the 1914–18 war, a Soviet republic was briefly set up in Bavaria, it had been headed by two intellectuals: Kurt Eisner as chairman and Ernst Toller as his deputy. The successful counter-revolution assassinated Eisner and sentenced the poet Toller to five years in prison. It was in prison that he had written his plays *The Machine-Wreckers* and *Masses and Man*, and from prison that they had been smuggled out together with the moving cycle of poems *Das Schwalbenbuch*, about the swallows who nested in the prisoner's cell and survived every effort of warders and governor to destroy them. Now his five year sentence was over.

On the way I diverted first to Leysin, where my cousin Davd, Carmel's son, was recovering from a bout of T.B. We spent the afternoon walking and talking, I the elder and, wrongly, supposedly the wiser. Then on for an ascent into the mountains north of the Rhône valley at Montana. In this sanatorium I spent three days. The T.B. patient here was Alexander Tudor-Hart and the doctor he was under a brother of Stephen Morland. Tudor-Hart was also being visited by his sister Beatrix. Beatrix, Andrew Morland and I set off for a walk up the nearest and lowest "mountain". It appears that in technical parlance anything may be dignified by that name that is over 8,000 ft. Only ascent of a peak above this limit entitles one to call oneself a "mountaineer" and our chosen objective did narrowly surpass it. For reasons that I have explained I cannot possibly do anything that can be called climbing. But this was only a walk; I love walking in the mountains and here moraines, rocks, glaciers, snowfields—everything was easy. Nevertheless, even here I just could not make the top and qualify, unable even on hands and knees to bring myself to surmount the last simple twenty-foot ridge over soft snow, however often my companions showed me.

The weather broke and Lugano, next, instead of being a beauty spot of lakes and islands, was nothing but one single downpouring sheet of water with streets squelching underfoot. Thoroughly soaked, I learned at the address I had obtained that Toller had just moved to Vienna.

I had planned to go on to Vienna too, not straight, but by a wide roundabout curve of railway that took me near another objective, Sonntagsberg. This tiny Austrian village is in not high but moderately hilly country. On one of these hills was a sort of hotel in which A. S. Neill had once kept school for a short time, before he had moved on to set up Summerhill at Leiston. I knew that Rolf Gardiner was now living there and his family had commissioned me to take him oranges.

Rolf was a considerable Cambridge figure in my day. He was large and blue-eyed, in appearance a sort of archetype of Nordic youth, active with *Wandervögel* and bubbling with strange ideas. He impressed me by telling me that only the best people could manage to wear blue, the next best had to content themselves with greens or browns; and gave me a first edition of *Ulysses* which he had had specially bound but afterwards decided that he did not like. His mother was small and brown, part Hungarian and part Finn; his father a large red Egyptologist with a hearty manner and energetic forehand—we used to play doubles in tournaments together. The young man had a friend named Roland, less earnest I suspect than Rolf, who claimed to have invented the oviform community and universal time. The former was an arrangement to provide for everybody around an oval: parents should live with their babies on one side, old people on the other, so that the young and old and busy should have least distance to travel to the centre; the youth and the maidens should live at opposite ends, though in whose interests they needed to be so far separated I am not at all clear. Universal time was more plausible. Mankind, Roland explained, was disunited because, owing to the rotation of the earth, at any given moment everyone living on a different longitude whom you asked the time must give a different answer. His system would unite them. Instead of asking: "What is the time?" you could henceforth ask: "Where is noon?" and everyone could at that moment answer the same: "Tokyo", "Calcutta", "Paris", "New York", as the case might be. Watches would have cities rather than figures marked upon them and it need not be very difficult to get used to, little more, say, than a decimal system.

Rolf had taken refuge in Sonntagsberg to write, and his parents' fear that he might not be getting enough vitamins—these mystery substances were just beginning to be talked off—was certainly justified. The house was a great big rambling castle of a place, half manor and half barn, built all at different levels, with echoing stone floors and staircases, bare walls and wooden benches. The furniture was bare, too, and sparse, but I was snug enough in my little room facing the sunrise and asked nothing better than to settle down, finishing my first draft of the *Le Cocu* translation in three weeks. There were not many persons staying in this simple place. The hosts were a blond, lantern-jawed young farmer and his wife, with a child whom Rolf called Minna von Barnhelm after Schiller's heroine, on account of her flaxen pigtails. The wife fed everyone consistently on delicious coarse soda-ey bread and huge steaming bowls of gravy, sinewy fragments of meat, crumbly potatoes and lumpy suet. There were no green vegetables available and no fruit. The times were still near enough to the end of the war and the madnesses of devaluation in the defeated Central Powers for life to be cheap for a foreigner. Lodging and board, all in, cost the equivalent of one and threepence a day.

Everything was still rainy and damp. Sometimes we set out by miry paths through the fields to the village in the valley where a small hall showed films one night a week (here I saw my first Soviet-made picture, one of battles and revolution). More often, all the inmates of the hostel stayed on in the evening in the dining-room after dishes had been cleared away, and two of us would play chess. Rolf did not play, and would sometimes go off to continue with his writing by candlelight. There was only one board and set of men, so everyone but the two players of the moment watched, rapt, the lamplight gleaming on the pieces and pawns and Minna's upturned nose and flaxen hair. No one's play was any good, despite the enthusiasm, and I found myself for the first time a champion and soon the unchallengeable master. Unchallenged, until one evening Rolf and I came in after a night's trudge and found, smiling and waiting for me over the board, a dark, bullet-headed close-cropped black-stubble-covered unshaven individual, a Russian "*ewige Student*" about forty years old or so whom I had never previously seen, because he had kept entirely to himself upstairs.

I was only too glad to get the game, and readily agreed when the stranger made a condition that he would not play except for money; it was he who set the stakes at what must have seemed to those present an enormous sum but in English currency was only half-a-crown. It appeared that my opponent was much hated in the hostel, probably because he held himself aloof and would not mix, though I suspect this was only because he was poor and could not pay his keep and was hence ashamed. Everyone crowded round, everyone hoped to see him beaten. The breathing was tense, I won the toss and chose white. The game followed conventional lines and I was soon in difficulties, as I knew I must be if he could play at all and, after not many moves during which but a few pieces were lost on either side, my position became hopeless and I resigned. There was a great collective sigh of disappointment and Rolf chided me angrily; he knew nothing of the balance of forces or position and it was clear that, in his estimation, by surrender I had let down the side, if not, indeed, our country. "What would you have done?" I demanded indignantly, feeling that I was being unfairly judged. It was clear from his reply that, if he had played chess he would have shoved forward his pieces to the last man and considered that no less should be undertaken by any being of spirit. He would not stay, and stumped off upstairs in dudgeon when I asked my opponent for a return. This time, with black, I played a gambit that I often used against Angus.

It is not a particularly good gambit. Indeed, it is probably because it is an unsound one that it is so rarely played, but by this very circumstance few people are familiar with it and this puts me on an equality with them because I do not know it either, whereas all the familiar openings are better known by anyone than by me. He blinked as he saw it and pondered a long time. After a difficult game that lasted many moves and left little on the board he agreed a draw. This meant of course that the stake for the first game had to change hands. The anger and disappointment of the company exploded. The farmer screamed at my late opponent, shouting that he would not allow his guests to be plundered under his roof. The "student" stood up, clasped chessman and board under his arm, declared he would not be insulted, that in future no one might use them (it turned out that they were his), and withdrew permanently back to his room. This was a pity; I should have been happy to have had the chance of playing more games with a better player at that cost, but how dare I explain to the company that a price big to them was small to me?

The translation finished, I shouldered my rucksack and resumed the long slow *Personenzug* rail journey through western Austria. Arriving in Vienna late at night, dirty and tired out with the laden Bergen on my back, I peered across the station square and threaded my way straight to the opposite side, where a neon sign blazed out the word HOTEL. I signed the register, handed over my passport, was given a small room with a double bed, threw myself down on it and at once dropped off to sleep. At three in the morning there was a knock on my door: "Open up—*Polizei*!" and several men came into the room. One of them had my passport and they started to ask me questions. My name? Nationality? Occupation? To this I answered "student", for so it appeared inscribed on the appropriate line. What was I doing in Vienna? I replied that I had come to go to the theatre, to the cinema, to look at the mice in the museum. (Half-asleep as I was, I had the sense not to add that I was looking for Toller.) "Those are not the occupations of a student!" the policemen said severely, but they handed me back my passport and left after searching my belongings. It was only when I could not get breakfast the next morning that I realised what had happened. By chance I had stumbled into a brothel and the management, which had probably never had a client book a room for a whole night before, let alone to sleep in, especially on his own, had panicked and sent for the police. If the reader still wants to know why, he should read a short story I chanced on somewhat later in the Bomb-Shop, written by Leonid Andreyev. Here a Nihilist student plans to assassinate a Grand Duke who is coming to visit a town on a certain date. How shall he be on the spot at the right time? To enter the town at the last moment will be difficult, as then the town will be packed out with police, every one on his guard. To enter early and walk about means to risk being recognised and picked up; so he decides to get in before the police guard and hole up in a brothel till the decisive hour. To avoid suspicion he, wiser than I, sent for one of the prostitutes, and the point of the story is that by refusing her services he humiliates her and, an argument resulting from her reproaches and she improbably convincing him that her life is purer than his, he becomes contrite and abandons his purpose. I am afraid that I had not yet read this story and on this occasion was the innocent abroad. However, after this experience I used to fill in on my hotel forms not "student" but "philosopher" for, as Voltaire said to the Englishman, everything is allowed once to a philosopher. (According to the legend, at the latter's suggestion they had tried homosexual intercourse. On the Englishman desiring to repeat the experiment Voltaire had refused, saying "*Une fois philosophe, deux fois bougre*".)

This time I moved into a more respectable hotel in an arcade in the Graben next to a toyshop, where I managed to buy inexpensive presents for the coming Christmas stockings at Townhill. It did not take me long to discover that I had missed Toller once again; he had gone on back to Germany only a few days before. I had time only to see in the Theater in der Josefstadt Reinhardt's production of Goldoni's *The Servant of Two Masters* with all three Thimigs (Hermann, Hugo and Helene) in the cast, which remains in my memory as the most perfectly balanced, the most delightful, production I have ever seen on the stage, and I set out again in pursuit.

The express took me smoothly into Prague. As I stood in the corridor beside a woman in her thirties whose straw luggage and packages were piled high on the rack of the compartment behind us, the train running slow as we approached the suburbs, I received an unexpected proposition. She was a countrywoman going to the city to be married, she said, and from then on would have to lead a quiet life. She knew she would not be met at the station, her fiancé was at work. This was her last chance. What did I say to the idea that we should both go off to an hotel? She would meet him the next day and explain simply that she had missed the train. There is a play or a film script here, I am sure, or at least a short story. No doubt part of the attraction of the idea for her was the fact that, I being a foreigner, we should never meet again and so there could be no possibility of complications. Of course I was terribly tempted and flattered as well, and I had no idea how to turn down such a proposal without hurting the lady's feelings and appearing, indeed being, a prig. But my schedule was tight and, worse, money was getting short. Besides, I was not at all sure of carrying off my role with proper sophistication. I put Satan behind me and remained a virgin.

A new train took me on across the Czechoslovak–German border. Now that I am old and a grump, I prefer on a train to work or read or best of all to enjoy my ability to shut my eyes and doze. Then, I strove heroically always to resist the natural inclinations towards sleep I have described, and try to miss nothing of the character of the countryside seen through the windows and whatever I could discover of the characters of my fellow-passengers.

A curious man got in at the petty frontier town and put his bundles on the rack. He was dressed in black, with a frock coat. He wore the tall, starched collar of a clerk and kept on his bowler hat. To talk he leaned forward with his hands resting on the crook of an imperfectly rolled umbrella, its ferrule insecurely pivoted on the floor. His frame was meagre, his tint a mixture of yellow and red, his sparse moustache bristled, his myopic eyes watered through pebble pince-nez, he was without doubt the ugliest man I ever saw. Making conversation, I had just mentioned the cheapness of living costs in Austria. He nodded sagely, and then agreed with the following remarkable words: "You are right, quite right. I have heard that one can buy three women in Austria for the price of two in Passau."

We were soon running into Berlin and here at last I overtook Toller, who was staying in the Excelsior, an impersonal place of glass and gilt and mirrors and many rooms, something like the Regent Palace behind Piccadilly. Ernst Toller was an extremely attractive personality. Dark, modest in manner, unusually handsome, he looked Byronically unhappy and yet would readily break into a smile as though eager to catch at every fleeting opportunity to be gay. Rigid *apparatchiks* used to say: "No wonder the Bavarian revolution failed if its leaders were all like Toller," but by this harshness they condemned themselves, for he was a truly good man and, if indeed not very practical, a tenacious idealist. He was a very open kind of person too, and received his young admirer from abroad warmly. We talked on far into the night. Option on his future output was quite rightly committed to Vera Meynell, whose translations of the works written in prison had already done such service to his reputation, but he promised me a second option, and then and later gave me some short sketches of *reportage*. One was observed remarkably: a drowning incident on the Italian coast. As the corpse was brought in one person stood stony on the shore, others flung themselves to and fro weeping—the hysterical ones were merely bystanders, the impassive figure was the bereaved mother. He also gave me an early verse romance of much less originality.

Toller and I became good friends throughout the succeeding years. He came several times to England and I introduced him to G.B.S., despite Shaw's sapient observation when I described his background before bringing him along: "A good many of my friends have been in prison and I know scarcely one who is the better for it." I took him behind the scenes at the Old Vic and introduced him to Lilian Bayliss. The latter obviously did not know him—why should she?—she was in the middle of the Vic complete cycle of Shakespeare and had her hands too full to keep up with contemporary plays. To someone who came by she presented Toller as "the Russian poet" and Toller, who had just enough English to catch it and thought of himself as a dramatist, German at that, was much deflated. I did my clumsy best to mend matters by explaining Lilian Bayliss as "*Eine einfache Dame*"—a simple lady. "*Ganz einfach*" ("thoroughly simple"), Toller kept muttering. It was not that he was conceited but, like others of us, he needed confidence.

My last meeting with Toller was in the lobby of the House of Commons in the spring of 1939. The Spanish Republic was at its last gasp, deliberately strangled by Britain, France and U.S.A. through the farce of "non-intervention". He had with him agonising pictures of Spanish civilians in the Republican zone suffering from pellagra and other deficiency diseases, and had brought them to melt the hearts of British cabinet ministers and induce them to ensure the passage of food and medical supplies. I knew by then only too well the kind of men he would have to deal with, and knew that to them the sight of such suffering on the Republican side would be what is now called "counter-productive", the last and final nail in the Republican coffin. The Foreign Office had all along been determined to end Republican resistance as rapidly as possible, and this evidence could only serve to satisfy it that its aim was now at last close to realisation. We have seen something of the same kind, from the calculators of like kidney, now in the sixties in relation to Nigeria and Biafra. But how could I persuade Toller? Such evil, even after all his experiences, was beyond his comprehension. He had married an exquisitely pretty, doll-like young wife, a "Nordic" blonde, and was blissfully proud of her. When the war came, they made their way, as did so many refugees from Hitler, to U.S.A. and Mexico. Here soon afterwards he cut his throat, and the usual horrible stories ran around among the emigré communities: the wife was supposed to have retained links with her Nazi family. I do not believe a word of it, Toller and his young bride had been so happy together, and when he died the tide of the war had not yet turned; the early overwhelming victories for Hitler's army would have been quite enough to drive a man like Toller to despair.

But all this then lay far ahead. Now, more theatres and then the immediate task was to get back to Townhill by Christmas. There were only a few hours and little money remaining. I studied the prices and time-tables. Cash in hand would just not make it third class to London, across London and then to Southampton, let alone provide food on the way. This was the first of three times I found myself in the same predicament trying to get home from Berlin. Once I had to drop into the Rumanian Embassy and borrow from Nicholas Mishu, by then transferred there, a pound which just sufficed. Once Hell and I together starved till we got on the steamer at Ostend and there a benevolent British Railways waiter, intimidated by a firm rule not to accept cheques from passengers, offered instead to stand us a meal out of his own pocket. I hope our embarrassed preference to starve on did not hurt his feelings. On this occasion I discovered from the timetable that I had just enough left if, instead of travelling Berlin–London–Southampton, I made the shorter rail journey to Hamburg and travelled steerage by the Hamburg–Amerika liner scheduled to put in at Southampton on the afternoon of Christmas Eve. Even steerage passengers had food included in the ticket price.

I bought the steerage ticket at the company's Berlin offices, then the railway ticket, and settled down to enjoy my ingenuity, only to discover when I had lugged my rucksack to the shipping offices in the port area of Hamburg that the scheduled Southampton call of the liner had been cancelled for want of passengers and freight. The clerks patiently explained that I was the sole passenger booked to get off at Southampton, to call there would cost the liner at least £300 in dock fees, let alone the time lost on the trip. The price of my ticket would of course be refunded. I as patiently explained that this sum was insufficient, it would not get me to my destination in time, or even at all, by any other carrier. A contract was a contract, I insisted. There was no small print on this ticket. If I were not put down as scheduled I should certainly sue. Deadlock. Excited conversations behind the counter and also "off". I settled down in a chair, filthy and travel-worn as I was and, to try to look unconcerned, worked away at the *Times* crossword puzzle. Suddenly there was a commotion in an inner office, the door broke open and a director appeared. Thrusting his top hat firmly on his head he grabbed my arm and, dragging me outside, raced me along the street, my rucksack bumping on my back, shoved me into a first-class carriage of the last train from Hamburg that could get to London in time to make the Southampton connection, handed me a five-pound note through the window and even waved to me as the train safely bore this irritating customer out of the station and off the company's back.

This is how I got home for Christmas.

Mother loved one of the presents I brought home from the Graben. It was for putting on her bathroom wall. When you pulled to tear the paper it played *La Donna è mobile*.

§ 14

THE NEW YEAR 1925 was due to bring about a fateful interview with my father. A confrontation was inevitable, with no quarter. Just how much allowance was he prepared to go on giving me, and what was it in life that I was going to do?

There could be no meeting point between us on these two questions. He wanted an answer from me on the second question before he decided the first. I, from my point of view, needed his answer to the first before I could usefully approach the second. My father held that it was his money that was in question, and before he ladled it out he had a right to foresee the use to which it would be put. I on the contrary considered that he owed me at any rate *some* moral obligation—magnitude subject to argument—in that the upbringing for which he had been responsible had accustomed me to a certain kind of life that it would be tyranny arbitrarily to end.

I have written further back of what I could name my Cordelia-complex, the barrier that destroys all sincerity of relationship and frankness of communication so long as the child's actions and possibilities are dependent on the degree of loyalty and respect it displays toward its parents. Above all I desired to end all element of uncertainty—and this, I think, not just out of arrogance or selfishness, or at least not that only; the hope to break this barrier and establish a frank relation untinged with self-suspicion of sycophancy certainly played its part. I demanded to know where I stood. Let us fix some permanent basis that no conduct of mine should cause to fluctuate; let it be whatever allowance he wished, or let it be none if that were his decision, but let the matter at least be settled and unalterable. This stability, the key as I saw it to any honesty or true filial feeling, was the one thing he would not allow. Then I saw in his attitude only the perversity of an ogre. As now I can perceive and acknowledge, any other would have seemed to him abandonment of the responsibility that love bade him retain.

Thus there could be no room for compromise. I still wanted to make my profession zoology and hoped that his decision would make research financially possible for me. He did not refuse outright but wanted proof of my capacity to be shown by a grant from others before (as in the Westminster exhibition and scholarship) he would be ready to replace or supplement the amount by any corresponding support. This condition I could not fulfil, and I think not only because of the equivocal, or rather, so far as their public result was concerned, merely moderate result of my examinations. I base this belief on a conversation during my final term with Professor Stanley Gardiner, who held the Cambridge Zoology chair. I had put in for a post on the whale research vessel *Discovery*—Scott's old expedition ship. This was going to the Antarctic for three years and, had I obtained it, would no doubt have settled my hash and my permanent professional direction. But the post had rightly gone instead to a far better zoologist and more capable research worker than I, my contemporary at King's, Leo Harrison Matthews. I had several other ideas for research: one a speculative piece of work on island subspecies still not yet undertaken, namely, to try to determine to what degree their characteristic skull shapes in adulthood could be modified by feeding the young on special foods and so affecting the growth of their jaw muscles. The B.M. was interested in the work, but the Treasury strictly defines the limits of its expenditure, and this experiment could be undertaken only independently with an outside grant. I had seen Gardiner to discuss the possibility of this or other schemes and he had answered me straight out: "It is impossible for you to expect a grant for research from any institute. Whatever project came before it, the committee concerned would ask why it should be expected to pay when you come from a background that could itself so easily afford to do so." Meanwhile my father, of course unable himself to judge the value of research in a field so far outside his ken, required as proof of its value just such an endorsement as was unobtainable. Impasse. Dead end.

In this clash of tears and frustration on one side, principled obduracy on the other, my mother obtained a concession for me. My father consented to continue the £500 allowance he had given me at University for just one year more. If he by the financial year's end approved of what I was by then doing, he might continue it. If not, not.

As I see it now, and considering the lights he lived by, this must have been for him a great effort of trust and tolerance. For me, however, it could provide no solution whatever. The crisis was shelved only, not resolved. It ended there and then my hopes of a career in Zoology. It was already clear between us that in the summer, being 21, I should allow nothing to prevent me from going to U.S.S.R., and he must have consoled himself, however reluctantly, with the fact that this enterprise at least was to be an expedition fully endorsed by and officially representing the B.M. (N.H.) itself. But after that, what then? In Zoology I could see no way of an assured income to sustain me; in the circumstances jobs at best could only be hoped to turn up unpredictably, by chance. The only way I could get out properly from under my father's thumb was by some assured income, which meant some other profession. Otherwise I must stand cap in hand in 1926 as I had in 1925.

When the time came I was in fact starting to earn, if little, in a career he could, if not precisely approve, at least understand. This was presumably enough to satisfy him, for the allowance was continued twice without renewal of show-downs or argument.

§15

THE FIRST thing I thought of was journalism and my parents helped, only for their initiative to be made fruitless by my wilful default. Having run journals at Cambridge, I naturally supposed I could make a go of it in journalism in London. I first tried a *démarche* of my own.

I knew Beverley Baxter, one of the young men Beaverbrook had brought over from Canada, now promoted to the editorship of the *Express*. My parents, on what introduction I do not know, had invited him to Townhill for the week-end while he was still a newcomer, and it is an index of the social attitude to "newspapermen" in those days that he had been placed on the lower floor of the secondary wing, a sort of congener of governesses, secretaries, architects and the like. It is perhaps an even more cogent piece of evidence that he had apparently not resented this at all. He had gone away and then written a few friendly paragraphs in the *Express* society column about the pleasant surroundings and the guests. My parents were astounded at such perfidy. They swore he must be an unspeakable cad and should never darken their doors again, etc. Baxter was perfectly innocent in the matter. While it never crossed my parents' minds that a guest could possibly betray to the public view, however harmlessly, what went on under a roof that was showing him hospitality, Baxter came from a country where it was already taken for granted that, if you were invited, you were expected in return to do exactly that.

Baxter, I think, was a little bit amused, even if considerably taken aback, by the unintended effect of his visit and its sequel. He knew I did not share my parents' view of his character as "rascal", and received me at once when I asked to call. He most amiably gave me many tips on the newspaper world, and at my request a trial as reporter to a Cambridge friend of mine who had been chairman of the University Labour Club. But to my surprise he advised me strongly against trying to get work anywhere as film critic. (I had written film criticisms at Cambridge, so why not in London?) His excuse was at least ingenious. "Critic on a daily paper is no job for a young man," he said. "Do you know how we choose our critics? When we have a reporter who grows too old to get about chasing news stories, instead of retiring him we buy him a dress suit and start sending him to first nights. You need something more active."

Perhaps, but what, did not appear. My parents' effort was at a higher level. John Walter, head of the family that had had the *Times* in ownership almost since its inception, came to dinner. My father opened his dilemma about me to him, and I was invited to visit the great man in his office the following Tuesday. It would then be up to me to sell myself. The upshot was: agreement on an ideal proposition, for £25 expenses advanced I would go to Berlin—*Caligari* had made this a mecca for all us young men of that generation interested in "film art"—and write an extensive report for the *Times* on the German film industry.

Neither of these careers thus begun succeeded. My protegé did not last long on the *Express*; I flopped altogether, did not even begin upon the *Times*. I fear that neither of us was properly cut out for journalism. I have been an N.U.J. member for nigh on forty years but let us face facts and, at least in my case, admit it.

Beverley Baxter, whom I liked—we always got on despite our political differences—was soon very scornful about my friend. "Do you know what happened last week?" he said. "The news of Kitty McKane's win came over the tape. I opened the door of my office and your friend happened to be passing. I called him and said: 'An English girl has just won the Women's Singles title at Wimbledon. Write me quickly a short leader about it, 120 words.' And do you know what he answered? 'I'm afraid, sir, I don't know anything about tennis.' The fellow's an idiot. No enterprise. Do you know what I should have done if anybody had asked me to write a short leader about anything I didn't know while I was a junior reporter? Grabbed the nearest messenger boy, of course, and got him to write it for me for half a dollar. I'm afraid we shall have to get rid of him. He's the sort of fellow who, if you sent him down to No. 10 Downing Street and asked him to investigate the truth of a story that the Prime Minister had a cold, would knock on the door and, when a footman opened it, ask him, receive the answer: 'No, Mr. Baldwin has not got a cold but he has just been beating his wife', and then come back to us and report: 'There is no truth in the rumour that Mr. Baldwin has a cold'."

Eventually my protegé found a possibly more congenial refuge in the Civil Service.

My own failure was worse. I went to Berlin, had a great time and then wrote nothing. I prepared well. I got several introductions, the most useful—as it turned out—from the woman publicity manager of the Stoll to the foreign editor of the German trade paper *Lichbildbuehne*. And I did not go alone. When he heard I was going, Angus MacPhail, who had been an accomplice at Cambridge in both journalism and films, decided to go too. I had booked third class to save money. Angus preferred to travel first but did not wish to travel alone; he offered to pay my supplement from third to first if I would play chess for half-a-crown a game with him all the way to Berlin. I am ashamed to say I lost on the deal.

We put down our bags in the Eden (I always stayed in the Eden from then on; I did not know it was boycotted by socialists because the right-wing officers had taken Liebknecht and Luxembourg there to murder them during the Spartacus days). Then we hurried off to beard the *Lichtbildbuehne* luminary with my first introduction. He turned out to be a small pleasant man, with nutcracker face and speaking perfect English. In the middle of the room was a mahogany pedestal table inlaid as a chess-board. "Do you play?" was Angus's obvious question. The host replied that he did and mentioned Thomas, Griffiths, White and other English "greats" as opponents with whom he evidently competed on equal terms. Angus collapsed on the sofa, open-mouthed. "And how many times have you beaten Lasker?" he managed to get out. "Only once," replied Heinz apologetically. Our host was Heinrich Fraenkel, now Assiac of the *New Statesman*. Heinz was a genuine amateur, more able at chess than films, more interested in films than chess. He had a curious history. In 1914 he had been a boy of 16 on holiday in England, cut off from return by the outbreak of the First World War. Isolated from all social intercourse he had obtained books from the library on, and *taught himself*, chess, never previously having seen a board. After three months' study he decided he was ready to play and, looking up addresses, made his way to the nearest chess club, which happened to be the City of London. Here it was he met Thomas, Griffiths and White and the rest and for long there were old members who remembered the German youngster who, at the beginning of the war, used to put the pieces out before anybody else arrived. For a time all went well, but after the *Lusitania* was torpedoed the club said to him that though they had nothing against him personally it would be better if he did not come any more. Soon after that he was rounded up and taken to the Isle of Man and for the rest of the war had to play his chess escorted by two soldiers with fixed bayonets from the junior to the senior camp, for only among the seniors could he get proper competition.

From this start Heinz learned to be fully bilingual. Later events caused him to throw up his *Lichtbildbuehne* job twice: once, from ambition, to go to Hollywood, the second time as a refugee from Hitler to try to gain a living in the British film industry. Neither excursion succeeded, but there is an irony in his relation to chess. In Hollywood he entered the Californian Open, played over a period, and then much to my indignation—for I was there at the time—dropped out half way while he was right up among the leaders, saying it took up too much time. I bullied him but could not get it into his thick head that prowess at sport and games, even if then written off as a frivolity in Continental Europe, was precisely the way to make friends and influence people for any career in U.S.A. or Britain. He could not believe any society could be so foolish. In England, after living insecurely on the periphery of films for several years, he met Kingsley Martin by chance across the chess board, became the first columnist on the subject the *New Statesman* ever had—and an exceptionally good one too—and brought up and schooled a family on the proceeds. "The stone that the builders rejected is become the keystone of the corner," etc.

Anyway, at that time Heinz could give introductions to everyone in Berlin and get one "In" everywhere. We saw the marvellous sets at Ufa—the houses were so stupidly solid and naturalistically (but totally unnecessarily) real that they must have cost as much or more than if they had been built to live in. We met Emil Jannings in his drawing-room and got an autographed portrait of him in his exact Holbein make-up as Henry VIII. We met all the stars, all the directors, and saw films medieval, rococo, contemporary, expressionist and futurist. We saw, before it was premiered, the just-finished triangle drama *Nju*, with Jannings as the husband, Elisabeth Bergner as the wife, Conrad Veidt as the lover; it struck us as a revelation (which it was in its day) of the possibilities of commenting profoundly on human relationships by cinema. Then I came back and wrote a letter to John Walter, returning my expenses advance, and saying I was sorry I should not be able to write on German cinema after all. What else could I do? Before I went to Berlin I would have been perfectly ready to write about the German cinema for I thought I knew plenty. When I had been there I could not possibly write, for I had now learnt enough to know I did not know enough. Was it my fault that I had been trained as a scientist and not a journalist? I should have wanted to spend another couple of years investigating before I felt competent to reach the judgements that earlier would have come so glib.

Something fruitful did happen on the journey back, however. After we had left Dover and were running into London I met in the corridor an English actor. This was Hugh Miller, an extremely handsome man with a beautiful wife who wrote pseudonymous satirical poetry in the *New Statesman*. Hugh Miller had been playing lead in a joint Anglo-German production in Munich in which Cedric Belfrage—also film-struck—had persuaded his Harley Street father to invest money to give him a start. (The film was, alas, not very successful.) Hugh Miller and I got into talk and before we reached Charing Cross decided that what London needed was a Film Society, to show pictures which were worth while for one or another reason but could not get commercial showing, just as the Stage Society did plays.

This was the route by which I stumbled into some forty years or so of films.

§ 16

THE PERIOD which this book must cover from now on is about two and a half years, from early 1925 to the middle of 1927. Then the end of the family group as I had known it will constitute a natural break.

This period is hard to recall in any coherent order. Its events are highly complex, for during it I led not merely a double, but a criss-cross multiple life.

I do not use the word "double" here in its usual sense of implying deception. Though it is possible that, when the reader has read what I have to write about it, his inclination may be to disagree. If I did anything at any time of which others, who may have considered themselves entitled to know about it, were not informed at the time, it was —I can swear it looking back with the utmost effort at objectivity— not by any deliberate deception, but simply, solely, because I was living my own life and did not consider my choices other people's business. "Thou shalt not lie but do you officiously have to tell everybody about everything all the time?"

The point is—I now had *two* rooftrees: I had got out of the family nest as fast as possible, in order to start my own, and yet not fully severed my connection with the old one. This duality was not for the sake of fleshpots—it is only fair to myself as a natural and trained sybarite and gourmand to make this clear—but because I knew my parents *wanted* me to keep contact. Their house was still a home with affection warmly open to me and never closed; it was surely little enough to expect of me to rejoin and use it gracefully from time to time. I repaid this generous and tolerant attitude by concealing nothing and myself volunteering information—though never beforehand, for that would have seemed subservient. And it is indicative evidence that this relationship was endured by my parents with open eyes, that, when the crises rose, there was never the slightest suggestion of reproach of me for duplicity however much they might be surprised or angered by the substance of what I did.

The second adjective, multiple, applies because during these two years I was doing and starting so many things that I am appalled at the task of disentangling them to get them into some sort of order as I dig them out of my memory. My energy must have been prodigious to be thus dissipated. As I contemplate my present lethargy I just cannot imagine how I got through a tithe of the jumble of activities, and yet at the same time it seemed perfectly natural to keep juggling all the balls in the air at once throughout the twenty-four hours and never get tired. Now, above all, the warning is needed that was set at the outset of these reminiscences: about the tricks of wrong sequence that memory in old age plays. Some few public events stand out like peaks above the mist to orient recollection, but it is certain that if the bundles of papers stacked higgledy-piggledy in my attics survive the spiders and foul weather long enough ever to fall victim to the industry of U.S. university graduates seeking diplomas, there will be several adjustments to be made; by that time, should it ever come, they will not matter.

The first territory the juvenile staked out on leaving the home range was a furnished flat in Lincoln's Inn at the top of an extremely narrow winding staircase: No. 19, Old Buildings. It is ironical, perhaps, that after evading living in college all through my university time, I should come to rest, in the first independent territory of my own, in a setting architecturally exactly like a college, with all the paraphernalia of courts and gates, guarded likewise by porters. The difference, of course, was that while here you had the antiquity and the architecture there was over you as tenant no authority and no discipline. The flat consisted of one long, narrow, low-ceilinged living-room, then went up a couple of steps through a tiny kitchen into a tiny bathroom, and then up a few more interior stairs into a poky tiny bedroom in which there was certainly no room to swing a cat, at least not while four-fifths of the room was occupied by a small bed. Through a window on these interior stairs one could easily get out on to a leaded roof where sloping eaves could protect a sun-bather from view, when there was a sun. I am not certain in remembering this but I think the rent was £120 a year.

A woman, thin, acidulous-looking, mournful, fond of drink, her softened complexion beset by lines of red and blue capillaries, with pointed nose, came in and "did" for me—a char who could cook a little something at a pinch. Despite this somewhat unpromising aura, Mrs. Henry was exceedingly kind, industrious, patient with quirks, totally uninterfering, a faithful friend to me and afterwards to Hell as well. She deserves blessings. I think she was recommended to me by Iris Barry.

This hole, then, was my base. It was from here I spun my webs: to prepare for the U.S.S.R. and to prepare the Film Society. This was the fortress from which to make my raids on a London not yet talked of as swinging.

It was a busy time. There were only a very few months before the collecting season. Before this took me abroad the Film Society must be assembled and launched. And as yet I cut down on nothing, maintained everything: politics—my first act was to join the Labour Party in my new locality, Holborn, and soon I was active enough to be on its executive: sport—I still had my duties in table tennis and pleasures, when I could spare time, in lawn tennis; and the bridge sessions had not yet been given up; social contacts—at No. 28, the 1917 Club and the Fabians—man is a social animal and can accomplish nothing on his own, without colleagues. Einstein somewhere recommends that young mathematicians should be given solitary jobs on lighthouses (would this up the rates of shipping insurance?). This may be ideal for thinking, but every achievement in action requires collaborators. And I had not abandoned the pursuit of Arcady, for which my new flat offered, or seemed to, fresh opportunity. Havelock Ellis said that maidens were less resistant—warmed perhaps and placid—before a gas fire. My flat had a gas fire and it was duly lit. Havelock Ellis said that those timid and myopic acquired new courage with their haziness of vision when spectacles were doffed. As my guests sat beside me on a pouffe or on the floor as near the gas fire as I could induce them to venture, my glasses would be duly laid aside.

No device profited. Young ladies came back with me for light refreshment after the theatre. I have never been at all sure what either of the American expressions then beginning to be current—necking or petting—respectively signify, but, whatever the limits of either, neither term could possibly be applicable to our chaste proceedings. *Le Cocu* was now finished and because of the quality of fey innocence with which she had ravished audiences in *The Immortal Hour* I appropriately fixed on Gwen Ffrangcon-Davies as the *must* for Stella, the heroine so utterly devoted to the husband whose jealousy obsesses him that she, pure from first to last, eventually obeys his commands to bed with the entire village in a vain effort to end at least the nagging, torturing anguish of his doubts. Miss Ffrangcon-Davies accepted to come and have all three acts read to her. I do not know what she made of the play or of my reading—I rather fancy she was a bit puzzled at being thought suited to the heroine (I was not wrong in this casting—when eventually the play was done at the Stage Society, Komisarjevsky as director cast Peggy Ashcroft who radiates just the same quality of purity invincible); but I do know that my guest departed with no contacts more intimate than the tips of the fingers from one to other at how d'you do and good-bye. With one young person, up from the country and living lonely in Chelsea, introduced to me by an older friend as a possible theatre companion, I did indeed get on excellently. So well, indeed, and so relaxed was our brief companionship, that she did stay several nights in Old Buildings. But, alas, the fatal and not very complimentary words used to me by our shared friend in explaining her introduction: "I am responsible and I know that I can trust you," stood—despite the gas fire being turned full on and the electric light off—between us like a drawn sword. Havelock Ellis was an old cheat.

The great event which solves such mysteries for a young man did, however, take place about that time and in the place traditional for dispersal of an Englishman's oats—Paris. To start, the Film Society required of course a choice of sufficient films for a first season. Also, they had not only to be chosen, but obtained. The principles of the Stage Society and its function were well established. The whole theatre world understood this Society as, of its nature and purpose, interested *only* in such plays as could obtain no other showing, either for reasons of censorship or novel and esoteric character, and a try-out at the cost of the society could only benefit everyone in every branch of the profession: the actors could widen their experience with fat parts otherwise unavailable, the authors see living on the stage works that would otherwise gather dust rotting in their desks, the managements find out the potentialities of new material without risking their money; only the critics might lose a week-end or two and they would be paid by their editors. This meant that actors, authors and managers mucked in; only theatre-hire, costumes and sets needed to be covered by the members' subscriptions to the Society.

We should have to operate the same way. We meant to show the films in no hole and corner fashion. We must have the best West End cinema for the purpose, the best orchestra and the best music. Remember—these were in the days of silent films and a special score well played was an intrinsic part of the impression that could make or kill a film. We—that is the group that eventually got together to do the job—could (and did) talk our heads off about benefiting film art by enabling interested persons to study the potentialities of cinema and introducing, to the cinema, circles and personalities who had never hitherto been attracted to it. But there is no doubt that—just as with my friends and I when we got *Caligari* to Cambridge—our real motive, unavowed perhaps even to ourselves, was that we liked pictures, and that without the subscriptions of the like-minded enthusiasts who joined the society, we should ourselves never have been able to afford to see them with a big audience and the right music—both essentials for proper appreciation—or maybe even entice their owners to send them to England at all. This is not to say that the Film Society did not have the seminal effect that we contended it would; it is only a reminder of the general rule that philanthropy often entails self-satisfaction, not sacrifice. The point here, however, is that so far as long films were concerned we were almost exclusively involved with imports, foreign language ones at that, because few British films were made without hopes of or even concrete prearrangements for commercial showing. At the outset foreign producers could not understand it when we approached them and asked to be allowed to show their films for nothing. It took a good deal of persuasion to convince them that we, eccentrically, were only interested in films if nobody else wanted them and that a showing by us would mean a copy in Britain that remained their property, duty paid, expertly titled in English, and so should at least do their export hopes no harm.

Correspondence was not enough. Selection and negotiation meant more visits to Berlin and to Paris. The Film Society in London was the forerunner of all the other ventures of the same kind which have now proliferated into federations of countless imitators in nearly every university and substantial town in Britain, and several continents outside. At that time these did not exist, the ground we ploughed was virgin. Our policy was to concern ourselves not only with "art" but with every use of film that did not reach the commercial screen in Britain at that time. Science concerned us—eventually we showed a film called *The Equation* $\ddot{x} + x = o$ and right at the beginning Shaw sent me with an introduction to the Institut Marey in Paris for photographs of fast motion slowed down; this institute was named after E. J. Marey, the biologist whose contribution to the eventual principle of recording and reproducing motion pictures was basic, and whom G.B.S. described as "my old friend who used to drop cats upside down out of the window and photograph them as they landed on all four feet". Technique concerned us—we early showed films of making films. Antiquity—if we found primitives that had been forgotten. Even what might be run-of-the-mill commercials in remote regions—if their exoticism kept them from the market for the British screen. In dedication to this task we were not, internationally speaking, quite pioneers, but seconds. First of all in the field was the Theatre du Vieux Colombier in Paris, which had already gone over from the stage not to the "society" idea, but to concern itself with regular showings of similar film material to small public audiences. We needed its experience and its contacts, which were liberally available. It was on one of these jaunts that, to show off my knowledge of Paris to my companions, I took them to the boulevard dance hall shown me by my commercial traveller friends three months before. Here a young girl, brunette, dark-eyed, round-faced smiled at and sat with us. I found her attractive and even made an effort at a dance. Back in London, making conversation between rubbers at the bridge table with former Cambridge friends I came to recital of this incident on my last trip and one of them observed that he supposed I had gone on and slept with her. On my replying in the negative, my friend exploded: "Why not? Are you a eunuch?" I could find no logical answer to the first of his two questions and so, I suppose, to find the answer to the second, set off at once back to Paris, found the young lady and made my proposition. Since I was now in the hands of a professional, all was simple. She knew the address to take me to, she knew how we should sign in the hotel register, she guided me in that and all else necessary besides. I liked her, we corresponded, I met her once again, she wrote me that she had a young man soldiering in North Africa and sent me a photograph of herself and their son, the friendship lapsed. Altogether an adventure unoriginal, even banal, but a step in life that autobiography should not omit.

Launching a body like the Film Society had many aspects besides determining policy and choosing films. First there were the contacts in the film world. Most important to me, because later my partner over several years, was Adrian Brunel. I met him through Hugh Miller and he was the ideal man to help. He was a good deal older than I, and a mentor ready to share his knowledge and experience with any neophyte. Adrian believed—I have no idea how rightly—that he was related to the great engineer. Certainly he could easily have made up and passed for his namesake. The film industry at the time mistrusted and, except for his friends, cold-shouldered him. He was accounted a dangerous intellectual, because he specialised in satirical one-reelers—they delighted the public all right but it was then axiomatic in the trade that audiences would not accept satire and that anyone intelligent enough to be satirical was dangerous; and he had made up to now but one feature (with Ivor Novello), *The Man without Desire*, whose theme —a hero with the gift of eternal youth become at last too jaded and too old for love—was then called—"highbrow" though it would now be thought trite. He was under contract to Mick Balcon's production company Gainsborough, but intrigues kept him ever from the floor. He bore this cross with a wry courage, almost gaily, and ran his own small company—of which much more later because I joined it—in a back street of Soho. He had a wife, Babs, dark, petite, good-looking and critical—still active and alive—and a son Christopher, whom he had made into a travel short of North Africa: *The Boy goes to Biskra*.

In their flat Adrian and Babs used to run social evenings called "hate parties", to which it was a great privilege to be admitted. The participants were regulars, all in films or on their fringes. We would come on after some première, take coffee, hard and soft drinks and, sandwiches, sit around and discourse in turn on everything in cinema that we most hated: renters or Wurlitzer organs or mottled title backgrounds. Among the regulars were Mick and Aileen Balcon, Herbert Wilcox, Victor Saville, Miles Mander, Sasha Stewart the photographer and his wife Leila (publicity manager of the then chief distributors in Britain, W. & F.), Vivian Van Damm and his wife (this was long before he started the Windmill; he used to organise a bus-load to Epsom every Derby and all of us tagged along), myself (very keen) and, of course, Hell with me as soon as we were together. The discussions were not only an admirable means of letting off steam, the steam itself was packed with expertise. Everyone favoured the idea of the Film Society and all promised backing. When it came to implementing promises it was a different matter and even Adrian had to drop out from letting his name appear among the founders: incredible as it sounds, he received clear intimation from the commercial interests associated with Gainsborough that to be associated on the notepaper with a long-haired enterprise like ours would be his final tombstone. He did much better for us, undertaking that all the essential technical work of import and preparation of every film should be done by his office for a fee so ridiculously nominal it was daylight robbery of himself.

The group to carry out the job had now to be collected and this was done at Iris Barry's. She was not yet the *Daily Mail* film critic—that came after, as result of her Film Society experiences, as did her much later departure for America, and initiation of the film archive and department of the Museum of Modern Art in New York together with acquisition there of a new husband. At this time she was married to the poet Alan Porter; she was dark, slender, capable and calm with extremely well-shaped features and a crop as tight as Beatrice Lillie's or a Dutch doll's. Iris had a gypsy mother and also two children who were not living with her. She and Alan had a small house in Guilford Street, which is just within the Bloomsbury ambience. Here she threw a party where the first plans were made.

The "originals" included—besides Iris, Hugh Miller, Adrian and myself—Sidney Bernstein, Frank Dobson, and W. C. Mycroft, this last the film critic on the *Evening Standard*. All these except Adrian are listed as members of the original Council. With us were also McKnight Kauffer—almost begetter of the modern poster of the twenties—and his equally tall and handsome wife Marion Dorn, as original in carpet design; Edmund Dulac—the delicate illustrator of fine editions—and his novelist wife Helen Beauclerk; Sidney's friend Jack Isaacs—don in English at King's, London—and Anthony Asquith.

Most of these came on to the Council later. It eventually received two waves of reinforcements: one, six or seven years afterwards on my return from Hollywood, when Jack and Anthony came on with Grierson and Thorold Dickinson, Ellen Wilkinson and my cousin Nancy Samuel, Herbert's daughter; the second only a few years before the advent of the Second World War brought the Society to an end—Sidney Cole, Robert Herring of *Close-up*, Basil Wright and Elsie Cohen, the first person in Britain to try to emulate Le Vieux Colombier with a public cinema for such programmes as ours. She started the Academy Cinema in Oxford Street and handed over to George Hoellering when ill-health made her retire.

But this is for the future. Throughout we were a happy and amiable band of colleagues. I don't think anyone ever left us but Hugh Miller—and that only because he went to U.S.A. We never had a single quarrel or disagreement about anything and there were no jealousies. I had no idea how exceptional this state of affairs was, for I had no experience, and even presumed it normal where a common objective is concerned. It is possibly less remarkable that I have seldom met it since.

The real indispensables were Iris, Sidney and Walter Mycroft.

It was a stroke of luck that Sidney's imagination was struck that night in Guilford Street. He was the only one of us on the real inside of films, as well as, probably, the only person in the industry of those days who shared our enthusiasm for "the arts". As second son of his father—the eldest died in Gallipoli—he had inherited the direction of, and much expanded, a small family business selling theatre equipment and a small chain of cinemas, by then—I think—numbering some dozen or so. In this latter role, he was active as an independent in the politics of the C.E.A. —the Cinematograph Exhibitors' Association—the organisation (largely ineffective owing to internecine wars) through which the then as yet "unchained" cinema owners strove to protect their interests in their perpetual battle against the "renters", those who distributed the films the exhibitors were bound to book to keep their cinemas open. It was not that in those days he was particularly rich. Like those whose capital is "working" he rarely carried ready money because credit was usually available when needed; Hell and I have been out with him in a Soho restaurant when all three of us were exposed as penniless, each having depended on the other, and he had to leave his watch to cover the bill. But he did have something, independence and booking power—trivial though the latter would be counted nowadays when the giant circuits rule (eventually he partially linked his small chain to the largest) —which the bigwigs both feared and wanted, and this made them deferential to anything he was known to be interested in and smoothed our way. He is sufficiently well known nowadays and completely unchanged, so I need not describe him in detail as he was then. His hair was not the grey it is now, of course. But he was the same slim, tall, elegant handsome creature, with humorous eyes and a boxer's nose, liberal and enterprising in his ideas, catholic, comfortable and choosy in his surroundings, generous and loyal to friends and family, an unpredictable and nerve-racking adventure to work for or—I should guess—to live with. In short, exactly as he is today. I do not know where the Film Society could have got to without him. Anyway, through him, it got the use of the Regent Street New Gallery Cinema on Sunday afternoons for a start.

Mycroft was invaluable because he knew the minds and ways of his fellow film critics, and what had to be done to get newspaper space. I don't know if many remember him now. He was tiny and hunch-backed. Unlike many others of his profession at the time, he was really interested in films. He was a loyal friend to the Society, and to Hell and me personally, even in his own despite, as we have good cause to remember. This will appear in due course. Later on, in the thirties, I saw less of him and was astonished to be told that, eventually victim of who knows what ambition of grandeur and tiny as he was, he had taken flying-lessons with some idea of being useful to Mosley and, when war came, sought refuge in Ireland for fear of being interned. He died soon after. I never had the slightest idea he harboured such aspirations, and I remember him with affection.

For secretary, really purser, we took on Miss J. M. Harvey, who ran a concert agency in Manchester Street. I don't know who suggested her, but she was perfect. For a minimal fee she took on all the paper work, the distribution of tickets, the keeping of files. It was a wonderful thing to have an expert so good that the rest of us could forget all this and just have fun with films. After years of running us, she went over to help Miss Cohen open the Academy, staying with us as Council member.

Our registration as a company "Not for Profit" was carried out by my solicitor cousin, Walter Hart. I had not realised that we must be "Ltd." in order to enter safely into contracts, nor that it would cost so much—near on £100, I think, before all was done. We did not wish the "Ltd." to appear in public relations, it had too commercial an air for our high-falutin' "art" image; but this is easily got round: all you need to do is for the "directors" to meet as "Film Society Ltd." resolve to form and own a body called "The Film Society", and Bob's Your Uncle. Of course this means that, legally speaking, if you wish, you can overrule the members and do whatever you like whomever they elect as Council or whatever they may vote or say or do, but if you act strictly as though you had no such power, and always obey their decisions, the problem never comes up. Try to thwart them, and you would have no Society, so of course you don't. I was fall guy again, and was made chairman. Here and in table tennis I learned by stern practise the arts of procedure and compromise, how to get through agendas without steam-rollering, etc. which were to stand me in good stead for a lifetime.

As shareholders, technically "guarantors", at £1 apiece, we enlisted all the most prominent V.I.P.s of our acquaintance. These were to bring us publicity, respectability, credit. I brought in G.B.S. and H.G., Julian Huxley and Haldane, Keynes, Roger Fry, H. F. Rubinstein (whom I had met through the Stage Society) and Anthony Asquith, who was just beginning to show a film interest. Also Angus, and Edith Craig, who used to lunch in Soho at the table next to ours, and she brought in her sister Ellen Terry. Father came in and brought Lord Ashfield, who was a most useful name as at that time he ran the Underground. I don't remember others so well, although I do recall Iris brought in J. St. Loe Strachey of the *Spectator*. The only hitch was with H. G. Wells who wanted the draft of our articles altered where we had him down as "writer"; he said he should be listed as "man of letters".

Now all was ready for a lunch at 28 Kensington Court for the critics and a press conference in the library afterwards to tell the world and start collecting members. I have already said enough to show that I did not much like a lot of the critics. There was nothing personal in this—"some of my best friends have been critics"—but in those days the opportunities for corruption and venality were not only rife but hard to resist. I do not know if the same was true of the theatre, but I should doubt it; the theatre had been going longer and had had more time to develop standards and tradition. Besides there was not in the theatre the same amount of money involved, or the same barbarous arrogance on the part particularly of the American film interests. I have not the slightest idea what the position is today and my remarks should not be regarded as applicable to present circumstances. But in those days the bribery would sometimes even be direct. For example a critic would be invited to see a film and suggest a page of titles or give some preliminary advice, with no intention on the renter's part of using either, and would be paid for it a substantial fee. Or some relative of his who wanted into the industry would be found a job. Some critics were quite notorious for falling in with such methods. Once we were discussing critics at dinner with H. Bruce Wolfe, the head of British Instructional, who gave Anthony Asquith his first chance of direction on the picture *Shooting Stars*. Anthony took up the cudgels for a man we had disparaged, recalling that his notice of the film had been a very good one. Wolfe replied: "I hate to tell you, Tony, but, seeing that it was your first picture and what was involved for you so important, we did not like to let it run loose so we gave him £100." The man was critic-columnist for one of the highest-circulation daily newspapers. But there was a much more subtle kind of corruption on all big circulation newspapers and this may well yet operate in some degree. Renters take space in advertising, plenty of it. They hold that the duty of a "critic" is not to parade his own views but simply to pass on to the readers what he is told, and that, if they advertise, they have a right to expect that such information shall not be confused by personal crotchety ideas. Throughout the years there have been defiant young critics full of ideas and determination to be honest and say what they really thought. Throughout the years there have been editors who stuck by them manfully when advertisers protested—stuck, that is, until the withdrawal of advertising had gone on long enough to become a bore. Ideals unbacked by colleagues and superiors have a way of yielding to "what's the use?" and withering (as with the police lieutenant a friend of mine knew in New York who, the day he was promoted, found a thousand dollars in his drawer and, when he took it to his chief was told to shut up, put it in his pocket and not play the fool). With experience, quite a lot of critics begin to learn which side their bread is buttered on and how much the market will stand. They begin to learn to distinguish between which films will carry the big advertising and which are friendless, so that the latter can safely be dismissed with a line or so of wisecracks and earn their contemner a safe repute for "wit". I write with glib distaste about this subject, but when I, too, later became a film critic—seriatim, on quite a varied lot of journals—I found out how difficult it was, be you never so honest in desire, to treat equally the films press-shown at Theatre A, where you would be provided afterwards with champagne and a caviare sandwich buffet, and those at Theatre B, whence I had been thrown out for complaining about having been invited on a press ticket and then made to stand at the back. Great hampers from renters at Christmas were easy to deal with on the *Daily Worker*. We would raffle the turkey and the gin bottles in aid of the Fighting Fund.

Anyway Iris Barry and I did our best at the press conference. We were ably supported not only by Mycroft but by other sympathisers among the pros: I count Pat Mannock of the *Daily Herald* and Ernest Betts as among the most decent and interested, and also Jympson Harman of the *Evening News*. The two trade papers, the *Cinema* and the *Daily Film Renter*, led by the latter's editor, Ernest Fredman, were cautious from the start. They seemed to regard our exploration of any other criterion of film judgement than box-office as an intrusion not only dangerous to their readers' interests but even immoral. C. A. Lejeune, bless her, disappointed us sadly. One of the first serious, non-gossip-monger film writers—she wrote then for the *Manchester Guardian*—we had hoped for her backing. But after we had explained that the society, even if a small and private body, would at least give a few of those interested a chance to see work that would otherwise be hidden entirely, she declared with red-hot obstinacy that nothing could be of any use that was not open to the public. In a sense she was not wrong, of course; that had to be the target and when the Academy Cinema was eventually opened and imitated, and the "film society" movement itself spread in the provinces, we were able to wind up with a sigh of relief and a sense of public taste and opportunity broadened and a job of work well done. But at that time was that possible? Is it ever right to make the better the enemy of the good?

However, the ship was now launched, and the organising donkey-work and circularisation for the first voyage could be left to Miss Harvey and her aides.

The date had come round for my twenty-first birthday (23 April 1925) and embarkation on the first voyage to U.S.S.R. I had had about eight weeks of assiduous learning Russian in an L.C.C. class, from a little old emigré lady who used Berlitz methods, and also gave extra teaching some evenings to me and the cousin of one of my friends, an extremely handsome lady whose daughters were called Ann, Barbara, Catherine, Dorothy and the like—she said that she had begun at the beginning of the alphabet as she was married to a Roman Catholic. The reader surely knows Berlitz: the teacher points to various objects or acts simple movements and you must repeat her words in the language you are learning, neither teacher nor pupil is allowed to utter anything in yours. At the end of this labour I was pretty eloquent indoors and able to talk fairly freely about tables, chairs and other furniture, but out of doors could not get on at all. However, with Hungarian experience in mind, I did learn as a side bonus the names of animals and once, when called on unexpectedly to make a speech in Moscow, managed to get away with it by declaring in Russian that before I came I had been told all kinds of things, for example that wild beasts—here I put in lions, tigers, bears, elephants and all the animals whose names I could remember—walked in the streets but now I knew that this was not so and, back in London, would say so. I am not sure what the audience made of this, but they applauded anyway.

So fantastic were the tales then current about Russia that this was not altogether so far-fetched a point in those days as the reader might suppose. Before I left, my father made one last effort. I was invited to the Bank and treated to the usual excellent lunch of juicy roast beef and crackly roast potatoes in the partners' dining-room. When my father got me alone he pleaded with me for the last time not to go, assuring me that disaster surely lay ahead. He and the other banks employed a network of informants in Russia, he explained, and it was quite certain that, as soon as I crossed the frontier, I should be seized and held to bring pressure on him to withdraw his signature to the recent "bankers' manifesto" in which he and others had joined to urge the British Government not to extend any trading credits to U.S.S.R.

until the Tsarist debts were recognised. It was not necessary for them to be paid, he explained to me. They needed only to be acknowledged. If once it were admitted that a state could ever repudiate its debts simply by staging a revolution and changing its government, all confidence of investors would be at an end and where would bankers be then? He also said that the spies had reported that pestilences were widespread all over Soviet territory, so that, whether arrested or no, I was certain to catch plague.

I would not be moved. Instead I acquired from my visit a lasting total scepticism about the conclusions of Kremlinologists. I am not sure that this has been useful, for even when guessing at their wildest, they sometimes hit the bull by chance. In a longish life I have had to learn also, that even when a liar tells nine lies it does not necessarily prove his tenth tale false.

§ 17

IN THOSE days there were two ways of travelling to U.S.S.R., by sea or by land. There was as yet no air connection. I chose sea.

My target was definite and I was to make two bites at it. Hinton was writing a big monograph for the B.M. on the voles and lemmings. There is an exceedingly primitive vole, *Prometheomys*, the "Prometheus mouse"—so called perhaps because it is found in only one place in the world, the Caucasus, which is Prometheus's legendary home. So far this mouse had been recorded only from one precise locality, the Krestovy Pereval or "Pass of the Cross"—the highest point on the Georgian military road. Only four specimens had been taken and these were all in Russian museums. There were none anywhere else. Hinton wanted to see some and our expedition was to get them. In the end we came back with forty. It is now known that the animal is rather more widely distributed than was then supposed.

I have described how, during his visit to Cambridge, Tomsky, then trade union chief in U.S.S.R., had promised to intercede with the Hunter's Union for the necessary sanction.

I planned the expedition for the autumn and once again Bancroft would go with me. But I thought it much better to go out first of all in the spring, study such material as there was on *Prometheomys* and other Caucasus specimens in the Academy of Sciences Museum—the Academy was still in Leningrad, it had not yet moved to Moscow—and then go on to Moscow for a short stay to collect the various permits and "sew the last button on to every uniform", returning to pick up Bancroft and the necessary equipment when the way was properly prepared.

I scouted round for documents. I had the B.M. (N.H.) credentials addressed to the Academy. I had a letter from the then Foreign Secretary, Austen Chamberlain, to the British Chargé d'Affaires in Moscow, and another from the Soviet Ambassador in London, Bogomolov, to whomever I wished to show it in U.S.S.R. But best of all I had a letter from Peter Kapitza, the physicist, to his mamma.

Kapitza had arrived in Cambridge during my last year. It should be emphasised that he was never a refugee, he just temporarily emigrated to seek facilities to carry on his work; through all vicissitudes he kept his red passport of Soviet citizen and renewed it regularly. When the civil war came to its end he found himself with only one passion and ability, physics, and no foreseeable opportunity to indulge it for the researches he had conceived. Clinging to the roof of a train—the way most people travelled in those days—he got out to Finland and then further on to Sweden. He arrived without prospects or resources but got into some advertised talk on mathematics, took part in the discussion and shone so brilliantly that soon he was invited to give a series of lectures there himself.

He next came on to London and, how exactly I do not know, eventually discovered himself in some government building, sprawling full-length on a table before some board of experts, expounding diagrams of experiments he wished to undertake related to some unprecedented means of momentarily concentrating overwhelming electric power to establish—if only for a flash—extraordinarily strong magnetic fields. The result was attachment to the Cavendish Laboratory at Cambridge under Rutherford and investment by the University in apparatus costing a small fortune. It was here I met him, now a Fellow of Trinity. Everyone liked and respected him, including Rutherford, and he in turn admired Rutherford and was glad to work in Cambridge. When, years later than the events I describe, Kapitza returned to U.S.S.R. for a brief visit, Stalin nobbled him and would not let him out again. There was naturally a terrible outcry in the British press: how could anyone do such a thing, the work was of no military value, science is international, it is a crime to separate the scientist and his apparatus, etc. "Uncle Joe", who was evidently no believer in allowing any brain drain, called that bluff by suggesting that, if that were so, why not send the specially-built research apparatus after its inventor, Kapitza, to join the latter in Moscow? The Cavendish, to its credit, was logical and did so. Stalin had a special research institute built to take it and there, though he does travel a bit again in these softer days, Peter Kapitza still remains and works, having proved a difficult kidnappee, passing in and out of favour in part according to his own alternating moods of patience and intransigence, a patriot and a scientist who has always retained his integrity and the world's regard throughout many complications; ultra-low temperatures near absolute zero are now, I believe, his particular speciality, he is *not*—as the popular press sometimes has it—the father of the Soviet atomic bomb.

But at this period he was still quite a young man and the grand result (for me) of his letter to his mother was that she put me up, for all my time in Leningrad, in a room in the family flat.

The Soviet steamship took four and a half days from the Port of London through the Kiel Canal to Leningrad, time enough to get a small foretaste of the new world through visits to the ship's "Red Corner" and conversations with the crew. The trip was the first of the season outward and homeward since ice-breakers had broken the way through the crumbling frozen surface of the Baltic and the Gulf of Finland. Homeward the vessel was taking a handful of British tourists for a sight of the May Day celebrations. Among my fellow-passengers was a pair of middle-aged Lancashire lads—brothers—business men who always took their holiday this time of year and had chosen this one by a pencil dab at the globe in the tourist office without the slightest idea of what it would be like. The elder recited Kipling's "If" at the ship's concert and, suddenly coming to a conclusion during the local demonstration and march past outside the Winter Palace for the festivity, observed with an air of discovery: "Red's their colour, is it?"

There was still snow on the streets and roofs of Leningrad, which is then at its most beautiful. The buildings were still pitted with gunfire and cobblestones were still loose beneath the tramlines. Would-be passengers waited in queue at the stopping places, blowing on their unmittened fingers or eating warm sausages from the street-vendors. One wrapped oneself up well and got used to tramping past, defying the nip in the air that grabbed one's unprotected nose. The Academy building was picturesquely sited on the Neva embankment near the old torch-flares of the Admiralty. I presented my credentials and worked at my material with Vinogradov, a modest but extremely competent young man whom I thought absolutely first-class. I have never been in touch with him since but I have heard he is still working at mammalian systematics somewhere in his modest way. I salute him for his aid and testify that I thought him a far better man than his better-known and more showy colleague in Moscow in the same field, the celebrated Professor Ognev, author of numerous lucrative best-sellers. There was too much of the "I am *le grand maître*, respect me" about the latter, a disease several Soviet scientists had taken over from the French and, comparing specimens in the Academy collection with new subspecies he had figured, I came to the conclusion—I fear—that some of these were based upon "immatures" and that he was an even worse splitter than I.

The Kapitza family lived in the suburbs, in a flat on the interminable

Kaminostrovsky ("Stone Island") Street, as everyone still called it, though its nameplates showed that it had even then been renamed *Krasnykh Zor* (the "Street of the Red Dawn"). But at that time old Leningraders-born could not get their tongues round the new names; Tomsky, for instance, could not even manage Petrograd, he always called the city "Peter". My hosts could not have been more hospitable. There was a grown-up son, ethnologist brother of the Cambridge Kapitza, and a daughter-in-law. Their health had been ruined by privations during the famine. He showed me the museum where he worked and I thought I had never dreamed of anything like its public galleries; they were an eye-opener in simplicity, though now every modern museum follows the trend that it pioneered. The public galleries of the ethnographical departments of the B.M. at Bloomsbury at that time were mere conglomerations by comparison, so multitudinous the layman could take nothing in. How can a non-expert detect the essential form of a particular style of spoon by viewing a case in which there are 100 different spoons, and very likely as many knives and necklaces as well? Indeed, how much better off is he when he can? Here in the new Leningrad Ethnographical Museum each tribe and period had its interior and exterior family grouping, a tent, building or room with figures dressed typically, using typical furniture, equipment, tools, conveyances—a whole mode of life could be perceived and appreciated at a single glance.

I loved the rich black bread of rye. I could never get used to buckwheat—Russians still use far too few green vegetables, especially in winter when they make do with pickled cucumber. In the Academy canteen I was introduced to a pink dessert like a gummy jelly, called *Kissel* and made of cranberry. "I suppose you never have cranberry in England," Academy colleagues said condescendingly and disbelieved when I told them that, on the contrary, sauce made out of cranberries is an accompaniment of the roast turkey that is our favourite Xmas dish. I especially liked the flat omelettes that Kapitza's mother cooked for my breakfast, flatter even than Spanish ones and much thinner, with little rectangular islands standing up in them made of black fried bread or green strips of onion shoot. Mrs. Kapitza was nearly always out late. She had been to Cambridge to visit her son the year before and, as a retired teacher, interested herself in the English schools. Now, if you please, though past 60 she was giving lectures everywhere on English education, in case there was any experience or method that might strike a spark here and be adaptable. I asked her directly: "How and why do you do it? Here you are, working yourself to exhaustion and you have surely no cause to love the Bolsheviks?" One son abroad if only for the time being, another son an invalid, her husband shot—he had been a Kadet Party member of the Duma and was executed during the Civil War. Madame Kapitza, a rubicund woman of infinite motherly energy, struggled for a moment to find the words she wanted in the unfamiliar tongue. Then she burst out: "It is not a case of loving or not loving. You do not understand. Here there is something new being built by our people. It is for everybody and by everybody. How can one not take part?"

There was time to see the sights: in the Hermitage the Rembrandts and in the Winter Palace itself the apartments of the Tsars. The first-floor rooms were kept just as Alexander III had lived in them; the heavy period of late Victorianism was everywhere, not undistinguished in its magnificence, and the upholstery maintained its richness in the smaller apartments to which he promoted his princess-mistress from her post as one of his wife's ladies-in-waiting. The floor above it, that of the more conventionally domesticated Nicholas II and his family, was of an incredible vulgarity. The gushing young lady guide was determined to draw moral lessons from every object to improve us group of gapers, but they were not always the aspects that occurred to me. In the throne room was a sad sight, a beautiful Renaissance Madonna slashed with bayonets, the only lovely thing among the hideous acreages of scarlet velvet set on gold furniture frames as tangled as spun sugar. The guide explained that the sailors had swarmed into the room through the window and in their rage destroyed the first thing they encountered, the damaged picture, but had then halted thunderstruck by the grandeur and complexities of the gold work and, saying to themselves that objects constructed by such labour must not be lightly cast aside, decided to spare all else. The small family breakfast room had a chandelier that revolved as it descended to the sound of music. The guide pointed to its luxury rather than its absurdity. As we went through the bathroom, the walls of which bore family photographs including one of George V and Nicholas II together, looking like twins, there on the broad sill was a really hideous soapstone Art Nouveau sculptured relief of a lily. The guide exclaimed in her schoolmarm voice: "Look, this exquisite object was presented to the Tsar and Tsarina by the Pope. Such was their wealth they could find no better place to put it than in the bathroom." For the first and last time I sympathised with the Tsar and his wife. I could just imagine any normal couple saddled with such an object saying to one another: "My dear, where can we put this thing where nobody will see it?" But after all the couple were not normal; as the husband's diaries show they were abnormally trivial, indifferent and callous, so perhaps after all the guide was right.

I saw films, too, a straightforward simple one about Stepan Khalturin, a revolutionary carpenter who put a bomb in the palace during repairs; and plays, one called *The Empress's Plot*, which was being shown in scores of theatres at once, and which had Rasputin, poisoned, shot, strangled and stabbed by his aristocratic murderers and writhing and cursing all over the stage and coming back for more. Also there was the children's theatre, and that *was* something. As you came into the auditorium you plunged into a cacophony like the zoo parrot house. When the curtain rose this was stilled for a moment, only for the din to break out again with Beatle-fan vehemence if a crisis occurred on the stage that made further restraint beyond human, or rather infant, power. The acting and the costumes were superb, but, long before Peter Hall, there was little scenery. This made no difference to the rapt excitement of the children. When Simon Legree was bidding for Topsy in *Uncle Tom's Cabin* the children were so determined to save her that they joined in the auction, the bids rising until they grew to heights so fantastic that, to gasps of horror and disappointment, those of the children died away. That scenery is not needed for realism, and that the children's imagination supplied it, was proved by a series of paintings the directress showed us in her office, made by the children at school after a performance of another play we saw, based on the fairy-tale of *Konyek Gorbunok* ("The Little Hump-backed Horse"). When the magic horse guides the youngest son and destined princeling on his journey "across seas seven times seven and over wide lands ten times ten" the two characters hand in hand had pranced to and fro across an empty stage, but the paintings showed stormy seas, deserts, mountains and tropical jungles.

Apropos of the realistic effect of the performances on children: the Kapitza daughter-in-law told us a good story about the child of a friend, who had gone to the theatre with her school but when the wolf appeared had screamed and struggled to get out of the auditorium. The child's granny was determined that her grandchild should be sensible and not alarmed by nonsense, and so she took her to another performance of the same play, after lecturing her on the difference between play-acting and reality. This time at the arrival of the wolf the child sat quiet and good, as though the lesson had sunk in. The granny, by her side, improved the occasion by whispering: "You do realise now, do you not, that this is make-believe and not really happening?" "Yes," replied the 6-year-old demurely, "and besides, this time we are sitting in the back row."

At the Academy I was thrilled to see on the floor rough wooden empty boxes painted with the name of the great explorer Kozlov, and it was even more odd to meet an aged Prince Semyonov-Tianshansky, collateral of the geographer of that name whose discoveries in Central Asia had led to his ennoblement and the addition of the name of the mountain range to his family surname. The present prince had followed up his forebears' explorations. He was a curious old man, languid, super-elegant, with the exaggerated long finger-nails that a mandarin grows to prove he is above any form of manual work.

A few fine sunny days made me think of swimming, but the request for an opportunity seemed to throw everyone into an unexpected tizzy, and I was surprised to be taken to consult the director, another nobleman, the famous scientist Oldenburg. When the latter failed to dissuade me, saying that in the Soviet Union nobody bathed till July and August and that this was only May, to which I replied boldly that Englishmen were not afraid of cold water, he did not seem to know what to do. Wisely he sent for the office boy, and the latter seemed equal to the situation for, after some rapid exchanges I could not follow, it was agreed I should visit the lad's rowing club for my bathe the following Sunday.

I memorised my directions and duly set out on foot along the Krasnykh Zor to its end and over fields till I came to the Neva, a bridge and, a little way down the opposite bank, the club, just as I had been instructed. A crowd of several hundreds awaited me. I had not realised, what a glance at the map would have told me, that the Neva springs out of Lake Ladoga almost on the Arctic Circle, that the ice on the lake was only just now cracking and beginning to break up, that this was why *nobody* bathed in Leningrad before midsummer, and that this collection of circumstances would naturally attract everyone informed by word of mouth to see the mad Englishman who proposed to swim.

Again what could A do? He obviously could not let the side down. And so, although the river clearly contained scattered ice-floes and even, to my further alarm, a few chilly seals, I let myself gingerly over the side of the landing-stage and started swimming up-stream in the coldest water and against the fastest current I had ever met. Fortunately I had the wit to enter at the up-stream end and, after the hardest possible effort up-stream for about five minutes, just had the strength to clutch the *down-stream end* of the landing-stage as it went by, and scramble out to the murmurs—I hope of admiration but I fear of some more pitying sentiment—of the crowd.

This was my last Leningrad exploit before going on to Moscow.

Yarotsky met me in Moscow and installed me in the Savoy Hotel. I did not like this at all. It was dingy and fantastically expensive. Five shillings for a bath, half a crown for an orange. The telephone kept ringing. This was confusing anyway, for in those days the Moscow telephone had every line crossed with every other, and whenever you lifted the receiver you could hear not only several distant conversations on the line but the simultaneous music of several different radio programmes. In general I did not get on well with the telephone on this my first visit to Russia. When I did manage to pronounce a wanted number intelligibly, the operator would always say something that sounded to me like "*Pasvanila*" and I would immediately hang up. I did not know what "*Pasvanila*" meant and could not find it in my dictionary, but came to the conclusion that it was a verbal adjective, feminine in ending, and must mean "Number engaged". Only when I got back to London and my teacher, did I learn that, though my grammatical guess about the ending was right, what it really meant was "I have rung" and the girl at the exchange always says it to mean you should hang on for the answer. Further, every time I responded to the ringing in this hotel, and picked up the telephone, I was startled to hear a mysterious feminine voice say "*Ya vas lyublyu*". I knew enough to know that this meant "I love you" and assumed instantly that there must be some mistake. No matter how much I tried to explain in my halting Russian that I was a foreign visitor, that I had only just arrived at the hotel, or to say my room number, there would come that low and inviting laugh and again: "*Ya vas lyublyu . . . Ya vas lyublyu.*" Even if I hung up, the phone would only be silent for a moment and then would come a new tinkle and the throaty overture would be repeated. It was an unhinging experience, thoroughly James Bond. I complained of the hotel to Yarotsky. He excused the prices by explaining that the hotel was especially for foreign business men and run as a device for extracting from them as much valuta as possible. The mysterious ladies were apparently a form of private enterprise—not prostitutes, oh no, prostitution had disappeared as socialism advanced, but enterprise by amateurs, office girls seeking to supplement their salaries by cheering foreign visitors in their loneliness.

Anyway, I was invited to shift my quarters to Yarotsky's own two-room flat, in a building close to the Trade Union offices in the Ploshchad Nogina, and henceforward slept comfortably on the Yarotsky floor, breakfasting with the aid of his tin-opener or off his bachelor cooking. With Yarotsky I met interesting people: the mighty-bearded Losovsky who looked like a ginger Viking and was then head of the T.U. international department and, out for a walk one day, a quizzical quiet man called Peters, the Chekist wrongly identified by popular Kremlinologists as the Sidney Street Peter the Painter.

It is amazing how much you can get through when you are young and life is fresh and everywhere you turn packed with impressions. I was only about five or six days in Moscow on this first visit and it almost frightens me to count the many things that happened.

I had two errands in Moscow and, these accomplished, could then swallow culture. First I must complete arrangements for the summer expedition. Secondarily I wanted to get Soviet pictures for the coming Film Society. All else would be bonus.

A call on Tomsky and a phone call. Then to the Hunters' Union, which had a small office near one wall of the "Kitaigorod", the Kremlin-like outer curve, now demolished, which once enclosed the Tartar traders visiting Muscovy. Here I obtained licences: to hunt—which would cover mouse-catching—and for firearms.

I needed to see the zoologists and called several times at the House of Scientists in Kropotkin Street (by now I had met Kropotkin's daughter, who then worked on the *Daily Express* as a reporter, but the old anarchist after whom the street was named was dead). Here I waited and from here made my further appointments. To cross Moscow in those days was far from easy. No taxis. No private cars. No buses or Metro to supplement the trams. You had the choice of an *izvoshchik*—a driver of the kind of open cab foreigners spoke of as a "*droshky*"—a good deal slower than the tram, of humping your rucksack on foot over the cobblestones, or of waiting till the tram came by and fighting for your place.

It was a fight, indeed, to get aboard. At the more popular stops you would press and nudge and shove to get on—this had to be at the rear—and shove and press to get through the human mass en route because exit was permitted only at the front. An exception was made for pregnant women and war-disabled, who might both mount and get off at the front end, but if you were not in that state or crippled already you had to calculate nicely: press too hard and you might be ejected before your journey's end; press too little and you might not get off at all. When the scrum at the stopping-place was settled and no more could worm themselves on to the platform, the more adventurous unsuccessful hanging to the outside of the tram like grapes, the bell would ring and the car set off at first hesitantly, picking up confidence and speed.

Often it would halt with a jerk. On one such occasion, while I was still on the entry platform, the crowd swayed, and a tall Red Army man carried back with the sway pressed the elbow of a small Jewish shopper, laden with parcels, through the plate-glass at the rear. The ensuing passionate argument resolved nothing, and the tram remained stationary while a militiaman was sent for. He arrived looking hesitant and unhappy and even smaller than the little Jew. I knew that new "Militia" was old "Police" writ large, for the function of preserving People's order was necessary however much hatred had been earned by those under the old title and in service of the old regime, but I did not know how different were the new methods and approach. The legend was current that militiamen were now particularly chosen *small*, so that they should not be able to intimidate the workers it was their duty to protect. Be this as it may, this one was dwarfish and certainly not out to intimidate anyone. He inspected the damage and then took out a notebook and wet the point of his pencil. "Twenty-five roubles," he announced. "It's not my fault", exclaimed the designated offender. "I couldn't help it. That man over there pushed me." "Who? Me?" demanded the soldier truculently and at once started wriggling backwards; being thin, he was soon lost to sight. "Twenty-five roubles," repeated the militiaman. "I haven't got twenty-five roubles," said the Jew. "I didn't do it on purpose and I can't pay." "You'll have to, or the tram can't go on," said the militiaman firmly. At this prospect the compressed passengers, who had hitherto been sympathetic, began to change sides. After voluble efforts to persuade the little Jew had failed, he was shoved off on to the street. I followed, Galahad-style again, for fear injustice might be done. The tram had moved off but the argument was still in progress. I weighed in as best I could in my dog-Russian, seeking to explain that the alleged defendant was right, it had not been his fault. Both men listened to me patiently for a moment, then they gave it up as a bad job and continued their argument. "Look here," said the Jew. "I haven't got twenty-five roubles. My wages are so small that if you took me to court it would be months before the damage was paid off. What good would that do anyone? If I were sent to prison, how would that help?" His logic was impeccable. The small militia-man pondered a few moments, then tore out the page he had been writing on and shut up his notebook. "You are right," he said. The two men shook hands and walked off in opposite directions. Justice had been arrived at after all.

I had myself occasion to transgress the traffic laws. At the corner of Kropotkin Street the tram slowed down for a turn, and if you were agile enough to jump on you were pretty sure to obtain a seat. At the next stop, two hundred yards further along its route, there was always a queue and you were not even sure of getting on board. One day I yielded to temptation and jumped aboard, rucksack and all, as the tram swept by the corner. The conductor, an elderly man with glasses, asked for my name and told me he would report me to the militia. I understood perfectly well, but pretended not to. I just held out the fare. The conductor then realised I was a foreigner. His face changed, he half-saluted and said that as I was a foreigner he would not report me to the militia, but make the punishment fit the crime. I must get off again. This was the last thing I wanted to happen. There was nothing else to do but go on sitting there smiling like a zany and holding out the fare. After a time he took it and handed me a ticket with a bad grace.

As ill-luck would have it, I was late for an appointment with the film people when I left the House of Scientists the very next morning at about the same hour. I jumped on at the same place and it was the same tram. When the conductor saw me he threw his cap on the floor and tore his hair. (He really did, people often do behave as convention has it on stage or film.) Then he turned round to the other passengers and shouted: "What shall I do? What can I do? This man persecutes me by jumping on my tram every day at the same time at the same place. I tell him it's forbidden but he cannot understand a word I say. What *can* I do?" Then he promptly punched me a ticket, took my kopeks and went off muttering. I felt a heel, but what could *I* do?

I had learned such tactics a day or two earlier at the Intourist office. I wanted of course to see the wonderful assembly of Matisses and Picassos collected by the Muscovite millionaire Shchukin, then forming the Shchukin Museum. Could I? No. This was not in the least a matter of official anti-impressionist hanky-panky at that time. Not at all. Actually, when I did get in I found a lively discussion in progress in the visitors' book. The last entry but one said: "This collection is a typical example of millionaire capitalist decadence." And the next said: "And the entry above is a typical example of ignorant doctrinaire rubbish." No, rather was the obstruction a matter of simple bureaucratic inertia. The place was just closed for summer redecoration, they said. I did not believe this and insisted on looking at the outside. The shutters *were* closed. There were ladders and whitewash all about. I had to retreat but argued that I had come from many miles away and might not have another chance. Would they not let me in? I would make allowances for the untidiness. No, it was against the rule. I showed the Soviet Ambassador's letter. No use. It meant as little as the Italian Ambassador's about the shotgun had meant on his frontier two years before. The Ambassador did not know when he wrote it, they said, that the Museum would be undergoing redecoration. At that moment, reinforcement arrived in the Intourist office in the shape of an American; he was an elderly New York connoisseur, I have sadly forgotten his name. "This afternoon," he said, "Shchukin Museum." Those present shook their heads. He took no notice. "This afternoon. Three o'clock. Shchukin Museum." They still shook their heads. They explained to him in English that it was closed, would be for the summer, could not be reopened. He took not the slightest notice although it is certain that he understood every word. He took them by the shoulders, repeating the words each time more loudly, as if talking to a deaf infant. "Three o'clock. Shchukin Museum. I tell chauffeur. Three o'clock." In the end he got to the Museum and they took the shutters down. Of course I latched on to him and got to see it too. It was marvellous.

So *not* knowing a language is sometimes better. It saves you from having to accept a negative.

The Tretyakov gallery was open in the ordinary way. Here I fell permanently in love with Serov's painting "The Girl with the Peach". I do not like Repin but I can understand his at-one-remove historical significance, not as a witness to subjects, but as an example of how these subjects seemed in the eye of his period. I saw over the Kremlin for the first time and also the rather excessively coloured-onion-domed Basil tourist-trap church in the Red Square outside. On its steps I got into a theological argument with a student who assured me that in Daghestan there were members of the Communist Party who believed in God. (He was quite right, as a matter of fact, I met one later that summer, a young dude in a train, dressed with true cossack smartness, elegant leather boots to the knee, rows of cartridges on the chest, who admitted he was a Mohammedan. He was rather shame-faced too, but whether this was because of his admission or because in all his finery he was taking a basket of unruly chickens to market, was not quite clear.) The granite mausoleum of Lenin had not yet been built; Lenin was still housed outside the wall in a dark wooden temporary lodging. It was a moving experience, since many times repeated, to join the slow-moving queue and gaze on the now waxen features so well known and so often thought of. I had not expected the red colour of his beard.

Meyerhold, whom of course I wanted to meet, was away; I had to content myself with photographs of his production of *Le Cocu*. Tairov, the other theatre experimentalist famous throughout Western Europe, was in Moscow; he was a friend of my fellow language-student, the multiple mother, and I took him a letter from her. I saw productions of *Pericoli* and *Lysistrata*—the second a superb one—in the studio attached to the Bolshoi; and in the Bolshoi I was bored by *Prince Igor*—except for the Polovtsian dances—and struck all of a heap and overwhelmed by the opulence and magnificence of its *Boris*. The theatre was packed and I was inserted in a last minute place standing three deep at the back of a box. Outside the cathedral in the first act, as the Tsar appears in procession to the thunder of the music, the vast stage filled with gorgeous colour on every robe and uniform, and everywhere glittering gold and jewels flashing back the brilliant spotlights, a peasant beside me asked who it was and, on being told it was the Tsar, said, "Who? Nicholas?" I am sure my wonderment was as great.

Mostly my host was busy, but he made time to come with me to see a court. In law administration there is always the problem of compromise between professional guidance and popular participation. In England in higher courts we have judge and jury; in our lower ones the clerk of the court jollys the lay magistrates along the road they should go. In those days in the U.S.S.R. the lower courts did the same thing with a difference through three judges all equal in decision-making: one, a trained lawyer providing the know-how in the very informal procedure; the other two, workers from local factories doing an elected stint. In the one we attended the professional was a dark, youngish man in his thirties, the lay judges on each side of him an elderly grizzled woodworker and a motherly female.

As Bancroft later sagely made the point to me, you can better tell how the ordinary person gets on under any regime by sitting in at civil or criminal cases—political ones may be misleading for they deal with the exceptions.

First came an application for an affiliation order. The plaintiff was a sturdy young blonde with a white kerchief on her head. She swayed slightly and rhythmically as she stood, for she was carrying the baby in her arms and soothing it to prevent it from waking up and taking part. This, however, did not prevent her from interrupting caustically whenever the spirit moved her. She was reinforced shrilly by her mother and various neighbours who deposed to the frequency and regularity of the defendant's visits. The defendant, a rather unsavoury bullet-headed character, tried to brazen the matter out by insisting that the child could not be his, he had never stayed longer than twenty minutes. "Long enough to make three children!" broke in the plaintiff fiercely. Catching the whispers of the strangers in the corner, the defendant, with swift presence of mind, grandiloquently demanded that, with the eyes of the workers of the entire world (presumably me) now fixed upon it, the court should demonstrate the quality of Soviet justice. It did. He was adjudged to pay the plaintiff one-third of his wages.

The second was a wry case of "morning after". Two workmates, bosom pals who shared a flat, had got drunk one night, quarrelled, grappled, rolled on the floor, and the smaller had unfortunately bitten off the tip of the larger one's nose. Both were repentant, both were crestfallen. The winner (of the fight, not the action) was sentenced to what I understood to be eighteen months' hard labour. This sounded pretty severe to me, but I soon got clear that in this case the phrase really meant that he would have to work one hour unpaid daily overtime for the period of the sentence, his pay for the extra hour going direct from the factory management to his friend in compensation for the latter's abbreviated nose. Anyway, neither appeared dissatisfied and they left the court arm in arm.

Yarotsky took me to a special evening at the Bolshoi: a conference of members of the Art Workers' Union. There was a gala performance afterwards at which I had the chance to see the over-50-years-old and already legendary ballerina Geltzer. The *clou* of the evening, which got by far the loudest applause, was an acrobatic turn by English tumblers—many of them brachydactyl dwarfs—named "Boot Villa", in which they impersonated the unruly family of the nursery rhyme old woman. I had seen it often in the music hall at home used as a "chaser"—the last item of the evening put on after the main turn while the theatre empties and the patrons go. For this modest function it was ideal, as the turn had no dialogue lines and whenever you went out you missed no plot; for the same reason—its immediate comprehensibility—combined for this audience with an element of exoticism, it was itself the star turn in Moscow. I was left reflecting on the truth in show business of the proverb about "one man's meat", etc.

For the meeting part of the proceedings the great stage, bedecked and criss-crossed with huge red flags and slogans, was filled with delegates in vari-hued costume. Incongruous in this atmosphere sat the bewildered and uneasy figure of a white-collared sober-suited British trade unionist, Monty Bailey, the then secretary of the Variety Artists' Federation, who had come to Moscow to try out the suitability of the ground for his members such as the "Boot Villa" company, and found himself swept into representing international art. When it came to his turn to speak he did his best with what he knew, starting with the conventional "funny story"—the hoary one about "fish and actors" —and going on to praise, as proof of the respect in Britain for things Russian, the success of a show like Nikita Balieff's "Chauve-Souris", which was not only, of course, an emigré one but as little regarded as star material in Moscow as our "Boot" friends in the British music-hall. Luckily he had the expert help of Yarotsky as interpreter, and the latter's resourcefulness was equal to the situation. I do not know exactly how he managed the "translation" but, as he delivered it and the audience broke into round after round of applause, Monty Bailey must have been wondering what he had said.

The situation reminded me of a tale told by my hostess during an evening I had spent with a fascinating couple in Leningrad. The husband was a Scottish printer who had taught himself Karait and spent a holiday studying the culture of these rare Crimean Jews; he was now producing a Karait-Russian dictionary. The wife was a Communist and teacher of economics who had just returned from a working tour in China. The interpreter there had insisted on translating her lecture sentence by sentence, and she had been alarmed to find herself applauded after each sentence with an enthusiasm that shook the hall. As there was nothing in what she was saying that should have evoked such a reaction, she expressed her disquiet to the interpreter who replied, quite unabashed: "We in China not like dry lectures, so after each sentence I put in slogan." Possibly Yarotsky was more subtle but to the same effect.

Kalinin was there, and when he left the hall I followed to see him go. In those days Soviet leaders did not claim or receive so much ceremony as some have done later. While on stage, when about to speak he had been so beset by the cameramen's spotlights that he had tried to wave the dazzlement aside, but quite fruitlessly, for the film men were merciless. The public had to be served. Occupying a post, that of a President of the Supreme Soviet (the Russian one of six equal Presidents, the others drawn from the equal components in the Union), equivalent to that of a joint Head of State, his manner was yet utterly benign and unaffected. As he was getting into his open car at a side-door, two soldiers in the street hailed him and I overheard what passed. "Hi, Kalinich," they called, using the diminutive, "which way are you going?" On his replying, they told him it was their way too, would he give them a lift? "Jump in," he answered simply and with no more ado they did and all went off together.

In the early mornings—I wake very early—two or three times I crept out for a less eventful before-breakfast bathe, this time in the low and muddy Moscow river. Young Muscovites nowadays will hardly believe it, but there where the Park of Rest and Culture now stretches used to be a desolate wilderness of untidy turf and shrubs, with willows at the waterside behind which you could undress and where you needed no bathing-clothes. I could hardly believe it myself when in 1949 for the first time I saw the present gleaming marble-white embankment terraces, the milling crowds in the sunshine, the happy bathers and skiff crews clad in blazing green and blue and scarlet, and the parti-coloured beach balls thrown from hand to hand.

My other athletic exercise was based on the British Embassy. I had duly presented myself with my credentials and the Austen Chamberlain letter, found hard clay lawn tennis courts and performed in bedroom slippers that I carried in my rucksack. I even found a Moscow tournament about to start and got into it with my borrowed embassy racket. My participation was undistinguished and brief, for the balls were old and would not bounce; besides, the bedroom slippers kept coming off.

Robert Hodgson, the Chargé d'Affaires, was an agreeable host and appeared to talk quite frankly. In Leningrad I had made acquaintance with two of Madame Kapitza's friends who wanted to visit England. One was Samuel Marshak, the children's poet and translator into Russian of Burns and Shakespeare's sonnets. The other was Lebedev, a painter whose flat colours and experimental patterns had found an attractive outlet in combination with Marshak as the outstanding partnership in children's literature of the day. While I was in the building a message was decoded and brought to Hodgson. Their visa applications had been refused in London. Hodgson exclaimed with annoyance and asked the clerk sharply: "You told them we had absolutely nothing against these two and thought the visas should be granted?" The reply was affirmative. "London is always doing this," he grumbled. "We might just as well save our breath." This was 1925, remember, and long before Goebbels thought of inventing, or Churchill copying, the picturesque phrase "iron curtain".

Over lunch I asked Hodgson about Georgia. It was some years after the unsuccessful Menshevik counter-revolution, but it was said in Britain that there had been renewed troubles and repression there, and Hodgson had just been allowed to tour the country to investigate and report to the Foreign Office. "There is no doubt there was trouble," he replied. "The rumour got round that we were coming with a new intervention and that everyone who wanted a change should make for the Black Sea to meet us. I don't know who started it, I should like to think nobody among our lot was ass enough. But anyway some local elders and those sort of people trekked westward to mountains near enough to the seacoast to look out for the Navy coming to set them free. Of course there was nothing at all there, couldn't have been. But the same rumour will never be believed a second time, that's finished."

I asked him about the twenty-six Commissars claimed on their memorial to have been shot by the British. "Oh, I went into that. The Foreign Office asked me to when that Labour delegation got home. We didn't give the order, I'm certain, but I can understand how these people thought we were responsible. There was a local government of Mensheviks in the town and when we caught this shipload of commissars we naturally put them into their hands. We don't interfere with what an administration does more than we can help in these cases, our object is just to be sure of the place strategically and give a chance for the locals to get the government they want. A British officer was in fact assigned to attend all the meetings and see no one got up to anything silly, but the records show quite clearly that when they held the meeting that decided on the executions our own fellow wasn't there. He was rather junior and I don't know why it was; he may have been playing the fool of course but on the other hand he might just have had a cold."

I do not remember word for word these passages I have rendered here in *oratio recta*, but I am quite certain of the sense.

From this the conversation turned to the general question of responsibility for what transpires when intervention occurs, and as its consequence. Hodgson told a story of the Siberian Far East, where he had been political officer. I wish I could remember the name of the Tsarist commander. It might have been Ungern-Sternberg, but I rather think it was someone else of similar type and record. "Here was this fellow there. Quite mad he was, and a brute. He had about 2,000 Whites who were always murdering and looting. There was an American there with 3,000 and a Japanese colonel with 7,000. As senior officer with the biggest contingent the colonel ranked on top as far as we Allies were concerned. I was on my own. This White Guard fellow would of course never have lasted a day if we hadn't been there to back him; nor would the local government—most of them Mensheviks or Social Revolutionaries—whom we had put in power. The White Guard said he wanted more soldiers and when the locals wouldn't let him have them, he rounded up all the young men he could find, took them outside the city and for some reason shot the lot. Then he raided the Swedish Red Cross train and murdered all the doctors and nurses and I suppose he felt he had gone rather far. He came to me and said there had been an unfortunate incident; his men had suspected the doctors of poisoning people with their injections and lives had been lost before he was able to interfere. I didn't believe a word of it, and suggested to the American that we should get the local government to put the man on trial. He was agreeable enough, but the Japanese colonel turned us both down absolutely flat. 'What, allow the civil arm to try an officer under my command?" he said. So nothing was done about the fellow and he carried on as before. Now, would you say we were responsible or not?"

Some time later, when diplomatic relations were momentarily interrupted between Britain and U.S.S.R., Jix (Joynson Hicks) started it by seizing tons of stuff from Arcos that never produced a mouse of evidence of wrongdoing. The Soviet authorities countered at the British Embassy in Moscow and claimed discovery of innumerable files showing espionage under Hodgson. Grains of salt are probably appropriate in such cases, but I must testify I found Hodgson (afterward Sir Robert) put his problem, now as old as 1918–21 but as fresh as Vietnam, rather well. His frankness was convincing. But then I have to remember that, as my later-on colleague Alfred Hitchcock used to say, not every person engaged in secret activity wears a cap with a little "SPY" on the brim as he has to do in films to help the audience.

It was in the film world that I encountered my only rebuff. I was in

U.S.S.R. just too early to hear of either Eisenstein's *Potemkin* or Pudovkin's *Mother*, then already in the pipeline—one for Sovkino, the other for Mejrabpom, the Workers' International Relief (the English section of which was called the I.L.D., "International Labour Defence"); these were the two main film production organisations of the time in Moscow, each maintaining rival studios. In Berlin on one of my Film Society scouting trips the previous January I had attended an evening anniversary show for Lenin's death, which had given Protozanov's *His Call*—an excellent film of the Red Guard in 1917—made by Mejrabpom. I had seen there its German international boss, Willy Munzenberg, and got introductions for the Moscow visit. These took me now around the Mejrabpom studio, where *Aelita*, a sci-fic story of a spacetrip to Mars, with futuristic costumes and a comic Russian accordion player who stimulated the downtrodden Martians to revolt, was the latest bright idea. From here, and with Tomsky's blessing, I got as far as the ruling administration of the film industry, and put my case to its then chief, Shvedchikov, an ancient warrior with shaggy grey hair, abundant grey moustache and sidewhiskers and shaggy pointed beard. In vain. Complete stymie. I tried hard to explain censorship restrictions on public shows in Britain, the commercial control of cinemas and all the familiar rest, but the idea of a special society that might be outside the operation of the market, and laws that might exempt it from control or censorship, was quite untranslatable into terms credible to Soviet understanding. Shvedchikov was polite enough, but a brick wall. "We are here only to buy or sell," was his refrain. I was to hear it in one form or another from Soviet film men for the next twenty years.

Frustrated only in this I returned to Leningrad and to a really delightful surprise. My friends of the Academy had waiting for me a bear cub, captured near Ladoga only a few weeks before. It was heavy to lift but just not too big and went with me on the steamer, sharing my cabin and sleeping in the lower berth. Before departure there was a brief, unexpected hold-up: Marshak had given me a complete list of his translations from English, hoping it might melt the hearts of the Home Office visa department men. (Incidentally, not until very many years later, through Robert Burns and Emrys Hughes, did those stony hearts relent at last.) A vigilant Soviet security officer, who did not know English but was riffling through my papers, caught on this list the name of Kipling, asserted that this was a notorious imperialist whose works were forbidden in the U.S.S.R., and at once all my notes and records were in jeopardy. However, with the aid of the friends seeing me off we convinced him that *The Jungle Book* and *Just-so Stories*—the translations in question—were really harmless, but it took quite a time.

The vessel was much smaller than the one I had come on; there were few passengers and the weather was horrible. In the end no one was left in the dining-room but myself and one companion—all others were laid low. My companion was a Jewish garment worker who had received permission to emigrate. He was very interesting on the situation in the factory in which the Revolution had opened to him the possibility to work. You could not expect, he said, a whole people incited for years to anti-Semitism not to show frequent relics of that behaviour, whether or no it was officially forbidden. In his factory shop he had been persecuted by a bully who would stand over him with insults, trying to provoke him to a fight. On his complaint, the bully had been not punished with imprisonment or fine—that my fellow-passenger seemed to think would have been too much to expect—but transferred to another department, and the little garment worker accounted it a tremendous triumph that it was not he who had been thus removed, but his persecutor. At the height of the storm my now sole companion was frightfully affected, but his suffering was never so great as to prevent him crawling to the table, even if he had to do so on hands and knees clutching at the cabin furniture. I wondered at this, but he told me without embarrassment or hesitation that his friends had clubbed together for his fare, food and drink was included in the ticket, and to miss anything would be to let them down. I tell this, not as a comic Jewish story, but, as anyone who has endured sea-sickness in the Baltic will appreciate, as a testimony to the steadfastness of the human spirit.

Whenever there was a fine day, the cub would be let out and would amble about the deck. As the sea grew calmer and the passengers reappeared he became highly popular with them, but not so apparently among the crew. He was a spoilt bear. Everyone had sweet biscuits or a suck of milk for him, and, if ever he was denied, he would howl, get up on his hind legs, and rout about, with as much of his nose and fore-paws as he could get in, at the bottom of the nearest human pockets. This babyish insistence was liable to occur at any hour of day or night. It became less frequent when we reached the North Sea, however. Here Bruin slept better and was more controllable.

We were heaved-to at night in the Thames Estuary, waiting for the right moment of tide to go on into our dock, and I got into conversation with the bosun, who happened to be a Finn. We were both leaning over the rail, and moonlight broke through the clouds and made us just able to see one another as he puffed upon his pipe. "I hope the bear has not been too much of a nuisance," I remarked. "I know it behaved badly at first, but it hasn't been so noisy since." The Finn slowly took the pipe out of his mouth and then spoke. "De boys not like its noise," he said slowly. "Dey give it some brandy dat dey buy in Kiel."

The poor brute had been dazed-drunk for about three days.

At the docks the Zoo had come in answer to my wire and were waiting to take the cub to quarantine. It grew to be a fine bear, very popular with the public and up to all sorts of tricks. It did not live for many years, however, dying in the end after a bank holiday. The post-mortem verdict was fatty degeneration of the heart due to over-feeding. Those were times when the bad custom of public feeding of animals in Zoos was still permitted. I hope the animal's infantile excesses had nothing to do with its demise.

§ 18

THE SECOND journey was made overland.

Bancroft was ready and not many extra preparations were necessary. I got another Churchill shot-gun, this time not a boy's .410 but a grown-up twelve-bore. In return for lugging it some ten thousand miles I fired exactly one shot with it, the last I have ever aimed at a living creature. It was the luckiest shot possible. We used to go down from our camp at the Krestovy Pereval to wash at a brook some four or five hundred yards below. One morning Bancroft hurried up with the news that a weasel was drinking at our watering place. Wiping the sleep from my eyes I seized the gun and scrambled down the hill. Not daring to risk scaring the creature I lay down and fired from extreme distance. Even so, the straight shot I intended might have blown it to pieces and destroyed the skin. One pellet, at the extreme edge of spread, struck it on the throat as it looked up and killed it instantly, not even penetrating the fur.

I had seen one football match in U.S.S.R., a fair open game of reasonable amateur standard. To help things forward I called on the then secretary of the Football Association, Sir Frederick Wall. He was a stiff high-collared walrus sort of man but very forthcoming. He gave me training manuals to take, and refereeing charts, and an F.A. handbook in soft leather tooled in gold as a special gift with a letter of presentation. He also gave permission, at my suggestion, for me to fix up Charlie Buchan, the ex-Arsenal forward then writing for the *News Chronicle*, to go out and coach. Buchan, a man with vision, was willing to go. But this idea did not come off; it was premature, no doubt, in those days. A good few years later, in the late 1930s when Soviet standards were already much higher, I also tried to arrange a League team to tour. West Ham was willing but the Foreign Office privately advised against it. It said it "could not guarantee repatriation in the event of the hosts going bankrupt". The F.A. would not consent without F.O. approval. The "financially unreliable" hosts would, of course, have been the U.S.S.R. central sports authorities. So much for "no politics in sport". But I hope at least that the manuals were of service in those formative days of Soviet soccer.

One more liaison effort was also abortive. The Hunters' Union was anxious to obtain male setters from Britain to breed from, as they looked on British gun-dogs as superlative. Through the good offices of the Zoo, the Kennel Club put me in touch with a breeder and Bancroft and I took out two potential sires, an Irish and an English. They had to travel in the guard's van. We fed and watered them on the way, coaxed the customs to stamp their health certificates and let them across every frontier, exercised them at the principal stops right up to Riga. But it was a fated project. The Irish, a young dog of perfect grace and beauty, was so well-bred it would not mate at stud when put to the Soviet bitches; the English, more mature and a splendid gun-dog the Hunters' Union was very pleased with, was killed in a hunting accident a few seasons later.

The trip from London was uneventful except for exercising the dogs and an unnecessary quarrel at one Baltic state frontier. Here the train was kept waiting for customs examination with windows closed in case contraband might be passed to smugglers on the track. It was hot and stuffy and our refusal to shut the windows led to the stationing of an armed guard outside with fixed bayonet to enforce obedience. As hour followed hour the situation became insupportable and I swung one of our steel-studded mountain boots through the glass of a window to admit the air. We got away with it—partly because the police did not know quite what value to accord our documents, mostly no doubt because Britishers were not so easily arrested in those days.

Bancroft and I did not stay long in Moscow beyond the few hours for necessary formalities. We engaged our berths on the railway and set out southward. Everything nearly went wrong at the start. I cannot think why, but our *izvoshchik* was late at the station. As the cab came in over the cobbles, we heard the train hooting for departure. It is no more allowable for a passenger to board a moving train than a tram in U.S.S.R., but we made a rush for it, gun trailing and rucksacks bobbing. We burst through the platform gates just as the train began pulling out, but trains are (were?) very long in U.S.S.R., they take a tremendous time to get up speed and we just managed to overtake it and be helped scramble up at the end of the last car when this had gone about a hundred yards. As foreigners, we were forgiven and this time not even chided.

Train seats in the Soviet Union of those days, maybe still, were soft or hard. Soft were sometimes of international wagon-lit standard, hard were of wood. On these long-distance journeys hard carriages were arranged with three tiers forward and aft. The bottom tier was a flat wooden bench. You could get baggage under it but this was not advisable as, if the heat were working, it might scorch. Another bench would go up at night for sleeping but in the day hung down to form a back. Topmost was a rack for bags and parcels. "Soft" had a restaurant that served meals of unknown quality to its passengers; they remained unknown for we never travelled that way. "Hard" passengers had to bring their own food with them, tins and boiled eggs, tea and utensils for brewing it with water from hot taps at the station stops, and they could supplement this with cucumbers, fruit, sometimes roast chickens, and bottled "limonad" (usually flavoured cranberry) or *kvas* bought from bargaining peasants at the railside. You would pile out of the train to stretch your legs, bargain—the gap between buyer and seller would narrow rapidly at the first warning hoot, as you had to scramble aboard again when the train started slowly after the second hoot before it gathered speed.

Incidentally, I do not know how I survived my diet on this expedition. I avoided water unless it was boiled, and soft fruit of which one usually eats the skin, but for some idiot reason I imagined that if you cut the rind off melons and cucumbers and ate ices while they were still frozen, you should escape typhoid. No more stupid error could be imagined. I devoured these substances in bushels yet remained unscathed as by some miracle.

At least we were young and fit and had our own eiderdowns packed in the rucksacks as usual. We travelled hard to save money and it was not uncomfortable. The trains were orderly by now. Each long-distance passenger out of Moscow had his numbered place, two to a bottom bench, to allow for stretching top or bottom when the top came down at night. This meant plenty of room in the day-time although you were expected to crowd up a bit and make room for elderly short-distance daytime passengers from among those who might crowd the corridors with their bundles, joining the train between intermediate stops separated by only a few hours or hundred miles.

The journey was quite agreeable. No one who has only travelled by railway in Britain can have any idea of its equivalent across the vast distances in Russia. I have never made the Trans-Siberian journey—this southward one was scheduled for some five days. The nearest thing to it in Britain is, I suppose, the stretch between Wick and Inverness that has to be enlivened with whisky, but even that is only some ten hours starting and stopping, not the endless forest or the interminable steppe. In Britain you pass the time behind your book or newspaper; a fellow-traveller is typically a resented interruption. A Russian train journey is like shipboard; you join a new community, you make friends. You struggle along the corridor and in a compartment two carriages away see two men engaged in a chess game. You stop to kibitz. After a time one of them looks up. "You play?" An appointment is made. The player looks at his diary. "Next Tuesday? No? Wednesday morning then?" There are no next Tuesdays or next Wednesdays on the few hours' journey that is all the narrow island of Britain can accommodate.

If you keep eyes and ears and mind open, humanity will be revealed to you. Bancroft had not prepared with even my few lessons, but he knew other languages as I did and, most important, a chore no intending visitor to the Soviet Union should neglect, he had of course mastered the Cyrillic lettering: what with words like "Restoran" and "Apteke" and "Parikmakher", anyone capable of applying himself to crossword puzzles will find the difficulties of orientation easier if he can only manage this much. We met interesting people; for example the chess-player was a quiet man, for all the world a sedentary, clerkly type with confident twinkling eyes, who had been a partisan hero in the Civil War and was now an economics expert with the budget of Moscow Soviet at his fingertips. Of contrasting kind were two brothers, Nepmen, who were able to tell us how local financial administration worked from the opposite side. It was still NEP time—that of the New Economic Policy that Lenin instituted to get quickly out of the hardships of "war communism" and utilise the services of old entrepreneurs and experts without letting capitalism return. The brothers told us that there was no fixed total of taxes. They would have to go regularly to the financial authorities, when their taxes, "voluntary contributions to the Red Cross" and the like would be assessed. If they found that their business really could not bear the impositions, and they took their books back to the tax departments and could prove that they really *would* have to shut up shop if the total burdens were not reduced, they might get an alleviation. But they had to be very convincing. Usually, if they asked: "What will happen to us if we do not pay the full 'voluntary' contribution?", the department experts would grin and reply: "Well, remember it's entirely voluntary." They would take a good look at one another, each side at each, and go on paying the full sum.

The only excitement occurred after we passed Rostov. The lights were put out and Red Army men came through the train, making us lie on the floor. There were bandits on the plain around here; they said, and sometimes these would take pot-shots at any lighted window. We passed Narzan in the North Caucasus foothills, a name of power for us because the best and purest mineral water—better said, the least flavoured, the likest to English sodawater—comes in small green bottles from that spa, and finally to Vladikavkaz, "Master of the Caucasus", now called Ordzhonikidze, after the famous one-time comrade of Stalin who was born there. The railway goes on eastward till it reaches the brink of the Caspian and flanks round the eastern edge of the Caucasus on the coastline there, descending southward past Baku, and coming back then westward towards Tiflis, the capital of Georgia, in the shape of a great horseshoe lying on its side. But we had now to get out at Vladikavkaz, for this was the northern end of the Georgian Military Road, built with such effort in the nineteenth century to subject the tribes—southern end being Tiflis. No railway directly crosses the mountains, the pass we sought is about half-way along the military road.

Vladikavkaz was a quiet, old-fashioned city. The stone walls of the big University building bore the usual pock-marks of revolutionary fighting. Here we added to our team a then youngish professor of zoology named Turov and his lab assistant, an old man with experience, to supplement our own labours in preparing skins.

We did not hire special cars for the road journey. Big lorries with jumbled passengers and luggage plied like buses from north to south and back. You could usually get on them and, if you did not wish to wait for them, for short stretches you could hire carts. The scenery was, I suppose still is, some of the most beautiful in the world. The road winds gradually along the mountainside, climbing with the river and above the riverbed, every here and there turning in hairpin bends above sheer precipices or disappearing into short tunnels, where steep slopes above are liable, in the wrong weather, to send avalanches tumbling down. Further south than the Swiss Alps, the Caucasus snow retreats higher, but the peaks too are higher, therefore even in midsummer the tops remain glittering white. Caucasus ranks as Europe, so the highest mountains in Europe are here, not in Switzerland: the No. 1 El Brus, not a difficult climb; the No. 2 Dikh Tau, on the record as having killed people; and the third, Kazbek, quite near the road here, symmetrical and almost sugar loaf, reputed easy. The lorry passed eminences on whose rocky crests are poised ruined fortresses, the haunts of chieftains who pounced down on travellers in the past. As it went through villages, barefoot children danced out behind it in the dust, shouting and clamouring: "*Davat dyengi!*" "*Davat kopeki!*" "*Davat karandash!*" "Give money! Give kopeks! Give a pencil! Give, give, give!" These words were not spoken in the children's own language, for they were Ossetians, but they were tamed enough even then to know Russian cries that the passengers would understand. At first I was embarrassed and considered priggishly: surely after as many as eight years from the revolution children should have more dignity than to beg? Then I reflected that, after all, what they were doing was simply helping to redress the imbalance of cultural and living standards between town and country, which was good Party policy, without putting extra weight on an overloaded transport system. Then I ceased being a fool and cut up pieces of pencil to throw overboard at the next village.

The pass lies at 8,000 feet. It had a single wooden hut with bare benches, a stove and a samovar. We unrolled our bundles within it for a longish stay. For under the turf exactly here had been taken the few *Prometheomys* so far known. This was the type locality, we must be able to find more. We did at once find burrows, long and complicated, not so deep as those of *Spalax* (*Prometheomys* is a much smaller animal and rather less adapted to its underground existence, its eyes are small and weak but do just open through the skin). Would it this time be the same story of frustration once again? We dug and dug. We enlisted four local poor peasants to help us, under a small man who had been to Mecca and was therefore suffixed with the name of Haj. In vain. The soil was not hard, the burrows were easy to uncover, we tried to outwit the voles by digging from several directions simultaneously, but they were always off and away before our trenches met.

The days passed. We lived hard but not insupportably. We had tins, and a special hard "expedition" bread we brought from Vladikovkaz, which starts hard and stays hard and never gathers mould. My only grumble was that as usual I did not like tea, I liked water. But this time I had to lump it, for either I must drink tea as everyone else did—or wait until others had drunk it, wash out the cooking vessel—we had only the one—reboil it full of water a second time for myself only and wait till *that* got cold.

A council of war. Time was passing and money going. I brought out a desperate plan: suppose I were to cadge a lift on the next passing lorry, go down into Tiflis, and try with my documents to coax out of the command there a dose of poison gas—surely they must have some—and bring it back for inserting down the burrows with piping, wouldn't that drive the animal before it into the fresh air? Surely that must do the trick?

It sounded rather a Heath Robinson idea but what other course was there? We so agreed, and I was waiting for the vehicle next morning when along came a bearded farmer with a captive in a huge earthenware vessel. He lifted the lid and there at the bottom was a cowering long-tailed field-mouse: interesting certainly but not what we had come so far to seek. Yet I felt the moment was crucial. We must not send our visitor away unrewarded. We tried again to describe the beast we needed but bought this one meanwhile. We paid 25 kopeks—about sixpence at par.

The lorry wound its way on and down through the hills into Georgia. First, as the river on this side broadened, the valley disclosed it trapped by a great hydroelectric station: a clear instance of the policy of that day of diverting Union funds for investment in the industrial expansion of the constituent peripheral republics beyond the measure of their own means and taxes. Further on the Georgian lowland becomes sun-hardened and semitropical. We stopped at an inn which boasted a pet bear, and, with revived talk of bandits, a posse of cavalry arrived to escort the lorry along the final stages into town.

In summer in Georgia the sunshine blazes, each day hotter than the last. Everyone is clad in white. It was the first such country I had ever visited and I, as a northerner, disapproved tropical ways, measuring what I saw in Tiflis by puritanical and energetic standards appropriate to a harsher clime, instead of making allowances for the hot rays beating down. I was shocked at the universal custom of the *siesta*. Shops would shut between twelve and three, office inmates look at you with positive hatred if you appeared between these hours. Flies covered all particles of food uncovered in the sunshine. Plump, motionless figures sat sheltering half visible in doorways, clad in singlets and seeking darkest shadow. Nevertheless my documents, particularly a letter from Tomsky, brought me into the building of the Party headquarters. I asked for, and was led into the presence of, the General Secretary of the Transcaucasian Federation (Georgia, Armenia and Azerbaijan were not yet separate Union Republics). The Secretary proved to be an elegant and extraordinarily handsome dark young man, as graceful as a Borzoi and with the same pointed features. It was siesta time and he was lying on a couch being massaged very expertly by a muscular man who looked like a wrestler. When I explained my errand, he sat up and laughed but by no means rejected the idea. He thought it should be possible and would speak to the military commandant. We agreed that I should return to the pass next day, find out if the position were unchanged and send him a telegram. He would then see what could be done.

After replenishing funds at the State bank next morning by means of a letter of credit, I boarded another lorry to go back the way I had come. It was evening by the time we reached Krestovy Pereval and outside the hut I could make out an extraordinary sight. Peasants of every shape and age, casting shadows far down the slope, were standing in queue bearing animals for us. Some had dead ones in bags, others live ones in pots. Inside the hut Bancroft and the Professor's elderly lab assistant were skinning for dear life, trying to keep up with the dead arrivals, or improvising accommodation or food and water for those that were still alive. My intuition had been sound. The twenty-five kopeks had been decisive: the field mouse had been a test case and its purchase had turned the tide. What I had not realised on this expedition was that you must understand your market: you can offer too much and arouse scepticism, just as you can offer too little to make it worth anyone's while. We had spread far and wide when we arrived that we were ready to pay five rubles for *Prometheomys*. What was ten shillings to us, in relation to the whole cost of the expedition or even the expense of waiting days in vain? But it was evidently a local fortune, impossible to credit, and the talk of such sums a proof that these strangers must be mad. Mad or not, when the cash proved real and not a rumour, we were clearly worth humouring.

The animals already brought included many of no great interest—specimens of species widely distributed, already in many collections and well-studied; but they also included *Prometheomys*. And so it continued on the succeeding days. Wider and wider spread the news that we really were mad, that we really were buying mice. We learned of pockets of *Prometheomys* in other alpine meadows, several miles away. More and more benefactors came, we could not keep up with them, and to cap all at last our digging party struck oil, Haj produced a captive of its forks and spades in triumph, we had to buy vodka and celebrate with a dance.

We were paying twenty-five kopeks for ordinary mice, from one ruble to five for the real thing, according to quality; we had by now young *Prometheomys*, adolescent and fully adult. What we would have liked also would have been embryos; but no females were pregnant and it seemed possible that their breeding might be seasonal. We had about two dozen or so skins and skulls, and a dozen healthy-seeming live ones, which we sent down to the Museum in Tiflis with careful instructions on how they should be kept alive. We ourselves fled back northwards to do some more collecting elsewhere. We wished to escape drowning in varieties of which we had already sufficient, though even then, for some days, optimistic peasants sent more sacks and parcels after us by the daily lorry.

The professor and his lab man went back to Vladikavkaz. We stayed on a few days about midway, in a meadow at the very foot of picture-postcard Mount Kazbek. There was an old mill there, long unused. Its innards were dark, cool, full of the fine scent of rotting wood and the dust of departed flour. I have never known anything like it outside fishing for mackerel. We had twenty or thirty breakback traps to put down and the rodents were so numerous that, long before you got to the end of the line of traps, you could hear the preceding ones you had set click-clicking as they snapped. If you did not complete your line and get back to the start quickly the voracious creatures had eaten every trace of their companions except perhaps a paw or foot that might have happened to get held beneath the sprung wire. The species present were long-tailed fieldmice, voles and smartly-patterned tiny light grey and black hamsters with exceedingly sharp teeth.

After two or three days of this, Bancroft and I went on to Vladikavkaz and then took a crowded train (where we met the Muslim from Dagestan) to try trapping in a new direction, westward along the flat plain north of the Caucasus as far as Nalchik.

This town was in a curious state in 1925. It is the capital of the autonomous region of Kabardaya-Balkarya. That summer at least it was unbelievably chaotic and disordered, backward and dirty beyond anywhere we had yet been. I was astonished to hear from Eisenstein not quite a dozen years later—he had just visited it in connection with some film project (I think *Bezhin Meadow*)—that by then it had become under its local leadership a sort of paradise on earth, the object of jealousy from all the regions round. When we were in Nalchik there were all kinds of odd people about, many of them foreigners, giving themselves out as Red Cross or some kind of philanthropists, speaking in various tongues and running down everyone. We did not find it easy to get facilities, either lodging or transport to work trapping lines outside the town. The weather north of the Caucasus had broken. Duckboards speedily became as sloshy as the puddles they were supposed to cross. While we were pondering our next move, Bancroft and I had a touching encounter. Filthy, mud-bespattered, dishevelled, with scrubby beards, we were standing more or less aimlessly outside the wooden fence of a barracks when a tall Red Army man under the decorated and slogan-clad entrance arch hailed us, and we got into conversation. He asked us what we were doing and we replied, truthfully: catching mice. At this he blushed deeply, said that he was a Pole and that he too knew what it was like to be in a far country and without money, thrust his hand in his pocket and gave us a ruble. He had evidently taken our remark in its literal Shakespearean sense. In this case A's course is clear; not to embarrass the maker of so human a gesture he must accept the gift and leave as soon as possible.

This we did, resolved to cut our losses, get down to Tiflis, assemble our collections and concentrate on getting them safe back to England.

In Tiflis we found it possible to clean up a bit and trim our beards, mine black and struggling to grow back into the skin as usual, Bancroft's blond and Saxon. It was still terribly hot—I learned here the Russian words for such weather: "*ochen zharka*", "very roasted". Only the night was bearable. By night amid bright lights a perpetual outdoor fête was held in a long pleasure ground, with sideshows and arcades, sticky sweetmeats and a great deal of gambling. A German trade union delegation was visiting the city and by day we saw a procession, headed by plump, sweaty white-clad Georgian office-workers with watch-chains, bearing a banner: "THE PROLETARIAT OF GEORGIA GREET THE PROLETARIAT OF GERMANY." In one point, Georgian nationalism had scored a notable triumph. In the museum the labels, formerly in Russian and Latin, had been replaced. All were now written only in Georgian, so that the whole collection of antiquities had become anonymous and useless to any outside visitor. To keep off the heat, Bancroft and I delightedly bought straw sun-hats with huge brims that we caught sight of hanging up outside some shops. It was only when children began to treat us like Elisha, and follow and point and laugh at us in the street, that we discovered they had never seen humans wearing such things before; these were the sort of sunhats you buy for *horses* and cut holes in for their ears to come through. Worse still befell when we tried to negotiate our tickets and make arrangements for the baggage transport. In whatever land I had been hitherto I had made a point of learning from the dictionary at least two expressions: "please" and "thank you". Of course I mastered these also in Georgia and it was only after many times the two of us going into offices, me bowing and delivering my polite opening gambit, only to find ourselves left to stew on our feet for hours without attention, that I learned that my phrases painfully memorized were used only by beggars, and that those hearing them—adding these to our appearance—had drawn the obvious conclusion.

We were standing in a line outside the ticket office of the main station one day, mercifully in the shadow of its roof, when we got into an argument about our answer: "Anglochanin" ("Britisher") to the question what nationality we might be. This seemed to puzzle our interlocutors. How could my companion and I each answer identically, he so fair and I so dark? An animated Jew with short black beard standing just in front of us seemed to understand and started explaining immediately. The Soviet Union was different from England, he said. It consists of many nationalities. All were Soviet citizens, but if asked for their nationality would reply "Russian", "Georgian", "Jew", "Ossetian"—whichever they happened to be. Whereas, in England, whatever you might be you always replied "Englishman". This account was near enough right, granting that our Georgian Jewish friend could not be expected to grasp the subtle differences of Scot and Welsh, etc., which must seem as meaningless at that distance as most of those in U.S.S.R. do to any of our B.B.C. commentators, who blanket everything with "Russian". However, it was so confusing to others in the queue that the affair grew heated and presently someone fetched a militiaman who demanded: "Political discussion—who is the ring-leader?" At this there arose a hubbub, utterly bewildering to the would-be guardian of order, and, in it all, the small and blinking Jew—just as on the Moscow tram—seemed likely to get thrust forward as the scapegoat. "Religious argument—just as bad," the militiaman announced when he managed to get a word in edgeways. Our Jewish neighbour protested even more excitedly. He had not been trying to arouse differences, he insisted. On the contrary, he was explaining that all should live together without them. At last the militiaman held up his hand and delivered a Solomonic verdict. "In the Soviet Union all are the same," he proclaimed. "Russian, Ukrainian, Georgian, Jew—all the same. This discussion will now cease." And he stalked away. Not one hundred per cent satisfactory, perhaps, but a good deal better than a pogrom.

In the end everything was fixed up, if not quite satisfactorily. The skins and skulls were safely packed. There was difficulty with the live *Prometheomys*, however. They had been confined in two big cages; fights had occurred, with dead and injured. Only eight or nine survived. We tried to solve the problem by having special cages made; each was smallish but with plenty of room to accommodate one alone and in these the survivors were placed separately. This took several days and gave Bancroft the chance to rush down to Yerevan in Armenia and see Ararat from afar, while I stayed to supervise the new vole accommodation. When he got back a battle ensued with the railway authorities. In no circumstances might we, as we had wished, transport the animals in our own compartment. They must go in the luggage van. Our documents were useless in this contest. No doubt the authorities were wiser than we and knew that, had we attempted to take them with us, either we or the animals would have been lynched by our fellow-passengers before we left the regions of fug and heat. The *Prometheomys* must travel as other baggage did, but it was granted, however, and signed and sealed in new documents, that we should be allowed to visit the van to water and feed our charges at every regular stop.

The railway to the east, then north at the Caspian through Baku, then west again and at last north-west up to Moscow runs for its first long hours across the arid desert. The carriage was packed and sweaty, the van an oven, a tin hell on wheels. One or other of us had to journey in this oven *the whole time*. What caused this was entirely our fault, mostly mine. *Prometheomys* is a big vole, not quite as big as a rat but a fair size. It probably uses incisors and front claws in burrowing. It has a nasty bite. I had felt this already, and did not want a repetition. Feeding the beasts too cautiously, I let one get out. Then another. Then I think Bancroft lost one. In the end several of our precious cargo were loose among the trunks and sacks and packing cases. We put down food and water for them but it was quite impossible to upturn everything in the hope of recapture. Nevertheless we dare not neglect any opportunity and stayed, watching, in the forlorn hope of a bit of luck, *locked in*, because the railwaymen, bound by regulations, were obliged to lock all doors of vans containing registered consignments. No luck at all, but whenever we reached a station at which something was taken out, the railwaymen, despite the difficulties this created for them, at our plea opened only one door each time, and here we poised like hawks ready to dart if any vole tried to exit.

I had wired ahead to notify Yarotsky of our predicament, but not even I had dared to hope for what actually happened when we reached

Moscow. The luggage van was detached, moved to a quiet siding, surrounded by a squad of Red Army men armed with rifles—they still wore those romantic Civil War cloth caps, patterned on ancient renaissance helmets, with a vertical cloth spike rising from the centre, and a cloth neckpiece simulating chain mail over the neck behind. The doors were opened and each sack or piece of luggage carefully lifted out one by one while we watched at the doors until the van was empty. The two or three loose voles remained in the bare van, safe and uncrushed, so that each in turn could easily be isolated and replaced in its proper cage. For that our national collection owes due thanks to the Soviet Trade Unions and Communist Party—as well as to the Red Army.

In the hotel we made two discoveries. First, that one or two of the voles had died: why? On examination the fur of every live vole was found to be covered, literally covered, with parasites, a seething crowd of fleas and ticks. What was causing this? The surviving beasts themselves seemed lively enough. Could, however, this state be connected with the fatal illness of the others? I came to the conclusion that this was a possibility. Maybe in nature the increase of parasites is held in check by rubbing off on the sides of the burrows, or even mutual grooming, as with monkeys. Each host alone in a relatively wide cage, there had been nothing to prevent multiplication of its passengers. I could get no advice from the Moscow zoologists, but I knew that insects could be killed by alcohol. I took a thin soft paintbrush and painted the coat of one of the surviving *Prometheomys* all over with 100 per cent alcohol. The poor creature shivered, and died within about ten seconds. Of course the evaporation rate of alcohol is so fast the animal must have been mortally chilled at once, and this I should have foreseen. I could think of nothing else to do but get home as fast as possible and hope.

The second disclosure was that we ourselves had become just as lousy as our charges. Writing up my notes on the desk in the hotel, I ran my fingers through my hair as usual and saw, in the light of the desk lamp, thick showers of crawling animals, mostly ticks, descending on the notebook. Frantic telephone calls conveyed warnings to, and made appointments with, the hotel hairdressing department. A courageous woman *parikmakher* handled the problem and shampoos were carried out by repeated kneadings with soapy water hotter than we could properly stand. This did the trick, but of course the voles could have borne such treatment of their whole surfaces no better than cold.

We were now presentable again, and down in the dining-room

found Keynes with Lopokova, who had brought him on his first visit to see her homeland. Keynes was boundless in his praises for the trains we had endured so long. He said that he had had no idea that a broad-gauge train that travelled so slowly resulted in so smooth and agreeable a motion. He proposed to reverse the tendency of British travel and introduce at extra prices ultra-slow ultra-comfortable specials for the ultra-rich. At any rate this seems more sensible than all the expensive rattle-trap haring about just to save an extra half-hour wasted at either end.

The formalities of exit papers took some days more. Bancroft spent these in exploring the shoe factories, then pretty rough. His reconnaissance paid off in benefits to the British balance of trade thirty years later. I loitered in a place called the "Ethnographical Shop", buying coloured silk-embroidered Central Asian skull-caps—"*tubetais*"—for souvenirs, and for a vast sum—nearly all my remaining rubles—a wondrous robe in broad stripe upon stripe of brilliantly blended hues and softly watered silks, reputedly once property of the last Emir of Bokhara—as a parting gift for my late inamorata, perhaps to prove to her that she was losing a man of taste. (I am ashamed to say that I now wish I had kept it; it would have just done me as a dressing-gown at my present size.) On our last day we got into talk with two nice girls in the hotel restaurant, and Bancroft improved the shining hour by an interrogation to discover how woman's rights worked out locally compared with Britain. We discovered, I think, that all jobs were open to Soviet women, except coal-mining and cavalry. With a touch of priggish Cambridge classicism Bancroft presently observed deadpan: "You know, of course, that women have no souls." The dark girl fixed him straight in the eye and returned: "Exactly like yourself."

Even these short delays were too long. Nothing arrested the fatalities among the *Prometheomys*. We preserved the bodies in alcohol for post-mortem dissection. The last victims died the night before we left Leningrad for London.

The post-mortem at home eventually produced a verdict of lung infection, similar to tuberculosis. It was conjectured that this might have been a result of taking a highly specialised underground animal to latitudes much higher, and therefore colder, than it was accustomed to, or else of taking a mountain animal down to lower levels.

Our difficulties were not yet quite over. The customs officers who boarded the boat in the Thames were adamant in demanding duty on our jars of alcohol. We argued that this was absurd. Our imports were clearly scientific specimens. Who would drink spirit with voles in it? They brushed aside the Austen Chamberlain letter although it had his signature and was on Foreign Office notepaper. What made them so aggressive and so obdurate? I have no idea. What I do know is that during an interval in our dispute two pressmen who had come on board the Soviet ship looking for copy sidled up to me. One said: "Bit of trouble, eh?" I replied in a loud voice: "No, nothing at all. Just a formality. It will be all right in a moment." The two withdrew. The customs officers, who had overheard, came back at once. The senior touched his cap: "Thank you very much, sir, for not talking to them. Your stuff is O.K., sir." And they chalked everything. From that day on I should have modified my aversion to what, when one is oneself its victim, inevitably appears the unnecessary vigilance of my press colleagues.

The end of our voles was sad, but that the expedition was not wasted may be verified by anyone who bothers to look up Hinton's monograph (pub. B.M.(N.H.), 1926), page three.

§ 19

THE AUTUMN of 1925 was taken up with two developments. I crept into the film business and I met Hell.

But first to speak of the opening of the Film Society's season and of two unexpected difficulties that had to be overcome. One related to film censorship. We were surprised, in our naïveté, to discover how the law stood on this. At the time it had been quite unknown to us, as indeed it was to most people. Censorship of plays had been specifically established, and exercised for centuries by a court official, the Lord Chamberlain. As readers will know, it has only recently been abolished. The Lord Chamberlain, while he could be relied on to protect the establishment from criticism or contempt, and those who cherished social convention and morality from shock, was broad-minded in other ways. Thus, in the late nineteenth and early twentieth century the Lord Chamberlain vetoed Bernard Shaw's *Widowers' Houses* and *Mrs Warren's Profession* and kept out of the regular theatre much of the septic influence of Ibsen. On the other hand when the tenant of that office happened to be staying at Townhill during a furore about a new spectacular called *Decameron Nights*, and had just paid a much-publicised visit to the theatre to see for himself what was going on, we asked him what he intended to do about it. "Nothing," he replied firmly. "Girls' bottoms are girls' bottoms wherever you see them."

The theatre owners and theatre managers loved the Lord Chamberlain because his existence and advice safeguarded them from prosecution and saved them from unwanted quarrels with their audience. For this reason they set themselves to oppose and succeeded in thwarting every movement for reform until 1968. But the Lord Chamberlain's writ ran only in the public domain. The situation was saved from being unbearable to ambitious young playwrights, and to highbrows wanting to stage and see notorious foreign importations, by the fact that the law remained uninterested in "private" performances, and the Lord Chamberlain—not out for work or trouble—was quite content that anyone who wanted to be, or even to pretend to be, a theatre club should act as a safety-valve to take the pressure off himself.

The Stage Society was the oldest and most respected of the private societies fulfilling this function. We had assumed that any enterprising public-spirited characters would be free to fulfil the same role for films. We were wrong. The law turned out to be quite different. There was, in fact, no law at all of film censorship. The British Board of Film Censors, which exercised the function, was simply a group appointed and paid by certain trade interests to exercise self-censorship, and was tolerated by the authorities as a convenience. This is still, roughly, the position. It had come about in the following way.

In the year 1909, in the wake of several cinema theatre fire disasters, my cousin Herbert Samuel, then Assistant Home Secretary, had piloted through the Commons a bill which later became law as the Cinematograph Films Act "to protect audiences against fire". To ensure that the design of buildings used for film showing should be adequate, that no obstructions should be left in the gangways, that standard fire-fighting applicances should be available, the local authority was given powers to licence the buildings in which film shows were given, and to lay down appropriate conditions for the licence.

Although nothing whatever was said about censorship in the bill, or in the debates on the bill when it was being discussed during its passage through parliament—as Herbert assured me and as *Hansard* confirms—nothing was said about censorship *not* being within the conditions that the authority laid down and, not for the first time, when eventually a test case was fought, the courts construed the bill not by what had been said about it during debate but by what appeared in it in the text, and the local authorities were held entitled to include conditions of censorship in the terms of their licence grants.

Only . . . Only, of course, it was impossible for the local authorities themselves to exercise such powers. Had they attempted to do so it would have meant for each a costly apparatus and staff for full-time viewing of many hundreds of films throughout the year, it would have meant the distraction of councillors all day from all their other business. Further, it would have meant film distribution becoming economically impossible; no cinema manager would be able to book a film ahead, not knowing in advance whether local quirks might not arise to prevent him showing it. Accordingly the local wiseacres put their heads together with the trade and came up with the answer: a private board paid and appointed by trade interests on whom the local authorities would devolve the task of viewing. This arrangement was qualified in two ways: first, the courts did hold that, though the local authorities might devolve their tasks, they could not devolve their responsibilities

—therefore the sponsor of a film might appeal to a local council against the trade board's ruling *if* he wanted to undertake the high expense of doing so in each separate area of local authority (it was sometimes commercially worth while with a film that had a special exploitation angle, e.g. an "educational" against V.D. for example); second, since there was no time to arrange Board or any other viewing of news reels before showing and keep them topical, for this class of film the requirement of censorship was just forgotten and no one bothered to submit news reels (this did not prevent, of course, the censor Board or local authority from coming down arbitrarily on anybody they disliked who might use the same material perhaps in a different arrangement at a later date).

To our surprise, we discovered that the Cinematograph Films Act, 1909, exempted not private performance, as did the theatre laws, but only performance in private houses. With an Act intended as a measure of fire protection this may be understood as reasonable. But since very few private houses possess rooms large enough to give an adequate projection throw and accommodate more than a few persons, this completely removed from the realm of cinema the freedom that such a body as the Stage Society enjoyed for enabling study of new work on the stage. This circumstance was even worse in cinema than it might have been in theatre, for two reasons. First, the Lord Chamberlain was often a cultured, educated man with civilised standards. The British Board of Film Censors, though some of its employee-examiners were men of great intelligence and wide knowledge, were employed on behalf of a trade concerned only with money; its dominant renters ruthless showmen who mostly made vulgarity and ignorance a virtue, its cinemas owned often by illiterates incapable of engaging in a contract otherwise than by subscribing their mark. The example of the urbane Mr. Trevelyan of today can provide no inkling of the crudity of his predecessors' modes of operation yesterday. For one thing, the Board of those days was unwise enough to make available a printed list of exceptions that would disqualify a film: miscegenation—*Othello*, for example, would have been precluded; no doctor, clergyman, schoolmaster, police official (there followed a long list of equally sanctified professions) might be represented in any role that might hold him up to derision or discredit—*The Doctor's Dilemma* or *The Private Secretary* would have been definitely out. "Notorious crimes" came under another ban, at least until many years after all concerned with them were dead; *The Great Train Robbery* of recent times would have been out of the question. Two persons of opposite sex, even if married and long past any imaginable age of effective performance, might not be represented together on one bed; unless—in obedience to what feat of mental gymnastics can hardly be imagined—one partner had at least one foot at all times on the floor. And here is where the second reason deriving from the difference in legal status came in. The Lord Chamberlain, being established by law, had authority beyond mere certification. He could allow certain plays as a whole or in part—i.e. gestures, phrases—conditionally, that is, provided their producers undertook to present them with modesty, in a particular way. The Board could not. Having no legally defined authority, operating on tolerance as servants of the industry only, with no direct excuse for existence except the tenuous reference in the licence clause, the film censors had themselves no means at all of controlling presentation. The Board foresaw, and here it was doubtless right, with the industry as it was in those days, that if it allowed the slightest exception to its rigidity this laxity would be exploited; one single scandalous frame overlooked and this would certainly be the one to be blown up on every poster and displayed in the "stills" outside the hall. Even the cuts themselves were often made use of in this way. Those who in 1968 have noticed the paperback of "Oedipus—the story of the man who married his mother" accompanied by a photograph of two pink nudes will no doubt get my point.

Things being so convenient for "commerce" in those days, the set-up so satisfactory for those who had enjoyed an exclusive management of films so unchallenged that they had taken their monopoly for natural law, those who might assert an interest in "art" were clearly an unnecessary, resented disturbance. We of the Film Society expected to be welcomed by all. Were we not bringing the industry new prestige, opportunities of research into novel methods of expression, a try-out ground, all at our own effort and expense? At its lowest, would we not introduce new talents to strengthen skills, new audiences to swell box office receipts? On the contrary, during the summer the industry had had time to think. We were condemned and hindered. I have described how Adrian Brunel was forced to retire into the background. George Pearson was the only then established British film director who supported us consistently and Mick Balcon the only producer.

It was not that our opponents were anti-art. They just did not think "art" had any place in their occupation. The secretary of the Board, Brooke Wilkinson, told me roundly that he had never known a film the making of which had not been determined in every respect and in every detail by money-making, and when I instanced *The Cabinet of Dr Caligari*, suggesting that the stylisation of sets might have represented a sincere effort by its makers to find novel graphic forms for portrayal of a strained and anguished mind, he pooh-poohed the conjecture as impossible. He explained to me that the Board had a rule forbidding the representation of lunatics in films because any audience was liable to contain people with relatives and friends in lunatic asylums, and a film like *Caligari*, for example, might distress these by making them think that that was how their patient-relations were actually confined.

In fairness to the Board and its attitude, it is only right to say that film-going in those days was far less selective than in modern times. Before television, a great proportion of cinemagoers were habitués, visiting a favourite local regularly even twice a week, regardless of the programme on show. The censor policy had a rational and practical basis. Though I ridicule here the absurder features of its operation, the fault lay in the inflexibility of the system—and the fact that the trade and some of its Board servants resented any development outside it as a diminution of their authority—rather than in the conscientiousness with which these latter approached their limited task.

I shall not deal further with the censorship here, for it befell me for many years to participate in conflicts with the B.B. of F.C. Many of the current reforms that make the situation nowadays less intolerable emerged from the fights we waged, but some of this may arise to be referred to in a later place.

It is sufficient here that there could clearly be no *modus vivendi* between an organisation with the objectives of the Film Society and a censorship exercised conscientiously to protect a non-selective general public. Of course times are different now; the public sees, the board passes, stars appear in, films that at the time, if made at all, could only have been bootlegged surreptitiously and with blushes in blue underground chambers on sub-standard stock. But this is not at all the point. We of the Film Society never needed to show, and never did, a film that could have caused a Lord Chamberlain a qualm. But we could not begin to work under standards prescribed to strait-jacket possible rogues, and that was the admitted and probably necessary motive of the Board's operation at the time.

Right away with our first-programme, we met trouble: Paul Leni's *Waxworks* was the centre piece. With the three acting "greats" of the German silent screen—Emil Jannings, Conrad Veidt, Werner Krauss—

the picture is recognised as a "classic" not only for these actors but particularly for its photography and composition (the director, Paul Leni, was an artist and we planned a simultaneous exhibition of his set designs). But one of the three episodes that comprises it is entitled "Jack the Ripper". Jack, played by Krauss, does nothing except walk in a few dark shots, muffled and with hands in pockets, menacingly along dark streets. As a matter of fact the young producers had run out of production money when the schedule reached this episode of their trilogy; they had been forced to scrap this part of the scenario and improvise a few seconds of such menacing "boding" scenes to round off their film, which, although a mild thriller in genre, was not horrific or even accused of "horror". The censor was not entirely obstructive. Jack the Ripper as a character could not be allowed; his crimes were real, and this came up against the list of bans. "Why not call him Spring-heeled Jack?", Brooke Wilkinson suggested helpfully, although admittedly the character never springs and you could not possibly see his heels.

We saw the compromise would mark a fatal precedent, and fought the issue, with every stop out, and pulling every string we knew, by a special appeal to the L.C.C. This was the authority for London; we took advantage of the judgement relating to appeals to ask it to licence to the New Gallery all programmes shown under our auspices and under bona-fide "private society" conditions of annual membership for eight performances, sight unseen and without benefit of censor. With so many sacred cows among our sponsors we won, but it was a close-run squeeze. According to my recollection the margin at the crunch was some 50 odd to 40 odd. Neither trade nor censor forgave us. Instead of being glad of getting rid of an embarrassment, they clearly resented our privilege.

No sooner over this pickle than we fell at once into another. The *Daily Express* anticipated our première by suddenly publishing on its eve a red-baiting article. The article was written and signed by its regular film critic, G. A. Atkinson. A group of prominent society figures, writers, artists, etc. had got together to communise the country by showing Soviet films, it alleged. Under the banner of art these persons—listed in the article—had secured exemptions from censorship and were going to introduce riot and revolution. Ivor Montagu had just returned from Russia. What had he been up to there? It was known he had a diplomatic passport—had he brought the films to Britain in the diplomatic bag? How many of those concerned were Communists? All must share responsibility for the plot.

There were many odd things about the article. I had no diplomatic passport. None of us was a Communist—at that time not even I. I had brought back no films from Russia, and I had no access at all to any diplomatic bag. There has never been any difficulty in importing any film into Britain, or so far as I know from anywhere. There is no law under which any can be excluded, unless it is obscene. It is quite true that I had tried to get hold of Soviet films for the Film Society but, as I have already mentioned, I had failed; and indeed it was not until several years later that we were to succeed in convincing the Soviet authorities that it would be sensible to let us show any.

But the interesting thing is that I had been earnestly advised that I *must* at all costs get hold of Soviet pictures for our programme. This had been in the course of a conversation I had had with somebody in the *Express* building itself shortly before my departure on the B.M. expedition. The somebody was G. A. Atkinson, who had, indeed, accepted the invitation himself to be one of the Film Society's one-pound-shareholder guarantors. His very words to me were: "It is no good you people starting off the Film Society with French and German Films. We've seen those before. You simply must succeed in getting Soviet pictures. Otherwise there'll be no interest and the papers will have nothing to write about."

In the upshot we had failed to get the pictures but he had found something to write about.

Since then, this kind of distortion has become a familiar experience. Then I was rather surprised. Sidney Bernstein, Iris Barry, Frank Dobson, Walter Mycroft and others were upset. Except for Mycroft—who could hardly do so since, being on the *Evening Standard*, he was employed by the same group of newspapers, they issued a writ. Sidney's solicitor took us to consult D. N. Pritt as counsel. It was the first time I ever met him. Later on I was to know him and admire him and be proud to share enterprises with him. Then he was just another lawyer in my eyes and I do not think that at that time he was yet active in politics. I refused to join in the writ. My own solicitor, my cousin Walter Hart, told me that, as I was the most seriously libelled, I should certainly collect the heaviest damages. But I explained that it was impossible for me to sue; although it was untrue to say that I was a Communist (at that time) or had engaged in surreptitious import of subversive pictures, I could not consider myself damaged by the former allegation and would, if I considered it in the interest of the country, have no hesitation anyway in importing anything. Therefore I would not claim to be libelled.

This was fortunate in a way, because not being a party to the case enabled me to see Beaverbrook and discuss a settlement. I got in touch with Beverley Baxter and told him the facts. Within a few days I was invited to Beaverbrook's office. It was a curious scene. In the corridor outside his office Atkinson came up to me and whispered, before we went in, that if what I really wanted was to have his job on the *Express* he was ready to give it up to me. I do not know what he had been put through in the building for this extraordinary idea to come into his head, but of course I took no notice of it. We entered and he stayed standing at the edge of the room during what followed, never speaking except once or twice answering "yes, sir" or "no, sir". Beaverbrook was sitting on the very edge of a low arm-chair, leaning forward. I do not recall, if I ever knew, exactly who were the several others present, but the room was crowded and I think I remember Lord Castlerosse and his cigar. Beaverbrook was short and to the point. The *Express* had consulted its lawyers, he said, looking to the others for confirmation, whereupon they nodded. The opinion was definite: the *Express* would lose the case, but the costs and any possible damages would be well worth it in view of the increased publicity and sales which would be sure to result from the public interest aroused. But he, Beaverbrook, did not want to make money that way. (Here a glare at the unfortunate Atkinson.) He would like to settle. Would my friends agree? As my colleagues did not want damages but only costs and a withdrawal, and we had agreed on this beforehand, this was easy to answer. A full retraction duly appeared.

Beaverbrook made a tremendous impression on me. Until that time I had never seen a being with such masterful gaze. As he looked at you he seemed to be trying to bully you, command you, hypnotise you, all in one. A few months later I met the only other human whom I ever saw look at people like that. This was Hell's daughter, Rowna, then five years old. A pity she did not keep it up.

§ 20

HELL AND I have been married now for forty years and a bit more. It is certainly not a day too much from my point of view. But the reader must not expect me here or later to enter into the same details about Hell, or our relationship, as I can about other matters. Fortunately the writer of an autobiography is not upon oath. He is under no obligation to tell the whole truth about everything (fortunately for the reader because otherwise his testimony would never end). It is enough that he should tell nothing but the truth. And this I try to do. On this part of my subject the reader must be content with that.

About how we met. Hell was working at the Celtic Typewriting Bureau, boss Miss Walters, Hell herself one of the most trusted typists and stenographers. It was a small concern that undertook typing jobs and sent out secretaries on daily assignments to businesses in the neighbourhood and was situated in the rabbit-warren of offices at the north end and east side of Chancery Lane. Hell remembers one of the first manuscripts I brought in. It must have been some sort of account of one of my travels for it described the countryside and local peasants somewhere as seen from a passing motor-car and contained the remarkable words: "each leaning on his or her hoe". Fowler himself admits the problem of syntax this illustrates as one of the most difficult in the English language to solve gracefully.

She also remembers, probably more vividly than I, our first meeting. I had burst into the office one morning when she was in charge and tried to borrow a pound. I have already explained that it was my habit to carry as little money as possible about me, and to borrow when I *had to* spend something, as the only way of not being extravagant, for any cash I had in my pocket immediately burned its way out again. I always paid back meticulously and speedily (when I remembered or was reminded), so my friends did not object. But in this case I was making my approach to a stranger. It would not have occurred to me as especially peculiar for, after all, did I not know myself as honest? Anyway Hell replied, truthfully, that she hadn't any money. My answer to that also was notable. Apparently I said: "Surely you have some petty cash. Can you not take it from the till?" Anyway this overture was unsuccessful. It may have been a case of love at first sight but this is doubtful.

Hell was just the same age as myself, short of three weeks. She had had as many adventures, of a different kind and in a different world. They had taught her, in a harder school, to be as self-reliant as I hoped to be and at the same time far more practical than I. She was a blonde, that is, what she afterwards taught me is certainly called blonde, namely a light mousy colour. (Until then I had been under the impression that the word was applied only to flaxen whiteness.) I learned her name from her closest friend at the Bureau, surnamed George, a tall and handsome girl whose black Eton crop was even tighter and sleeker than Hell's brown. It appears that Hell's surname was Hellstern, and that she had been known by its first syllable ever since her schooldays, in every job or circle in which she found herself. It is a good name, easy to say, easy to remember and I have always used it. She does not specially like her real first name, Eileen, and except that after we were married, when I had some vague notion that woman's dignity should be preserved by her not submerging her surname in her husband's and I stamped out nameplates on one of those machines on railway platforms that said IVOR MONTAGU EILEEN HELLSTERN, and stuck them outside our room with completely misleading consequences, we have never used the Eileen. HELL has given no trouble, except in explaining to friends who on first introduction are sure they must have heard wrong, or convincing telephonists who are confused when you spell it out as part of a joint signature at the end of a telegram.

George might be handsome, but I had no eyes for anyone but Hell. She was peaches and cream with a round, marsh-mallow beauty, deceptively soft but concealing an occasional and devastating frankness of speech and an honesty of judgement that has made her throughout these forty years at once the admiration and terror of all who know her. She is a walking conscience for everyone and, without her needing to utter anything but only so that they may survive with honour her pellucid gaze, everyone adores and wishes to stand well with her. A certain Roman Emperor was reputed to have been accompanied at his triumphs by a slave ever whispering in his ear "You are mortal". Just so has Hell's company spared me many follies. Besides, she can read my handwriting. I will say no more about why it has been my topmost good fortune in life that we have been young, and fated to grow old together.

Anyway, from this time forth, at my incessant solicitation and in response to my clumsy attempt to forget egotism long enough to appear thoughtful for the first time of another, by her hardwon consent and overlooking of my frequent failures in this regard, she still living south of the river, I in Lincolns's Inn, we began at last to see more of each other and to "keep company". Off and on and more and more we went about together. My closest friends became her friends. We quarrelled, made things up, separated by great renunciations, became inseparable once more because we could not help it. So, I suppose, the course of true love flows ever. This process continued for about two years. And this in spite of the warning she received at the outset from Miss Walters who, on examining a fresh revision of *Le Cocu Magnifique* that I had brought in for copying, advised Hell firmly that she must not be worried by what she found in it—the Bureau bore no responsibility for, and must be neutral toward, the oddest products of its clients.

§ 21

The Brunel "organisation" was insinuated into a narrow staircase giving off Dansey Yard. This is a cobbled alley running east-west between Shaftesbury Avenue and Gerrard Street. At the time of which I speak it had just outside its front door a green *pissoir*, romantic because it had been the scene of the arrest in the twenties of one of the more popular newspaper padres and a small boy. Later on, when the firm became Brunel & Montagu Ltd., I designed for us a staff tie, green with thin diagonal streaks of gold.

Giving off the small doorway of No. 6 were a few rooms in which the late C. Francis Parkins and his companions had a primitive laboratory, weaving their chemical mysteries of development, printing, trick and title-making to our advantage, until, about the time we ourselves closed down, they moved to their present premises in Dean Street and Wardour Street as one of the best firms in the business, Studio Film Labs., retaining a staff who have maintained the old original friendships.

Up a flight a tiny office, small enough to be crowded by one desk, one file and a couple of chairs even with no one in it, but sometimes occupied by Adrian and some caller-friend such as Vyvyan Holland, fought for first floor space with an equally claustrophobic projection theatre seating some four or five. The floor above had tiny cutting rooms. And above that was an almost inaccessible chamberlet where tea was brewed by a boy named Garbett, but whom we called Truscott because the first office-boy had been named so, just as Victorian maids were arbitrarily dubbed with their predecessor's names to avoid their mistresses having to remember new ones. Truscott, an obliging boy with fair curly hair, combined his tea-making with projecting and film-joining, in fact he did almost all the donkey-work about.

Everyone who ever worked, or had worked for Adrian, joined the circle of friends and became an in-and-out occasional. Dropping-in regulars were his most recent cameraman, the tall thin Henry Harris, a curious blend of caustic amiability, and the still taller and thinner Edwin Greenwood who later directed films and wrote novels and was a militant Roman Catholic. So militant was the latter that he used to go to Paris and take part, in a mild, benevolent way, in the riots of the Camelots du Roi, and a favourite saying of his was: "I am a Catholic, and no one shall f—— the Pope in my presence but myself."

The two chief steadies, and excellent cutters both of them, were Lionel ("Tod") Rich, an upright lugubrious type of man with a strong sense of humour that he would die rather than allow to appear in his demeanour, and J.O.C. ("Jock") Orton whom I have already mentioned, shorter and heavier, with a rosy complexion and hair receding from the forehead, ex-Captain R.F.C. These two had entered the film business in an odd fashion. They came out of the 1914–18 war, invested their demobbed officers' gratuities in a film venture with Adrian, and lost every penny because it was too successful. This may sound strange, but should be clear enough when explained. The film they backed was the silent version of *Owd Bob*, one of the best of the old pictures, and this had been so well received at the trade show that exhibitors' bookings arrived in such abundance that they had not capital enough to pay for prints to cope with the demand. Exhibitors' forward contracts are the most gilt-edged paper in film business, but banks were so allergic to any form of film financing in those days that these small-scale impresarios could raise nothing on them, and were forced, by the very volume of the valuable commitments they had received, to sell out, for a song, to better-capitalised distributors who could cope until, months after booking, payment would mature.

After that the pair had nothing to do but hang around the office. Adrian could hardly throw them out in the circumstances and so they graduated to the staff—if so regular a name can be applied to colleagues who have to hope that the weekly business will be solid enough to divide up into salaries for all. I came in by somewhat of the same avenue, and so, later, after me, did, first Angus—who also decided to try his luck in films, and later still Sergei Nolbandov. Sergei was a Russian refugee, and Nalbandov—as he was called when I first knew him—is the Turkish for Smithson. He was a peculiar man, with a fund of peculiarly amusing stories. When we first knew him he had been working for the Moscow Narodny Bank, and was now scraping a living in complex enterprises such as promoting carpet sales, or inducing all of us to invest in hundredweights of Soviet honey that had got over-ripe in the docks—it was marvellous stuff, slightly fermented and intoxicating, but how do you sell such quantities even as Christmas presents via your friends? His wife, an optimistic Scotswoman named Grace, had great schemes for selling tombstones. I hung about to watch the Film Society pictures being processed. Angus, later, because he too was interested in them; Sergei, because he "represented" in London the emigré film producer Yermoliev, famous owner of a pre-revolutionary studio in Yalta, who wandered about Europe setting up vast super-spectacles without knowing how to dispose of them to the markets when they were finished, and with whom we were trying to do deals for the Film Society or for titling. Later, incidentally, Sergei and I, Grace and Hell, became great friends and "S.S.N." and "I.M." translated many novels and stories together from Russian. Later still Sergei consulted a numerologist, who advised him that the letters of his name would add up to a more favourable total if they had one more "o" and one less "a"; he changed it accordingly and thenceforward never looked back.

Tod, Jock, Angus and I came into No. 6 all in the same way. It is surprising how much knowhow you absorb if you simply sit around and watch, especially if, like Adrian, the watched one is able, talkative and congenial. After a time, too, he begins to notice that you have been passing him paper-clips, fetching him film tins, getting him shots off the pins on which they were hanging, and tidying up the cuts out of the bins. When the boss notices this has been going on a few weeks he begins to be ashamed that you are not on the payroll, asks if you would like some arrangement, and then you are *in*. This was no doubt a more haphazard way of entering the industry than in these days of unionisation. Heaven forfend such casual entry should return to allow exploitation of the filmstruck now that computers check the expenditure of every giant corporation to see where they can scrape an extra penny for the shareholders. But in those days it worked because the boss was Adrian and he was never a boss but shared every scrap of knowledge he had and every commission that came in. And the same continued, when Adrian and I turned ourselves into a limited company at the same address, and the same also about a year onward when, Adrian at last getting started directing for the big companies, presently Frank Wells joined as a third, active, partner in running the firm.

There was very much to keep me busy at first on the Film Society pictures. This is no more a history of the Film Society than of world table tennis, and so I have no intention of discussing in detail the influence we exercised or the quality of the films we showed.

Looking through the programmes of the first two years, however, gives me an idea of the nature of the editing and titling in which Dansey Yard must have been involved for it. The revivals we showed, such as the Chaplins and early one-reel D. W. Griffiths, a *Maria Marten* by Elvey, *Tillie's Punctured Romance*, the entire *Caligari*, a Lubitsch and as much of *Greed* as we could get hold of, required little working over. The scientific films, often not designed for public showing in that particular form, did. The first "*absolute*" films (Ruttman's) from Germany, the first "abstracts" from France (Chomette's *A Quoi rêvent les Jeunes Films*, Man Ray's *Emak Bakia* and Leger and Murphy's *Ballet Mecanique*), the first surrealist (Réné Clair's *Entracte*) required only good main titles and the music planned for them. But most of the big features were imported and had to be fitted with translated titles. Lupu Pick's *New Year's Eve* was a film without any at all, but *Waxworks* and *Nju*, two of the films Robert Wiene made after *Caligari* (a *Raskolnikov* and *The Hands of Orlac*), a baroque *Cinderella* (according to Grimm), Greta Garbo's first international picture (Pabst's *Joyless Street*), and the first Japanese film to appear in Britain were all big jobs. Most copious of all, and done in a big rush, was a show of the two parts of Fritz Lang's *Dr. Mabuse*, which we put together in short order to show as one. The copies had come from France, and Angus, who had undertaken to work all night through on the eve of the show, to put in our English titles and take out the originals, slipped up and overlooked one, with the result, received with applause, that the villain, making up to the innocent heroine, suddenly dropped into appropriate French as he whispered seductively in her ear: "*Voulez vous diner avec moi dans un endroit discret*?" I can only match that error with a title of mine in the film of the *Dytiscus* (Giant Water Beetle) larva, designed to show its predaciousness, "It attempts an adult newt," but I am afraid that, foolishly innocent on my part, was just an ambiguous in-joke appealing to my colleagues's dirty minds.

Of course not all of any season's programme was completed in advance. We were lucky if we had a few pictures and dates lined up. We had to keep hunting and there were many more trips abroad. In Berlin I had to see Elisabeth Bergner to negotiate for *Nju*. I had already marvelled at her in *Die Heilige Johanna* and made her acquaintance by waiting at the stage door. I had told G.B.S. how wonderful I thought her performance was, but also that I did not like the production at all. I consider that a producer spoils Shaw, as also Shakespeare, by having characters with angry speeches primarily display their anger by volume, so that they shout and the words themselves are often lost in the raised voice. (The Germans always do this, but I am afraid inadequate producers fall back upon this method in our country too.) Shaw and

Shakespeare did not write their words to be lost, but to be heard; their *content* expresses sufficient anger when the character is to be portrayed as angry and the play must be so directed: inchoate noises, you or I could write. Now Hell made some excuse for a holiday and came with me and I have not forgotten that, when Bergner gave us lunch, she put an orchid on Hell's plate, and she afterwards presented Hell with what we liked best in her house, a Nefertiti reproduction, not the gaudy coloured one, but the chaste sandstone one.

Jock Orton came with Iris and me to Paris. We found our expeditions grow increasingly social. *À Quoi rêvent les Jeunes Films* had been financed by a Comte Etienne de Beaumont, and he had to be approached directly in a huge and elegant Paris mansion standing in its own grounds, via an introduction from a Marquise friend of my mother's whose mansion was even bigger and slightly decayed—she herself wore a lace mantilla—and very Proust indeed. We wanted a film with Mosjoukine made by Marcel L'Herbier from the Pirandello novel *Feu Matthias Pascal*. Marcel L'Herbier took me upstairs to show me his latest, called *L'Inhumaine*, but after three reels, when the projectionist, who had only one projector, was changing over, I stupidly asked a question that was bothering me: why was there this contrast between natural clothing and acting on the one hand, and, on the other, arbitrary patterns of architecture and decoration Caligari-style. He screamed and rushed into the projection box, emerging with all the reels embraced in his arms, declaring that he would stop the show and that he had never been so insulted in his life. It was some time before I could discover the corn I had trodden on in my ignorance and then make the peace. Apparently the sets had been strictly natural too, patterns of that kind had just become all the mode in Paris life.

Another gaffe was made by Jock at a party thrown for us by very "society" characters indeed. Somebody asked him what we were here for and, his French not being equal to explaining that the Film Society was interested in unusual products of film art, he blundered into saying that we had come "*pour chercher les films curieux*". Alas, the word in French means not what it does in ordinary English, but what it does in the book catalogues, and immediately all the drawing-room crowded round him asking where he expected to find them, he must tell the addresses, etc. etc.

A worse, indeed somewhat disillusioning, episode occurred at the New Gallery when we showed Réné Clair's *Entracte*. I called the film surrealist just now because it is inconsequent, but I am confident it was not made with the intent, and indeed the significant, if veiled, overtones, of the serious surrealists. It is made for a giggle, and so we on the Council had taken it. Not so the audience at the New Gallery. Some started to boo, others to scream and cheer, people got up and shouted, others shook their fists and even their neighbours—I have never seen an English audience so passionate, all over a logically inconsequent series of images that we had thought rather fun. I remember how pensive Frank Dobson was at tea afterwards. He had been sitting behind Clive Bell, who had been among the most violent and vociferous in denunciation of those who had had the temerity to boo. Blasphemers of artistic experiment, he had called them. "Makes you think twice, doesn't it, about what these fellows say in praise of your own work," said Dobson ruefully, and then had the grace to laugh.

Meanwhile, at around the turn of the year 1925–26, I had thrown away an opportunity. Hinton had approached me with the proposal that I should undertake completion of the text part of Barrett-Hamilton and Hinton's *History of British Mammals*. This was perhaps the first really systematic study plus natural-history-reportage plus traditional lore modern review of the subject. It is a much more scientific proposition than its nineteenth-century predecessors—which are written mainly from the sportsman's point of view—and it had been appearing in irregularly-issued serial parts over a number of years. Begun by an Irishman, Barrett-Hamilton, with Wilson, the artist-zoologist who died with Scott, and both of its originators having perished in the course of publication, it had been continued by Hinton and the Museum artist, a dark, handsome man called Dollman. Now, with Hinton succeeding to Oldfield Thomas's responsibility for the department, he found himself without time to continue and a fresh continuer was needed. I hesitated. There was an element of cowardice in my refusal, I am sure; it was a book I cherished, and rightly—although unfinished, it has remained standard for the parts that were completed (Bats and Rodents and Insectivores) almost to the present day, when Harrison Matthews and the Mammal Society volumes have taken over—and I had an inward doubt about my capacity not to make a botch of it. But, six months earlier, I am sure I should have had a try at any cost. Now I had undertaken responsibilities, and was working among colleagues, my father had raised no trouble about my work in films; I was still determined to be independent and had no idea how he would take a change back to zoology; Hinton was not at all sure what guarantee he could get for me from the publishers or grant from elsewhere. I turned it down and was ashamed. It was my last chance to become a professional zoologist.

During the winter months and the spring of 1926 Hell and I on our excursions sometimes found ourselves become a foursome, particularly on outings to the music hall. We went with Angus and with us came also a calm and jolly woman of maturer age. Her name was Marjorie Russell, she worked in publicity, and she and Angus had decided to go halves together in a flat.

We made a sort of lunch club for the Dansey Yard outfit and other friends in a small restaurant in Lisle Street called Alexis; besides ourselves Jack Gielgud, Kate Cutler and Edith Craig were the regulars. Most of us were members also of Elsa Lanchester and Harold Scott's Cave of Harmony in Charlotte Street. But whatever else united our foursome it worshipped goddesses in common, elevated above all other idols in the world of entertainment: Renee and Billie Houston.

For a year or more we attended their every engagement within reach, often following them in their commutings across London when they were playing in two halls at the time time, or, when they were content with one, spending the interval between their appearances in the two houses in their dressing room. Renee was the little girl in this child act, her golliwog hair "stained Kiwi" or she so pretended; Billie, in real sooth her sister, played the deep-voiced sober fraternal influence with a short golden crop. George Balharrie, who was or was not Renee's first husband—in the act this relationship was left surrealistically obscure—took over the orchestra for the stage performance, and the contrast between the incredible skill with which Renee burlesqued a spoilt little girl in dialogue with Billie, and a merciless termagant in her treatment of George, was the heart of the show. Renee, of course, is still alive and kicking actively in show business and her eventual stage and domestic marriage was a lasting, secure and happy one for nearly a generation. Her figure has changed, and few today will imagine that this currently ample matron was once as dainty as a sylph. What has not changed an atom is her capacity to act, better put, her incapacity to do anything but act, utterly convincingly, on or off the stage. I heard her the other day on radio, as fascinating as ever, discussing her early days; the ceaseless flow of anecdote, fact and fiction, innocence and sophistication—mingled inextricably—is unaltered by an iota from that which made her company and her domination of every scene an unparalleled delight to sit back and listen to in the dressing-room as behind the footlights forty years before. Every word and gesture was always delivered with complete aplomb. Take as many grains of salt as you cared to while she was holding forth, the tales themselves were never a whit the worse. We were all fans and followers of both the sisters and I fancy that Renee must have been partial to us four also or we should certainly not have been tolerated for so long. One week-end they came back from an engagement in Belfast and Renee announced that she and George—as they could not have children—had together adopted an infant son they proposed to christen in our honour: Angus Ivor Russell Balharrie. His subsequent progress was graphically described at intervals. I sometimes have qualms in case somewhere he still exists, and his putative godparents have all his life neglected him, but then equally I have no idea whether indeed he ever existed.

These halcyon days on the fringe of show business were roughly interrupted by the General Strike.

§ 22

AT THIS time was I Labour or Communist? It may come as a surprise to those who have grown up for a generation in an "either-or" situation in which, in the order of things, one is supposedly Labour *or* Communist, and in which these two categories are mutually exclusive and this is apparently part of the natural order of things, that it was not always so. Hence the question is not immediately capable of a simple answer.

In the technical sense, and this is the only one that has real meaning nowadays, when in nearly every country Communist Parties with precise policy and organisation have come into being, I was certainly at this time not a member of the Communist Party. I did not become one until the early thirties of the century. But, as we have seen, it chances that I had been a member of one of the political groupings (the British Socialist Party) that came together to form the Communist Party. For domestic reasons, rather than considered political choice, I had not immediately joined the latter. But in those days one had no particular reason to need to make formal choice. I have already explained the Labour Party was not, as is now pretended by its right-wing, originally a body with a particular philosophical, ethical or political outlook, "traditional British" or otherwise. The Labour Party was not "Social-Democratic" or "Socialist as opposed to Communist" or anything like that in its conception and tradition. Quite the contrary. It was, in its original conception, its foundation, and its operation for many years, a *class coalition*, the *working class as a political movement*, and so deserved the adherence of every socialist of every hue.

In those days the Right Wing was only beginning to get going in its innovation of expulsion and ostracism of critics and opponents, their disqualification from individual membership of the Labour Party and even attack upon their rights in the trade unions. The transformation of the Labour Party from its traditional coalition character to an orthodoxy that split the working class and progressive movement sharply into sheep and goats was only just starting. So it was fully possible at this time to find in the *Weekly Worker* or the *Sunday Worker* the most sense, to respect Communist leaders as wise and honest, to despise such as MacDonald and Thomas on their record, to share the critical views and *Weltanschauung* of Communists, and this all with full frankness, and yet be an honest, enthusiastic Labourite, hard-working for the victory of party and cause. And many were, among them I.

This narrative, in the diversity of its branchings, the irrelevance if not frivolity of its asides, may shade the fact that not only at this time and since, but even earlier, politics has always had priority for me. By this I do not in the least mean that, as portrayed in the slanderous warning picture of Communists held up in vulgar red-baiting, I have ever put "party" before loyalty to associates in my various jobs, social or professional. Communists would deserve, and receive, short shrift from their associates if they were thus unreliable. On the contrary, it is a fact of experience that Communists are most mistrusted where they are known only from the stereotypes peddled by their enemies (e.g. as shown in their low votes in elections where the opponents' monopoly of press, radio, etc., deprives them of proper contact with the electorate), and most enjoy confidence and affection where they are best and most truly known, e.g. in the factories and union branches where they work, among the neighbours where they live. It is quite clear that duty as a Communist requires being reliable in any responsibility you assume, any obligation of office you accept, and that the Communist must look at the problems of such organisations as he voluntarily joins and the associates he voluntarily works with from this point of view. But what is equally clear is that, consistent with such obligations, when the chance does come to do something effective in the political field, this takes precedence over private interest or personal pleasure.

So now the developing situation presaged calls that could not be ignored.

When I came back from U.S.S.R., though deeply impressed, above all, by the sense of comradeship there and, in the current cant phrase, the evidence of the wind of change, I still did not join the Communist Party of Great Britain. I still did not know enough about Communism or Marxism. I admired both Lenin and Trotsky, and could not understand the issues between the Soviet Party and Trotsky which were then reaching the surface. I did join the scientists' trade union (the National Union, now the Association, of Scientific Workers) as soon as it was formed and, as a trade unionist, the Minority Movement. I consorted with Communists and found among them the only political friends of like approach. But my only organised political links were with the Fabian Society, the Holborn Labour Party and the latter's committee;

and, as at Cambridge, I represented the constituency party on the Holborn Trades Council.

All the signs of the coming clash could be seen from afar: Baldwin's treacherous tactical device to postpone the issue, paying a subsidy to the miners to hold back their strike while he completed his preparations to defeat them; then the beheading of the left with the trumped up charges against the Communist Twelve. I was present at the trial and heard the petty magisterial baiting of G.B.S. and H. G. Wells when they came forward to offer bail.

When Baldwin was ready he forced the conflict, encouraging the coal owners to close the mines and put the miners on the stones. For them the long hard struggle thus begun, for the latter part of which they had to fight alone abandoned by the Labour leaders, was technically not a strike but a lock-out.

After all that they had said in support of the miners, the General Council of the T.U.C. could not refrain at first from calling the General Strike to defend them, nor the Labour Party leadership from pretending at first to support it. What we of the rank and file did not know was that from the outset these leaders were only desperately seeking the first plausible pretext to call it off.

A mighty wave of solidarity swept the country. No section of the workers called out refused the summons. The miners' case was unanswerable. The Baldwin government's determination to crush it by force in the interest of the coalowners no less obvious. Only when the waters have been muddied are the organised workers confused. In such a moment as May 1926 they do not hesitate.

Our trades council in Holborn, plus the constituency L.P. executive, was transformed into a Council of Action. Delegates of all affiliated Unions sat in almost permanent session in a small local hall. We dealt with incoming news, sent representatives where they were needed, exchanged messages with other parts of the country. I remember the impatience of the representatives of the essential services whom the T.U.C. had told to stay at work—electricians, gasworkers, telephonists and the like. The mood was one of eagerness to stand united. Money was collected from those still working for those on strike. It poured in. Resolutions were passed expressing readiness to respond to any further call of solidarity.

My contempt for the standards of the conventional politicians was not diminished when one of the most egregious of the latter—Sir John Simon—pretended to be giving an "objective" legal opinion on the "constitutionality" of sympathetic strikes, and types like Baldwin pretended that such an opinion, from that tainted source, was judicial rather than *ex parte*.

The Council of Action executive had an office in a second-floor Bloomsbury flat. All public transport was halted, except for a few vehicles manned by blacklegs which of course we boycotted. I had a bicycle and acted as courier. Our office was watched all day by obvious police spies. So clumsy were they that to show our contempt we sent out hot cups of tea to cheer them in the drizzle. I remember a trick that was played by a comrade in the International Labour Defence, situated a few streets away. I had taken a message and he asked me in returning to carry back a parcel to our headquarters. Like a fool I consented and, as I unhooked my bicycle from the railings, felt a tap on my shoulder. I turned round and was confronted by a plain-clothes man. My heart sank. I did not know what might be in the parcel. "Open it," he said. "Show me your warrant", I replied. He brought out his wallet and proved his identity. "I can make you open it," he insisted. "You cannot," I replied, using the same tactics as I had with the customs invigilator at Dover, "if you insist that it be opened, you must open it yourself."

He made a knee by crooking his leg against the railings and started to undo the parcel. One knot, one string, one paper wrapper. Inside was another string, another knot around another wrapper. And another. And another. And another. As he went on, the detective's face began to work. He struggled vainly to preserve his dignity. He could see what was going to happen but he was as one obsessed. He was unable to stop. He managed to keep his face straight as at last he unfolded the last wrapper and there inside was—a small scrap of red crêpé paper. His face worked again. He must have known that he was being watched by those inside. He said: "I suppose you want me to do it up." "Of course," I answered. And do it up again he did, every wrapper, every string, every knot in its turn. As he struggled with the last he gave his first, and only wintry smile. "There," he said, patting it. "Neat enough. You can tell I was once a shop assistant."

If he sees these words he will know the joke was on me as well as on him. I had been scared stiff. But fair is fair. I realised that, if I had known what was in the parcel, I could never have acted realistically enough to bring it off.

A courier's job was in general not a cakewalk. Most difficult was the morning collection of the *British Worker*. The Labour leaders came to some sort of gentlemanly bargain with the establishment they were supposed to be fighting and, though they stopped the press in general, allowed trade unionists to print a rag for Churchill called the *British Gazette* in exchange for the authorities not interfering with production —on the *Daily Herald*'s presses—of a *British Worker*.

This latter was the means by which the strike leadership kept in contact with the rank and file. With no public transport, the Councils of Action had to improvise the means of distribution. Sometimes we had to fetch our parcels of papers from the *Herald* premises themselves. Their old building had a narrow entrance and this was always blocked by street newsvendors. It was perfectly natural that we couriers for the strikers should find our priority of collection resented and, so far as these rivals were concerned, be looked on as scabs in all but a technical sense, indeed be the object of physical molestation. We had to run the gauntlet of a rugger scrum of newsvendors as we went in and as we came out with our packages. It was easy to strip a man of his spectacles so that they became lost amid the packed and jostling mass and trampled underfoot, especially easy if his arms were occupied with clinging to the bulky block of newspapers. I cannot see properly without glasses—certainly not well enough to recognise a face across a room—so that afterwards, when I had recovered the bicycle from some distant point at which it had been hidden for safety, it was not so easy to cycle purblind back across London with the package balanced on the handlebars amid a traffic that was largely improvised and amateur.

After a time the distribution point was shifted to Labour Party headquarters in Eccleston Square, and there we couriers from each Council of Action waited in queue along the corridors and up the stairs until we reached the counter where Herbert Morrison and others were doing up the packages and asking each of us to identify his constituency, ticking it off against a roster to avoid impersonation and duplication. It was my fate to come to Morrison and reach him as he was struggling to tighten a knot that he was pulling in the binding twine, and his forehead was puckered with the effort. When I answered "Holborn" to his question, he screwed up his bad eye socket and turned on me such a face of hate as I have never forgotten. "You're the people who keep sending resolutions to us," he snapped and pulled so savagely on the twine that it broke and he had to begin again. And all we wanted to do was to assure the National Executive and T.U.C. General Council of our support!

It was not an auspicious beginning of my acquaintance with this man, nor the last brush I had with him. Nor was I now entirely surprised when the N.E.C. and G.C. tricked us all a few days afterwards. Casting around, as they had been ever since the first day, for a means of getting themselves out of the predicament they had landed themselves in by their desire to control a movement in whose aims they had no faith and whose mood they feared; their bluff called by Baldwin, they were frantic somehow to cage again the tiger they had invoked. The straw they clutched at to save themselves was my cousin Herbert, who had obligingly headed a commission of investigation into the coal industry for Baldwin during the six months previously. That Baldwin was merely using the Commission as a mask to gain a breathing-space for his strike-breaking preparations would never have mattered to Herbert, a man of perfect integrity and uprightness, one of those aggravating creatures in whose character you can find no fault but who are themselves so certain they can do no wrong that often they serve blindly as a means of wrongdoing in others. He had simply done his duty as he saw it, which was to produce an honest report, one that had more or less come down in favour of moving towards nationalisation of the coal industry and which, of course, the Tory Government had not had the slightest intention of implementing. Now, consulted by the Labour Party National Executive and the T.U.C. General Council, he did a similar job for them, responding with an "opinion" about what would be a fair and suitable compromise solution, and the N.E.C. and G.C. immediately announced it to the nation in terms that implied victory and made it a pretext for calling off the strike. For his part in the affair my upright cousin, whom I justly respected so much for that uprightness when a boy and whose virtues I still recognise though I respect them less, earned not unjustly thereafter the sobriquet of "Slippery Sam". The General Council did not say that "Sam's" was a purely *personal* opinion. Otherwise they would never have got the strikers back. Of course it in no way bound the government, which ignored it, and no doubt always intended to, though in the first hours of confusion after the calling-off this was not apparent to the rank and file. However, the N.E.C. and G.C. had attained their object, which was: to get the monkey of responsibility for a semi-revolutionary situation off their own backs at any cost, even though that meant the desertion of the miners and their abandonment to a grim war of attrition that they were bound to lose.

As for my family relationships during this period, they began in melodrama and ended in farce. I have already described how a welcome was always ready for me at both Kensington Court and Townhill during this period 1925–27, despite the fact that I had gone away to live by myself in Lincoln's Inn. When the General Strike started I made it quite clear that I was a member of the local Council of Action in Holborn and should be too busy to visit my parents until the strike was over. The reactions of my father and mother were quite different. My mother was so angry that she forbade me ever to return should I now cross the threshold to rejoin my comrades. My father was equally upset but not thrown off his bearings. He expostulated with my mother, saying: "If he has assumed obligations to his friends, which he should not have done of course, then he will have to carry them out." My mother was obdurate. If she had not taken with full patriotic earnestness the appeal of Baldwin after the strike was over for "no victimisation" I might indeed never have been asked back under the parental roof and this might have saved many complications.

The vindictiveness came from Eccleston Square, however. The Communist leaders were released from prison after the few months of their sentences, but the Labour Party N.E.C. were determined that as soon as possible their flock must be decontaminated from any intercourse with them. Sheep, if they are to remain safely sheep . . . must be kept away from goats. The Communist Party had earlier been disaffiliated as a Party, now individual Communists were declared ineligible for Labour Party membership and the constituency parties ordered to expel them all. Although no C.P. member, I was of course against this. In fact, the majority of the Holborn Labour Party refused to operate the order and the constituency party was itself dissolved.

Since then, though a dues-paying affiliate of the Labour Party many times over through stumping-up the political levy in my trade unions and through other bodies, I have been excluded, as an individual, by such anathemas.

§ 23

THE NEXT six months were "action-packed".

Atkinson's whisper to me outside Beaverbrook's office had not been so nonsensical as I had supposed. Several of the Film Society supporters did find their way to newspapers as film critics, notably Iris Barry who, on the *Daily Mail*, became one of the best "outsiders" of her time. I say "outsider" because one day, after sitting in with us at the cutting rooms, and perhaps for the first time passing film stock through her hands, she remarked to me with surprise that she had not known that stock (as it was in those silent days) was tinted—amber, lavender, blue for night effects, red for fires, etc.—to produce the colour effects she saw on the screen. She admitted that, without thinking about it, she had imagined the colour changes were effected by change in glass screens or lamps within the projector. In any case it is perhaps arguable how far technical know-how is an advantage to the critic. G. A. Atkinson had been off target in thinking I might yearn for the *Express* (Beverley Baxter's remarks had been sufficiently off-putting) but I had, in the spring, applied for and obtained a post as the first film critic the *Observer* ever had. It was a grievance among us enthusiasts for film "art" that the "quality" press at that time in general ignored the cinema, it was a rarity for the better weeklies or dailies to notice a moving picture, and there was no counterweight to the cheap gossip and rehashed distributors' publicity material that so often masqueraded as film journalism. I wrote to the *Observer* editor, was interviewed, and authorised to write weekly short notices that, it was agreed, should be paid for at space rates if printed or at a minimum if crowded out. There was nothing like a regular column. It was usually a matter of two or three paragraphs at the most.

This arrangement broke down towards the end of the same May that saw the end of the General Strike. The outstanding M.G.M. 1914–18 war film *The Big Parade*, with John Gilbert, which had been made the subject of much advance ballyhoo, was press-shown prior to its first British run at the Tivoli. For some reason which I considered unwarranted by the picture itself, a group of my leading press colleagues launched a concerted attack on the film as an insult to Britain, an ignoring of Britain's part in the 1914–18 war, in which "we bore the brunt" (as of course we did) for years before "at last they came in and reaped the fruits". It is well known that this kind of American rewriting of history has taken place, and no doubt even more frequently in recent times than in those days. Political motive is sometimes attributed, but probably wrongly; it is simply the natural result of film-making with commercial motive primary, the scraping around for subjects and the need—in terms of the relation of films and audiences—to give the home market spectators characters to identify with in order that their emotions may be engaged. The ground of objection is better directed to political *effect*, rather than the uncertain and unprovable sphere of motive; it is obviously unjustifiable, even for the sake of gain, so to misrepresent history as to persuade peoples and generations unfamiliar with the facts that American airmen were essential in winning the Battle of Britain or that G.I.s in tanks were victorious in the Desert War. But *The Big Parade* was nothing whatever of this kind. No particular battle was identified, it was a purely personal story which, though shaped as romance, stood up as a generalisation without exclusive national application, depicting civilians of many levels of occupation swept up into uniform by war hysteria, welded into comradeship, enduring the trials and casualties of warfare, and the indelible mark left by his experiences on the survivor. It is an outstandingly smooth and powerful piece in its genre, and in no way deserved the dead set of patriotic flag-waving directed against it at the time by so much of the British press. I looked on the matter as so important I went specially round to the *Observer* and explained personally the issues involved, which in my view transcended a mere brief description of the film and must oblige a responsible newspaper to appraise its quality and take a stand. I kept my review to five paragraphs but found them cut to one. I would not continue a job which the paper so determinedly regarded as insignificant, gave notice and recommended Angus MacPhail as my successor.

Though Angus succeeded in holding the job only a few months, it is pleasant to record that it then passed to C. A. Lejeune, in whose hands cinema was granted a full column and the importance it deserved, and who made the *Observer* for years one of the outstanding weightier influences that film criticism needed. Our clumsy skirmishes may well have served to prepare her victory in the common battle.

Adrian came for a week-end to Townhill and brought a camera. We used the garden, innocent guests and often unwilling family to make another of his burlesques—this one, so far never shown to trade or public, called *Life, Love and Laughter at Swaythling Court.* (The title combined those of the latest Betty Balfour comedy and of a current detective best-seller.) We were taking on yet more staff at Dansey Yard—this was around the time when Ian Dalrymple joined us—and, on the strength of this week-end, my sister Joyce, now getting on towards 18 years of age and hoping to see life at last, was allowed to come in and lend an occasional hand. If I had been frustrated in my childhood wish to teach her reading, at least I could now introduce her to living, or rather that corner of it represented by meals at Alexis, the second and upper floors of No. 6, passing paper clips, and Soho generally.

The major firm to which Adrian had been under contract as a director all this time, though without yet reaching the floor, was Gainsborough Pictures. Their studio was at Islington, off New North Road; it is now a furniture depository. Its producer-chief was M. E. Balcon. He was in turn dependent on his distributors, W. and F., bossed by C. M. Woolf. I already knew Mick. As I have noted, he and his wife Aileen were part of the regular gang at Adrian's hate parties. But friendship is not always a sure link in the film rat race. It can sometimes be the reverse—a handicap. Mick and Islington had started auspiciously a few years before with an immensely successful picture, *Woman to Woman*, starring an American actress, Betty Compson, which they had taken over for completion when an American company that had started it slid out. This picture had been directed by Graham Cutts and he had followed it up with several other successes, the most recent being *The Rat*, a popular monstrosity in which Ivor Novello with his consistent charm had played a misunderstood Apache. With this record, the sufficiently competent Cutts was naturally the White-Headed Boy of C. M. Woolf, for, whether by pose or conviction, C. M. Woolf always chose to adopt an aggressive attitude of anti-intellect and anti-art. Unfortunately, Cutts was jealous of all other directors under contract to the firm and his idea of self-protection was to thwart their projects by pouring cold water on them within earshot of Woolf, to denigrate their work to friendly pressmen, and to snatch their subjects for himself. This was one of the reasons why Adrian had had to wait so long for an opportunity. *The Man without Desire* was, in Woolf's eyes, not a credit but a debit, and the trouble was—as ever in such circumstances when personal conflicts arise in a big organisation—the closer the friend the more often he is called on to make concessions if the boss, in a tight corner, seeks compromise. Cutts was much cleverer than Adrian at this rivalry game. He would never even speak to Mick when a dispute arose, or even just a question of his own contract and salary. "My dear Mick, that's business, and business should not be mixed with friendship." He kept a personal agent in the studio and any would-be interlocutor on the subject would be diverted to the latter. I watched on the fringe and learned useful tactical lessons; though they were such as my temperament forbade me to employ myself, at least they did not come as total surprises when later I recognised them employed against me.

One day that summer Adrian relayed to me from Mick an urgent invitation to lunch. I went at once. The lunch was in the Monico off Piccadilly Circus, and I even remember ordering (and enjoying) mashed potatoes and fried onions. The problem confronting Mick was, he said, an urgent one. Mick had on his hands a picture he could not use because W. and F. would not show it. It had been completed, cut and titled but they did not like it. This picture, *The Lodger*, had been made by a new young director under contract to Gainsborough, Alfred Hitchcock. But the situation was even worse than this. It was not Hitchcock's first, but third. He had made two others, *The Pleasure Garden* and *The Mountain Eagle*—the latter a joint production shot in Munich—and W. and F. liked neither of these, either. So Mick had been holding them up because he had thought it important that Hitch's first picture should be a winner. Then the other two might be good enough to get booked in the wake of the first one's success. From the business point of view, Gainsborough could not put out a picture that would give Hitch a weak start. That would do no good to those that followed. What was to be done? An investment not only in one but in three pictures and in a man's career was in jeopardy. *The Lodger* was a mystery thriller, obviously high-class and possibly that was why W. and F. were objecting to it. Yet there did seem to be something wrong with it. Would I look at it and see what I could do? It was a long chance, in view of my inexperience—this was, in fact, my first film assignment outside Dansey Yard—but Adrian had suggested that in view of my having handled Film Society pictures of odd style and thriller content, I might come up with something.

Of course I jumped at the chance. The fee was, I think, £60.

I had not hitherto met Hitch, although I had heard of him. He looked rather as he does now, but plumper and younger, a somewhat enlarged edition of Harry Langdon. He had an absolutely warranted confidence in his own taste and judgement as far as technical matters of film-making were concerned. He had a rationalist's eye for consecutive story-telling, a logician's ability for economical scripting to carry the narrative, and—nearly if not entirely uniquely among the British film directors of his day—an artist's eye for meaningful compositions of the image (he had started in a studio as a title-writer; not a literary deviser of the texts but the craftsman who graphically composes the text in the rectangle and actually hand-writes the letters). His particular talents of suspense and, what I would rate even higher, his observation of familiar and unfamiliar pictorial detail and their weaving into the treatment to make unlikely events appear realistic—these had not yet fully developed. But there was certainly no other director ready to analyse and dissect a problem before solving it in a way which made collaboration with him such a pleasure for me throughout many years. Not that at that moment, though our paths then crossed, we did much collaborating. At that moment Hitch was troubled, anxious and diffident with good reason. There is no barrier to a young man of talent like the fatal "I knew him when . . ." of a senior rival insinuated in the ear of an employer or prospective employer, referring to some past humble capacity from which at last the young man's ability gives him deserved opportunity to rise. Hitch had not only hand-written titles when he started at Islington, he had served as an assistant-director to Cutts on a whole number of the latter's pictures there. Cutts could recognise the threat to his primacy and Woolf lent a ready ear to the poison Cutts injected.

Hitch was introduced to the spoiled young outsider who was to "improve" his picture. This was a bad start indeed to cooperation, for the situation was as humiliating for the one as it was embarrassing for the other. He generously left me to look at the film and set about its reconstruction on my own—to do it, with Mick's consent, as I saw fit. He carried out, with an excellent grace, the retakes I requested—although I never have quite understood why they, principally fresh long-shots of the lynching chase, did not tone better with the close-ups to be embodied in them; perhaps the same cameraman was not available. But gradually we began to talk about the problems together. He accepted my ideas without demur, I his with pleasure. We became friends, and although we later had disputes—or rather one major dispute—before eventually we came together again in a still closer and more fruitful collaboration—this first time turned out luckily for us both.

My solution to the immediate problem was that, as *The Lodger* was an "unusual" film, we must go the whole hog and make it more unusual. There was not the slightest point in toning it down and making it neither one thing nor the other, to please W. and F. or anyone else. If we did, it would lose any distinction it might have and certainly not please the public. More than any other director in Britain at that time, Hitch told his story sufficiently in pictures. So I cut down the titles as far as possible. Except in one respect. I had noticed the effectiveness in *The Gold Rush*, which had just been shown, of Charlie's device of frequently using the name of his heroine as a one-word emotive refrain title: "Georgia." "Georgia." Each time an echo evoking a mood. I did the same here with Hitch's picture: "Daisy." "Daisy." I have no idea why the plagiarism was missed by the critics, but it seems to have been. *The Lodger* could not be made a wholly titleless picture, but the titles were got down to eighty instead of the usual from three hundred and fifty to five or six hundred, And we had McKnight Kauffer do mysterious and dramatic backgrounds for the main titles. Hitch was pleased. So was Mick. C. M. Woolf was overborne and washed his hands of us. The press went gooey-eyed over *The Lodger* and Mick's gamble paid off. The log-jam broke, the two earlier films could now come out and the original "Hitchcock touches" in their treatment got their full meed of attention.

This episode coincided with the breaking of the other Gainsborough deadlock. Adrian at last got his assignment to direct. He relates in his autobiography that he had wanted to do, and been promised, *The Rolling Road*, the story of a boy and girl love affair after a shipwreck on a desert island in the Pacific. Instead, at the last moment this was snatched away. Cutts eventually did it instead (and a right mess he made of it, too, as you shall hear). Adrian was told to think of a war subject.

He did not want to do a conventional chauvinistic war film of "bangs and gunpowder", but I had an idea. Hell was ill at the time and I remember visiting her with flowers in her sick-room and sitting beside the bed while we worked out notes together on a half sheet of paper.

The idea was no more original than "Daisy." "Daisy." Nevertheless it had not been exploited, at any rate in British cinema, before. This was simply to make a *non-battle* picture, a story of the home front, bringing in all the things that people would remember, recruiting and blackouts and ration cards and home leave and air raids and the armistice and so forth. As hackneyed skeleton to stick this on, we wrote down on the half-sheet a novelettish sequence of events, the well-to-do family with a daughter (Lilian Hall-Davis) marrying an officer (Jameson Thomas) who was killed at the front, a clean, fresh, young-looking son (Godfrey Winn) who was missing believed killed and had picked up a French peasant girl wife who had befriended him in his loneliness in France and, turned up, their baby in her arms, on the doorstep during the fireworks of the November 1918 armistice celebrations, and so forth.

Adrian liked it, Mick liked it and it went straight ahead. This was the film that we called *Blighty*. I sold Mick the half-sheet of paper for £25, because we were so keen for him to let Adrian do it, only we made two reservations to the sale. I retained the novel rights in case I should ever want to write it up and, as Adrian rather thought he might one day like to try a play out of it, the contract provided that play rights should be his. The sequel must go here although it happened rather later. A fair time afterwards when I had left Islington and was hard up, I was reading the book reviews in one of the more respectable Sunday newspapers, and among the new novels the title *Blighty* caught my eye. I read the review, which was rather favourable, and the plot seemed familiar, the characters' names identical. I got on to the publisher who referred me to Gainsborough. It appears that they had forgotten all about the contract and their publicity office had got a young fiction writer to undertake the novel on commission to help publicise the film. Gainsborough grudgingly consulted its files and admitted that they had disposed by error of a property not theirs. What was I to do? The situation was complicated: first, Adrian was still working for the firm and I knew how vindictive film interests can be; second, I knew Mick was innocent of the mistake and did not want to make trouble for him; three, it was exceedingly unlikely I would ever get round to writing a novel out of it anyway; four, the author was said to be a young man, the review praised the novel, and the position was not his fault either. The simplest way out seemed to be to agree that the contract between Gainsborough and the publishers should stand; it should merely be altered to substitute me as owner and beneficiary. I was unlucky, but there it was.

I was also, the event proved, a fool. The day after this had been arranged I got a letter from Woolworth's saying that in view of the success of the film they would like to have a paper-back novel written up from its story. They would have it done and printed in a first imprint of a quarter of a million copies. Terms offered: a farthing a copy.

Easy mental arithmetic will show that this would have meant a first payment to me of over a thousand pounds. But it was too late. The infernal hard-back publishers refused to consider, on any conditions, releasing paperback rights. To cap all, only now did I discover that the hardback was just as hackneyed as my original story outline, that its author was an employee of the very newspaper in which I had read the favourable review, and that this last had been written by a colleague. The novel died the death. This is the nearest I have ever come to literary fortune.

However, back to the film. A hard-boiled professional, Eliot Stannard (chiefly notable as the original of *Bootle's Baby*) was engaged to write the scenario. His method, which caused me wonderment, was to sit down and tap it straight out on the typewriter as he thought of it, without change or erasure. I appreciate that today this is more common.

We cast, as our star and Roman matron with stiff upper lip against misfortune, Ellaline Terriss. She was rightly a great name in the English theatre and cost a lot; but alas, when we had finished casting, we had no money left in the budget for the father, and the nearly anonymous bit-part actor who played her husband was so intimidated at the idea of appearing opposite her that he did not dare take lunch with his film wife in the studio and used to bring a packet of sandwiches to consume modestly hidden behind parts of the scenery. We included Renee and Billie Houston in small roles, I think in the scenes of armistice rejoicing; it was their first appearance before the camera. For the French girl, with Mick's assent, I went over to Paris to get Nadia Sibirskaia who, a few months earlier, had impressed all the Film Society members with a deeply moving performance in a film called *Menilmontant*. I am not quite sure, however, whether the tremendous effect of that film owed more to the fine acting and direction or to the appearance, in scarcely lit double or treble photography, of a momentary vision then unique to all of us, the actress's nude back view. She was no more Siberian than you or I, but as Parisian as the waif she portrayed, and had taken her *nom de guerre* because the young man who had set the film up with her and directed it was an emigré called Kirsanoff. I had much difficulty in persuading her to come, for she spoke no English and had never been out of France. Besides, she would clearly miss Kirsanoff, who joined his entreaties to mine because he unselfishly considered the publicity abroad might help forward her career. She agreed in the end on condition that her contract included joint top billing with her name in type of size equal to that of Terriss.

This was fair, the one famous on the British stage but devoid of film experience, the other unknown in England but having proved herself a film actress to rave about. I saw that this was done.

In the upshot her experience was unhappy. Sibirskaia was bitterly lonely in London. She gave an excellent performance, but lacked what she needed, masculine company and admiration. She grew more and more miserable and perked up only as her ordeal neared its close. When the last day on the studio floor was reached, and, as befits the end of a voyage, toasts were drunk in champagne, Godfrey Winn—whose first and, I think, last film part this was—picked her up and gaily waltzed her round the floor. If only this had come about earlier things might have been different. The end of the story is abominable. When the film was distributed, Nadia Sibirskaia's name was entirely omitted from every poster and advertisement. I protested at once, but Gainsborough's lawyers explained that *the company* had breached no contract; it had included her name with everyone else's in the cast list on the film itself; Gainsborough, producers, could not be held responsible for what W. and F., distributors, might choose to do in conducting their own business, and all the posters and advertisements were theirs. W. and F. for their part said the name Sibirskaia was unnecessary, it was unknown in Britain and was too long; it would clutter up any advertisement. I took legal advice but was helpless. I was told that, when seeing to her contract, I should have insisted on a sub-clause requiring that the company's obligations respecting publicity be transferred to any distributor or purchaser of the film.

This did not give me any better liking for my associates on the "business" side of the industry. Mick had quite a hard job keeping the peace. The mutual animosity was ill-disguised. About this time Mick called me in as editing retriever a second time. Now it was Graham Cutts's South Sea epic, pinched from Adrian, that was in trouble. The cutting was not finished, but it was already a worry. Some of the action was insufficiently clear and the big scenes did not come off effectively.

Some points for repair seemed obvious enough in the projection theatre. The shipwreck scene, which involved a sort of mutiny and panic taking to the boats imperfectly quelled by the captain, was unclear because no one could see that, when he threatened the crew, the captain was armed with a revolver, or how and when he became disarmed in the mêlée. I asked for extra close-ups to be taken, but Cutts was in a bad mood. All conversation had to be conducted through his agent and, when he finally agreed to take the shots, they came out angled so that the new close-up revolver was just as invisible as before, and I had to retake the scenes once again myself. These retakes were my first time of film directing.

The second problem was worse. I thought it could be lessened, though not eliminated. There was a lot of bareskin mutual chasing of the hero and heroine, slightly though always respectably clad (in essentials at least), along the sandy shores of the deserted island. It was obviously intended to be titillating. I found it only repellent. These scenes could not be eliminated, but they could be shortened. C. M. Woolf himself was brought down to the studio to hear my verdict. He kept saying: "Of course, Mr. Montagu is a gentleman, he would not understand." I was furious. The last thing I wished anyone to suppose me was a gentleman, in this or any other sense (save that of G.B.S., of which Woolf would not have heard). I really do believe he thought I was objecting to the scene because it was erotic. Quite the contrary. Not only I but anyone else must have found it profoundly anaphrodisiac. The hero, who—I understand now—had found part of the capital for the film and was really a very nice man, was middle-aged and far too mature in appearance for this sort of boy-and-girl *Blue Lagoon* stuff; the girl was an ingenue all right but, where she should have been voluptuous, was, alas, ladylike.

This time Mick stood by me. The facts were only too painfully bare, they stared you in the face. The trims were done. And I found myself more or less transferred to Islington, responsible for supervising both scripts *and* editing, at a wage of £40 a week. Tod, with Jock, Angus and the rest carried on by themselves at Dansey Yard for the time being; they were quite capable enough to do without Adrian and me.

It was now December 1926 and Hell and I decided, at least I suppose I kept urging and she finally agreed, that we would get married.

§ 24

We decided on this although I had just dissipated my grand-patrimony.

That is, my grandfather had left me £300. I had got my hands on it and spent it. This is how it happened.

The last time we spoke of table tennis I had become Chairman of the Table Tennis Association in 1922. I was still Chairman, but not a quite happy one. Our two most energetic and ingenious pioneers in the revival quarrelled, threats of slander writs flew in all directions. My attempts at conciliation ended, as all too often do such good intentions, in both parties resigning, leaving us rather bare. For a time we functioned just as a loose link of almost self-selected executive members, trying to gather under our umbrella any group that we heard of that had continued or started up playing. There were elections, certainly, but in the nature of things those who got elected were mostly a few personalities well known to followers by their past prominence in the game or residence near London, with a sprinkling who could afford occasional journeys from the north to meetings in the south.

In 1926 a new recruit set out to change all that. He was W. J. Pope and he was hardly even an Englishman, being born in Newport, Monmouthshire. Nevertheless, he had a vision that within twelve months he successfully imposed on us, of creating a new kind of body, nationally representative, by restricting the election of the executive to nominees from separate area constituencies into which the country became divided. The new body was eventually called (in 1927) the "English Table Tennis Association" and I became its first President and Chairman. At first I did not understand the necessity for all this, and hesitated to support him. Later I saw he was right and he became my best friend for twenty years, until just after the Second War he died from a cerebral lesion. Anyway, his conception turned us into a real national body and was the making of the game in this country. He had gained the knowledge of this necessity from experience of trade union organisation, being an office worker in Unity House, the headquarters of the National Union of Railwaymen. W. J. Pope was small, with hairline receding far beyond his forehead, almost pop-eyes, enormous energy, a fierceness that could as readily become a shy diffident smile, and a frank way with people that was winning and even compelling. Though now retired from active politics, he had been a lifelong socialist and rebel. He learnt his own table tennis—he was a first-class attacking player in the old Welsh style with penholder grip wipes on the forehand—in Bradford gaol where he had been confined during the war as a conscientious objector. And I think that in my own political work and development he found a vicarious satisfaction.

Pope qualified at the trials that year for a place in the England team in our annual match against Wales. This was the only international played in those days, for the game was not properly organised anywhere outside Britain. But he gave up his place to come with me on a trip to Berlin. We took with us a scratch team composed of some veterans outside the charmed ranks of top selection and some boys from his office club at Unity House. The previous year, a Dr. Lehmann of Berlin had invited there the current English champion, a tall and athletic Indian student named P. N. Nanda, and held a tournament with lawn tennis scoring. Nanda won every round by the score of 6–0 6–0. Now in summer 1926 Dr. Lehmann repeated his invitation to every centre in Europe—there were few enough—where he had heard of players. The lesson we learned was that though the players we had brought might still be well ahead of Germany, they were no match for the two or three visitors from Budapest and Vienna.

The result was that, as chief officers of the oldest association participating, Bill Pope and I then and there extended a provisional invitation to those present to come to London in December for a European Championships, subject to confirmation by our executive committee at home. Pope and I found a hall—the old Memorial Hall in Farringdon Street—where the event could be staged. We should have to build tiered seating, but even with hospitality offered to all teams we hoped to lose not too much money. The Committee was scared of the commitment, however, and their reluctance could only be overcome by my offering a guarantee. This is where the £300 had to go. I could not guarantee more for it was all I had. The place was packed and we got out just inside the guarantee. Yet when I think of the championships as they are nowadays—we made them into "world" titles retrospectively at a foundation meeting of the "International Table Tennis Federation" held afterwards—with forty or more associations participating and guarantees from host city or host country necessarily running into scores of thousands of pounds, I do not think we did badly.

Sometimes we wasted money. To tempt teams to come from abroad we had offered a contribution to the travelling expenses of each. At the preliminary meeting each foreign country concerned sent a diplomat and I, more tactful than wise, politely handed each his due in a sealed envelope addressed to him but without asking for a receipt. The day after the meeting the Czechoslovak legation representative—an elegant young man from Sudetenland who twelve years later joined Hitler—after much hum-ing and ha-ing asked me for his cash. It turned out that the ass, used to diplomatic conferences and above treating lesser documents of importance, had thrown it away with all the other material that had been given to him, dropping it into the first waste-paper-basket he met so that it was irrevocably lost. I had been an ass too of course and had to reimburse him. On the other hand, mother graciously saved us money by presenting us with a cup, which we used for the men's team championships of the world, the table tennis equivalent of the Davis Cup, and my father took me once more to the bullion room at Samuel Montagu and Co., where I chose a fine fat-bellied design in old English style which has survived the intervening years and cost £35 secondhand.

At the foundation meeting in the library at Kensington Court, I was elected chairman of the new International Federation. The delegates had little alternative because I was the only one present who could speak all the languages we needed. I held this post, and its succeeding title "President" (introduced when my back was turned so to speak, at the first meeting I missed), for nearly forty-one years. I used to comfort myself with the thought that not all this effort was waste, that the game has provided a lot of fun and exercise in a lot of parts of the world through its expansion, and perhaps built just a few friendships, but now I dismiss such vanities as only guesswork. It is just as often that things people happen to do are able to be done simply because the time is ripe and, if one had not been there oneself, some other character could have come along and done them better.

Anyway, I have promised the reader not to be technical about the sport, so that I will record only that Hungarians in the end won nearly everything, that we thought ourselves well repaid by the respectable and reasonably respectful publicity gained, *The Times* through the father of the present Peter Wilson, an expert on ball games, being particularly good on the Men's Singles final. We had usually found it hard to get any newspaper reporting at all, unless derisive. It is an ironical memory that, while I was still writing for the *Observer*, I asked a news editor once whether there was not any way at all we could get articles printed on our young players, and he replied to me unhelpfully that nobody was interested in any of the names I mentioned, such as (e.g.) Fred Perry, and that we must first get them known (how?) before we could expect any newspaper to print anything about them.

This is related to show that if we decided to get married, in spite of Hell's misgivings, it was not because we had any capital. There was also no *assured* income and the prospects in my chosen occupation were highly dicey. The reason for our decision was that twice during the previous twelvemonth we had made up our minds to separate for good and all and never see each other again, but had not been able to. We found we could not be happy parted and were content together. And that seems to me a good reason.

I must now tell the reader more about Hell. This cannot be a biography until she chooses to write it herself, when it will be exciting and instructive enough. But a few details are necessary as background to what follows. Hell was a tiny baby, the youngest child of an over 40-year-old mother who had eight children over the years. When Hell was born her eldest sister was already 23 years old. When we first met, her father was already dead; he had died suddenly one night. He was a master made-to-measure bootmaker for bespeaking clients in South London. Some years ahead of when I write, we went with Marjorie Russell to a week-end with Constance Spry and her husband Henry, a retired judge from India; it turned out that he used to get boots from her father and now, thirty years later, was still wearing them, which shows how good they must have been. There are Hellstern bootshops too in Bond Street, the Rue de la Paix and Fifth Avenue. I have seen them. A family legend says these were founded by the *good* members of the family, all pious Jews, but that Hell's father's father was the *bad* one, the atheist cobbler of medieval tradition, who was content to be cut off in his infidelity and instead of sharing the family fortune work as craftsman for himself. It is pleasanter not to disturb this legend than to try to verify it. The mother, Kate, was a girl from Surrey. Faced suddenly by such responsibilities and complications as her husband's death involved, she could not cope with them and had some years of breakdown in an institution. Hell went to work early and for years earned her living in the most varied occupations, in sweets manufacture at Pascall's and in the rag trade, as well as by typewriting and shorthand. The father of her daughter was an older man who came from Leicester. The daughter, ours since, is called Rowna. This was probably some mistake because there is no such name, but whether it was intended to be Rona or Rhona or even Rowena, all perfectly possible names, and whether the slip was Hell's fault or the registrar's, remains uncertain. Anyway it is nicer than any of these and should have started a fashion. Her mother, back with the family, and an unmarried milliner sister, helped Hell to look after Rowna. I had met Rowna, who was now 5 years old as I have described, and she seemed prepared to tolerate me, however reluctantly.

As soon as we had reached our decision and were sure of it I pressed that it should be carried out as soon as possible. But how? You may think you can get married easily after you come of age but things are not so simple as that. It appears that you can only give notice to the registrar, even of just a secular marriage, if one of the parties is qualified by residence in the appropriate parish for at least one day immediately previously. This was a dreadful hurdle. Hell did not wish to inform her people and get married from Brixton any more than I intended to inform mine and get married from Kensington. But it turned out that Lincoln's Inn, being one of the Inns of Court, is in some way extra-territorial, it belongs to no parish. Nobody who lives there can get married at all, unless they qualify by staying at least one night somewhere else—from midnight to 6 a.m. are the magic hours, just as for residence at Cambridge—and then notify the registrar appropriate to this temporary address.

Now came the greatest absurdity. It ought to have been easy. We took advice from the nearest available Registrar, at St. Giles, between Holborn and Tottenham Court Road. (The site of his office has since been destroyed by bombing.) All that had to be done was for me to get into an hotel nearby at the appropriate time. But I was working harder than I ever had before. There were no unions in the film industry in those days and I worked nearly right round the clock. During daytime I had to be in conference with Mick or the film directors, arguing about scenarios, or sometimes keeping actual or prospective cast sweet; nights—when I could be quiet and undisturbed, either alone or with an assistant—I worked at cutting, over at Islington, perpetually on the treadmill to maintain the schedules. More than once we made a tentative date for the wedding and then I missed getting to the hotel by midnight because something urgent cropped up. What idiots we can be!

Finally we managed to get everything in order for 10 January. I remember the date partly because it was my sister's birthday and partly because that year it was the date of one of Southampton's cup-ties.

We both got to St. Giles registry office in time, I from Wardour Street, Hell from the same direction, for she was now working at a rag trade shop north of Oxford Street. The witnesses met us there: Angus and Marjorie. Owing to my ignorance and impracticality, there was yet another hitch. This was at the final seconds of the twelfth hour itself. I had read somewhere that the ring is a ritual relic of the chain—the first link in fact—with which the husband in some period attached his wife to symbolise that henceforth she was to be his property. It seemed an odious ritual to which no woman should be subjected. I had no intention that, at our wedding, Hell should endure such an humiliation. So I had no ring, not accidentally but intentionally. I supposed that the ring was only a part of the religious service. That it was a legal necessity of the secular ceremony in the registry office was undreamed of by me. Accordingly, when the registrar asked me for the ring I smiled blandly and explained that we were not going to use one. There followed argument in which I was discomfited—I had to borrow one from Marjorie; in fact she pulled it off her finger and made Hell a present of it so that I could perform the actual process of putting it on the bride. Later I got Hell a jade one, but that lasted only until she caught something hard that somebody threw to her to catch. Indeed, Hell did not have a proper wedding ring until, after my father's death, my mother gave me his beautifully ornate, almost filigree, old fashioned tie-ring. Reduced in bore, it makes a lovely wedding ring and is real gold.

We kissed, for we were, I dare claim, in love, but there is even more yet for me now, as an old man, to be ashamed of. I had managed to squeeze into the schedule the hotel at the right date, and the wedding, but now the manifold burdens of all that I let preoccupy me caught up again. Mick had at the last moment bidden me lunch with and chat up some actress he wanted in a coming picture. I had to push off and leave Angus and Marjorie to lunch the bride. That Hell neither wept nor swore never to see me more is due perhaps less to a forgiving nature than to the fact that she already knew what she was taking on. There are some advantages in marriage partners getting to know each other thoroughly beforehand.

§ 25

THE SECRET marriage, thus begun, did not long remain secret.

Yet it was no leak that revealed it to my family, but I myself, deliberately.

At first the wedding made no difference to the outward relationship between Hell and me. She continued to live in Brixton and work in the West End, I to live in Lincoln's Inn, work in Soho or Islington and visit Kensington Court.

It was after one such visit to Kensington Court that I was leaving, late, and going downstairs to return to Lincoln's Inn after all others in the house had gone to bed, when my father emerged from his dressing-room to call me back upstairs. He was in his vest, I remember, and the braces of his trousers were undone and hanging down the back.

What he had to say was epoch-making. He had decided to come with me to see Southampton play in the next round of the Cup.

I was inexpressibly moved. Those who have read so far will realise that this was the first time in my life he had ever made a gesture towards even an appearance of respect for any of my ideas—I dare say towards an idea or liking of any of his children—that he did not himself share and approve.

Football he thought vulgar, and beyond any decent pale. It is an interesting fact that the Southampton Football Club directors had some years before invited him to take shares in the club and become one of them. He had replied: No, thank you, he spent quite enough on sport already, supporting county cricket and lawn tennis. The truth was, it was precisely because of this, which was of course generally known and appreciated, that the Saints directors had decided to reward this local philanthropy by their offer. The Saints, at that time season after season heading or near-heading the table first of the Southern League, then of the Third Division of the Football League, to which it was transformed, were doing very well and profitably.

There are, I hope, many instances of my father's generosity or indulgence to his children in these pages. To me, for example, the transference (a sensible business deal but one of which I was beneficiary) of his Zoo membership, his underwriting by £1 guarantee of the Film

Society, his backing of various expeditions, at B.M. solicitation, his cooperation in provision of the Swaythling Cup. But then none of these acts transcended what he considered, in his own code, actions appropriate to our family status. This code was liberal enough. Art he could understand as a U occupation, if an eccentric one, but not science, which still smacked of handicraft. Like his father before him, he saw making money as the true occupation, not—I should be precise—certainly for itself, but as an opportunity for service by contributing to the stability of society, to philanthropy and culture. This could conceivably be attained to a degree by following the arts or literature; experience proved it—my mother for example had taken me as a child to visit the studio of Alma Tadema. The size of the mansion and the place recognised in society for the artist, as well as his title, would have satisfied my father for any of his children. In that he was far more tolerant and less tyrannical in imposing his own standards than his father was before him. But he had no taste at all for mice and such, and hence the long passionate battle which I had been forced to accept as lost. I knew what he meant by offering to come with me to a football match, what it counted for in hidden and unexpressed affection, and how much it must have cost him.

After thanking him and saying "Good-night" I went on downstairs. For the first time I was troubled at having a secret from him. My impulse at once was to drop all barriers between us, to make a new effort to communicate, to repay his gesture by my frankness.

Still pondering, I reached the hall, where Woolven was waiting to let me out. I told him what I was thinking about. His reply was the only one possible for a perfect butler. "You had better tell his Lordship," he said.

I went back upstairs and knocked on father's dressing-room door. He called "Come in!" I entered and told him that, incidentally, I thought he might like to know, I had recently married.

The moment of intimacy was lost, for ever. How could I have expected anything else?

He led me at once into the library and demanded an explanation. I remember exactly his disconcerted look, the heavy, not quite walrus moustaches. I haltingly told him of Hell's virtues and qualities, of what we meant to each other and of our happiness.

He asked me if she were a Jewess. I was able to reply that though she had not been brought up as one, she was certainly of Jewish origin. This was quite true, for there was no doubt of this in respect of her father. I knew this meant a lot to my father because one of the few arguments I had overheard between him and my mother had been on this subject. He had reproached her for asking Harold and Frida Laski to the house, saying of this marriage "outside the faith" that one could not run with the hare and hunt with the hounds, it must either be one thing or the other. My mother had replied with unwonted fierceness that in this respect he was "the sort of thing that made the Christian religion necessary"; despite her pride in her own father's return to Judaism and her dutiful teaching of her children, and in complete contrast to her narrow political blinkers, she had no religious bigotry. My father appeared quite satisfied by my reply on this point, and it was never raised again, but he kept muttering at everything else I said:

"Yes, but why did you have to marry her?"

This attitude shocked me, and reminded me once more of the gulf of incomprehension that I should never really be able to cross. My reply was the worst possible. I said:

"I do not know."

At that moment it appeared to me the natural, the only right and truthful thing to say.

I now realise, of course, that we were speaking on—as they say now—totally different wavelengths. What I meant was that I was not prepared to justify sociologically the institution of marriage. I had brought myself up on the healthy dialectics of Shaw and Wells, who—as I have already indicated—by questioning the most sacred assumption of the Victorians about marriage and all other family relationships, forced a re-examination by their generation from which our present society now benefits. What I meant by my words was: whatever our feelings for each other I would not presume to suggest that it necessarily followed, from the viewpoint of an ideal society, that they should result in marriage. All he understood, and I did not in my naïveté realise this until long afterwards, thinking it over, was simply that I already regretted what I had done.

Had I instead simply uttered the conventional words appropriate to his own set of ethics and values, the three simple words: "I love her"—then indeed, I think now, his reactions would have been quite different. He would have doubted, he would have dismissed my judgement, but then, grumbling, his sense of respect for the individual integrity of all but his children—perhaps even, in the end, of his children also—would have made him approach the situation quite differently. But I did not say these three words. They could never have occurred to me. Not because they were not, and indeed have remained till today, the mainspring of my life, but because I should immediately have denied that, in themselves, they provided an adequate logical motivation for marriage in the year 1927.

My father called my mother from her bedroom and she came in wearing her dressing-gown. My mother, however surprised, was much less floored by the situation. She did not reproach, so much as seek details. I remember her saying: "But I thought you were fond of one of the Houston sisters, the younger one with the short hair." I think I irrelevantly replied: "Yes, but Hell has just the same haircut." This was a completely absurd remark of course, but the situation had gone beyond rational conversation. I think I was surprised at my mother's knowledge of my doings and acquaintances shown by her mention of Billie. Where she was wrong, of course, was in guessing that my admiration there was anything but the relationship of fan to idol, or rather, one of four fans to a double idol: the target of my true feelings had been unsuspected. Even at that moment I noticed, with some irony, the contrast between my parents' respective reactions to the two crises within a twelvemonth: the General Strike and now the surprise news of my marriage. In the former case it was my mother whose intolerance was boundless, she even showed a certain venom; my father who respected my stand as a fulfilment of obligation, however wrong-headed and misguided he considered the views that had led to it. Now it was my father who was struck down by what he clearly regarded as an irremediable calamity, my mother, who was distressed more for his sake than by the deed itself, sought chiefly to mollify and console him.

Obviously, the matter could be taken no further then. I went downstairs and let myself out.

§ 26

MY FATHER'S first step was to send for his youngest brother, Lionel, then wintering in Monte Carlo. After all, was he not a bachelor, the family "man of the world"? Was he not the one familiar with cards, racehorses and therefore presumably with women, at least such a woman as Hell was supposed to be?

Lionel invited us to dinner in his flat. It was a nice flat, comfortable and not too crowded, with furniture in excellent taste, and a piano. The food was good, He was friendly and cheerful, doing his utmost to put Hell at her ease. His mission was plain. It was to look Hell over. This mission was faithfully accomplished. If, as we later heard rumoured in the family, it was also to buy her off, the conversation did not get round to the point of anything so vulgar. I have never dared during this last forty years to ask Hell whether she is sorry this was so, or no.

Nevertheless, the matter soon emerged into the public domain. But not through the fault of any confidant. Hell and I were driving back from somewhere Kent way when we saw the posters: "BARON'S SON WEDS SECRETARY". The story was now out, the fat was in the fire. We bought an *Evening News* and there it was, bannered across the front page with my picture (the latter worth no more than a one-column block of course). They had no photograph of Hell.

The paper had got its beat, though belatedly, in the ordinary way of business. It was the duty of special reporters to watch the registry offices in the West End for news stories, just as it was the duty of others to keep an eye on the police courts. The St. Giles man, luckily for us, had missed the statutory advance notice of our marriage, but had caught up with it thumbing through back records. It was as simple as that.

I suppose times have changed. How can such a private incident of relations between two not very important people become a nine days' nonsense for the newspapers? It would not happen today, would it? Or would it still?

The first objective was to get Hell down to Brixton, quick. Her family must be reassured in case there were worries. I hurried on from there to Lincoln's Inn.

The telephone rang incessantly. Where was Mrs. Ivor Montagu? Had I a photograph of Mrs. Montagu I would give to the press? Where could this or that agency take a photograph? Had I any statement to make?

I was obtuse, stubborn. I would give no information. No, they should NOT have a photograph. These were private matters. I disapproved of publicity about what was nobody else's business. I would not cooperate in any way. The jackals, of course, only returned the hungrier to the fray. I held them off.

The next day I was at Gainsborough when a telephone call came from Lubliner's, the dressmakers in Berners Street where Hell was now working. The press had discovered the address and photographers were congregating outside. What should Hell do? By now I was raging. We should not be put upon. Why should we be pestered into doing something we did not want? Her face should NOT become public property. Those responsible for this importunity should NOT be rewarded. Mick was consulted and remembered that the premises of Willy Clarkson, the theatrical costumier, were also in Soho, not too far from Hell. I rushed off there and when I went on into Lubliner's I had a parcel under my arm. When we emerged Hell was wearing a mask and a black wig.

Next morning, when we looked out of the window down into the courtyard outside Old Buildings we could see a young man waiting there with camera. We were now besieged.

I have spoken of the way out of No. 19 through a window on to a lead flat among the roof-tiles. We found now that we could wriggle on beyond there, and climb over projections and similar leads across the roofs, with no damage to clothes other than the dirtiness incurred by sliding on roof-tiles, and no difficulty or danger, to another staircase. So this is how, still stubborn, we now came and went. That lunchtime we ate at Pinoli's, in the lower part of Wardour Street. The place, which was cheap, had the most numerous *hors d'œuvres* in London, and while we tucked into these and discussed strategy, Mycroft told us that we were being stupid.

"By refusing them, you have only got their backs up. They will never let you go so long as you stop them. If you let them have a photograph, they'll forget about you both in half a day. The longer you obstruct them the more frantic they'll be."

He was obviously right and I was a fool. He went on: "What is more, sooner or later they will get a picture of Hell, you can't keep them off for ever. When they do get it you don't want it to be a newspaper flash with shut eyes and her mouth agape." He chuckled: "When the public do see Hell you want her to be looking her best. Why not get on to Sasha?" (This was Alex Stewart, the husband of Leila Stewart, W. and F.'s publicity chief, whom I have mentioned way back as a society photographer. His studio was in Suffolk Street.) "He'll do it for you and give the photographs out as well so that you will have no bother. There is only one thing. If you do let him distribute them, which would be the most sensible thing, you might consider suggesting to him to offer it to the *Evening Standard* first. When the story broke in the *Evening News*, the editor sent for me and asked me if I had known about it. He knew I must know you because of the Film Society. I said yes, certainly I had known, but that you were a friend of mine. You may imagine he wasn't pleased."

When I talked about Walter Mycroft earlier I mentioned that whatever he might have been or done later, he had given me reason to be thankful to him. I was thinking of this act of loyalty and also of his good advice.

Sasha did the trick immediately. I will not say the pictures do show Hell at her best. At least he managed to give her a satisfying languishing and romantic look. Coloured, they would have looked very nice on chocolate boxes. And that suited their purpose.

We had no further need for concealment and made our way openly back to Lincoln's Inn. As we approached the staircase at Old Buildings, the waiting besieger came forward with his camera and a smile. He was quite a young man. As he prepared to take his photograph we told him that it was unnecessary: the *Evening Standard* with the portrait on its front page were already on the streets. The effect was unanticipated. He immediately burst into tears.

He told us that he was a freelance, the sole support of his widowed mother, or something of that kind. That it was not easy for a freelance to sell pictures to the newspapers unless they were something out of the ordinary. That he had got his mother to pack sandwiches and taken up his stance at the foot of the staircase, for he knew we lived there, and if he stayed there long enough we must appear sooner or later and then at last he would have a picture that every editor wanted. I remained silent. There was nothing to say. What could I do, except once again feel a heel?

Meanwhile a veritable blizzard of correspondence had been showered on Kensington Court from my mother's numerous and widespread acquaintances—all sympathy letters.

When I plucked up courage to call some time later she sat there with her secretary, still opening them, answering them, filing them. They struck a fairly monotonous note. One she showed me, a letter from a young intimate of hers I did not like, forever at Townhill, the daughter of a general, said: "I always think there is something so parrot-like in the idea of a secretary." A cutting came from U.S.A. It seems Hell and I had reached immortality in comic strip. There we were, both of us in immaculate evening dress throughout the adventures illustrated, I looking like David Niven and Hell like Beatrice Lillie. My father was sternly resentful and dignified, definitely a Lewis Stone casting, my mother burly and dewlapped like a Daughter of the Revolution. Then the Queen was shown writing a letter that ordered the family to soften and eventually brought reconciliation.

Believe it or not, there actually was among my mother's huge snowfall of letters one from Queen Mary and she showed it me. I do not know how wind of it had got across the Atlantic but evidently it had. However, the Queen was much too tactful to express commiseration on the occasion of an alliance with one who, after all, held equal claim to respect as one of her husband's subjects. She wrote simply: "Dear Gladys, I feel for you, May."

Only one sign of life came from Rowna's father and it should be recorded to his credit. Hell had not heard from him for some years. But now he turned up at her Brixton home, knocked on the door and asked, rather thickly, whether the child was "all right". Hell's sister answered the door of the flat and would not admit him. She must have answered affirmatively. He went away and did not reappear.

§ 27

AFFAIRS AT Islington were now not quite so pressing. Several new projects were safely on the stocks and the finishing ones under control. Adrian was beginning—not his own choice of subject—on *The Vortex*. As he foresaw, the censor was certain to eviscerate any guts it might have possessed at birth, and Noel Coward's plot: "Mother, will you give up lovers if I give up drugs?" necessarily became: "Mummy, will you give up going to teas and dances if I give up cigarettes and aspirins?" not the most compelling of dramatic issues. Mick was ready to give me leave and Dansey Yard was ticking over. So a honeymoon became feasible. Where?

Any expedition abroad was invariably associated in my mind with being useful. The selfishness of the fact that what I considered useful always, or almost always, coincided with what *I* considered enjoyable and that Hell's tastes and priorities might not always, even if nearly always, coincide with mine, had not yet penetrated to my consciousness. So naturally I consulted Hinton at South Kensington. Was there anything the B.M. specially wanted anywhere in Europe? "Yes," replied Hinton, "porcupines from Sicily."

So Sicily it had to be.

We got no porcupines. All we got was paratyphoid for Hell and jaundice for me. Yet our marriage has survived even that beginning.

We went by rail through Paris and Rome. Air travel was not then (in early 1927) nearly so common as it is now. In Palermo I presented credentials at the University, received advice from the Zoology professor about our target area, and the company of one of his students, a stocky young man who was studying divinity as well as science, to act as guide-interpreter. I did not like Sicily. Every destination had to be reached along hard-surfaced dusty roads on foot under the parching sun. Palermo had never before seen a girl with a short-cropped head and knee-length skirts and, in the centre of the city, crowds used to follow us along the streets, laughing and pointing. Some of our troubles we brought on ourselves. I have already sufficiently described how, in my folly, I had regarded marriage as a private affair between the parties only; and looked on rings, wife's altered surname and the like as degraded symbols of female subjection that equal partners should eschew, not, as they are, necessities imposed either by law or custom which forbid, or exact a price for, nonconformity. But in any case we should have had no time between opportunity and departure to change our passports which were still, as originally issued, single.

From Palermo we set out eastward in a hired car along the coast road to a point about half-way between Sicily's east and west. The bumps in the roads were so unbelievable that when we tried to eat our hard-boiled picnic eggs without stopping and losing time they were flung out of our hands. At midway distance we turned abruptly to the right, southward towards the interior, and, after a journey that can only have been five miles by map but most likely was three or four times that in curly winding twists up into the hills, arrived at the town chosen for us by the professor.

Castelbuono was (is?) an extraordinary place. At least it resembled nothing I had hitherto dreamed of or experienced. For all I know it may be typical of the culture that built it and preserved it. The best answers I could find to questions about its total population ran into several thousands. But it did not, as in the case of an urban unit of this size familiar from northern, especially Protestant, Europe, spread over a wide area, with streets and people and vehicles, and grade insensibly through suburbs into the countryside.

Not at all. Like a compressed pimple it sat on the top of a hill, its stone streets, stone dwellings, churches, walls, piazzas, continuous, tight, mysterious even in sunlight, and impenetrable. Around it the town immediately became fields, an investing army rising to the town walls, descending to the twisted corkscrew valleys, into which every morning numerous menfolk from the nature-surrounded stone fortress descended to cultivate cereals or rootcrops or tend olives. In the day-time sun-baked Castelbuono appeared sparsely populated. You would see, aside from occasional carts dragged by reluctant and dejected donkeys, only old women, black-clad, black kerchiefs or scarves tight round their foreheads as headgear, sometimes dragging bundles or pitchers, and little girls. We scarcely saw a female between 6 and 60 during the whole time of our stay in Castelbuono. If we are to suppose that such existed, they must have been locked away in purdah, safe in each dwelling from prying eyes that might violate their prison-citadel.

We put up at an inn in the centre of the town. It had cool, but not quite clean, rooms. There were many fleas and the middle-aged hostess stridently complained that we had brought these to her fine hotel with our dirty animals. (I should recall, for the non-zoological reader that most mammalian parasites are fairly specific, that is to say they do not seek, and cannot survive upon, hosts others than those to which evolution has adapted them; the fleas that were the cause of dissension were certainly familiar human ones, unlikely to have entered her sacred inn on any other carrier.) Our animals were of course mice that I culled from the lines of traps I put down and visited in the fields around while we waited and hoped for news of porcupines. I used to get up and go down each day with the morning light to check the traps before it got too hot and this led to another difficulty. Our embryo priest had brought a French-Italian pocket dictionary with him, to eke out our conversation (it was a smattering of French, not English, that he was able to communicate in). Hell is often a tease to keep things going and make the atmosphere and talk cheerful as well as bearable. Explaining some remark of hers I must unfortunately have said she was a "coquette" (even that it is not true, but in most settings would have served, and dissipated itself on the air, as small-talk); the student must have mistaken the word in his dictionary for "cocotte"—he was certainly aware that our passports were made out in different names because he had handed them in at the inn for registration—and the supposed opportunity aroused his appetite. He soon took to letting me go down the slopes of the fields on my morning rounds alone, while he stayed behind and tried his luck at coaxing, or even forcing, his way into our bedroom before Hell was up. Ever denied and, at last reaching the bed, finally convinced by the one French word she then knew: "*Imbecile!*", he took her refusals as a personal affront, and sulked.

A worse ordeal in some ways was the local Chief of Police, who was simultaneously both Fascist principal and Commissioner in charge of the district that included Castelbuono. His French was better than the student's and he too took to coming into our room, which was a big one, lounging on the side of one of the beds, and making conversation while Hell and I were busy skinning away with our scalpels or sewing up the skins of the day's haul from the trap-lines.

He was a young man about twenty-five, lithe and extremely good-looking in an operatic sort of way. He liked to boast. He could do anything he liked, he said, arrest anyone in the district, imprison them as he wished. (I had never heard of the Mafia, which must, then as before and as now, have wielded real power in the area, so I cannot venture even a conjecture about its relationship at that time with the fascist administration of which the young man was king-pin.) Did we know, he asked—slapping his thighs—that he knew everything about us? He read all our letters, made a point of having them passed to him from the post-office. (We could take this with a grain of salt, for he knew no English and we certainly never met anyone in Castelbuono who could have translated them for him.)

From this he would go on to grin and lick his lips about how, quite soon now, Italy would put Yugoslavia in its place. "From the moment we declare war," he said, "it will take us only twenty-four hours to occupy the whole country." When I begged leave to doubt this, remarking that Yugoslavia had an army too, he brushed the objection aside. "It is nothing, nothing," finally remarking: "Well—forty-eight hours then," as generous offer of compromise. If only wars could dispose exclusively of such odious fire-eaters as he, and leave others unharmed, they would be an institution worth preserving.

Alas, all the days we were there, no one reported porcupines, not even a wild-goose-porcupine-trail worth pursuing. Baffled, we were about to retire with our mice, when someone did bring to the inn a splendid animal, one of the most graceful and beautiful in its movements of all the mammals of Europe, a marten.

We did get it on to the train at Naples, and allowed to travel first-class with us right through to Paris, of course in a cage, for such an animal is too savage, too supple and too swift just to have been let loose in our sleeping compartment. Securing sanction for the embarkation was a feat in itself. At the ticket office I met the same blank wall of refusal based on printed regulations as I had with the *Proteus* at the railway station at Dover. The rule book covering animals allowed in a sleeping compartment spoke only of cats and dogs. It was in vain I insisted that the marten is a form of cat. (A pretty remote form I am afraid, but it should have done for any railway official even half-inclined to be obliging to a passenger.) Unfortunately this official seemed unwilling to be obliging at all and read me a virtuous lecture on the difference between pre-Mussolini Italy, which was lax, and the Italy of Mussolini, which insisted on the maintenance of regulations that were fair to all. Fuming and frustrated, I was tapped on the shoulder by a friendly dragoman who took me behind a pillar and whisperingly asked me if I did not realise that all the booking-clerk wanted was a tip. Such a thing had never occurred to me, I had taken quite seriously the stories by British sympathisers with Fascism of how Mussolini was eliminating corruption from Italy. But there was no more difficulty after I had passed a trivial 200 lire above the fare through the ticket office window and given a like sum to the dragoman.

The journey home was not a relaxing one. We fed the marten with meat solicited from the dining car and gave it water and, when we got to Paris, the Jardin des Plantes took care of it for a few days further. But it got no further and this is a sad story. Almost immediately after arriving in Paris the marten ate its feet off and had to be destroyed. Such tragedies do seem to occur with carnivores that are kept in captivity without proper knowledge and lacking the right vitamins in the diet. The animal seems somehow to sense a lack, though of course it cannot *know* in the human sense what it is that it is seeking. Rather should I say these things used to happen. Now, when all reputable zoos exchange information, sharing available experience on the preservation of their charges, such fates for confined animals are more rare and these are in general far healthier (more long-lived, free of parasites and livelier) than in the wild. In this case we could realise that, if a dietary deficiency was indeed the cause of the animal's self-devouring, this must have been of longer standing than the few days in our possession, and our attempt at bring it away from Sicily the only chance it could have had of recovery.

Our return from Paris to London was uneventful but within a few hours after getting back it was realised that we ourselves too were both ill.

§ 28

I APPROACH the end of this volume. It is perhaps hard to imagine an ordeal more disagreeable to a young woman placed as Hell was, than that which now befell her. Fortunately, throughout most of it she was only partly conscious.

It had been arranged that I was to bring Hell to Kensington Court for dinner as soon as we got back. We came, but she felt ill, and Norman Haire, whom we both knew well and I consulted, was sent for. He told my mother that Hell was pregnant, but why he thought so I do not know. Maybe he was relying on his expectations of us and his examination therefore was cursory. In any case the opinion was quite erroneous as a natural circumstance proved within the next hour. My mother, who had been not at all hostile to the idea, but pleased, was now worried and sent for her doctor, for it was apparent that Hell's temperature had soared to the heights and her condition become a high fever. The new doctor was not very clever about it either, but he had her put to bed at once, in my old room off the landing, the one done up in black and yellow checks. In fact Hell's illness never was identified precisely—her maladies are mostly untypical. It showed all the symptoms of typhoid and so was called a paratyphoid, but was not recognised as any of the familiar forms. Meanwhile the doctor had taken one look at me, lifted my eyelids, said "*You* have jaundice", and packed me off to a nursing-home.

The thoughtless might say: lucky Hell, to be diagnosed under circumstances in which she could be sure of careful nursing, quiet surroundings, even luxuries as she got better.

The thoughtful will be ahead of me. Here is a girl, desperately ill, her temperature in the high hundreds, surrounded by in-laws whom she has hardly met and who have been associated with unwelcome and denigration in a setting of fantastic public scandal, isolated completely from every background and person that she knew. Even her new-wed husband had been whisked away. The reader of these pages will appreciate that, to whatever degree now tamed and domesticated by use, I was not, at the opening of our partnership, the most thoughtful and protective of cavaliers; yet a girl when marrying, even if she must expect sooner or later to encounter her in-laws, is surely entitled to hope that that will happen with her husband-of-choice, such as he is and whatever his limitations, by her side.

Yet here she was, on her own among strangers certain above all others to eye her critically. Merciful heaven provided that, as I have said, for a long time she should be unconscious.

Gradually she must have become aware of my mother, who would without doubt have been constantly there, considerate and tender; of the nurse; of Mabel; of Joyce, whom she already knew. As she began to improve she became aware also of a daily visit. My father, with his unfailing sense of duty, came upstairs every afternoon as soon as he got back from the city. He sat silent, for ten minutes regularly, in the armchair in the corner of the room, unable to think of anything to say, mutely determined that she should understand through the speechlessness that he yet wished her well.

To have survived, she must have been tough. The experience left her with only one mark for life: a detestation of chicken in any form and of lemon jelly.

It is easy to conjecture why the results of the inward battle conducted during this period, during which my family had to contrast the image they had formed beforehand with the reality of the young woman before them were not unsatisfactory. It may be that their guest's physical helplessness was itself in a sense an advantage, and created a situation in which prejudice had to be dropped, truth could stand out more starkly and be appreciated. By the time that Hell was convalescent and I was back from nursing home, the war was over. Hell was already one of the family and willing to put up with it.

My mother, whose qualities I can never praise too highly, however much our own relations were bedevilled by the fate that kept us at loggerheads until the end, took her right under her wing. She searched through her wardrobe and gave Hell dresses—to my mind an odd way of NOT patronising somebody—but in my mother I am certain it was intended as a sign of intimacy and honour, not of condescension. She praised Hell and tried to make her feel happy in every possible way. But here again, as so often, what was intended as the utmost warmth, without the slightest reservation or alloy, did not always come out and sound exactly as it was meant to. She said: "Dear, you do have such a lot of charm. I should love to have you with me at my dinner parties. Would you—would you be willing to—I would pay—take lessons to change your accent? You know, darling, when I'm abroad, I always try to learn a little of the other people's language." It was good that Hell does not like dinner-parties. Better still, that she did not misunderstand Mother, but on the contrary understood her, and also responded to her warmth. However, so far as she was concerned, the services of Professor Higgins remained uncalled upon.

There was still another, closer confidence: "My dear, if you want your marriage with Ivor to be a success, you must start from the beginning as you mean to go on. You must keep him there"—with a light downward pressure of the thumb—"as I have Louis. He does not need to realise it. That is why Louis and I have been so happy together."

The historian will be wiser to take this injunction less as reliable testimony of her real relations with my father than as evidence of what she thought good for me. Anyway, Hell did not misinterpret her motive, which was undoubtedly only eagerness to help her new daughter in the trials ahead, and made some conciliatory reply about not marrying someone because you want to change him into someone different. Whether Hell did indeed take this injunction to heart, however, I cannot tell, for, if she has, her touch has been soft as silk and light as thistledown.

My father's attitude had altered too. In one of our rather inarticulate twosomes, he yet made it clear that, now he knew Hell, his doubts were at an end. He accepted the marriage and wished me to regard ourselves as reconciled. We must come down to Townhill as soon as we felt better.

Whatever one's own feelings, one does not hurt others by rebuffing them when their overtures are so manifestly intended as acts of goodwill. The week-end itself went well. But Father went out once again with the mayfly. This time the trout won. He caught a chill from which he never recovered.

It was not apparent at first that the end would be fatal. He was then 57 years old; this would not be considered a great age in these days, though, it is true, as late as the 1920s the expectation of life was rather less. His illness was then called "a cold in the kidneys". My father suffered seriously from gout. This is an hereditary disease in our family. In old tradition, and hence still in contemporary folklore, gout—which is a "joke" disease because the untreated victim becomes ill-tempered as well as anguished and wears comical bandages—is a physiological aftermath of good living, and to be kept under by dieting the sufferer. I myself have had a doctor telling me solemnly to abstain from port, although I never touch the stuff or anything like it. This idea is now known to be incorrect, or at least a very minor and almost irrelevant part of the story. Gout, which is accumulation of uric acid in the joints (opening its campaign usually in one or other of the big toes, or both), comes of an hereditary disposition of the organism not to eliminate sufficient uric acid by normal metabolism in the ordinary processes of bladder and digestive tract. If the subject lives long enough, he is bound to suffer from it, when the uneliminated accumulation throughout his life has grown enough in proportion to his body-size to become a nuisance. My father, my eldest brother and I have all been gouty. My lot attacked suddenly when I was over fifty and bound that evening to fulfil an engagement to talk on films to a Staff College club down at Camberley, a pledge I had to fulfil seated in a chair and wearing a huge white swathe of bandages romantically around one foot. Nowadays, however, drugs have been discovered that can completely subdue the condition. The research people are working on drugs to prevent those hereditarily so disposed from accumulating the surplus uric acid in the first place. The ones I take were worked out slightly earlier; they operate quite adequately in pairs, one to get the uric acid out from the pockets in which it has accumulated and put it back in circulation, the other to combine with the circulating acid and form a compound that the metabolism will eliminate. I take as prescribed four pills, two of each kind, every day of my life and now—fingers crossed—have no trouble whatever I eat.

I have gone into all this medical detail because I find it interesting that my father's was one of those cases that need never have ended fatally if medical knowledge then had been what it is today. (Whether medicine, in thus saving life and contributing to the population explosion, as well as prolonging it and keeping old people on in positions of authority while the younger ones are excluded and alienated, has done humanity a real service is quite another question that does not arise here.) At this time these remedies were not known. My father used to have phases of drinking water and eating Melba toast and suffering recurrent agonies when he could hardly be spoken to. From the symptoms of his final illness it is extremely probable that the direct cause was gout: his kidneys had been so strained or injured by the effort to deal with the attacks that they could not cope with or eliminate even ordinary liquids.

Back at 28 Kensington Court and confined to bed he speedily became swollen and dropsical, as well as unconscious for long periods. Famous doctors, including the King's own physician and other specialists in the organs affected, consulted around his bedside. They could do nothing, except, as they always do with V.I.P.s, keep him alive as long as possible, even beyond reasonable hope.

In my father's case this fitted in with an odd Jewish superstition: that only the good die on Saturdays. My relatives on my father's side did mention this during his illness and, so infinite are the astonishing quirks of human nature, it appeared to comfort them that the doctors' devices succeeded in that he did last the week out and life was pronounced extinct only on the night of Friday to Saturday, in the early hours of the Sabbath.

There had been no opportunity for any realisation by him that his condition must end fatally, nor for any farewells.

We children were standing by. When he was dead my two brothers and I went down into my father's and mother's bedroom to say "Kaddish", the Hebrew prayer that begins "Holy! Holy Holy!" and is recited on all occasions of mourning. I remember the scene vividly. Neither my mother nor my sister was present; even at home women do not participate in orthodox Jewish ceremonial for the dead. Visualise the three tall brothers; both my elders were over 6 feet and I only half an inch under. We wore pyjamas and dressing-gowns, I think—at least Stuart and I did, Ewen lives near to No. 28 and may not have spent the night there. Did we wear top-hats? I still kept one at Kensington Court for occasions of pomp although, as it was too big for me, I had to keep it off my ears by folding a *Daily Express* inside the crown. One or other of us may have had on a black velvet prayer cap. We certainly wore *taliths* and held prayer-books in our hands, standing tall and sombre besides the silken bed on which lay the scarce cold body of our father, never wakened from an unconsciousness that had lasted several days.

Into the room hurried panting from his run up the stairs a tiny gnome-like figure with a small black bag, the sacred officer hastily summoned for preparation of the corpse.

The gnome came to a stop, peered at us over thick spectacles from under the bowler perched dangerously on the back of his head, looked round enquiringly and asked in a hoarse whisper:

"Vere's de deader?"

If he had not been blind as a bat the query should have been quite unnecessary, for my father lay a yard in front of him.

The scene was pure Mile End Pavilion.

It broke the tension. Let the curtain fall here, for we all realised that our lives would henceforth fall into a new pattern. The family had lost its linch-pin and would not be the same.

INDEX